LENIN READER

Hoover Institution Studies, No. 15

LENIN READER

Selected and Edited by

Stefan T. Possony

HENRY REGNERY COMPANY

CHICAGO

In conjunction with

The Hoover Institution on War, Revolution, and Peace

STANFORD UNIVERSITY

TABLE OF CONTENTS

INTRODUCTION

In thirty-odd years of his career as a writer and political leader, Lenin (Vladimir Ilych Ulyanov, 1870–1924) wrote as many as ten million words, and perhaps more; these include several books, a considerable number of brochures, many magazine articles and literally hundreds of newspaper articles. As chief of government, he was the author of official documents and diplomatic notes. Moreover, he made dozens of speeches and maintained a voluminous correspondence.

Lenin's writings have been published in the form of individual books, pamphlets, several editions of "selected" works and four editions of "collected" works. The *Leninskii Sbornik* (or Lenin miscellany) contains some forty volumes of notes, memoranda and other informal writings, as well as letters; still other letters have been published in *Sochineniya* and in special editions devoted to Lenin's correspondence with persons such as Maxim Gorky. The various editions of Lenin's works show considerable differences in their completeness and editorial comment: the fifth edition[1] will be the most complete, since it will contain a good deal of heretofore unpublished material; however, in respect to scholarship and pertinence of editorial comment, the second and notably the third editions are superior.

---

[1] In 1965, the fifth edition of his *Sochineniya* (*collected works*) was still being published.

ix

Although not all of Lenin's texts were originally written in Russian, most of them are available only in Russian—on the other hand, some of the articles that he wrote in German have never been published in Russian. The German and French translations of the second and third editions of *Sochineniya* have remained incomplete, and only very few volumes were published in English. Publication of the fourth edition, presently being issued in English,[2] is very slow, but materials are being included which were released after the completion of the fourth Russian edition. *Leninskii Sbornik,* however, has never been translated.

Most of the writings which were released for the first time during the last years of the Khrushchev regime, including Lenin's so-called testament, pertain to the role of Joseph Stalin and the "co-existence" concept. They also include a few letters addressed to Inessa Armand: heretofore this correspondence had been suppressed to conceal Lenin's relationship with her. Yet the larger part of the Lenin-Armand correspondence, including her letters to him and the organizational letters she penned under his guidance, remains to be published. And it is particularly noteworthy that hardly any of the hundreds of letters which N. K. Krupskaya, his wife and secretary, wrote upon his instructions have been released. Unless we make the improbable assumption that Lenin never wrote important official documents, we must conclude that hardly any important text which sheds light on his activities as chief of government has been disclosed thus far. Nor is there much documentation concerning Lenin's activities in the Central Committee and the Political Bureau of the Communist party.

There is no reason to believe that major works of the period before 1917 have been withheld from publication. However, some minor writings undoubtedly have been lost, and there are indications that numerous letters and perhaps some lengthier manuscripts have vanished. According to one story, Lenin, before departing from Switzerland in 1917, left a whole trunk of papers

---

[2] V. I. Lenin, *Collected Works,* Moscow, Foreign Languages Publishing House, 1960–

in Geneva. It has been asserted but not confirmed that several years after his death this trunk was transferred to Moscow. It is reasonably certain that not all the manuals and letters that are available in Russian archives have been released; furthermore, several Western libraries hold unpublished Lenin papers.

Since only a small portion of Lenin's writings can be reproduced in this *Reader,* our selection is to serve merely as a primer. It is hoped that this *Reader* will familiarize the student and the interested public at large with those ideas that commanded Lenin's central interest and will help the student grasp Lenin's chief arguments and understand their development in his own thinking. However, those who want to study Lenin's thoughts thoroughly have no choice but to work their way through fifty-odd volumes of his *Collected Works.*

The extracts which appear in this volume have been chosen on the basis of their continuing significance. Those who are interested in the context from which they were taken will in most instances find the complete texts in the twelve-volume edition of *Selected Works* (1943), which is generally accessible in the United States. Texts which were taken from other sources can also be located without difficulty: all extracts are dated, and the various editions of Lenin's works are, on the whole, chronologically arranged. The readers who want to study the full texts will be well advised to check related writings from the same period.

The dates will also facilitate an investigation of the circumstances in Lenin's career which influenced or conditioned a particular train of thought. Since he was mostly preoccupied with practical political problems, real comprehension of his arguments presupposes a knowledge of the situation to which they were addressed. It may be mentioned in this connection that this *Reader* was originally intended to be introduced by a short biographical sketch which, before it was finished, had grown into a full length biography.[3]

---

[3]Stefan T. Possony, *Lenin, The Compulsive Revolutionary* (Chicago: Henry Regnery Co., 1964).

Lenin was a first-rate columnist and an excellent public speaker, and his pamphlets are usually written in a forceful style. However, his books tend to be pedantic and pedestrian: he often was repetitious and dogmatic, and he indulged in too many quotations as though the authority of Marx and Engels, rather than fact and logic, could prove the validity of his point. But when all this ballast of polemical citation is thrown overboard, Lenin's thinking comes through fresh, direct and often original.

Lenin was a poor economist but a good economic historian; his contributions to the theory of socialism, however, are debatable. As a philosopher his accomplishments range from unbelievably low to astoundingly high. But as a writer on politics and political action he is uniformly interesting and in many ways unsurpassed. It is, therefore, not surprising that in this century he has exercised an influence that is far more profound that that of Machiavelli in earlier times.

To be sure, Lenin was more than a craftsman of politics and conquest. Under different circumstances he might have become a creative social scientist or a great philosopher. But under any condition inner compulsion would have driven him to political action: he was a political activist by nature, talent and inspiration.

The interpretation of Lenin which still predominates originated with Stalin, and the Communist infatuation with dogmatism—an affliction for which Lenin must bear much of the blame—has resulted in simplistic, one-track interpretations of him as a thinker. Communist writers like to present Lenin as though he must be considered "in one piece." According to them, although Lenin's ideas may have been evolving, "Leninism" was essentially established when the master in his early youth became politically conscious. Even anti-Communists and critics of Lenin have often quite uncritically accepted this interpretation. The fact remains, however, that Lenin's thinking has many dimensions and many facets. His ideas were not always well organized, nor were they static or free of contradiction; his documentation was often fragmentary and his evidence willfully interpreted.

But if he had had a chance to read the works on "Leninism" that were published after his death, he undoubtedly would have remembered Marx's well-known reply to an uncritical admirer: *"Moi, je ne suis pas Marxiste."* Lenin hardly was a Leninist.

At least three major periods can be distinguished in Lenin's intellectual life. The first lasted from the inception of his interest in revolution (1887) and his subsequent adoption of Marxism (1893) to the publication of *What is to be Done?* (1902). This period did not come to an abrupt end: in some aspects it terminated as early as 1900, and in others it lasted till 1905, when Lenin still showed himself sensitive to problems of democracy and the concept of revolution as a predominantly social and techno-economic) process.

During the second period, which lasted from 1902 (or more accurately from 1900–1905) to early 1921, he was the Lenin as most of the world has come to know him—the organizer, conspirator, power-politician, practitioner of violence, leader of insurrection, dictator and conqueror. This was the Lenin that served as Stalin's model.

Much of this "Leninist" Lenin remained alive during the last two years of his active life. But by March, 1921, the uprising of the Kronstadt sailors against the iniquities of Bolshevik rule and the New Economic Policy, through which "war communism" was replaced by a partial restoration of "capitalism" in agriculture and trade, had demonstrated the failure of earlier policies. At that point a third period began, with a very different Lenin coming to the fore. In this period—it lasted but two years because he was incapacitated by illness in March, 1923—Lenin sketched a new approach to the theory and practice of communism. It is this Lenin of the third period about whom the world—which includes the Communist party—knows least and, at this juncture of history, it should know most.

Nikolai Ivanovich Bukharin, the theoretician who was personally closest to Lenin, insisted on the fundamental importance of Lenin's last writings—he was promptly purged by Stalin, falsely accused of having plotted twice to assassinate Lenin, and was executed. Bukharin's rehabilitation in March, 1965, suggests that in the Soviet Union, too, a new interpretation of Lenin may be in the making. The truth is everywhere beginning to assert itself that, as Lenin departed from Marx and Engels, so Stalin departed from Lenin, at least from the Lenin of the last period and the Lenin who was trying to learn the lessons of his experiences.

In many respects, the political and economic structure of the Soviet Union originated with Lenin, but the Soviet Union as we have known it since the mid-1920's is mainly a Stalinist creation. "De-Stalinization" and the great emphasis placed by current Soviet leaders on Lenin constitute a half-hearted attempt to remove the excesses and excrescences of Stalinism and to return to Lenin. However thus far, this "Leninist counter-revolution" has remained inconclusive, because Soviet leaders still are mentally conditioned to interpret Lenin in the Stalinist fashion and because they have refused to face up to the fact that Lenin *did* change.

Lenin's partial restoration of capitalism was an oblique—and not fully avowed—confession that the nature of the economic problem, and hence the challenge of the building of socialism, had not been understood by the Bolshevik school. Therefore, policies that would be based on Lenin's last phase might open the door to real progress or, at least, to the normalization of conditions within the Soviet Union. Strict adherence to Lenin's advice that the Communists should cease to praise themselves and should instead exceed the economic accomplishments of "capitalism" would indeed result in a "revolution," especially if solid scientific analysis could persuade the Communists that there are intrinsic reasons that "communism," especially in its Stalinist form, limits productivity and slows socio-economic development.

Such is the irony of history that within the Soviet Union an abandonment of Lenin's destructionism in favor of the conservative and constructive concepts of his last phase may mark the beginnings of a breakthrough to freedom.

Lenin's writings constitute a body of significant historical documents, but they are also a rich repository of living political thought. This *Reader* should help to stimulate the study and *critical analysis* of Lenin.

Gerhard Loose
Boulder, Colorado

Stefan T. Possony
Stanford, California

March, 1965.

HISTORICAL DATES

1825	——	Dekabrist Rising.
1825–55	——	Nicholas I.
1830–31	——	First Polish Revolution.
1853–56	——	Crimean War.
1855–81	——	Alexander II.
1857	——	Slavonic Welfare Society (a Pan-Slav group) formed.
1861	——	Emancipation Edict liberates serfs.
1863–64	——	Second Polish Revolution.
1864	——	Zemstvo Laws establish local self-government in Russia.
1865–76	——	Russian conquests in Central Asia.
1867	——	Pan-Slav Congress at Moscow.
1870	April 22	Birth of Vladimir Ilyich Ulyanov (Lenin) at Simbirsk.
1874	——	Reform of Russian Army.
1876	——	*Land and Liberty* (secret revolutionary society) formed.
1879	——	Establishment of *Will of the People,* a revolutionary group.
1879	August 28	Lenin enters Simbirsk gymnasium.
1881	——	Russian expansion into Trans-Caspian region.
1881	March 13	Alexander II assassinated.
1881–94	——	Alexander III. Reaffirmation of autocracy. Persecution of minorities. Accelerated industrialization. Marxism becomes influential in Russia.

1884–87	——	Continued Russian advance in Central Asia.
1886	January 24	Ilya Nikolayevich Ulyanov (Lenin's father) dies.
1887	May 20	Alexander Ulyanov (Lenin's elder brother) executed for planning the assassination of Alexander III.
1887	June 22	Lenin graduates from Simbirsk gymnasium, winning a gold medal.
1887	September	Lenin enters Kazan University.
1887	December 17	Lenin arrested for alleged participation in a student demonstration at Kazan.
1887	December 19	Lenin expelled from the University and goes to Kokushkino (his grandfather's estate).
1888	October	Lenin returns to Kazan.
1889	——	Lenin in Samara. Undertakes self-study of law, attempts farming, meets with revolutionaries of older generation, also studies revolutionary literature.
1890	May	Lenin permitted to take university examinations as an external student.
1890	August–November	Lenin in St. Petersburg auditing law courses.
1891	March–November	Lenin in St. Petersburg to prepare for examinations.
1891	November 21	Lenin passes final law examinations at St. Petersburg University.
1891–92	——	Famine in Volga region.
1891–94	——	Conclusion of Franco-Russian Alliance.
1892	January 26	Lenin awarded diploma.
1892	August 4	Lenin granted right to practice law.
1893	spring–summer	Lenin participates in Marxist study circle.
1893	September 12	Lenin moves to St. Petersburg.

1894	first half year	Lenin active in Marxist circles in St. Petersburg. Henceforth he devotes himself exclusively to politics.
1894	March–June	Lenin writes his first brochure.
1894–1917	——	Nicholas II.
1895	spring–summer	Lenin in Switzerland, France and Germany. Meets Russian exiled revolutionaries and European Marxists.
1895	November–December	Lenin prepares publication of *Rabocheye Dyelo,* an illegal newspaper, in St. Petersburg.
1895	December 7	Lenin arrested.
1895	December 15	League of Struggle for the Liberation of the Working Class established at St. Petersburg.
1896	entire year	Lenin held for interrogation. Does extensive study and much writing while in prison.
1897	February 10	Lenin exiled to Shushenskoye, Siberia.
1897	during year	While in exile Lenin actively studies and writes, keeps contacts with Marxists throughout Russia.
1898	March	Russian Social Democratic Labor Party (RSDLP) founded in Minsk.
1898	July 22	Lenin marries N. K. Krupskaya.
1899	April	Lenin's *The Development of Capitalism in Russia* published. He uses the pseudonym "Vladimir Ilyin."
1900	January 29	End of exile. Lenin and Krupskaya depart from Siberia.
1900	March	Lenin settles in Pskov. Krupskaya, on police orders, forced to live in Ufa.
1900	May	Conference with leaders of RSDLP. Decision to start extensive publishing activity abroad.

1900	July 16	Lenin leaves Russia to implement this decision.
1900	September	Lenin settles in Munich.
1900	December 24	First issue of *Iskra,* a newspaper initially edited and largely written by Lenin.
1901	March 23	First issue of *Zarya,* a short-lived magazine connected with *Iskra.*
1901	May	Krupskaya rejoins Lenin.
1901	December	The pseudonym "Lenin" is used for the first time.
1902	March	Lenin publishes *What Is To Be Done?* in Stuttgart. This book establishes his reputation among the revolutionaries.
1902	April 12	Lenin and Krupskaya move to London.
1903	May	Lenin and Krupskaya move to Geneva.
1903	July 30—August 23	Second Conference of RSDLP. The Party divides into Bolshevik and Menshevik factions. Lenin, leader of the Bolsheviks, becomes isolated within the party and is separated from *Iskra.*
1904–05	——	Russo-Japanese War.
1904	August	Bolshevik conference held in Switzerland. Lenin activates an organization of his own, but officially remains within the RSDLP.
1905	January 2	Fall of Port Arthur.
1905	January 4	Lenin, probably with Japanese help, publishes his own paper *Vperyed.*
1905	January 22	Bloody Sunday: In St. Petersburg demonstrators, trying to petition the Tsar, dispersed and shot at by military units, initiating first Russian revolution.
1905	April 25—May 10	Third Congress of RSDLP (without Menshevik participation).

1905	May 27	Russian naval disaster at Tsushima.
1905	June–July	Lenin writes *Two Tactics of Social Democracy in the Democratic Revolution.*
1905	August 20	Tsar publishes manifesto creating the Imperial Duma (parliament).
1905	September–October	Mass strikes.
1905	October 20–30	Mass strikes spread to most major cities. St. Petersburg in state of disorganization.
1905	October 26	First meeting of the Soviet of Workers in St. Petersburg.
1905	October 30	October Manifesto institutes a semi-constitutional regime in Russia.
1905	November 2	Amnesty for political exiles and political criminals.
1905	November 11	Lenin returns to Russia, settles in St. Petersburg.
1905	December 16	Dissolution of the Soviet.
1905	December 18–22	Mass strikes.
1905	December 22–30	Abortive insurrection at Moscow.
1906	April 23—May 8	Fourth Congress of the RSDLP, with Menshevik participation. Lenin elected to Presidium.
1906	May 10	Inaugural Session of First Duma.
1906	May–November	Lenin under the name of "Karpov" unsuccessfully runs for Duma seat.
1906	July 21	Dissolution of First Duma.
1906	November	Extensive agrarian reform.
1906–7	——	Partisan warfare and "expropriations" conducted under Lenin's direction.
1907	January–April	Lenin moves from Russia to Kuokkala, Finland, for security reasons.
1907	May 13—June 1	Fifth Congress RSDLP. Lenin elected to Presidium.
1907	summer	For security reasons Lenin moves to Styrsudd, Finland.

1907	June 16	Dissolution of the Second Duma. New electoral law promulgated.
1907	August 18–24	Lenin participates in Stuttgart Congress of Socialist International.
1907	late August	Lenin returns to Finland.
1907	August 30	Anglo-Russian Entente.
1907	December	Lenin leaves Finland for Western Europe; spends several days in Stockholm and Berlin.
1908	early January	Lenin and Krupskaya settle in Geneva.
1908	August	Lenin undertakes philosophical research in London.
1908	late fall	Lenin returns to Geneva. Finishes his book *Materialism and Empiriocriticism*.
1908	December 12	Lenin and Krupskaya move to Paris.
1909	——	Revival of Pan-Slav agitation.
1909	spring	Lenin meets Inessa Armand.
1909	summer and fall	Lenin concentrates on writing, tries to strengthen his position with the RSDLP.
1909	November 5–8	Lenin participates in Eleventh Session of International Socialist Bureau at Brussels.
1910	Jan. 15—Feb. 5	Lenin participates in meeting of RSDLP central committee at Paris.
1910	spring	Beginning of close friendship with Inessa Armand.
1910	August 1–8	Lenin visits Maxim Gorky at Capri, Italy.
1910	Aug. 28—Sept. 3	Lenin participates in Copenhagen Congress of the Second International.
1911	——	Italo-Turkish War.
1911	summer	Lenin runs a Party school at Longjumeau, near Paris.
1911	December 27–30	Lenin presides over Bolshevik meeting at Paris.

1912	January 18–30	Lenin runs Prague Conference, which establishes the Bolsheviks as a *de facto* separate group.
1912	April	Unrest in Russia resumes.
1912	May 5	First issue of *Pravda,* a legal Bolshevik daily, published in St. Petersburg.
1912	June–July	Lenin moves from Paris to Cracow, Austrian Poland.
1912–13	——	Balkan War.
1913–14	——	Lenin devotes most of his time to writing for *Pravda.* Travels several times to Switzerland, Germany and France. Krupskaya ailing.
1914	——	St. Petersburg changed to Petrograd.
1914	May–July	Strike movement and unrest in Russia.
1914	August 1	Germany declares war on Russia.
1914	August 6	Austria declares war on Russia.
1914	August 8	Lenin arrested in Austrian Poland.
1914	August 19	Lenin released. Austrian authorities allow him to depart for a neutral country.
1914	September 5	Lenin settles in Berne, Switzerland.
1914	late 1914	Indirect contacts between Lenin and Austrian psychological warfare agencies.
1914	Sept. 1914—May 1915	Severe defeats of Russian army.
1915	Feb. 23—Mar. 3	Lenin directs Bolshevik conference at Berne.
1915	September 5–8	Lenin participates in Zimmerwald Conference of anti-war Socialists.
1915	mid 1915–mid 1916	Indirect contacts between Lenin and German psychological warfare agencies.
1916	January–July	Lenin writes *Imperialism.*
1916	February	Lenin moves to Zurich.
1916	during year	Stabilization of Russian front.

1916	April 24–30	Lenin participates in second "Zimmerwald Conference" at Kienthal.
1916	July–September	Lenin takes long vacation.
1917	early January	Lenin in serious financial trouble.
1917	March 8	Strikes and riots in Petrograd.
1917	March 12–14	Provisional Government in Russia. Tsar abdicates. Soviets activated throughout Russia.
1917	March 30	Provisional Russian government recognizes independence of Poland.
1917	April 6	United States enters World War I.
1917	April 9	Lenin, Krupskaya, Inessa Armand and other exiled Bolsheviks leave Switzerland for Russia. Despite the state of war between Russia and Germany, they are allowed to pass through Germany.
1917	April 16	Lenin and his party arrive in Petrograd.
1917	April	Lenin presents his April Theses, defining Bolshevik tactics and calling for continuation and intensification of the revolution.
1917	May 7–12	Lenin takes leading part in Seventh All-Russian Conference of the Russian Social Democratic Labor Party (Bolsheviks) in Petrograd.
1917	May 17	Trotsky returns from the United States.
1917	June 7	Resolution of All-Russian Soviet of Peasants to transfer the land to the peasants without compensation.
1917	June 16—July 7	Lenin attends First All-Russian Congress of Soviets of Workers and Soldiers.
1917	early July	Russian offensive in Galicia.
1917	July 11	Russian army defeated, subsequent German counter-offensive.
1917	July 15–18	Bolshevik uprising.

1917	July 18	Lenin goes into hiding.
1917	July 19	Arrest of Bolshevik leaders ordered.
1917	July 20	Alexander Kerensky appointed Prime Minister.
1917	July 22	Lenin flees from Petrograd.
1917	August 3	Lenin indicted for high treason.
1917	August 8–16	Sixth Congress of RSDLP (Bolsheviks) in Petrograd takes place in Lenin's absence. Trotsky and his organization join Bolsheviks.
1917	August–September	Lenin escapes to Finland.
1917	September 9–14	Abortive *coup d'état* by General Kornilov.
1917	mid-September	Lenin proposes uprising.
1917	October 8	Trotsky elected chairman of Petrograd Soviet.
1917	October 12 or 19	Lenin returns secretly to Petrograd.
1917	October 23	Bolsheviks undecided about uprising.
1917	October 29	Lenin insists on immediate insurrection counter to intra-Party opposition.
1917	November 3	Selected Party leaders decide to launch uprising.
1917	November 7	Bolsheviks seize power. Decree of peace.
1917	November 11	Rump Congress of Soviets accepts Lenin as head of government.
1917	mid-November	Armistice negotiations with Germans.
1917	November 20	Ukraine proclaimed independent people's republic.
1917	November 25	Free and general elections to Constituent Assembly. Socialist revolutionaries obtain 54% of the vote, Bolsheviks with 24% are in minority.
1917	November–December	Various decrees establish Bolshevik dictatorship and a radically socialist economic system.

1917	December 6	Independence of Finland.
1917	December 15	Armistice with Germany.
1917	December 17	Lenin orders demobilization of Russian Army.
1918	January 8	President Wilson proclaims Fourteen Points.
1918	January 18	Constituent Assembly in session preparing basic legislation to establish a socialist democracy.
1918	January 19	Lenin dissolves Constituent Assembly.
1918	January 28	Ukraine declares its independence.
1918	February 10	Trotsky breaks negotiations with Germany declaring that there would be neither peace nor war between Germany and Russia. Germany resumes hostilities. Residual Russian army retreats.
1918	February 19	Nationalization of the land.
1918	March 3	Treaty of Brest-Litovsk between Germany and Russia.
1918	March 6–8	Lenin defends peace treaty before Seventh Congress of now renamed Communist Party.
1918	March 10	Lenin and his government move to Moscow. Lenin and Krupskaya later live in Kremlin.
1918	March 15–16	Fourth Congress of Soviets ratifies Treaty of Brest-Litovsk.
1918	June–August	Allied British and French forces land at Murmansk and Arkhangel to prevent a Bolshevik alliance with Germany.
1918	July 4	Fifth Congress of Soviets.
1918	July 6	German Ambassador Mirbach murdered in Moscow. Anti-Bolshevik uprising by Social Revolutionaries.

1918	July 6	Bolsheviks organize terror on large scale. Civil War raging in Western Siberia, Urals, Northern Caucasus and Volga area.
1918	July 10	Promulgation of first Soviet Constitution.
1918	July 17	Assassination of Tsar Nicholas II and his family on Lenin's orders.
1918	August 30	Fanya Kaplan, an idealistic Socialist, inflicts two bullet wounds on Lenin.
1918	September 4	Fanya Kaplan executed.
1918	September 5	Decree of Red Terror.
1918	September–October	Lenin recuperating.
1918	October 5	Decree of labor conscription of members of bourgeoisie.
1918	October 31	Decree instituting universal compulsory labor service.
1918	November 9	Revolution in Germany.
1918	November 11	World War I comes to an end. The Russian civil war spreads to areas of southern and western Russia evacuated by German troops.
1919	January	Communist uprising in Germany fails.
1919	March 2–6	Communist International (Comintern) founded.
1919	March 18–23	Eighth Congress of Russian Communist party.
1919	March 21–August 1	Communist regime in Hungary.
1919	April 4—May 1	Communist regime in Bavaria.
1919	April 28	Covenant of the League of Nations.
1919	April–May	Caucasian states declare their independence.
1919	spring	U.S. troops join Allied forces in Russia.
1919	June 28	Treaty of Versailles.

1919	September–October	Western Allies abandon Arkhangel and Murmansk.
1919	October	Petrograd threatened by anti-Bolshevik forces who are defeated.
1920	February 2	Soviet government recognizes independence of Estonia.
1920	March 1 and 6	Lenin warns that war with Poland is impending.
1920	March 11	Lenin orders military units to Polish borders.
1920	March 29—April 5	Ninth Party Congress.
1920	April 25	Poland launches preventive war.
1920	May 7	Polish troops conquer Kiev.
1920	June 10	League of Nations established. Lenin publishes *Left Radicalism: An Infantile Disorder.*
1920	July 12	Soviet government recognizes independence of Lithuania.
1920	July 19—August 7	Second Comintern Congress in Petrograd. Lenin presides over first session.
1920	May–August	Soviet troops advancing toward Warsaw and East Prussia.
1920	August 11	Soviet government recognizes independence of Latvia.
1920	August 17	Red Army crushed near Warsaw. Communist forces retreat from Poland.
1920	September 22–25	Lenin participates in Ninth All-Russian Conference of Communist party.
1920	October 1 or 2	Inessa Armand dies.
1920	October 12	End of Soviet-Polish war.
1920	October 14	Soviet government recognizes independence of Finland.
1921–22	——	Famine in Russia; wide-spread epidemics.

1921	February–April	Bolsheviks seize Caucasus.
1921	Feb. 23–Mar. 17	Kronstadt uprising against Bolsheviks.
1921	March 17	On Lenin's recommendation, New Economic Policy is inaugurated by Tenth Party Congress. "War Communism" is abolished.
1921	March 18	Treaty of Riga with Poland delineating Soviet-Polish borders.
1921	July 11	Third Comintern Congress convenes.
1921	July 13	Upon Lenin's request, Maxim Gorky appeals to Europe and America for food.
1921	September 7	Distribution of American food commences under Herbert Hoover's direction. Russian economy slowly recovering on a basis of state capitalism.
1922	March 27	Eleventh Party Congress under Lenin's leadership.
1922	April 2	Lenin appoints Stalin to post of Secretary General of the Communist party.
1922	April 10—May 19	Soviet government participates in International Economic Conference at Genoa.
1922	April 16	Treaty of Rapallo between Germany and Soviet Russia.
1922	May 26	Lenin's first stroke.
1922	June–July	Lenin incapacitated.
1922	October 25	Vladivostok falls into Bolshevik hands. End of civil war.
1922	November 13	Lenin speaks to Fourth Comintern Congress.
1922	November 20	Lenin, before Moscow Soviet, delivers his last public speech.
1922	December 15–16	Lenin suffers second stroke.
1922	December 24	Politbureau decides to keep Lenin in political and personal isolation.

1922	December 25	Lenin writes first part of letter with recommendations on Party leadership.
1922	December 28	Lenin continues work on his letter to the Party.
1922	December 30	Formation of the Union of Socialist Soviet Republics (U.S.S.R.).
1922	December 30–31	Lenin writes article on national question.
1923	January 4	Lenin writes post scriptum to his letter to the Party and suggests Stalin's dismissal as Secretary General. (This letter is known as Lenin's "testament.")
1923	January–March	Lenin's last writings adumbrating new approach to socialism.
1923	March 4	An article by Lenin with sharp, implied criticism of Stalin published in *Pravda*.
1923	March 5–6	Lenin breaks Party and personal relations with Stalin and prepares for a showdown fight.
1923	March 7–8	Data on Lenin's activities during these days are still undisclosed.
1923	March 9	Lenin suffers third stroke and loses faculty of speech.
1923	April 17–25	Twelfth Party Congress meets in Lenin's absence.
1923	May 12	Lenin transported to Party sanatorium at Gorki.
1923	May–October	Intensified power struggle between Stalin and Trotsky.
1923	June 4	Distribution of American food in Soviet Union ceases.
1923	October 18–19	After remarkable recovery, Lenin makes unannounced trip to Moscow and Kremlin. Press is silent about Lenin's initiative.
1923	October 19	Lenin transported back to Gorki.

1923	October–November	Communist and Nazi uprisings in Germany.
1923	October 22	Communist revolution in Germany cancelled by Moscow.
1923	November–December	Lenin visited by Party leaders.
1923	December 18	*Pravda* announces that Trotsky is ill.
1924	January 7	Lenin participates in a combined Christmas and New Year's party.
1924	January 8	*Pravda* discloses that Trotsky, for reasons of health, is temporarily relieved from all duties and goes on vacation.
1924	January 17–18	Before Thirteenth Party Conference, Stalin makes speeches to Congress with strongly implied criticism of, and ill-concealed personal remarks against, Lenin.
1924	January 18	Trotsky departs from Moscow.
1924	January 20	Lenin complains about visual disturbances.
1924	January 21	Lenin's health takes a sudden turn for the worse. Lenin dies from a fourth stroke.
1924	January 22	Autopsy and first embalmment.
1924	January 23–27	Lenin lies in state at Moscow.
1924	January 27	Lenin buried in temporary mausoleum.
1924	April	Lenin's body embalmed for the second time.
1925	——	Establishment of an institute for research on Lenin's brain.
1927	January	Soviet government invites foreign observers to view Lenin's body exhibited in the mausoleum in order to dispel rumors about his remains.
1927	November 15 and 19	*Pravda* reports results of research on Lenin's brain.
1928	——	Lenin's body is deteriorating; mausoleum is closed temporarily; body is treated for third time.

1929   November 10   Institute for research on Lenin's brain
                            reports its results.

1939   February 27   N. K. Krupskaya dies.

During World War II   Lenin's body (?) is transferred to Kui-
                            byshev, later to Tyumen (Siberia).

After World War II   Lenin's remains returned to Moscow
                            mausoleum.
                            The question of whether the mauso-
                            leum houses Lenin's body or an arti-
                            fact remains undecided.

I

BASIC PRINCIPLES

1. LENINISM AND MARXISM

"Leninism": This amazing expression is Comrade Martov's. Comrade Martov waited till they were five strong to raise the "revolt" against my single self. Comrade Martov is not a skillful polemicist: he wants to destroy his opponent by paying him the greatest compliments. (*One Step Forward, Two Steps Back,* May, 1904, *Selected Works,* II, 458.)

Marx considered the whole value of his theory to lie in the fact that it is "by its very nature a critical and revolutionary theory." And this latter quality is indeed completely and unconditionally characteristic of Marxism, for this theory directly sets itself the aim of *revealing* all the forms of antagonism and exploitation in modern society, following their evolution, demonstrating their transient character, the inevitability of their transformation into a different form, and *thus serving the proletariat so that it may as quickly and easily as possible put an end to all exploitation.* The irresistible force of attraction which draws the Socialists of all countries to this theory consists indeed in the fact that it combines a strict and supreme scientific spirit (representing as it does the last word in social science) with a revolutionary spirit, and combines them not by chance, not only because the founder of the doctrine combined in his person the qualities of a man of learning and a revolutionary, but does so intrinsically and inseparably within the theory itself. Indeed, the purpose of

1

theory, the aim of science, as directly laid down here, is to assist
the class of the oppressed in its actual economic struggle.

> We do not say to the world: Cease struggling — your whole
> struggle is valueless. All we do is to provide it with a true slogan
> of the struggle.

Hence, according to Marx, the direct purpose of science is
to provide a true slogan of the struggle, that is, to be able to
present this struggle objectively, as a product of a definite system
of production relations, to be able to *understand* the necessity
of this struggle, its meaning, course and conditions of development. It is impossible to provide a "slogan of the struggle"
unless every separate form of the struggle is minutely studied,
unless every one of its steps in the transition from one form to
another is followed, in order to be able to define the situation
at any given moment, without losing sight of the general character of the struggle and its general aim, namely, the complete and
final abolition of all exploitation and all oppression. (*What the
"Friends of the People" Are and How They Fight Against the
Social Democrats,* 1894, *Selected Works,* XI, 605 f.)

. . . We take our stand entirely on the basis of the theory of
Marx: it was the first to transform socialism from a utopia to a
science, to fix the firm foundation of this science and to indicate
the path along which it is necessary to proceed, while developing
this science further and elaborating it in every detail. It laid
bare the essence of modern capitalist economy, explaining the
manner in which the hire of the laborer, the purchase of labor
power, masks the enslavement of millions of propertyless people
by a handful of capitalists, the owners of the land, factories,
mines, etc. It showed that the whole trend of development of
modern capitalism is toward the ousting of small production
by large, and the creating of conditions which make a socialist
system of society possible and inevitable. It taught us to see under
the veil of rooted customs, political intrigues, subtle laws and
artful doctrines, the *class struggle,* the struggle between all species
of propertied classes and the masses of non-possessors, *the*

proletariat, which stands at the head of all the propertyless. It made clear the real task of a revolutionary socialist party: it is neither drawing up plans for the reconstruction of society, nor preaching sermons to the capitalists and their hangers-on about improving the lot of the workers, nor making conspiracies, *but the organization of the class struggle of the proletariat and the leadership of this struggle, the final aim of which is the winning of political power by the proletariat and the organization of a socialist society....*

... There can be no strong socialist party in the absence of a revolutionary theory uniting all the socialists, from which they draw all their convictions and which they apply in their modes of struggle and methods of activity. To defend such a theory, which you absolutely feel to be the truth, against unfounded attacks and attempts to deteriorate it, does not by any means imply that you are an enemy of *all* criticism. We do not by any means look upon the theory of Marx as something final and inviolable; on the contrary, we are convinced that it only laid the cornerstones of the science which Socialists *must* advance in all directions, if they do not want to lag behind events. We think that the *independent* elaboration of Marx's theory is especially necessary for Russian Socialists since this theory provides only the general guiding principles which in *detail* must be applied in England in a manner different from that applied in France, in France in a manner different from that applied in Germany, and in Germany in a manner different from that applied in Russia. We will therefore gladly afford space in our paper for articles on theoretical questions and invite all comrades to a frank discussion of controversial points. *(Our Program,* 1899. Compare with *Collected Works,* IV, 210–212.)

And now we very clearly perceive the two lines of Engels' (and Marx's) recommendations, directions, corrections, threats and exhortations. They most insistently called upon the British and American Socialists to merge with the labor movement and to eradicate the narrow and hidebound sectarian spirit from their organizations. They most insistently taught the German Social

Democrats to beware of succumbing to philistinism, to "parliamentary idiotism"... to petty bourgeois intellectual opportunism.

Is it not characteristic that our Social Democratic gossips have noisily proclaimed the recommendations of the first kind and have kept their mouths shut, have remained silent over the recommendations of the second kind? Is not *such* one-sidedness in appraising Marx's and Engels' letters the best indication, in a sense, of our Russian Social Democratic . . . "one-sidedness"? . . .

In countries where there are *no* Social Democratic members of parliament, *no* systematic and consistent Social Democratic policy either at elections or in the press, etc., Marx and Engels taught that the Socialists must *at all costs* rid themselves of narrow sectarianism and *join* with the labor movement so as to *shake up* the proletariat *politically*. . . . In a country where the bourgeois-democratic revolution was still incomplete, where "military despotism, embellished with parliamentary forms". . . prevailed, and still prevails, where the proletariat had long ago been drawn into politics and was pursuing a Social Democratic policy, what Marx and Engels feared most of all in such a country was parliamentary vulgarization and philistine compromising of the tasks and scope of the labor movement.

.   .   .   .

Marx and Engels erred much and often in determining the proximity of revolution, in their hopes in the victory of revolution (e.g., 1848, in Germany), in their faith in the imminence of a German "republic" ("to die for the republic," wrote Engels of that period, recalling his sentiments as a participant in the military campaign for an imperial constitution in 1848–49). They erred in 1871 when they were engaged in "raising revolt in Southern France," for which "they . . . sacrificed and risked all that was humanly possible. . . ." The same letter says:

> If we had had more means in March and April, we would have roused the whole of Southern France and would have saved the Commune in Paris.

But *such* errors—the errors of the giants of revolutionary thought

who tried to raise and did raise the proletariat of the whole
world above the level of petty, commonplace and trifling tasks—
are a thousand times more noble and magnificent and *historically
more valuable and true* than the puerile wisdom of official
liberalism, which sings, shouts, appeals and exhorts about the
vanity of revolutionary vanities, the futility of the revolutionary
struggle and the charms of counterrevolutionary "constitutional"
fantasies. . . .

The Russian working class will win its freedom and give a
fillip to Europe by its revolutionary action, full though it may be
of mistakes—and let the philistines pride themselves on the in-
fallibility of their revolutionary inaction. *(Letters of J. F. Becker
and Others to F. A. Sorge and Others,* preface to the Russian
translation, April 6, 1907, *Selected Works,* XI, 731 f., 736 f.)

The Marxian doctrine is omnipotent because it is true. It is
complete and harmonious and provides men with an integral
world conception which is irreconcilable with any form of superstition, reaction or defense of bourgeois oppression. It is the
legitimate successor of the best that was created by humanity in
the nineteenth century in the shape of German philosophy,
English political economy and French socialism.

.   .   .   .

After the overthrow of serfdom, when a *"free"* capitalist society
appeared, it was at once discovered that this freedom signified a
new system of oppression and exploitation of the toilers. Various
socialist doctrines immediately began to arise as a reflection of
this oppression and protest against it. But socialism in its first
origin was *utopian.* It criticized the capitalist society, it condemned it and damned it, it dreamed of its destruction, it drew
fantastic pictures of a better order and endeavored to convince
the rich of the wickedness of exploitation.

But utopian socialism was unable to show a real way out. It
could not explain either the essence of wage slavery under capitalism, or discover the laws of its development, or find the *social
force* which was capable of becoming the creator of a new society.

In the meantime, the stormy revolution which accompanied
the fall of feudalism and serfdom everywhere in Europe, and
especially in France, revealed ever more clearly the *struggle of
classes* as the basis of the whole development and its motive force.

Not a single victory of political freedom over the class of feudal
lords was won without desperate resistance. Not a single capitalist
country was established on a more or less free and democratic
basis without a life and death struggle between the different
classes of capitalist society.

Marx was a genius because he was able before anyone else to
draw from these facts and consistently elaborate the conclusion
which world history teaches. This conclusion is the doctrine of
the *class struggle*.

People always were and always will be the stupid victims of
deceit and self-deceit in politics, as long as they have not learned
to discover the *interests* of one or another of the classes behind
any moral, religious, political and social phrases, declarations
and promises. The supporters of reforms and improvements will
always be fooled by the defenders of the old, as long as they will
not realize that every old institution, however absurd and rotten
it may appear, is kept in being by the forces of one or the other
of the ruling classes. And there is *only one* way of breaking the
resistance of these classes, and that is to find, in the very society
which surrounds us, and to enlighten and organize for the
struggle, the forces which can and, by their social position, *must*
form the power capable of sweeping away the old and of establishing the new. (*The Three Sources and Three Component
Parts of Marxism,* March, 1913. Compare with *Selected Works,*
XI, 3, 7–8.)

The standpoint of life, of practice, should be first and fundamental in the theory of knowledge. And it inevitably leads to
materialism, brushing aside the endless fabrications of professorial scholasticism. Of course, we must not forget that the
criterion of practice can never, in the nature of things, either
confirm or refute any human idea *completely*. This criterion
also is sufficiently "indefinite" not to allow human knowledge to

become "absolute," but at the same time it is sufficiently definite to wage a ruthless fight on all varieties of idealism and agnosticism. If what our practice confirms is recognition that the only path to this truth is the path of science, which holds the materialist point of view ... the sole conclusion to be drawn from the opinion of the Marxists that Marx's theory is an objective truth is that by following the *path* of Marxian theory we shall draw closer and closer to objective truth (without ever exhausting it) ; but by following *any other path* we shall arrive at nothing but confusion and lies. (*Materialism and Empirio-Criticism*, 1908, *Selected Works*, XI, 205.)

2. DIALECTICAL MATERIALISM

The great Hegelian dialectics which Marxism, after having put it on its feet, made its own, must never be confused with the vulgar procedure of justifying the zigzags of politicians who swing over from the revolutionary wing to the opportunist wing of the Party, or with the vulgar habit of lumping together all the individual statements, the individual moments in the development of the various stages of a single process. Genuine dialectics does not justify individual errors; it studies the inevitable turns and proves their inevitablity by means of a thorough, detailed analysis of the process in all its concreteness. The fundamental thesis of dialectics is: There is no such thing as abstract truth, truth is always concrete. (*One Step Forward, Two Steps Back*, 1904, *Selected Works*, II, 463.)

Just as man's knowledge reflects nature (i.e., developing matter) , which exists independently of him, so man's *social knowledge* (i.e., the various views and doctrines—philosophical, religious, political and so forth) reflects the *economic system* of society. Political institutions are a superstructure on the economic foundation. (*The Three Sources and Three Component Parts of Marxism*, March, 1913, *Selected Works*, XI, 5.)

DIALECTICS

. . . In our times, the idea of development, of evolution, has almost fully penetrated social consciousness, but it has done so in other ways, not through Hegel's philosophy. Still, the same idea, as formulated by Marx and Engels on the basis of Hegel's philosophy, is much more comprehensive, much more abundant in content than the current theory of evolution. A development that repeats, as it were, the stages already passed, but repeats them in a different way, on a higher plane ("negation of negation") ; a development, so to speak, in spirals, not in a straight line; a development in leaps and bounds, catastrophes, revolutions; "intervals of gradualness"; transformation of quantity into quality; inner impulses for development, imparted by the contradiction, the conflict of different forces and tendencies reacting on a given body or inside a given phenomenon or within a given society; interdependence, and the closest, indissoluble connection between *all* sides of every phenomenon (history disclosing ever new sides) , a connection that provides the one world process of motion proceeding according to law—such are some of the features of dialectics as a doctrine of evolution more full of meaning than the current one. (*Karl Marx,* November, 1914, *Selected Works,* XI, 17 f.)

MATERIALIST CONCEPTION OF HISTORY

Realizing the inconsistency, the incompleteness, and the one-sidedness of the old materialism, Marx became convinced that it was necessary "to harmonize the science of society with the materialist basis, and to reconstruct it in accordance with this basis." If, speaking generally, materialism explains consciousness as the outcome of existence, and not conversely, then, applied to the social life of mankind, materialism must explain *social* consciousness as the outcome of *social* existence. "Technology," writes Marx in the first volume of *Capital,* "reveals man's dealings with nature, discloses the direct productive activities of his life, thus throwing light upon social relations and the resultant mental conceptions."...

. . . .

The discovery of the materialist conception of history, or, more correctly, the consistent extension of materialism to the domain of social phenomena, obviated the two chief defects in earlier historical theories. For, in the first place, those theories, at best, examined only the ideological motives of the historical activity of human beings without investigating the origin of these ideological motives, or grasping the objective conformity to law in the development of the system of social relationships, or discerning the roots of these social relationships in the degree of development of material production. In the second place, the earlier historical theories ignored the activities of the *masses*, whereas historical materialism first made it possible to study with scientific accuracy the social conditions of the life of the masses and the changes in these conditions. At best, pre-Marxist "sociology" and historiography gave an accumulation of raw facts collected at random, and a description of separate sides of the historic process. Examining the *totality* of all the opposing tendencies, reducing them to precisely definable conditions in the mode of life and the method of production of the various *classes* of society, discarding subjectivism and free will in the choice of various "leading" ideas or in their interpretation, showing how all the ideas and all the various tendencies, without exception, have their roots in the condition of the material forces of production, Marxism pointed the way to a comprehensive, an all-embracing study of the rise, development and decay of socioeconomic structures. People make their own history; but what determines their motives, that is, the motives of people in the mass; what gives rise to the clash of conflicting ideas and endeavors; what is the sum total of all these clashes among the whole mass of human societies; what are the objective conditions for the production of the material means of life that form the basis of all the historical activity of man; what is the law of the development of these conditions—to all these matters Marx directed attention, pointing out the way to a scientific study of history as a unified and true-to-law process despite its being extremely variegated and contradictory. (*Karl Marx,* November, 1914, *Selected Works,* XI, 17–20.)

The elements of dialectics may be represented in detail as follows: (1) *objectivity* of approach (no examples, no digressions, but the thing itself) ; (2) the totality of this thing's manifold *interconnections* with other things; (3) *development* of this thing (or phenomenon) , its individual movement and life; (4) the internally contradictory *tendencies* (*and* aspects) in the thing; (5) the thing (phenomenon, etc.) as a sum and *unity of opposites;* (6) *conflict* or disclosure of these opposites, contrariety of tendencies, etc.; (7) union of analysis and synthesis—dissecting the individual parts and the whole, synthesizing all these parts; (8) the relationships of every thing (phenomenon, etc.) are not only manifold, but general, universal. Every thing (phenomenon, process, etc.) is bound up with *every* other; (9) not only unity of opposites, but *transformation* of *every* degree, quality, feature, aspect, trait into *every* other (into its opposites) ; (10) endless process of deducing new aspects, relationships, etc.; (11) man engaged in the endless process of deepening the knowledge of things, phenomena, processes, etc., from appearance to essence, and from superficial to deeper layers of being; (12) from co-existence to causality, and from one form of interconnection and reciprocal dependence to another, deeper, more general one; (13) recapitulation of specific traits, properties, etc., on the lower level at the higher one, and (14) apparent reversion to the old form (negation of the negation) ; (15) conflict of content and form and *vice versa*. Discarding of form, transformation of content; (16) *transformation* of quantity into quality and *vice versa*. ([15] and [16] are *examples* of [9].) (*Conspectus of Hegel's* SCIENCE OF LOGIC, 1914. Compare with *Collected Works*, XXXVIII [*Philosophical Notebooks*], 221–222.)

Comrade Bukharin talks about "logical" grounds. The whole of his argument shows that he—perhaps unconsciously—holds the point of view of formal, or scholastic, logic and not of dialectical, or Marxian, logic. In order to explain what I mean, I shall start with the very simple example which Comrade Bukharin himself has given. During the discussion on December 30, 1920, he said:

Comrades, perhaps the controversy that is going on here is making the following impression upon many of you. Two men meet and ask each other: What is the glass that is standing on the rostrum? One says: "It is a glass cylinder, and he who says it is not, let him be anathemized." The other says: "A glass is a drinking vessel, and he who says it is not, let him be anathemized."

As the reader will see, Bukharin wanted, with the aid of this example, to explain to me in a popular manner the harmfulness of one-sidedness. I gratefully accept this explanation and, in order to prove my gratitude with deeds, I will reciprocate by giving a popular explanation of what eclecticism is, as distinct from dialectics.

A glass is undoubtedly a glass cylinder and a drinking vessel. But a glass not only has these two properties, or qualities, or sides, but an infinite number of other properties, qualities, sides, inter-relations and "mediations" with the rest of the world. A glass is a heavy object which may be used as a missile. A glass may serve as a paperweight, as a jar to keep a captive butterfly in; a glass may have value as an object with an artistic engraving or design, quite apart from the fact that it can be used as a drinking vessel, that it is made of glass, that its form is cylindrical, or not quite so, and so on and so forth.

To proceed. If I now need a glass as a drinking vessel, it is not at all important for me to know whether its form is com-pletely cylindrical and whether it is really made of glass; what is important is that its bottom shall not be cracked, that it should not cut my lips when I drink from it, etc. If I need a glass, not for drinking purposes, but for some purpose that any glass cylinder could serve, then even a glass with a cracked bottom, or even with no bottom at all, would do.

Formal logic, which schools confine themselves to (and which, with modifications, the lower grades should confine themselves to), offers formal definitions and is guided exclusively by what is most customary, or most often noted. If in this two or more dif-ferent definitions are combined quite casually (a glass cylinder and a drinking vessel), we get an eclectic definition which points to various sides of the object and nothing more.

Dialectical logic demands that we go further. In the first place, in order really to know an object, we must embrace, study all its sides, all connections and "mediations." We shall never achieve this completely, but the demand for all-sidedness is a safeguard against mistakes and rigidity. Secondly, dialectical logic demands that we take an object in its development, its "self-movement" (as Hegel sometimes puts it), in its changes. In relation to a glass this is not clear at once, but even a glass does not remain unchanged, particularly the purpose of the glass, its use, its *connections* with the surrounding world. Thirdly, the whole of human experience should enter the full "definition" of an object as a criterion of the truth and as a practical index of the object's connection with what man requires. Fourthly, dialectical logic teaches that "there is no abstract truth, truth is always concrete," as the late Plekhanov was fond of saying after Hegel. . . . Why is this argument of Bukharin's lifeless and vapid eclecticism? Because Bukharin does not make the slightest attempt, independently, from his own point of view, to analyze the whole history of the present controversy. . . . Bukharin . . . approaches the subject without the faintest attempt at a concrete study, with bare abstractions, and takes a little piece from Zinoviev and a little piece from Trotsky. This is eclecticism.

In order to illustrate this more graphically, I will quote an example. I know nothing about the insurgents and revolutionaries of South China (except two or three articles by Sun Yat-sen and several books and newspaper articles which I read many years ago). Since insurrections are taking place there, there are probably controversies between Chinese No. 1, who says that insurrection is the product of the most acute class struggle which embraces the whole nation, and Chinese No. 2, who says that insurrection is an art. I could write theses like Bukharin's without knowing any more: "On the one hand . . . on the other hand." One did not sufficiently take into account the "art factor," the other did not sufficiently take into account the "acuteness factor," etc. This will be lifeless and vapid eclecticism, because it lacks the *concrete* study of the *given* controversy, of the given question, of the given approach to it, etc. (*Once Again the Trade Unions, The Present Situation,* and *The Mistakes of Trotsky and Bukharin,* January 25, 1921, *Selected Works,* IX, 65–67.)

3. NATURE AND FUNCTION OF MARXIST THEORY

The case of the Russian Social Democrats strikingly illustrates the fact observed in the whole of Europe (and long ago noted also by the German Marxists) that the notorious freedom of criticism implies, not the substitution of one theory for another, but freedom from any complete and thought-out theory; it implies eclecticism and absence of principle. Those who are in the least acquainted with the actual state of our movement cannot but see that the spread of Marxism was accompanied by a certain lowering of theoretical standards. Quite a number of people with very little, and even totally lacking, theoretical training, joined the movement for the sake of its practical significance and its practical successes. We can judge, therefore, how tactless *Rabocheye Dyelo* is when, with an air of invincibility, it quotes the statement of Marx: "A single step of the real movement is more important than a dozen programs." To repeat these words in the epoch of theoretical chaos is like wishing mourners at a funeral "many happy returns of the day." Moreover, these words of Marx are taken from his letter on the Gotha Program, in which he *sharply condemns* the eclecticism in the formulation of principles: "If you must combine," Marx wrote to the Party leaders, "then enter into agreements to satisfy the practical aims of the movement, but do not haggle over principles, do not make 'concessions' in theory." This was Marx's idea, and yet there are people among us who strive—in his name!—to belittle the significance of theory.

Without a revolutionary theory there can be no revolutionary movement.

.   .   .   .

. . . The role of vanguard can be fulfilled only by a party that is guided by an advanced theory.

.   .   .   .

All subservience to the spontaneity of the labor movement, all belittling of the role of "the conscious element," of the role of Social Democracy, means, *whether one likes it or not, the growth of influence of bourgeois ideology among the workers.* All those who talk about "exaggerating the importance of ideology," about exaggerating the role of the conscious elements, etc., imagine that the pure and simple labor movement can work out an independent ideology for itself, if only the workers "take their fate out of the hands of the leaders." But this is a profound mistake.

.   .   .   .

Since there can be no talk of an independent ideology being developed by the masses of the workers in the process of their movement,[1] *the only choice is:* either bourgeois or socialist ideology. There is no middle course (for humanity has not created a "third" ideology, and, moreover, in a society torn by class antagonisms there can never be a non-class or above-class ideology). Hence, to belittle socialist ideology *in any way, to deviate from it in the slightest degree* means strengthening bourgeois ideology. There is a lot of talk about spontaneity, but the *spontaneous* development of the labor movement leads to its becoming subordinated to bourgeois ideology, leads to its developing *according to the program* of the *Credo,* for the spontaneous labor movement is pure and simple trade unionism . . . and trade unionism means the ideological enslavement of the workers to

---

[1] This does not mean, of course, that the workers have no part in creating such an ideology. But they take part not as workers, but as socialist theoreticians, like Proudhon and Weitling; in other words, they take part only to the extent that they are able, more or less, to acquire the knowledge of their age and advance that knowledge. And in order that workingmen *may be able to do this more often,* efforts must be made to raise the level of the consciousness of the workers generally; care must be taken that the workers do not confine themselves to the artificially restricted limits of *"literature for workers"* but that they study *general literature* to an increasing degree. It would be even more true to say "are not confined," instead of "do not confine themselves," because the workers themselves wish to read and do read all that is written for the intelligentsia, and it is only a few (bad) intellectuals who believe that it is sufficient "for the workers" to tell them a few things about factory conditions and to repeat over and over again what has long been known.

the bourgeoisie. Hence, our task, the task of Social Democracy, is to *combat spontaneity*, to *divert* the labor movement from its spontaneous, trade unionist striving to go under the wing of the bourgeoisie, and to bring it under the wing of revolutionary Social Democracy.

. . . .

The question now arises: What does political education mean? Is it sufficient to confine oneself to the propaganda of working class hostility to autocracy? Of course not. It is not enough to *explain* to the workers that they are politically oppressed (no more than it was to *explain* to them that their interests were antagonistic to the interests of the employers). Advantage must be taken of every concrete example of this oppression for the purpose of agitation (in the same way that we began to use concrete examples of economic oppression for the purpose of agitation). And inasmuch as *political* oppression affects all sorts of classes in society, inasmuch as it manifests itself in various spheres of life and activity, in industrial life, civic life, in personal and family life, in religious life, scientific life, etc., etc., is it not evident that *we shall not be fulfilling our task* of developing the political consciousness of the workers *if we do not undertake the organization of the political exposure of autocracy in all its aspects?* In order to carry on agitation around concrete examples of oppression, these examples must be exposed (just as it was necessary to expose factory evils in order to carry on economic agitation). (*What Is To Be Done?* 1902, *Selected Works,* II, 46–48, 61–63, 78–79.)

Marxism differs from all other socialist theories in that it represents a remarkable combination of complete scientific soundness in the analysis of the objective conditions of things and of the objective course of evolution and the very definite recognition of the significance of the revolutionary energy, the revolutionary creative genius and the revolutionary initiative of the masses—and also, of course, of individuals, groups, organizations and parties which are able to discover and establish contact with these classes. The high estimation of revolutionary periods in the development of humanity follows logically from the sum total of Marx's historical views, viz., that it is precisely in such periods that the numerous contradictions slowly accumulating in periods of so-called peaceful development find their solution. It is precisely in such periods that the direct role of the various classes in the determination of the forms of social life manifests itself with the greatest force, and the foundations are created for the political "superstructure" which for a long time after rests upon the new productive relationships. Unlike the liberal bourgeois theoreticians, Marx regarded these periods, not as a deviation from the "normal" path, a manifestation of a "social disease," the sad result of extremes and mistakes, but as the most vital, important, essential and decisive moments in the history of human society. In the activities of Marx and Engels, the period of their participation in the mass revolutionary struggle of 1848–49 stands out as a central point. This served as their starting point in determining the destiny of the labor movement and of democracy in different countries. They always returned to this point in order to determine the internal nature of the various classes and their tendencies in the most striking and purest form. It was from the point of view of the revolutionary epoch of that time that they always evaluated the later, smaller political formations and organizations, political tasks and political conflicts. (*Against the Boycott,* July 9, 1907, *Selected Works,* III, 414 f.)

4. CAPITALISM

The question was precisely whether Russia was striving to become a capitalist nation, whether the ruination of her peasants was the process of creation of the capitalist system, of the capitalist proletariat, and Marx replied that "if" she is striving to become a capitalist nation she will have to transform a good proportion of the peasantry into proletarians. In other words, Marx's theory insists on investigating and explaining the evolution of the economic systems in certain countries and its "application" to

Russia merely means *investigating* Russian relationships of production and their evolution by *utilizing* the accepted methods of *materialism* and *theoretical* political economy.

The working out of a new methodology and politico-economic theory marked such gigantic progress in social science, such a tremendous stride in the socialist movement that the principal theoretical problem that rose up before Russian Socialists almost immediately after the appearance of *Capital* was the problem of the "destiny of capitalism in Russia." Around this problem the most heated controversies arose, and in accordance with it the most important program postulates were decided. And it is a remarkable fact that when a separate group of Socialists appeared (about ten years ago) which answered the question regarding the capitalist evolution of Russia in the affirmative and based this decision on the data of Russian economic conditions, it did not encounter any direct and definite criticism of the material issue, any criticism which, based on the same methodological and theoretical principles, gave a different explanation of this data. (*What the "Friends of the People" Are and How They Fight Against the Social Democrats,* 1894, *Selected Works,* I, 293 f.)

There are three main stages in this development [of capitalism in Russian industry]: small commodity production (petty, mainly peasant trades); capitalist manufacture; and the factory (large-scale machine industry). The facts utterly refute the opinion that is widespread among us that "factory" and *"kustar"* industry are isolated from each other. On the contrary, their division is purely artificial. The connection and continuity between these two forms of industry are most direct and intimate. The facts very clearly prove that the main trend of small commodity production is toward the development of capitalism, in particular toward the rise of manufacture, and before our very eyes, manufacture is very rapidly growing into large-scale machine industry. Perhaps one of the most striking manifestations of the close and immediate connection between the consecutive forms of industry is the fact that a number of big and very big manufacturers were, at one time, the smallest of small tradesmen and passed through all the stages from "people's industry" to "capitalism." Savva Morozov was first a serf peasant (he purchased his freedom in 1820), then a shepherd, carter, weaver in a mill, then a *"kustar"* weaver, walking to Moscow to sell his cloth to merchants; then he became the owner of a small establishment for giving out work to outdoor workers, and finally a factory owner. At the time of his death in 1862, he and his numerous sons owned two large cotton mills. In 1890, the four factories which belonged to his descendants employed 39,000 workers and produced goods to the value of 35,000,000 rubles.

[After adducing additional examples, Lenin concludes:]

It would be interesting to know where, in these and similar cases, the Narodnik economists would define the beginning of "artificial" capitalism and the end of "people's" industry.

The three main forms of industry enumerated above are distinguished from each other by the different technical methods employed. The characteristic feature of small commodity production is its very primitive, hand technique that has remained unchanged from time immemorial. The craftsman remains a peasant who adopts the methods handed down by tradition of working up raw material. Manufacture introduces division of labor, which fundamentally changes the form of technique and transforms the peasant into a "detail worker." But hand labor remains, and, on this basis, progress in methods of production is inevitably very slow. Division of labor springs up spontaneously and is adopted by tradition just as in peasant labor. Large-scale machine industry alone introduces a radical change, throws hand labor overboard, transforms production on new, rational principles and systematically applies the knowledge of science to industry. Until capitalism organized large-scale machine industry in Russia, we observed—and still observe in those industries in which it has not yet organized large-scale production—almost complete stagnation in technique; we see the employment of the same kind of hand loom, the same kind of water mill or windmill that was employed in production a century ago. On the other hand, in those industries which the factory has conquered, we see a complete technical revolution and extremely rapid progress in the methods of machine production.

Owing to the difference in the technical methods employed, we see different stages of development in capitalism. The characteristic feature of small commodity production and manufacture is the prevalence of small enterprises from among which only a few large ones stand out. Large-scale machine industry completely squeezes out the small enterprises. Capitalist relationships arise also in the small trades (in the form of small workshops employing wage workers, and merchant capitalists), but these are only slightly developed and are not marked by a sharp line of antagonism between the groups of persons taking part in production. Neither big capitalists nor broad strata of proletarians have yet arisen. In manufacture we see the rise of both the one and the other. The gulf that divides the owner of the means of production from the worker has already become fairly wide. "Wealthy" industrial centers spring up, the mass of the inhabitants of which represent entirely propertyless workers. A small number of merchants, who do an enormous business in the purchase of raw materials and the sale of finished goods, and a mass of detail workers living from hand to mouth, such is the general picture which manufacture presents. But the multitude of small establishments, the preservation of contacts with the land, the preservation of tradition in production and in the whole system of life—all this creates a mass of intermediary elements between the extremes of manufacture and retards the development of these extremes. Large-scale machine industry sweeps away all these retarding factors, the extremes of social antagonism reach their highest development. All the gloomy sides of capitalism, as it were, concentrate together; the machine, as is well known, gives a powerful impetus to the undue lengthening of the working day; women and children are drawn into industry; a reserve army of unemployed is formed (and must be formed to suit the conditions of factory production); etc. However, the socialization of labor, which the factory brings about to an enormous degree, and the change it brings about in the sentiments and understanding of the people it employs (particularly the destruction of patriarchal and petty bourgeois traditions) give rise to a reaction: unlike preceding stages, large-scale machine production imperatively calls for the planned regulation and public control of production (a manifestation of the latter tendency is factory legislation) .

The very character of the development of production changes at various stages of capitalism. In small trades this development follows in the wake of the development of peasant economy; the market is extremely restricted, the distance between the producer and the consumer is small, the insignificant dimensions of production easily adapt themselves to barely fluctuating local demands. That is why the characteristic feature of industry at that stage is its stability, but that stability is tantamount to stagnation in technique and the preservation of patriarchal social relationships enmeshed in all sorts of remnants of medieval traditions. Manufacture works for a wide market—sometimes for the whole nation and, in conformity with this, production acquires the character of instability that is peculiar to capitalism and which reaches its greatest dimensions under factory production. The development of large-scale machine production cannot proceed except in spurts; periods of crisis alternate with periods of prosperity. This sporadic growth of the factory accelerates to an enormous degree the ruination of the small producers; and the workers are drawn into the factory in masses at one moment, in busy seasons, and thrown out at another. The formation of a vast reserve army of unemployed, who are prepared to take any kind of work, becomes a condition for the existence and development of large-scale machine industry. . . . [In a previous chapter] we showed the strata of the peasantry from which this army is recruited and in subsequent chapters the main occupations for which capital keeps this army in reserve were indicated. The "instability" of large-scale machine industry has always given rise, and now gives rise, to reactionary complaints among those who continue to look at things through the spectacles of the small producer and who forget that it is this "instability" alone that put an end to the stagnation of the past and stimulated the rapid change in methods of production and in all social relationships.

One of the manifestations of this change is the separation of industry from agriculture, the release of the social relationships in industry from the traditions of serfdom and the patriarchal system that hover over agriculture. In small commodity production the tradesman has not yet completely emerged from the peasant shell; in the majority of cases he remains a tiller of the soil, and this connection between small industry and small agriculture is so strong that we observe an interesting law of the parallel disintegration of the small producer in industry and in agriculture. The rise of a petty bourgeoisie and of wage workers is proceeding simultaneously in both spheres of national economy and thus preparing, at both poles of disintegration, the divorcement from farming of those engaged in industry. Under manufacture this divorcement assumes considerable dimensions. A number of industrial centers arise which do not engage in agriculture. The chief representative of industry is no longer the peasant, but the merchant manufacturer on the one hand and the "artisan" on the other. Industry and the relative development of commercial intercourse with the rest of the world raise the standard of living and culture of the population; the worker working for the merchant manufacturer begins to look down upon the peasant farmer. Large-scale machine industry completes this change, finally separates industry from agriculture, creates, as we have seen, a special class of the population which is totally alien to the old type of peasantry and which differs from the latter in its manner of living, its family relationships, in its higher standard of material and spiritual requirements. In small industry and in manufacture we always see remnants of patriarchal relations and a variety of forms of personal dependence which, in the general conditions of capitalist economy, extremely worsen the position of the toilers, degrade and corrupt them. Large-scale machine industry, by concentrating together masses of workers who frequently come from various parts of the country, cannot possibly tolerate remnants of patriarchalism and personal dependence, and is marked by its "contempt for the past." And it is precisely this rupture with obsolete tradition that served as one of the important conditions which made possible and created the necessity for the regulation and the public control of production. Particularly, in speaking of the changes the factory has brought about in the conditions of life of the population, it is necessary to observe that the drawing of women and adolescents into the factory[2] is, in the main, a progressive phenomenon. Unquestionably, capitalism extremely worsens the conditions of these categories of workers and it becomes particularly necessary to regulate and shorten their working day, to guarantee hygienic conditions of labor, etc.; but to strive to prohibit completely women and adolescents from going into industry, or to preserve the patriarchal system which prevented them from doing so, would be reactionary and utopian. By destroying the patriarchal isolation of these categories of the population who formerly never emerged from the narrow circle of domestic, family relationships, by drawing them into direct participation in social production, large-scale machine industry stimulates their development and increases their independence, i.e., creates conditions of life that are incomparably superior to the patriarchal immobility of pre-capitalist relationships.

The characteristic feature of the first two stages of development of industry is that the population is settled. The small tradesman, remaining a peasant, is bound to his village by his farm. The worker under manufacture is usually restricted to the small industrial district which is created by manufacture. There is nothing inherent in the system of industry in the first and second stages of development that disturbs the settled character and isolation of the producer. Intercourse between the various industrial districts is rare. The transfer of industry from one place to another takes place only in the form of the migration of

---

[2]According to *Index,* the factories and works in European Russia in 1890 employed 875,764 persons of whom 210,207 (27 per cent) were women, 17,793 (2 per cent) were boys and 8,216 (1 per cent) were girls.

individual small producers who establish small trades in the out-lying parts of the state. Large-scale machine industry, however, necessarily creates mobility among the population; commercial intercourse between various districts grows enormously; railways greatly facilitate travel. On the whole, the demand for labor increases, now rising in the period of boom, now falling in the period of crisis, so that it becomes necessary for the worker to go from one factory to another and from one part of the country to another. Large-scale machine industry creates new industrial centers which, with unprecedented rapidity, arise sometimes in unpopulated places—which would be impossible without the mass migration of workers. . . . The facts show also (we will add) that mobility among the industrial workers bears the same features that we observed in the mobility of the agricultural workers, viz., that the industrial workers, also, not only migrate from those districts where there is a surplus of labor, but also from those districts where there is a shortage of labor. . . . The workers leave, not only because they cannot find "local occu-pations," but also because they strive to go to those places where conditions are better. Elementary as this fact is, it is worthwhile reminding the Narodnik economists of it again, for they idealize local occupations, condemn migratory trades and ignore the progressive significance of the mobility among the population which capitalism creates.

The characteristic features described above, which distinguish large-scale machine industry from preceding forms of industry, may be summed up in the words "socialization of labor." Indeed, production for an enormous national and international market, the development of close commercial contacts with various parts of the country and with various countries in the purchase of raw materials and auxiliary materials, the enormous technological progress, the concentration of production and the population by enormous enterprises, the destruction of the outworn traditions of patriarchal life, the creation of mobility among the population and the raising of the standard of requirements and the develop-ment of the worker—all these are elements of the capitalist process which more and more socialize the production of the country and at the same time socialize those who participate in production.[3]

In regard to the question of the relation of large-scale machine industry in Russia to the home market for capitalism, the data given above lead to the following conclusion: The rapid development of factory industry in Russia creates an enormous and continuously increasing market for means of production (building material, fuel, metals, etc.); it increases with particular rapidity the *proportion of the population engaged in producing* items to be used in production and not for personal consumption. But the market for items for personal use also grows rapidly owing to the growth of large-scale machine industry, which draws a growing proportion of the population away from agriculture into commercial and industrial occupations. (*The Development of Capitalism in Russia,* 1896–1898, *Selected Works,* I, 203–212.)

We must now . . . sum up the question which in literature has come to be known as the "mission" of capitalism, i.e., of its historical role in the economic development of Russia. To admit that this role is a progressive one is quite compatible . . . with the fullest admission of the negative and gloomy sides of capitalism, with the fullest admission of the inevitable, profound and

---

[3]The data prove, in our opinion, that the classification of the capitalist forms and stages of industry given by Marx is more correct and sound than that classification which has gained currency at the present time and which confuses manufacture with the factory and regards working for the merchant as a special form of industry.... To confuse manufacture with the factory implies taking the purely superficial symptoms as the basis for the classification and ignoring the essential features of technique, economics and social life which distinguish manufacture from the machine period of capitalism. Undoubtedly, capitalist domestic industry plays a great role in the mechanism of capitalist industry. There is no doubt also that working for the merchant is a special feature of pre-machine capitalism, but it is to be met with (and in by no means small dimensions) in the most varied stages of the development of capitalism. It will be impossible to understand the significance of working for the merchant unless it is studied in connection with the whole structure of industry in the given period, or in the given stage of the development of capitalism....

all-sided social antagonisms which are a feature of capitalism and which reveal the historically transitional character of this economic system. It is the Narodniki who try with all their might to make it appear that if one admits that capitalism is historically progressive, one thereby becomes an apologist of capitalism, and it is precisely the Narodniki who underestimate (and sometimes ignore) the most profound contradictions of Russian capitalism, gloss over the disintegration of the peasantry, the capitalist character of the evolution of our agriculture, the rise of a class of rural and industrial wage workers with allotments, and gloss over the complete predominance of the lowest and worst forms of capitalism in the notorious *"kustar"* industries.

The progressive, historical role of capitalism may be summed up in two brief postulates: increase in the productive forces of social labor and the socialization of labor. But both these facts manifest themselves in very diversified processes in various branches of national economy.

The development of the productive forces of social labor is observed in complete relief only in the epoch of large-scale machine industry. Until that high stage of capitalism was reached, handicraft and primitive technique was preserved and developed quite spontaneously and at a very slow pace. The post-Reform epoch differs sharply from previous epochs in Russian history in this respect. The Russia of the wooden plow and the flail, of the water mill and hand loom, rapidly began to be transformed into the Russia of the steel plow and the threshing machine, of steam driven mills and looms. There is not a single branch of national economy that is subordinated to the capitalist mode of production in which a similarly complete transformation of technique has not been observed. Owing to the very nature of capitalism, this process of transformation cannot take place except through a series of unevennesses and disproportionalities: periods of prosperity alternate with periods of crisis, the development of one branch of industry leads to the decline of another, the progress of agriculture affects one branch in one district and another branch in another, the growth of trade and industry is faster than that of agriculture, etc. A number of errors the Narodniki commit are due to their effort to prove that this disproportionate, sporadic, feverish development is not development.

Another feature of the development of the social productive forces by capitalism is that the growth of means of production (productive consumption) is much faster than the growth of individual consumption: we have pointed out more than once how this manifests itself in agriculture and in industry. This feature is the result of the operation of the general laws of the realization of the product in capitalist society, and is in complete harmony with the antagonistic nature of this system of society.

The socialization of labor by capitalism manifests itself in the following processes: Firstly, the very growth of commodity production destroys the fragmental character of small economic units that is the feature of a natural self-sufficient economy and unites the small local markets into an enormous national (and then into a world) market. Working for oneself is transformed into working for the whole of society, and the more capitalism is developed, the greater is the contradiction between the collective character of production and the individualist character of the appropriation of the results of production. Secondly, in place of the formerly scattered production, capitalism creates production, both in agriculture and in industry, that is concentrated to a degree never witnessed before. This is the most striking and outstanding manifestation of the feature of capitalism that we are examining, but it is not the only one. Thirdly, capitalism squeezes out the forms of personal dependence that were an inseparable part of preceding systems of economy. In Russia, the progressive character of capitalism in this respect is particularly marked, for in Russia the personal dependence of the producer existed (and partly continues to exist to the present day) not only in agriculture but also in the manufacturing industries ("factories" employing serf labor), in the mining industry, in the fishing industry, etc. Compared with the labor of a dependent or bonded peasant, the labor of a free laborer is a progressive phenomenon in all branches of national economy. Fourthly, capitalism necessarily creates mobility among the population which was not required in previous systems of social economy and was impossible on any large scale under those systems. Fifthly, capitalism constantly diminishes the proportion of the population engaged in agriculture (in which the most backward forms of social and economic relationships usually predominate), and increases the number of large industrial centers. Sixthly, capitalism increases among the population the need for union, for association, and gives these associations a special character compared with associations in previous times. While breaking down the narrow, local estate associations of medieval society and creating fierce competition, capitalism at the same time divides society into large groups of persons who occupy different positions in production, and gives a tremendous impetus to the organization of the persons within each of these groups. Seventhly, all the changes referred to, which capitalism brings about in the old economic system, inevitably lead also to a change in the spiritual make-up of the population. The spasmodic character of economic development, the rapid change in the methods of production and the enormous concentration of production, the disappearance of all forms of personal dependence and patriarchal relations, the mobility of the population, the influence of the big industrial centers, etc.— all this cannot but bring about a profound change in the very character of the producers. . . .

. . . .

. . . The question as to whether the development of capitalism in Russia is slow or rapid depends entirely upon what this development is compared with. If we compare the pre-capitalist epoch in Russia with the capitalist epoch (and this is precisely the comparison that should be made if a correct solution to the problem is to be found), then we will have to admit that the development of social economy under capitalism is extremely rapid. If, however, we compare the present rate of development with the rate that would have been possible at the modern level of technology and culture generally, then we would have to admit that the present rate of development of capitalism in Russia is really slow. Nor could it be anything else but slow, for there is not a single capitalist country in the world in which ancient institutions, which are incompatible with capitalism, which retard its development, which immeasurably worsen the conditions of the producers who "suffer from capitalism as well as from the insufficient development of capitalism," have survived in such abundance as they have survived in Russia.

. . . Capitalism during the present war has developed beyond its prewar stage. It now controls whole branches of production. As far back as 1891, i.e., twenty-seven years ago, when the Germans adopted their Erfurt Program, Engels maintained that capitalism could no longer be regarded as planless.[4] That idea is antiquated; as soon as there are trusts, planlessness ceases. The development of capitalism has made gigantic strides, particularly in the twentieth century, and the war has done more than had been done in twenty-five years. State control of industry has advanced not only in Germany, but also in England. Monopoly in general has evolved into state monopoly. Objective conditions show that the war has accelerated the development of capitalism, which advanced from capitalism to imperialism, from monopoly to state control. (*Report on the Current Situation* . . . . May 7, 1917, *Selected Works,* VI, 99.)

It is time to abandon the prejudice that only Communists, among whom there are excellent people without question, can perform any definite piece of work. It is time to abandon this prejudice; we need workers who know their job, and we must enlist them all in the work.

Capitalism has left us a great heritage; it has left us its big experts. And we must unquestionably utilize them, utilize them

---

[4]Lenin is referring to the following words of Engels: "When we pass from joint stock companies to trusts which control and monopolize whole branches of industry, it is not only private production that ceases, but also planlessness." These words are contained in a letter to Kautsky dated June 29, 1891. (*Selected Works,* VI, 540.)—*Ed.*

on a broad and mass scale; we must find work for every one of them. We have absolutely no time to spend on training experts from among our Communists, because everything now depends on practical work and practical results. (*Speech Delivered at the Second All-Russian Congress of Councils of National Economy,* December 25, 1918, *Selected Works,* VIII, 217.)

5. SOCIALISM

Socialism[5] is a protest and struggle against the exploitation of the toilers, a struggle for the complete abolition of this exploitation. (*Selected Works,* I, 300.)

When Narodism first arose . . . the theory was a rather symmetrical one; starting out with the concept of a special form of national life, it was based on the belief in the communist instincts of the "village commune" peasant and for that reason regarded the peasantry as the direct champions of socialism. But it lacked theoretical analysis—confirmation by the facts of Russian life, on the one hand, and experience in applying a political program based on these assumed qualities of the peasant, on the other.

The development of the theory proceeded along these two lines, theoretical and practical. Theoretical work was directed mainly toward studying the form of *landownership* in which they wished to see the rudiments of communism; and this work resulted in the accumulation of a wealth of facts of the most varied kind. But this wealth of material, which dealt mainly with the forms of *landownership,* completely obscured from the eyes of the investigators the *economics* of the countryside. This was all the more natural, firstly, because the investigators lacked a fixed theory regarding the method of social science, a theory that would explain the necessity for singling out and giving special study to relationships in production and, secondly, the

[5]The following passages (pp. 29–37) are selected from *What the "Friends of the People" Are and How They Fight Against the Social Democrats,* 1894. Only volume and page from *Selected Works* are acknowledged in the text.

material collected served as direct evidence of the immediate needs of the peasantry, their immediate misfortunes which had a depressing effect upon peasant economy. All the attention of the investigators was concentrated on studying these misfortunes —the lack of land, the high taxes and other payments, lack of rights, the wretchedness and oppression of the peasants. All this was described and studied and explained with such a wealth of material, in such minute detail that had our government not been a class government, had its policy been determined not by the interests of the ruling classes, but by an impartial consideration of the "needs of the people," it would, of course, have been convinced a thousand times of the necessity of removing these misfortunes. The naive investigators, believing in the possibility of "persuading" society and the state, were completely submerged in the details of the facts they had collected and lost sight of one thing, the politico-economic structure of the countryside; they lost sight of the main background of the form of economy that was really being depressed by these direct and immediate misfortunes. Naturally, the result was that defense of the interests of the system of economy that was being depressed by the lack of land, etc., turned out to be the defense of the interests of the class in whose hands this system of economy was concentrated and which was the only class that could hold on and develop in the given social and economic relationships prevailing *within* the village commune under the economic system prevailing in the country.

Theoretical work directed toward the study of the institution which was to serve as the basis and support for the abolition of exploitation led to the drawing up of a program which expresses the interests of the petty bourgeoisie, i.e., the very class upon which the exploiting system rests.

At the same time, practical revolutionary work also developed in an altogether unexpected direction. Belief in the communist instincts of the muzhik naturally demanded that the Socialists abandon politics and "go among the people." A large number of energetic and talented people undertook to carry out this program, but practice proved to them how naive was the idea about the communist instincts of the muzhik. Incidentally, it was decided that it was not a matter of the muzhik, but of the government—and the whole of the work was then concentrated on fighting the government, but it was only intellectuals, and *workers* who sometimes joined them, who carried on this fight. At first this fight was waged in the name of socialism and was based on the theory that the people were ready for socialism and that it would be possible, merely by seizing power, not only to bring about a political revolution but also a social revolution. Lately, however, this theory is apparently becoming discredited and the fight the *Narodnaya Volya* waged against the government is being transformed into a struggle waged by radicals for political liberty.

Hence, from the other side also, the work led to results which were the very opposite to the starting point; from the other side also, there emerged a program which expressed only the interests of radical bourgeois democracy. Strictly speaking, this process has not yet been completed, but it has already become clearly defined. This development of Narodism was quite natural and inevitable, because the doctrine was based on the purely mythical conception of a special (communal) system of peasant economy; the myth dissolved when it came into contact with reality, and peasant socialism was transformed into radical democratic representation of the petty bourgeois peasantry. (*Selected Works*, I, 303–305.)

The petty bourgeois theories we discussed above are *absolutely* reactionary in so far as they are put forward as socialist theories.

But if we understand that there is absolutely nothing social-istic about these theories, that they utterly fail to explain the exploitation of the toilers and, therefore, are totally useless as a means for their emancipation, that as a matter of fact all these theories reflect and vindicate the interests of the petty bourgeoisie—then our attitude toward them must be different, then we must put the question: *What should be the attitude of the working class toward the petty bourgeoisie and its program?* And it will be impossible to reply to this question unless the dual character of this class is taken into consideration (in Russia, this duality is particularly marked owing to the fact that the antagonism between the big bourgeoisie and the petty bourgeoisie is less developed). It is a progressive class in so far as it puts forward general democratic demands, i.e., fights against all survivals of the epoch of medievalism and serfdom; it is a reactionary class in so far as it fights to maintain its position as a petty bourgeois class and to retard, to turn back the general development of the country from the bourgeois direction. Reactionary demands, as, for example, the inalienability of allotments, as well as the many other projects for placing a guardianship over the peasants, are usually put forward on the plausible pretext of protecting the toilers; as a matter of fact, of course, they only make their conditions worse while at the same time they hamper them in their struggle for their emancipation. A strict distinction must be drawn between these two sides of the petty bourgeois program and, while denying that these theories in any way bear a socialistic character and while combating their reactionary sides, we must not forget about the democratic part of their program. I will quote an example in order to show that the complete repudiation of petty bourgeois theories by Marxists does not prevent them from including democratic demands in their program; on the contrary, it calls for stronger insistence on these demands than ever. Above, we mentioned the three main postulates which were the stock-in-trade of the representatives of petty bourgeois socialism, viz., lack of land, high land purchase payments and the tyranny of administration.

There is absolutely nothing socialistic in the demand for the abolition of these evils, for they do not in the least explain the causes of expropriation and exploitation, and their removal would not in the least affect capital's oppression of labor. But the removal of these evils would purge this oppression of its medieval attributes, which serve to intensify it; it would facilitate labor's direct struggle against capital and, for that reason, as a democratic demand, will be energetically supported by the workers. Speaking generally, the question of payments and taxes is one to which only a petty bourgeois would attach particular importance, but in Russia, in many respects, the payments made by the peasants are simply remnants of serfdom: such, for example, are the land payments, which should be immediately and completely abolished; such, for example, are those taxes which the peasants and the urban petty bourgeoisie have to pay, but from which the "nobility" are exempted. Social Democrats will always support demands for the removal of these remnants of medieval relationships which cause economic and political stagnation. The same thing must be said in regard to lack of land. I have already proved in detail the bourgeois character of the complaints on this score. But there is no doubt that the land enclosures permitted under the Peasant Reform positively robbed the peasants for the benefit of the landlords and rendered a service to this great reactionary force directly (by seizing the peasants' lands) and indirectly (by the artful manner in which the peasant allotments were apportioned). Social Democrats will most strenuously insist on the immediate return to the peasants of the land of which they have been deprived, and the complete expropriation of the landlords—the bulwark of serf institutions and traditions. This latter point, which coincides with the nationalization of the land, contains nothing socialistic because the farmer relationships, which are already arising in this country, would flourish much more quickly and to a larger extent if the land were nationalized, but it is extremely important in the democratic sense as the only measure that will finally break the power of the landed nobility. Finally, only people like Messrs. Yuzhakov and V. V., of course, can talk of the peasants' lack of rights as being the cause of the expropriation and the exploitation of the peasants; but not only is the tyranny of the administration over the peasantry beyond a doubt, it is something more than simply tyranny, it is treating the peasants as the "base rabble" who, by their very nature, must be subject to the noble landlords, to whom the right to enjoy common civic rights is given only as a special favor (colonization,[6] for example), and whom any pompadour[7] can order about as if they were inmates of a workhouse. Social Democrats will unhesitatingly join in the demand for the complete restoration of the civic rights of the peasants, for the complete abolition of all privileges for the nobility, the abolition of the bureaucratic tutelage over the peasantry and for self-government for the peasantry.

Generally speaking, Russian Communists, the followers of Marxism, should more than anyone else call themselves *Social Democrats* and never, in their activities, forget the enormous importance of democracy.[8]

In Russia, the remnants of medieval, semi-serf institutions are still so very strong (compared with Western Europe), they impose such a heavy yoke upon the proletariat, and upon the people generally, and retard the growth of political thought among all estates and classes, that one cannot refrain from urging the tremendous importance for the workers of the struggle against all serf institutions, against absolutism, the estates and the bureaucracy. Every effort must be made to explain to the worker in the greatest possible detail what a terrible, reactionary force these institutions represent, how they increase the power of capital over labor, how they degrade the workers, how they retain capital in its medieval forms which, while conceding nothing to the modern, industrial forms as far as the exploita-

---

[6]One cannot help recalling here the purely Russian insolence of a serf owner with whom Mr. Yermolov, now Minister of Agriculture, in his book, *Bad Harvests and National Calamities,* protests against the settling of the peasants on new territory. This, he says, cannot be regarded as rational from the point of view of the state when in European Russia the landlords are suffering from a shortage of labor. What indeed do the peasants exist for, if not to feed by their labor the idle landlords and their "high placed" hangers-on?

[7]"Pompadour," a word used by the satirist Saltykov-Shchedirn, means petty tyrant, stubborn administrator or willful bureaucrat.—*Ed.*

[8]This is a very important point. Plekhanov is quite right when he says that our revolutionaries have "two enemies: old prejudices which have not yet been eradicated, on the one hand, and a narrow conception of the new program, on the other."

tion of labor is concerned, add to this exploitation enormous difficulties in the struggle for emancipation. The workers must understand that unless these pillars of reaction[9] are overthrown it will be utterly impossible for them to wage a successful struggle against the bourgeoisie, because as long as they exist, the Russian rural proletarian, whose support is absolutely essential if the working class is to attain victory, will never cease to be a wretched and cowed creature, capable only of acts of sullen desperation and not of sensible and sturdy protest and struggle. And that is why it is the imperative duty of the working class to fight side by side with radical democracy against absolutism and the reactionary estates and institutions—and Social Democrats must urge the workers to do this while not for a moment ceasing to explain to them that it is necessary to wage a struggle against these institutions only as a means of facilitating the struggle against the bourgeoisie, that the achievement of general democratic demands is necessary for the working class only as a means of clearing the road to victory over the chief enemy of the toilers, viz., capital, an institution which is purely democratic in its nature but which, in Russia, is strongly inclined to sacrifice its democracy and enter into alliance with reaction in order to

---

[9]A particularly imposing reactionary institution, and one our revolutionaries have paid relatively little attention to, is our native bureaucracy, which *de facto* rules the Russian state. Its ranks reinforced mainly by members of the middle class, this bureaucracy is both in origin and in the purpose and character of its activities profoundly bourgeois, but absolutism and the enormous political privileges of the landed aristocracy have given it particularly harmful qualities. It is a weathercock which sees its supreme task in combining the interests of the landowner and the bourgeois. It is a Yudushka who takes advantage of his serf-owning sympathies and connections to fool the workers and peasants and, on the pretext of "protecting the economically weak" and acting as their "guardian" to protect them from the kulak and usurer, passes measures which reduce the toilers to the position of "base rabble," surrenders them completely to the serf-owning landowner and makes them more defenseless against the bourgeoisie. It is a most dangerous hypocrite who, having learned from the experience of the Western European masters of reaction, skillfully conceals its Arakcheyev designs with the figleaf of phrases about loving the people. [Yudushka is a character in Shchedrin's *The Golovlov Family*, typifying the pious hypocrite Arakcheyev, a police expert of the time of Alexander I.—*Ed.*]

suppress the workers and to retard the labor movement still further. (*Selected Works,* I, 315–319.)

The Social Democrats are often reproached with wanting to monopolize the theory of Marx whereas, it is argued, his economic theory is accepted by all Socialists. But the question arises, what is the use of explaining to the workers the form of value, the nature of the bourgeois system, and the revolutionary role of the proletariat if, in Russia, the exploitation of the toilers is not due to the bourgeois system of organization of economy, but, say, to the lack of land and income, and the tyranny of the administration?

What is the use of explaining the theory of the class struggle to the workers if that theory cannot even explain their relationship to the manufacturers (capitalism in Russia is artificially implanted by the government), let alone the relationship of the mass of the "people" which does not belong to the factory worker class which has arisen?

How can the economic theory of Marx and the deduction drawn from it, viz., the revolutionary role of the proletariat as the organizer of communism through the medium of capitalism, be accepted, if efforts are made to find ways to communism other than capitalism and the proletariat which it has created? (*Selected Works,* I, 321.)

The socialist intelligentsia can expect to perform fruitful work only when it abandons illusions and begins to seek support in the actual and not the desired development of Russia, in the actual and not the possible social and economic relationships. Moreover, its theoretical work should be directed toward the concrete study of all forms of economic antagonisms in Russia, the study of all their connections and sequence of development; it must expose these antagonisms wherever they have been concealed by political history, by the peculiarities of legal systems and by established theoretical prejudices. It must present a complete picture of our conditions as a definite system of relationships in production and show that the exploitation and expropriation of the toilers are inevitable under this system, and point to the way out of this system that has been indicated by economic development. (*Selected Works,* I, 324.)

DRAFT OF THE PROGRAM OF THE SOCIAL DEMOCRATIC PARTY (1895–1896)

A

1. Large factories and works are developing more and more rapidly in Russia, ruining the small *kustars* and peasants and converting them into propertyless workers, driving more and more people into the towns and into factory and industrial villages.

2. This growth of capitalism implies an enormous increase in wealth and luxury among a handful of manufacturers, merchants and landowners and a still more rapid increase of poverty and oppression among the workers. The improvements in production and machinery introduced by the large factories, while serving to increase the productivity of social labor, at the same time serve to increase the power of capital over the workers, to increase unemployment and, simultaneously, the defenselessness of the workers.

3. But, while increasing the oppression of labor by capital to the highest degree, the big factories have created a special class of workers who obtain the opportunity of waging a struggle against capital because the very conditions of their lives destroy all their ties with their own enterprises and, combining the workers by common labor and shifting them from factory to factory, unite together large masses of workers. The workers begin to wage their struggle against the manufacturers by means of strikes, and a strong desire to unite springs up among them. Out of separate uprisings of workers arises the struggle of the Russian working class.

4. The working class struggle against the capitalist class is a struggle against all classes that live on the labor of others, and against all exploitation. This struggle can end only in the

transition of political power to the hands of the working class and the transference of all the land, implements, factories, machines and mines to the whole of society for the purpose of organizing socialist production, under which all that which is produced by the workers and all improvements in production will be for the benefit of the toilers themselves.

5. In its nature and aims, the Russian working class movement forms part of the international working class movement.

6. The principal obstacle in the struggle of the Russian working class for its emancipation is the absolutist, autocratic government with its irresponsible officials. Relying on the privileges enjoyed by the landlords and capitalists and pandering to their interests, it keeps the lower orders in a state of complete lack of rights and thereby hampers the labor movement and retards the development of the whole of the people. For that reason, the struggle of the Russian working class for its emancipation inevitably gives rise to a struggle against the absolute power of the autocratic government.

B

1. The Russian Social Democratic party declares its task to be—to assist in this struggle of the Russian working class by developing the class consciousness of the workers, by helping them to organize and by teaching them the real aims of the struggle.

2. The struggle of the Russian working class for its emancipation is a political struggle, and its first aim is to achieve political liberty.

3. For that reason, the Russian Social Democratic party, while remaining part of the labor movement, will support every social movement against the absolute power of the autocratic government, against the privileged class of landed aristocracy and against the remnants of serfdom and the estate system which restrict free competition.

4. On the other hand, the Russian Social Democratic party will wage war against all attempts to bestow on the toiling classes the guardianship of the absolutist government and its

officials and to retard the development of capitalism and, hence, the development of the working class.

5. The emancipation of the working class must be the task of the working class itself.

6. The Russian people need, not assistance from the absolutist government and its officials, but emancipation from their tyranny.

C

On the basis of these views, the Russian Social Democratic party demands first of all:

1. The convocation of a *Zemski Sobor* of the representatives of all citizens for the purpose of drawing up a constitution.

2. Universal and direct suffrage for all Russian citizens who have reached the age of twenty-one without distinction of religion and nationality.

3. Freedom of assembly, right of association and the right to strike.

4. Freedom of the press.

5. Abolition of the estates and complete equality of all citizens before the law.

6. Liberty of conscience and equal rights for all nationalities. The transference of the registration of births and deaths to independent civil officials who shall be independent of the police.

7. The right of every citizen to lay a charge against any official in the courts without having first to complain to the higher officials.

8. The abolition of passports, complete liberty to move from place to place and to settle in other parts of the country.

9. Liberty to engage in any trade or occupation and the abolition of the guilds.

D

For the workers, the Russian Social Democratic party demands:

1. The establishment of industrial courts in all branches of industry, the judges to be elected in equal number by the capitalists and the workers, respectively.

2. The legal restriction of the working day to eight hours.

3. The legal prohibition of night work and night shifts. Prohibition of the employment of children under fifteen years of age.

4. The legislative enactment of rest days and holidays.

5. The extension of factory laws and factory inspection to all branches of industry over the whole of Russia and also to state factories and to *kustars* working in their own homes.

6. That factory inspectors occupy an independent position and shall not be subordinate to the Ministry of Finance. That members of the industrial courts enjoy equal rights with factory inspectors in regard to the supervision of the application of the factory laws.

7. That payment of wages in goods be completely prohibited everywhere.

8. That representatives of the workers be elected to supervise the proper drawing-up of wage rates, the rejection of bad work, the expenditure of money collected in fines, and the housing conditions of the workers at the factories.

That a law be passed to the effect that the total deductions from wages for whatever purpose (fines, deductions for bad work, etc.) shall not exceed ten kopeks per ruble of wages earned.

9. That a law be passed making the employer responsible for injury to the workers, the onus of proof that the injury was due to the fault of the worker to be placed on the employer.

10. That a law be passed making it compulsory for employers to maintain schools and provide medical service for the workers.

E

For the peasants, the Russian Social Democratic party demands:

1. The abolition of land purchase payments, the peasants to be compensated for payments already made. The peasants to be compensated for all payments made to the state in excess of what was due.

2. The restoration to the peasants of the land that was cut off from their holdings in 1861.

3. Complete equality of dues and taxes imposed on peasant and landowner lands.

4. The abolition of the system of collective responsibility[10] and the repeal of all laws that restrict the peasants in the disposal of their land. (*Selected Works,* I, 341–345.)

Social Democracy is a combination of the labor movement with socialism. Its task is not passively to serve the labor movement at each of its separate stages, but to represent the interests of the movement as a whole, to point out to this movement its ultimate aims and its political tasks, and to protect its political and ideological independence. Isolated from Social Democracy, the labor movement becomes petty and inevitably becomes bourgeois. In conducting only the economic struggle, the working class loses its political independence; it becomes the tail of other parties and this runs counter to the great slogan: "The emancipation of the workers must be the task of the workers themselves." In every country there has been a period in which the labor movement existed separately from the socialist movement, each going its own road; and in every country this state of isolation weakened both the socialist movement and the labor movement. Only the union of socialism with the labor movement in each country created a durable basis for both the one and the other. But in every country this combination of socialism with the labor movement took place historically, was brought about in a special way, in accordance with the conditions prevailing at the time in that country. In Russia, the necessity for uniting socialism with the labor movement was proclaimed in theory long ago, but it is only now being put into practice. The process of uniting the two movements is an extremely difficult one, and there is therefore nothing surprising in the fact that it is accompanied by vacillations and doubts.

What lesson should we learn from the past?

The whole history of Russian socialism has so brought it about that the most urgent task of the day is to fight against the autocratic government to win political liberty. Our socialist

---

[10]In the event of a peasant failing to pay taxes or other imposts, the whole village was held responsible.—*Ed.*

movement has concentrated, so to speak, on the struggle against the autocracy. On the other hand, history has shown that the isolation of socialist thought from the advanced representatives of the working class is greater in Russia than in other countries, and that as long as this isolation continues, the revolutionary movement in Russia is doomed to impotence. From this emerges automatically the task which Russian Social Democracy is destined to fulfil: to imbue the masses of the proletariat with the ideas of socialism and with political consciousness, and to organize a revolutionary party closely allied with the spontaneous labor movement. (*The Urgent Tasks of the Movement,* December, 1900, *Selected Works,* II, 11 f.)

DRAFT OF A PROGRAM FOR THE SOCIAL DEMOCRATIC PARTY OF RUSSIA (FEBRUARY 1902)

A

1. Commodity production is developing in Russia at an increasing rate, and the domination of the capitalist system of production is becoming more and more complete.

2. The continuous advance of technology results in small production being squeezed out by large-scale production. The important part of the means of production (land and factories, tools and machinery, railways and other means of communication) is becoming concentrated in the hands of a relatively insignificant number of capitalists and big landowners as their private property. Independent small producers (peasants, home workers, artisans) are being ruined more and more, losing their means of production and thus becoming transformed into proletarians, or else into the servants and tributaries of capital. An ever-increasing number of workers are compelled to fall back on the sale of their labor; they become wage laborers dependent on the owners, and by their labor create the wealth of the latter.

3. The greater the advances made by technological progress, the more does the growth of the demand for labor lag behind the growth of its supply, and the greater become the possibilities of the capitalists of raising the rate of exploitation of the

workers. Insecurity of existence and unemployment, the burden of exploitation and every kind of humiliation become the lot of increasingly wide strata of the working population.

4. This process is still further aggravated by industrial crises, which are the inevitable outcome of the fundamental contradictions of capitalism. The poverty and destitution of the masses go hand in hand with the waste of social wealth as a consequence of the impossibility of finding markets for the commodities produced.

5. Thus the gigantic development of the productive forces of social, and increasingly socialized, labor is accompanied by the fact that all the chief advantages of this development are monopolized by an insignificant minority of the population. The growth of the wealth of society is accompanied by the growth of social inequality; the gulf between the class of owners (bourgeoisie) and the class of the proletariat becomes deeper and wider.

B

6. But while all these inevitable contradictions of capitalism grow and develop, the numbers and the solidarity, the discontent and the indignation of the proletariat also grow, the struggle between the working class and the capitalist class is aggravated, and the desire grows to throw off the intolerable yoke of capitalism.

7. The emancipation of the working class can only be the task of the working class itself. All the other classes of contemporary society stand for preserving the foundations of the existing economic order. The real emancipation of the working class requires a social revolution—which is being prepared by the whole evolution of capitalism—i.e., the abolition of the private ownership of the means of production, their transformation into the property of the state and the substitution of the socialist organization of the production of commodities for the capitalist production of commodities for the benefit of society as a whole, with the object of securing the greatest benefit and the free and all-around development of all its members.

8. This proletarian revolution will completely abolish the division of society into classes and, consequently, all the social and political inequality arising out of that division.

9. In order to carry out this social revolution, the proletariat must win political power, which will make it the master of the situation and allow it to remove all obstacles that stand in the way of its great objective. In this sense, the dictatorship of the proletariat is the necessary political condition of the social revolution.

10. Russian Social Democracy sets itself the task of laying bare before the workers the irreconcilable antagonism between their interests and the interests of the capitalists, of showing to the proletariat the historical significance, character and condition of the social revolution it is destined to carry out, and of organizing a revolutionary class party capable of directing all the manifestations of the struggle of the proletariat.

11. But the development of international exchange and of production for the world market has created so close a link between all the nations of the civilized world that today the working class movement had to be, and long ago became, an international movement. Russian Social Democracy regards itself as a unit of the world army of the proletariat, as part of international Social Democracy.

12. The immediate objectives of Russian Social Democracy are, however, considerably modified by the fact that in our country numerous remnants of the pre-capitalist, feudal social order very greatly retard the development of productive forces, render impossible the complete and all-around development of the class struggle of the proletariat, keep down the standard of living of the working population, determine the barbarous Asiatic forms under which the peasantry, numbering many millions, is eliminated, and keep all the people in a state of ignorance, inequality and subjection.

13. The most important of these remnants of the serf system and the most powerful bulwark of all this barbarism is the tsarist autocracy. It is the worst and most dangerous enemy of

the movement for the emancipation of the proletariat and the cultural development of the whole of the people.

C

For these reasons[11] the Russian Social Democratic Labor party sets itself as an immediate political task: to overthrow the tsarist autocracy and to supplant it by a *republic* on the basis of a democratic constitution that would secure:

1. The sovereignty of the people, i.e., the concentration of all the sovereign power in the state in the hands of a legislative assembly composed of the representatives of the people.

2. Universal, equal and direct suffrage in the elections to the legislative assembly as well as to all the organs of local government for every citizen having attained the age of twenty-one; secret ballot at the elections; the right of every elector to be elected to any of the representative assemblies; payment of the representatives of the people.

3. The inviolability of the person and homes of citizens.

4. Unrestricted freedom of conscience, speech, of the press, of assembly; the right to strike and to organize unions.

5. Freedom to move from place to place and to engage in any trade desired.

6. The abolition of estates; complete equality of rights for all citizens, irrespective of sex, religion or race.

7. The recognition of the right of self-determination for all nationalities in the state.

8. The right of every citizen to bring suit against any official, without having first to file charges with the latter's superiors.

9. The abolition of the standing army and the latter's replacement by the universal arming of the people.

10. The separation of the church from the state and of the schools from the church.

11. Universal, free and compulsory education up to the age

---

[11]Here begins the text adopted by the commission as a whole (i.e., the Program Commission of the editorial board of *Iskra*).—*Ed.*

of sixteen; poor children to be furnished with food, clothes and school supplies at the cost of the state.

D

For the purpose of protecting the working class and of increasing its fighting power,[12] the Russian Social Democratic Labor party demands:

1. The limitation of the working day for all wage laborers to eight hours in every twenty-four.

2. The legal enactment of a continuous weekly rest period of not less than thirty-six hours for all wage laborers of both sexes in all branches of the national economy.

3. The prohibition of all overtime work.

4. The prohibition of night work (from 9 P.M. to 5 A.M.) in all branches of the national economy except those in which it is absolutely necessary for technical reasons.

5. The prohibition of wage labor for children under fifteen.

6. The prohibition of female labor in occupations particularly harmful to women's health.

7. The legal responsibility of employers for the complete or partial disablement of workers if this disablement is due to accident or to harmful working conditions; the workers to be freed from the onus of proof that the disablement was the employer's fault.

8. The prohibition of payment of wages in kind.[13]

9. State pensions for aged workers who have lost the capacity to work.

10. That the number of factory inspectors be increased; that female inspectors be appointed in those occupations in which

---

[12]Moved by Lenin to amend the beginning of the paragraph: "For the purpose of preserving the working class from physical and moral degeneration, as well as for the purpose of increasing its power in its struggle for its emancipation . . ."—*Ed*.

[13]Moved by Lenin to insert here: "The compulsory inclusion in all contracts concerning the hiring of workers of a clause guaranteeing weekly payment of wages."—*Ed*.

female labor predominates; that the observance of the factory laws be placed under the supervision of representatives elected by the workers and to be paid by the state; fixing of piece rates and deductions for spoiled work to be supervised by elected representatives of the workers.

11. That the organs of local government set up bodies, to include representatives of the workers, to inspect the sanitary condition of the dwellings assigned by the employers for the workers, as well as the regulations concerning these dwellings and their conditions of lease—with the object of protecting the wage laborers in their lives as private persons and citizens from the interference of the employers.

12. That a properly organized all-around system of health inspection of the conditions of work in all enterprises employing wage labor be established.

13. That factory inspection be extended to artisan, home and rural industry, and to state enterprises.

14. That breach of the factory acts be deemed a criminal offense.

15. The prohibition of all deductions from wages, on any pretext or for any object whatsoever (fines, spoiled work, etc.).

16. The establishment of industrial courts in all branches of the national economy, on which the workers and the employers shall be represented in equal numbers.

E

In addition to this and with the object of democratizing Russia's state economy, the Russian Social Democratic Labor party demands: the abolition of all indirect taxation and the establishment of a graduated income tax.

With a view to removing the remnants of the old serf system, the Party will strive to obtain:[14]

1. The abolition of land compensation payments and quit-

---

[14]Proposed by Lenin to be inserted here: "and for the purpose of facilitating the free development of the class struggle in the countryside, the Russian Social Democratic Labor Party will strive to obtain...".—*Ed.*

rents as well as of all obligations at present imposed on the peasantry as the taxpaying estate.

2. The abolition of mutual responsibility[15] and of all laws restricting the peasants in the free disposal of their land.

3. The restitution to the people of all sums taken from it in the form of land compensation payments and quitrent; the confiscation with this object of the property of the monasteries and of the appanage estates, and the imposition of a special land tax on the big land owning nobility who received land compensation loans, the revenue from this tax to be placed into a special people's fund for the cultural and charitable needs of the rural communities.

4. The establishment of peasant committees (a) for the restitution to the rural communities (by expropriation, or, in cases where the land has changed hands, with compensation) of the land which at the time of the abolition of serfdom was taken away from the peasant and serves in the hands of the landlords as an instrument for keeping the peasants in a state of bondage, (b) for the abolition of the remnants of serfdom in the Urals, in the Altai, in the western region and in other parts of the country.

5. That the courts be empowered to reduce excessive rents and declare invalid all contracts that entail bondage.

While striving to achieve its immediate political and economic aims,[16] the Russian Social Democratic Labor party supports every opposition and revolutionary movement directed against the social and political order existing in Russia, but emphatically rejects all those reform plans which represent an extension of police tutelage over the toiling masses as a step toward the solution of the social problem.[17]

---

[15]All the members of the village commune were jointly held responsible for the payment of taxes, etc.—*Ed.*

[16]Proposed by Lenin to amend the beginning of the paragraph as follows: "While fighting for these demands, the Russian Social Democratic Labor Party," etc.—*Ed.*

[17]Proposed by Lenin to amend the end of the paragraph as follows: "projects implying any extension or consolidation of the tutelage of the police and the officials over the toiling masses."—*Ed.*

On its part, the Russian Social Democratic Labor party is firmly convinced that the complete, consistent and durable fulfillment of the political and social changes set out above can only be achieved by overthrowing the autocracy and convening a constituent assembly freely elected by the whole people. (*Selected Works*, II, 224–230.)

. . . Marx deduces the inevitability of the transformation of capitalist society into socialist society wholly and exclusively from the economic law of the movement of contemporary society. The chief material foundation of the inevitability of the coming of socialism is the socialization of labor in its myriad forms, advancing ever more rapidly, and conspicuously so, throughout the half century that has elapsed since the death of Marx—being especially plain in the growth of large-scale production, of capitalist cartels, syndicates and trusts; but also in the gigantic increase in the dimensions and the power of finance capital. The intellectual and moral driving force of this transformation is the proletariat, the physical carrier trained by capitalism itself. The contest of the proletariat with the bourgeoisie, assuming various forms which grow continually richer in content, inevitably becomes a political struggle aiming at the conquest of political power by the proletariat ("the dictatorship of the proletariat"). The socialization of production cannot fail to lead to the transfer of the means of production into the possession of society, to the "expropriation of the expropriators." An immense increase in the productivity of labor; a reduction in working hours; replacement of the remnants, the ruins of petty, primitive, individual production by collective and perfected labor—such will be the direct consequences of this transformation. Capitalism breaks all ties between agriculture and industry; but at the same time, in the course of its highest development, it prepares new elements for the establishment of a connection between the two, uniting industry and agriculture upon the basis of the conscious use of science and the combination of collective labor, the redistribution of population (putting an end at one and the same time to rural seclusion and unsociability and savagery, and to the unnatural concentration of enormous masses of population in huge cities). A new kind of family life, changes in the position of women and in the upbringing of the younger generation are being prepared by the highest forms of modern capitalism; the labor of women and children, the breakup of the patriarchal family by capitalism necessarily assume in contemporary society the most terrible, disastrous, and repulsive forms. . . . The socialism of Marx propounds the problems of nationality and the state. The nation is a necessary product, an inevitable form, in the bourgeois epoch of social development. The working class cannot grow strong, cannot mature, cannot consolidate its forces, except by "establishing itself as the nation," except by being "national" ("though by no means in the bourgeois sense of the term"). But the development of capitalism tends more and more to break down the partitions that separate the nations one from another, does away with national isolation, substitutes class antagonisms for national antagonisms. In the more developed capitalist countries, therefore, it is perfectly true that "the workers have no fatherland," and that "united action" of the workers, in the civilized countries at least, "is one of the first conditions requisite for the emancipation of the workers" (*Communist Manifesto*). The state, which is organized oppression, came into being inevitably at a certain stage in the development of society, when this society had split into irreconcilable classes, and when it could not exist without an "authority" supposed to be standing above society and to some extent separated from it.

. . . .

This condition of affairs persists even in the democratic republic, the freest and most progressive kind of bourgeois state; there is merely a change of form (the government becoming linked up with the stock exchange, and the officialdom and the press being corrupted by direct or indirect means). Socialism, putting an end to classes, will thereby put an end to the state. (*Karl Marx*, November, 1914. Compare with *Selected Works*, XI, 33 f., 35 f.)

We must repeat that we are Marxists and that we take as our basis *The Communist Manifesto,* which has been perverted and betrayed by the Social Democrats on two important points: (1) the workers have no country; "national defense" in an imperialist war is a betrayal of socialism; and (2) the Marxist doctrine of the state has been perverted by the Second International.

The term "Social Democracy" is scientifically incorrect, as Marx frequently pointed out, in particular in the *Critique of the Gotha Program* in 1875, and as Engels reaffirmed in a more popular form in 1894. From capitalism, mankind can pass directly only to socialism, i.e., to the social ownership of the means of production and the distribution of products according to the amount of work performed by each individual. Our Party looks farther ahead: Socialism is bound to pass gradually into communism, upon the banner of which is inscribed the motto "From each according to his ability, to each according to his needs."

That is my first argument.

Here is the second: The second part of the name of our Party (Social Democrats) is also scientifically incorrect. Democracy is but one form of the state, whereas we Marxists are opposed to all and every kind of state.

The leaders of the Second International (1889–1914), Messrs. Plekhanov, Kautsky and their like, have vulgarized and perverted Marxism.

The difference between Marxism and anarchism is that Marxism recognizes *the necessity of the state* for the purpose of the transition to socialism; but (and here is where we differ from Kautsky and company) *not* a state of the type of the usual, parliamentary, bourgeois, democratic republic, but a state like the Paris Commune of 1871 and the Soviets of Workers' Deputies of 1905 and 1917. (*The Tasks of the Proletariat in Our Revolution,* April 23, 1917, *Selected Works,* VI, 73.)

What, then, are the tasks of the revolutionary proletariat? The main defect and the main error in all socialist discussions is that the matter is put in too general a form—the transition to socialism. What we should discuss is concrete steps and measures. Some of them are ripe, others are not. We are in a period of transition. We have created forms that patently differ from the forms of bourgeois states. The Soviets of Workers' and Soldiers' Deputies are a form of state without parallel. This form represents the first step toward socialism, and is inevitable at the inception of a socialist society. This is a fact of decisive importance. The Russian revolution created the Soviets. No bourgeois country in the world has, or can have, such state institutions, and no socialist revolution can function with any other form of state power. The Soviets of Workers' and Soldiers' Deputies must take power not for the purpose of an immediate transition to socialism. That is impossible. For what purpose, then? They must take power in order to accomplish the first concrete steps toward the transition to socialism, steps that can and must be taken. In a case like this fear is our deadliest enemy. (*Report on the Current Situation Delivered at the May Conference of the Russian Social Democratic Labor Party,* May 7, 1917, *Selected Works,* VI, 100 f.)

DRAFT OF THE DECREE ON THE SOCIALIZATION OF THE NATIONAL ECONOMY

The critical food situation and the danger of famine created by the speculation and sabotage of the capitalists and government officials, as well as the general state of disorganization, make it essential to adopt extraordinary revolutionary measures for combating this evil.

In order that all citizens of the state, and particularly the toiling classes, shall take up the fight against this evil immediately and comprehensively, and address themselves to the proper organization of the economic life of the country, stopping at nothing and acting in the most revolutionary manner, under the leadership of their Soviets of Workers', Soldiers' and Peasants' Deputies, the following regulations are decreed:

Draft of the Decree on the Nationalization of the Banks and the Adoption of the Measures Necessitated Thereby

1. All joint stock companies are declared to be the property of the state.

2. Members of boards and directors of joint stock companies, and also all shareholders belonging to the wealthy classes (i.e., possessing property exceeding 5,000 rubles, or an income exceeding 500 rubles per month) are obliged to continue the systematic conduct of the affairs of these enterprises, observe the law relating to workers' control, surrender all shares to the State Bank and submit to the local Soviets of Workers', Soldiers' and Peasants' Deputies weekly reports of their activities.

3. State loans, foreign and domestic, are hereby annulled.

4. The interests of small holders of bonds and shares, i.e., holders belonging to the toiling classes of the population, shall be fully protected.

5. Universal labor service is hereby introduced: All citizens of both sexes between the ages of sixteen and fifty-five shall be obliged to perform work assigned to them by the local Soviets of Workers', Soldiers' and Peasants' Deputies, or by other organs of the Soviet power.

6. As a first step toward the introduction of universal labor service, it is decreed that persons belonging to the wealthy classes (see paragraph 2) shall be obliged to possess, and make proper entries in, consumers'-workers' books, or workers' budget books, which must be presented to the competent workers' organizations or to the local Soviets and their organs for weekly notations of the performance of the work undertaken.

7. For the purpose of proper control and distribution of food-stuffs and other necessary commodities, every citizen of the state shall be obliged to join a consumers' society. The food boards, committees on supply and similar organizations, and also the railway and transport unions, shall, under the guidance of the Soviets of Workers', Soldiers' and Peasants Deputies, enforce the observation of the present law. Persons belonging to the wealthy

classes, in particular, shall be obliged to perform any work assigned to them by the Soviets in the sphere of organizing and conducting the affairs of the consumers' societies.

8. The railway employees' unions shall be charged with the duty of expeditiously drawing up and immediately carrying out *extraordinary* measures for the better organization of transport, particularly as regards the transport of foodstuffs, fuel and other items of prime necessity, being guided by the instructions and orders firstly of the Soviet of Workers', Soldiers' and Peasants' Deputies and then of the bodies empowered for this purpose by them and by the Supreme Council of National Economy. Similarly, upon the railway unions, working in conjunction with the local Soviets, shall devolve the duty of energetically combating petty food profiteers and mercilessly suppressing speculation, if necessary resorting to revolutionary measures for this purpose.

9. Workers' organizations, unions of office employees and the local Soviets shall immediately set about engaging closed and demobilized enterprises, and also unemployed workers, in the performance of useful work, the production of articles of necessity, raw materials and fuel, and the processing of sales and orders. While under no circumstances postponing the performance of this work, and while likewise proceeding to the exchange of country products for city products without awaiting special instructions on the subject from superior bodies, the local unions and Soviets shall be strictly guided by the orders and instructions of the Supreme Council of National Economy.

10. Members of the wealthy classes shall be obliged to keep all their monetary possessions in the State Bank and its branches, or in the savings banks, withdrawing not more than 100–125 rubles per week (as shall be established by the local Soviets) for living purposes; withdrawals for purposes of production and trade shall be made only with a written certificate of the organs of workers' control.

For the purpose of supervising the due observation of this present law, regulations shall be drawn up providing for the exchange of the present currency bills for new currency bills.

Persons guilty of defrauding the state and the people shall be liable to the confiscation of all their property.

11. Violators of the present law, saboteurs and government officials who go on strike, and also speculators, shall be liable to a similar penalty, and to imprisonment, or to dispatch to the front, or to compulsory labor. The local Soviets and their organs shall with all due speed decide upon the most revolutionary measures to be taken for combating these real enemies of the people.

12. The trade unions and other organizations of the toilers, acting in conjunction with the local Soviets and with the participation of reliable persons recommended by Party and other organizations, shall organize mobile groups of inspectors to supervise the carrying out of the present law, to inspect the quantity and quality of work performed and to bring to trial before the revolutionary courts persons guilty of violating or evading this law. (December, 1917, *Selected Works,* VI, 442–444.)

Socialism does not extinguish competition; on the contrary, it for the first time creates the opportunity for employing it on a really *wide* and on a really *mass* scale, for drawing actually the majority of the population into an arena of labor in which they can display their abilities and reveal their talents, which are an untapped spring among the people, and which capitalism crushed, suppressed and strangled in thousands and millions.

. . . .

The Paris Commune gave a great example of how to combine initiative, independence, freedom of action and vigor from below with voluntary centralism free from stereotyped forms of rule. Our soviets are following this example. But they are still "shy," they have not yet got into their stride, have not yet "bitten into" their new, great, creative task of creating the socialist system. The Soviets must set to work more boldly and display greater initiative. Every "commune," every factory, every village, every consumers' society, every committee on supplies must *compete* with its neighbors as a practical organizer of accounting and control of labor and distribution. The program of this accounting and control is simple, clear and intelligible to all. It is: everyone to have bread; everyone to have sound footwear and good clothing; everyone to have warm dwellings; everyone to work conscientiously; not a single rogue (including those who shirk their work) to be at liberty, all to be kept in prison or put to compulsory labor of the hardest kind; not a single rich man who violates the laws and regulations of socialism to be allowed to escape the fate of the rogue, which should, in justice, be the fate of the rich man. "He who does not work, neither shall he eat"—this is the *practical* commandment of socialism. This is how things should be organized *practically*. These are the *practical* successes our "communes," and our worker and peasant organizers, should be proud of. And this applies *particularly* to the organizers among the intellectuals, because they are *too much, far too much* in the habit of being proud of their general instructions. (*How To Organize Competition*, January 10, 1918, *Selected Works*, IX, 413, 420 f.)

Introduce accurate and conscientious accounting of money, manage economically, do not be lazy, do not steal, observe the strictest discipline during work— it is precisely such slogans, which were justly scorned by the revolutionary proletariat when the bourgeoisie concealed its rule as an exploiting class by these commandments, that now, after the overthrow of the bourgeoisie, are becoming the immediate and the principal slogans of the moment.

.　.　.　.　.　.　.　.　.　.　.　.　.　.

The socialist state can rise only as a network of producers' and consumers' communes, which conscientiously calculate their production and consumption, economize labor, steadily raise the productivity of labor and thus enable the working day to be reduced to seven, six and even fewer hours per day. Nothing will be achieved unless the strictest, nationwide, all-embracing accounting and control of *grain and the production of grain* (and later of all other necessities) are organized. Capitalism left us a heritage of mass organizations which can facilitate our transition to the mass accounting and control of the distribution of goods, viz., the consumers' cooperative societies. (*The Immediate Tasks of the Soviet Government,* April, 1918, *Selected Works,* VII, 317 f., 328 f.)

Socialism cannot be built unless advantage is taken of the heritage of capitalist culture. There is nothing communism can be built from except what has been left us by capitalism. (*Report of the Central Committee of the Russian Communist Party at the Eighth Party Congress,* March 18, 1919, *Selected Works,* VIII, 36.)

In the last analysis, productivity of labor is the most important, the principal thing for the victory of the new social system. Capitalism created a productivity of labor unknown under serfdom. Capitalism can be utterly vanquished, and will be utterly vanquished, by the fact that socialism creates a new and much higher productivity of labor. This is a very difficult matter and must take a considerable time. (*A Great Beginning,* June 28, 1919, *Selected Works,* IX, 438 f.)

Socialism means the abolition of classes.

In order to abolish classes one must, firstly, overthrow the landowners and capitalists. That part of our task has been accomplished, but it is only a part, and, moreover, *not the most difficult* part. In order to abolish classes one must, secondly, abolish the difference between workingman and peasant, *one must make them all workers.* This cannot be done all at once. This task is incomparably more difficult and will of necessity be a protracted one. This task cannot be accomplished by overthrowing a class. It can be solved only by the organizational reconstruction of the whole social economy, by a transition from individual, disunited, petty commodity production to large-scale social enterprise. This transition will of necessity be extremely protracted. This transition may only be delayed and complicated by hasty and incautious administrative legislation. The transition can be accelerated only by affording such assistance to the peasant as will enable him to improve his whole technique of agriculture immeasurably, to reform it radically.

In order to solve the second and most difficult part of the problem, the proletariat, after having defeated the bourgeoisie, must unswervingly conduct its policy toward the peasantry along the following fundamental lines: The proletariat must separate, demarcate the peasant toiler from the peasant owner, the peasant worker from the peasant huckster, the peasant who labors from the peasant who profiteers.

In this demarcation lies the *whole essence* of socialism. (*Economics and Politics in the Era of the Dictatorship of the Proletariat,* October 30, 1919, *Selected Works,* VIII, 8 f.)

The victory of socialism over capitalism, the consolidation of socialism, can be regarded as assured only when the proletarian state power, having utterly suppressed all resistance of the exploiters and having secured complete stability for itself and complete subordination to itself, reorganizes the whole of industry on the basis of large-scale, collective production and on a modern technological foundation (based on the electrification of the whole national economy). This alone will enable the towns to render such radical technical and social assistance to the backward and scattered rural districts as will help to create the material basis for enormously raising the productivity of agriculture, and of agricultural labor in general, and thereby stimulate the small tillers of the soil by the force of example and their own interests to adopt large-scale collective mechanized agriculture. (*Preliminary Theses on the Agrarian Question,* July, 1920, *Selected Works,* X, 227.)

We can build communism only on the sum of knowledge, organizations and institutions, only on the stock of human forces and means left to us by the old society. Only by radically remolding the work of instructing, organizing and training the youth shall we be able to assure that the result of the efforts of the young generation will be the creation of a society unlike the old, i.e., of communist society.

. . . .

We call ourselves Communists. What is a Communist? The word "Communist" is derived from the Latin word for "common." Communist society is a society in which all things—the land, the factories—are owned in common. Communism means working in common.

Is it possible to work in common if each works on a separate plot of land? Common labor cannot be created all at once. (*The Tasks of the Youth Leagues,* October 2, 1920, *Selected Works,* IX, 467 f., 479.)

"Freedom and equality *within the limits of toiler democracy* is freedom for the small landowner (even if he farms nationalized land) to sell his surplus grain at profiteering prices, i.e., to exploit the worker." Anyone who talks about freedom and equality within the limits of toiler democracy—conditions under which the capitalists are overthrown while private property and free trade remain—is a defender of the exploiters. And in exercising its dictatorship, the proletariat must treat these defenders as exploiters, even if they call themselves Social Democrats and Socialists, or even if they admit that the Second International is putrid, and so on and so forth.

As long as the private ownership of the means of production (e.g., agricultural implements and livestock, even if the private ownership of land is abolished) and free trade exist, the economic basis of capitalism will exist. The dictatorship of the proletariat is the only means of successfully destroying this basis, the only means of abolishing classes (without which there can be no thought of real freedom for the individual—*and not for the property owner*—of real equality, in socio-political relations between man and man—*and not the hypocritical equality between the property owner and the propertyless,* between the well-fed and the hungry, between the exploiter and the exploited). On the one hand, the dictatorship of the proletariat leads to the abolition of classes, leads to it through the overthrow of the exploiters and the suppression of their resistance; on the other hand, it leads to it by neutralizing, rendering harmless the small property owner's vacillation between the bourgeoisie and the proletariat. (*False Speeches About Freedom*, December 11, 1920, *Selected Works*, X, 226 f.)

Our last—but most important, most difficult, and still most uncompleted—task is economic construction, the laying of an economic foundation for the new, the socialist, edifice, the replacement of the feudal edifice, which has been destroyed, and the capitalist edifice, only half of which has been destroyed. In this most important and most difficult of tasks we have suffered the most failures and committed the most errors. And how could one expect a task so new to the world to be begun without failures and without mistakes? But we have begun it. We are continuing it. By our "New Economic Policy" we are just now engaged in correcting a number of our mistakes. We are learning how to continue the building of a socialist edifice in a small-peasant country without committing such mistakes.

The difficulties are immense. But we are accustomed to grappling with immense difficulties. . . . But we master also, at least to some extent, another art essential in revolution, namely, flexibility, the ability to effect swift and sudden changes of tactics if changes in objective conditions demand it. . . . We calculated—or perhaps it would be truer to say that we presumed, without sufficient calculation—to organize the state production and the state distribution of products on communist lines in a small-peasant country to direct orders of the proletarian state. Experience has demonstrated our mistake. A number of transitional stages proved necessary: state capitalism and socialism, so as to prepare, by many years of work, for the transition to communism. Not directly relying on enthusiasm, but aided by the enthusiasm born of the great revolution, and on the basis of personal interest, personal benefit and business principles, you must set to work in this small-peasant country to build solid little bridges leading to socialism by way of state capitalism. Otherwise you will never get to communism, you will never bring these scores of millions of people to communism. That is what experience has taught us. . . . The proletarian state must

become a cautious, assiduous and shrewd "businessman," a punc-
tilious *wholesale merchant*—otherwise it will never succeed in
putting this small-peasant country economically on its feet. Under
existing conditions, living as we are side by side with the capitalist (capitalist for the time being) West, there can be no other
way of transition to communism. A wholesale merchant would
appear to be an economic type as remote from communism as
heaven is from the earth. But that is one of the contradictions
which in the actual conditions of life lead from a small-peasant
economy, by way of state capitalism, to socialism. Personal interest will develop production at all costs. Wholesale trade economically unites the millions of small peasants; it gives them a
personal interest, binds them together and leads them on to the
next step, namely, to various forms of association and union
in production itself. . . . We are already, in the field of this new
science, finishing our preparatory class. . . . We shall move up
into the higher classes. We shall go through "the whole course,"
although the circumstances of world economics and world
politics have rendered that course much longer and much more
difficult than we should have liked. No matter what the cost, no
matter how severe the sufferings of the transition period may be
—despite disaster, famine and disruption, we shall not lose heart
and shall carry our cause to a triumphant conclusion. (*The
Fourth Anniversary of the October Revolution,* October 14, 1921,
Selected Works, VI, 506–508.)

We must admit that a radical change has taken place in our
point of view concerning socialism. This radical change lies in
that, formerly, we placed, and had to place, the main weight of
emphasis on the political struggle, on revolution, on winning
power, etc. Now we have to shift the weight of emphasis to
peaceful, organizational, "cultural" work. I would be prepared
to say that the weight of emphasis should be placed on educational work, were it not for our international relations, were it
not for the fact that we have to fight for our position on a world
scale. However, if we leave that aside and confine ourselves en-

tirely to internal, economic relations, the weight of emphasis in our work is certainly shifted to educational work. (*On Co-operation,* January 6, 1923, *Selected Works,* IX, 408.)

6. CLASS, INTELLIGENTSIA, LIBERALS, WOMEN.

A. CLASS

To look for the fundamental distinguishing feature of various classes in society in their source of income is to give precedence to relations of distribution, which in reality are only a consequence of relations of production. This error was long ago pointed out by Marx, who described those who were unable to see it as vulgar Socialists. The fundamental feature that distinguishes classes is the place they occupy in social production, and, consequently, the relation in which they stand to the means of production. The appropriation of a part of the social means of production and their application to private enterprise, enterprises organized for the sale of the product, is the fundamental feature that distinguishes one class in modern society (the bourgeoisie) from the proletariat, which is deprived of all means of production and sells its labor power.

To proceed: "The basis of the existence of both groups is *labor,* as a definite category of political economy." It is not labor that is a definite category of political economy, but the social form of labor, the social organization of labor, or, in other words, the mutual relations of people arising from the part they play in social labor. The same mistake of vulgar socialism which we have analyzed is repeated here in another form. When the Socialist Revolutionaries say: "Essentially—the relations between farmer and farmhand, on the one hand, and between independent peasants and the money lenders, the kulaks, on the other are exactly the same," they reproduce wholesale the mistake of German vulgar socialism, which . . . stated that essentially the relation of employer to worker is the same as that of landlord to tenant. Our own . . . [vulgar Socialists] are equally incapable of distinguishing between the basic and the derivative forms of exploitation, and only declaim on the subject of "exploitation" in general. . . . They are equally incapable of understanding that it is precisely the exploitation of wage labor that forms the basis of the whole predatory order of today, that it is wage labor that leads to the division of society into irreconcilably hostile classes, and that it is only from the point of view of *this* class struggle that all the other manifestations of exploitation may be consistently gauged, without becoming vague and devoid of principle. (*Vulgar Socialism and Narodism Revived by the Socialist Revolutionaries*, November, 1902, *Selected Works*, II, 198–199.)

What does the "abolition of classes" mean? All those who call themselves Socialists recognize this as the ultimate goal of socialism, but by no means all ponder over its significance. Classes are large groups of people which differ from each other by the place they occupy in a historically definite system of social production, by their relation (in most cases fixed and formulated in laws) to the means of production, by their role in the social organization of labor, and consequently, by the dimensions and method of acquiring the share of social wealth that they obtain. Classes are groups of people, one of which may appropriate the labor of another owing to the different places they occupy in the definite system of social economy.

Clearly, in order to abolish classes completely, it is not enough to overthrow the exploiters, the landowners and capitalists, not enough to abolish *their* property; it is necessary also to abolish *all* private ownership of the means of production, it is necessary to abolish the distinction between town and country, as well as the distinction between manual workers and brain workers. This is a very long process. In order to achieve it an enormous step forward must be taken in developing the productive forces; it is necessary to overcome the resistance (frequently passive, which is particularly stubborn and particularly difficult to overcome) of the numerous remnants of small-scale production; it is necessary to overcome the enormous force of habit and conservativeness which are connected with these remnants.

The assumption that all "toilers" are equally capable of doing this work would be an empty phrase, or the illusion of an ante-diluvian, pre-Marxian Socialist; for this ability does not come of itself, but grows historically, and grows *only* out of the material conditions of large-scale capitalist production. The proletariat *alone* possesses this ability at the beginning of the road from capitalism to socialism. (*A Great Beginning,* June 28, 1919, *Selected Works,* IX, 432 f.)

General talk about freedom, equality and democracy is in fact but a stereotyped repetition of conceptions which actually derive from the relations of commodity production. To attempt to solve the concrete problems of the dictatorship of the proletariat by means of such general talk is to accept the theories and principles of the bourgeoisie all along the line. From the point of view of the proletariat, the question can be put only in the following way: Freedom from the oppression of which class? Equality between which classes? Democracy based on private ownership of the means of production, or on the struggle for its abolition?—and so forth.

Long ago Engels in his *Anti-Duehring* explained that the conception of equality derives from the relations of commodity production and becomes transformed into a prejudice if equality is not understood to mean the *abolition of classes.* This elementary truth regarding the distinction between the bourgeois-democratic and the socialist conceptions of equality is constantly being forgotten. But if it is not forgotten, it becomes obvious that, by overthrowing the bourgeoisie, the proletariat takes a decisive step toward the abolition of classes, and that in order to complete the process the proletariat must continue its class struggle making use of the apparatus of state power and of all methods of combating, influencing and bringing pressure to bear on the overthrown bourgeoisie and the vacillating petty bourgeoisie. (*Economics and Politics in the Era of the Dictatorship of the Proletariat,* October 30, 1919, *Selected Works,* VIII, 12 f.)

What distinguishes our revolution from former revolutions

is that there is no utopianism in our revolution. The new class, having replaced the old class, can maintain itself only by desperate struggle against other classes, and will finally triumph only if it can bring about the abolition of classes in general. That is what the vast and complex process of the class struggle demands; otherwise, you will sink into a morass of confusion. In what does the domination of a class consist? In what did the domination of the bourgeoisie over the feudal lords consist? The constitution spoke of freedom and equality. That was a lie. As long as there are toilers, property owners are capable of profiteering, and indeed as property owners they are compelled to profiteer. We declare that there is no equality, that the well-fed man is not the equal of the hungry man, that the profiteer is not the equal of the toiler.

In what does the domination of a class consist now? The domination of the proletariat consists in the fact that ownership of means of production by landowners and capitalists has been abolished. The spirit and foundation of all former constitutions, even the most republican and democratic, lay in private owner-ship of means of production. Our constitution has the right, has won itself the right, to a place in history because the abolition of private ownership is not confined to paper. The triumphant proletariat has abolished private ownership and completely destroyed it—and therein lies its domination as a class. The prime thing is the question of ownership. When the question of ownership was solved practically, the domination of the class was assured. When after that the constitution in-scribed on paper what had actually been effected, namely, the abolition of capitalist and landlord ownership, and added that the working class, according to the constitution, enjoys more rights than the peasantry, and the exploiters have no rights whatsoever—that was a record of the fact that the domination of our class had been established and that we had bound to our-selves all strata and all small groups of toilers. The petty bour-geois property owners are disunited; those among them who have more property are the enemies of those who have less property, while the proletarians, by abolishing private ownership, have declared open war on them. (*Report of the Central Committee at the Ninth Congress of the Russian Communist Party* [Bolsheviks], March 29, 1920, *Selected Works,* VIII, 89 f.)

What are classes in general? Classes are sections of society, one of which is permitted to appropriate the labor of the other. If one section of society appropriates all the land, we have a landowner class and a peasant class. If one section of society possesses the factories and works, has shares and capital, and the other section works in these factories, we have a capitalist class and a proletarian class. (*The Tasks of the Youth Leagues,* October 2, 1920, *Selected Works,* IX, 476.)

B. INTELLIGENTSIA

There is nothing terrible in the influence of the landowners over the people. They will never succeed in fooling any large numbers of workers or even peasants for any considerable length of time. But the influence of the *intelligentsia,* who do not take a direct part in exploitation, who are trained to play with general phrases and concepts, who go in for every "good" idea and who sometimes from sincere stupidity elevate their mid-class position to a *principle* of non-class parties and non-class politics —the influence of this bourgeois intelligentsia over the people is dangerous. Here, and here alone, do we find an infection of the masses which is capable of doing real harm and which demands the exertion of all forces of socialism in an endeavor to counteract this poison. (*In Memory of Count Heyden,* 1907, *Selected Works,* XI, 694.)

History knows all sorts of metamorphoses. To rely on firmness of convictions, loyalty and other excellent spiritual qualities is not being serious in politics. A small number of people may possess excellent spiritual qualities, but the issues of history are decided by huge masses, which, if the small number of people do not suit them, sometimes treat the small number none too politely. (*Political Report of the Central Committee to the*

Eleventh Congress of the Russian Communist Party [Bolsheviks], March 27, 1922, *Selected Works*, IX, 347.)

C. Liberals

One need not be a prophet to be able to prophesy that our revolutionary movement will reach its apogee and the liberal ferment in society will increase tenfold, and that then new Loris-Melikovs and Ignatyevs will appear in the government and inscribe on their banner: "Rights, and an authoritative Zemstvo." But if this should come to pass, it would be to the extreme disadvantage of Russia and to the extreme advantage of the government. If any considerable section of the liberals put their faith in this banner, and, allowing themselves to be carried away by it, attack the revolutionary "termagants" in the rear, the latter may find themselves isolated, and the government will try to restrict itself to a minimum of concessions in the form of an advisory and aristocratic constitution. Whether this attempt will be successful or not depends upon the outcome of the decisive battle between the revolutionary proletariat and the government. But of one thing we may be certain, and that is that the liberals will be betrayed. With the aid of slogans like those advanced by Mr. R. N. S. ("Authoritative Zemstvo," or "Zemshchina," etc.) the government will decoy them like puppies away from the revolutionaries and then will take them by the scruff of the neck and thrash them with the whip of the so-called reaction. And when that happens, gentlemen, we shall say: *serves you right!*

Why, instead of demanding the abolition of absolutism, are such moderate and carefully worded desiderata put forward in the form of concluding slogans? First of all, for the sake of the philistine doctrinairism which desires to render a "service to conservatism" and which believes that the government will be mollified by such moderation and become "subdued" by it. Secondly, in order to "unite the liberals."

.   .   .   .

Russian Social Democrats have never closed their eyes to the fact that the political liberties for which they are fighting will *first and foremost* benefit the bourgeoisie. Only a Socialist who is steeped in the worst prejudices of utopianism or reactionary Narodism would object to carrying on the fight against the autocracy for that reason. The bourgeoisie will benefit by these liberties and rest on its laurels. The proletariat, however, needs liberty in order to develop the fight for socialism to the utmost. And Social Democracy will persistently carry on the fight for liberation, no matter what the attitude of the various strata of the bourgeoisie toward this fight may be. In the interest of the political struggle, we must support every opposition that is raised against the oppression of the autocracy, no matter on what grounds it may be raised and by what social stratum it is expressed. For that reason, we are by no means indifferent to the opposition expressed by our liberal bourgeoisie generally, and by our Zemstvo-ists in particular. If the liberals succeed in organizing themselves in an illegal party, so much the better. We shall welcome the growth of political consciousness among the propertied classes; we shall support their demands, we shall endeavor to work so that the activities of the Social Democrats and the liberals mutually supplement each other. But even if they fail to do so (which is more probable), we shall not give them up in disgust. We shall try to establish contacts with individual liberals, make them acquainted with our movement, support them by exposing in the labor press all the despicable acts of the government and the local authorities, and try to induce them to support the revolutionaries. Such an exchange of service between liberals and Social Democrats is going on already; it must be extended and made constant. But while always ready to carry on this exchange of services, we shall never, under any circumstances, cease to carry on a determined struggle against the illusions which are so widespread in politically undeveloped Russian society generally and in Russian liberal circles in particular. In regard to the Russian revolutionary movement we may say, paraphrasing the celebrated statement of Marx in regard to the Revolution of 1848, that its progress lies not so much in the achievement of positive gains, as in emancipation from harmful illusions. We have emancipated ourselves from the illusions of anarchism and of Narodnik socialism, from contempt for politics, from the belief that Russia will develop in its own peculiar way, from the conviction that the people are ready for revolution, and from the theory of the seizure of power in single combat between the heroic intelligentsia and the autocracy.

It is time our liberals emancipated themselves from the illusion which would appear to be theoretically bankrupt, but which reveals extreme vitality in practice, viz., that parleys with the Russian autocracy are possible, that some sort of Zemstvo is the embryo of the constitution, and that the sincere adherents of the latter can fulfil their vow of Hannibal by patient legal activity and patient appeals to the enemy to become subdued. (*The Hannibals of Liberalism,* July, 1901, *Selected Works,* II, 218, 221–223.)

The whole course of the historical development of the Social Democratic movement is characterized by the fact that regardless of all obstacles it has won for itself more and more freedom of action, in spite of tsarist laws and police measures. The revolutionary proletariat, as it were, surrounds itself with a certain atmosphere, impenetrable by the government, of sympathy and support, both within the working class and within other classes too (which, of course, agree with only a small part of the demands of labor democracy). At the beginning of the movement a Social Democrat had to do a great deal of educational work, or concentrate his efforts almost exclusively on economic agitation. But now these functions, one after another, are passing into the hands of new forces, of wider masses who are being attracted to the movement. The revolutionary organizations are concentrating more and more on the work of actual *political* leadership, the work of indicating the Social Democratic conclusions to be drawn from the manifestations of labor protest and of popular discontent. In the beginning we had to teach the workers the alphabet, both in the literal and in the figurative sense. Now the level of political literacy has risen so enormously that it is possible, and it is our duty, to concentrate all our efforts on the more direct Social Democratic aims of giving organized leadership to the revolutionary torrent. Now the liberals and the legal press are doing a great deal of the "preparatory" work upon which we have had to spend a great deal of effort up to now. Now the open advocacy of democratic ideas and demands, without being persecuted by a weakened government, has spread so widely that we must adapt ourselves to an entirely new sweep of the movement. Of course, in this preparatory work there are both weeds and wheat! Of course, Social Democrats will have to pay greater attention to the struggle against the influence of bourgeois democracy on the workers. But this very work will have much more real Social Democratic content than our former activity, which was directed mainly toward rousing the politically unconscious masses.

The more the popular movement spreads, the more the true nature of the different classes becomes revealed and the more pressing is the task *of the Party* to lead the class, to be its organizer, and not to drag at the tail of events. The more all kinds of revolutionary activity develop everywhere, the more obvious become the emptiness and the inanity of *Rabocheye Dyelo* catchwords about activity in general, which are so readily taken up by the new *Iskra*-ists, the more apparent becomes the meaning of *Social Democratic* activity, and the greater are the demands which events present to our *revolutionary initiative*. The wider the new streams of the social movement become, the more important is it to have a strong Social Democratic organization which is capable of creating new channels for those streams. The more the democratic agitation and propaganda, which is going on independently of us, works to our advantage, the more necessary does organized Social Democratic leadership become in order to preserve the independence of the working class from bourgeois democracy.

A revolutionary epoch is to Social Democracy what wartime is to an army. We must extend the ranks of our army, increase it from peace to war strength, mobilize the reservists, call up all those on furlough, organize new auxiliary corps, units and services. (*New Tasks and New Forces,* March, 1905, *Selected Works,* III, 435 f.)

What is a philistine? A hollow gut, full of fear and hope, that God have mercy! What is the Russian liberal democratic philistine of the Cadet and near-Cadet camp? A hollow gut, full of fear and hope, that the counterrevolutionary landowner have mercy! (*In Memory of Count Heyden,* 1907, *Selected Works,* XI, 699.)

D. WOMEN

Notwithstanding all the liberating laws that have been passed, woman continues to be a *domestic slave,* because *petty housework* crushes, strangles, stultifies and degrades her, chains her to the kitchen and to the nursery, and wastes her labor on barbarously unproductive, petty, nerve-racking, stultifying and crushing drudgery. The real *emancipation of women,* real communism, will begin only when a mass struggle (led by the proletariat which is in power) is started against this petty domestic economy, or rather when it is *transformed on a mass scale* into a large-scale socialist economy.

Do we in practice devote sufficient attention to this question, which, theoretically, is indisputable for every Communist? Of course not. Do we devote sufficient care to the *young shoots* of communism which have already sprung up in this sphere? Again we must say emphatically, No! Public dining rooms, day nurseries, kindergartens—these are examples of the shoots, the simple everyday means, which assume nothing pompous, grandiloquent or solemn, but which can *in fact emancipate women,* which can in fact lessen and abolish their inferiority to men in regard to their role in social production and in social life. These means are not new; they (like all the material prerequisites for socialism) were created by large-scale capitalism. But under capitalism they remained first a rarity, and second—and what is particularly important—either *profit-making* enterprises, with all the worst features of speculation, profiteering, cheating and fraud, or the "acrobatics of bourgeois philanthropy," which the best workers quite rightly hated and despised.

There is no doubt that the number of these institutions in our country has greatly increased and that they are *beginning* to change in character. There is no doubt that there is far more *organizing* talent among the working women and peasant women than we are aware of, people who are able to organize in a practical way and enlist large numbers of workers, and a still larger number of consumers, for this purpose without the abundance of phrases, fuss, squabbling and chatter about plans, systems, etc., which our conceited "intelligentsia" or half-baked "Communists" always suffer from. But we do not *nurse* these new shoots with sufficient care. (*A Great Beginning*, June 28, 1919, *Selected Works*, IX, 441 f.)

In the most advanced countries, advantage is taken of woman's weaker position to make her inferior and to degrade her; and it is precisely in this sphere that the Soviet government has destroyed every trace of the old, unjust laws, which were intolerable for the representatives of the toiling masses. And we can now proudly say without the slightest exaggeration that except for Soviet Russia there is not a single country in the world in which there is complete equality between men and women and in which women are not placed in a degraded position, which is particularly felt in everyday family life. This was one of our first and most important tasks. . . .

We, the representatives of the Soviet government, the Bolshevik Communists and adherents of Soviet government, are constantly being accused of having violated democracy, and the evidence advanced to prove this is that the Soviet government dispersed the Constituent Assembly. Our usual reply to these charges is: We have no use for the kind of democracy and constituent assembly which arose under the system of private ownership of land, when people were not equal, when those who owned capital were the masters and the rest worked for them, were their wage slaves. This kind of democracy has served as a screen to conceal slavery even in the most advanced states. We Socialists are adherents of democracy only to the extent that it alleviates the position of the toilers and oppressed. All over the world socialism pursues the aim of fighting against all exploitation of man by man. We attach real significance to the democracy which serves the exploited, those who are placed in a position of inferiority. If non-toilers are deprived of the franchise, that is real equality. He who does not work shall not eat. In reply to these accusations we say that the question that should be put is: How is democracy carried out in this or that state? We see that equality is proclaimed in all democratic republics: but in civil law, and in the laws governing the position of woman, her position in the family and in regard to divorce, we see inequality and the degradation of women at every step. And we say: This is violation of democracy, and precisely in regard to the oppressed. The Soviet government has applied democracy to a greater extent than any other country, even the most advanced, by the fact that in its laws not the slightest hint of any inferiority of women is left. I repeat, not a single state and no democratic legislation has done even half of what the Soviet government did for women in the very first months of its existence.

Of course, laws are not enough, and we cannot under any circumstances be satisfied merely with what we say in our laws; but we have done all that was expected of us to make women equal with men, and we have a right to be proud of what we have done. The position of women in Soviet Russia is now an ideal position from the point of view of the most advanced states. But we say to ourselves: Of course this is only a beginning.

As long as women are engaged in housework their position is still a restricted one. In order to achieve the complete emancipation of women and to make them really equal with men, we must have social economy, and the participation of women in general productive labor. Then women will occupy the same position as men.

This, of course does not mean that women must be exactly equal with men in productivity of labor, amount of labor, its duration, conditions of labor, etc. But it does mean that women shall not be in an oppressed economic position compared with men. You all know that even with the fullest equality, women are still in an actual position of inferiority because all housework is thrust upon them. Most of this housework is highly unproductive, most barbarous and most arduous, and it is performed by women. This labor is extremely petty and contains nothing that would in the slightest degree facilitate the development of women. (*The Tasks of the Working Women's Movement in the Soviet Republic,* September 23, 1919, *Selected Works,* IX, 494–496.)

7. REFORMS, REFORMISM, REVOLUTION

Revolutionary Social Democracy always included, and now includes, the fight for reforms in its activities. But it utilizes "economic" agitation for the purpose of presenting to the government not only demands for all sorts of measures, but also (and primarily) the demand that the government cease to be an autocratic one. Moreover, it considers it to be its duty to present this demand to the government not on the basis of the economic struggle *alone,* but on the basis of all manifestations of public and political life. In a word, it subordinates the struggle for reforms to the revolutionary struggle for liberty and for socialism, as the part is subordinate to the whole. (*What Is To Be Done?* February, 1902, *Selected Works,* II, 83.)

Reformism, in general, means that people confine themselves to agitation for changes which do not require the removal of the main foundations of the old ruling class, changes that are *compatible* with the *preservation* of these foundations. The eight-hour day is compatible with the preservation of the power of capital. The Russian liberals, in order to attract the workers, are themselves prepared to endorse ("as far as possible") this demand. On the other hand, those demands for which *Luch* does not want to "agitate" are *incompatible* with the preservation of the foundations of the pre-capitalist period, the period of serfdom.

Luch eliminates from the agitation precisely that which is not acceptable to the liberals, who do not want to abolish the power of the landowners, but want only to share their power and privileges. *Luch* eliminates precisely that which is incompatible with the point of view of reformism.

That's the whole point!

Neither Muranov, nor *Pravda,* nor any Marxist rejects partial demands. That is nonsense. Take insurance, for example. We reject the *deception* of the people by idle talk about having partial demands met by means of *reformism.* We reject as utopian, self-seeking and false the *liberal reformism* in present-day Russia, the reformism based on constitutional illusions and full of the spirit of servility to the landowner. That is *the* point which *Luch* tries to confuse and hide by phrases about "partial demands" in general, although it itself admits that neither Muranov nor *Pravda* rejects certain "partial demands."

Luch curtails the Marxian slogans, tries to fit them into the narrow, reformist, liberal measure, and thus carries bourgeois ideas into the ranks of the workers. (*Controversial Questions,* June, 1913, *Selected Works,* IV, 145.)

Socialists do not repudiate the struggle for reforms. For example, even now they must vote in parliament for improvements in the conditions of the masses, however slight, for increased relief to the inhabitants of devastated regions, for lessening national oppression, etc. But it is sheer bourgeois deception to preach reforms as a solution to problems for which history and the actual political situation demand revolutionary solutions. (*Proposals . . . ,* December, 1916, *Selected Works,* V, 233.)

Marxists are absolutely convinced of the bourgeois character of the Russian revolution. What does this mean? It means that the democratic changes in the political regime and the social and economic changes which have become necessary for Russia do not in themselves imply the undermining of capitalism, the undermining of bourgeois domination. On the contrary, they will, for the first time, properly clear the ground for a wide and rapid European, and not Asiatic, development of capitalism; they will, for the first time, make it possible for the bourgeoisie to rule as a class. The Socialist Revolutionaries cannot grasp this idea, for they are ignorant of the rudiments of the laws of development of commodity and capitalist production; they fail to see that even the complete success of a peasants' uprising, even the redistribution of the whole of the land for the benefit of the peasants according to their desires ("the Black Redistribution" or something of that kind), will not destroy capitalism, but on the contrary will give an impetus to its development and will hasten the class disintegration of the peasantry itself. . . .

But it does not at all follow from this that the *democratic* revolution (bourgeois in its social and economic content) is not of *enormous* interest for the proletariat. It does not at all follow that the democratic revolution could not take place in a form advantageous mainly to the big capitalist, the financial magnate, the "enlightened" landowner, and in a form advantageous to the peasant and to the worker.

The new *Iskra*-ists are radically wrong in their interpretation of the sense and significance of the concept of bourgeois revolution. Their arguments constantly reveal the underlying idea that the bourgeois revolution is a revolution which can only be of advantage to the bourgeoisie. And yet nothing is farther removed from the truth. The bourgeois revolution is a revolution which does not go beyond the limits of the bourgeois, i.e., capitalist, social and economic system. The bourgeois revolution expresses the needs of capitalist development, and not only does it not destroy the foundations of capitalism, but, on the contrary, it widens and deepens them. This revolution therefore expresses the interests not only of the working class, but also the interests of the whole bourgeoisie. Since, under capitalism, the domination of the bourgeoisie over the working class is inevitable, we are entitled to say that the bourgeois revolution expresses not so much the interests of the proletariat as those of the bourgeoisie. But the idea that the bourgeois revolution does not express the interests of the proletariat is altogether absurd. This absurd idea reduces itself either to the old-fashioned Narodnik theory that the bourgeois revolution runs counter to the interests of the proletariat and that, therefore, bourgeois political liberty is of no use to us, or to anarchism, which rejects all participation of the proletariat in bourgeois politics, in the bourgeois revolution and in bourgeois parliamentarism. Theoretically, this idea ignores the elementary postulates of Marxism concerning the inevitability of capitalist development as the basis of commodity production. Marxism teaches that at a certain stage of its development a society that is based on commodity production and has commercial intercourse with civilized capitalist nations inevitably takes the road of capitalism itself. Marxism has irrevocably broken with all the nonsense talked by the Narodniki and the anarchists about Russia, for instance, being able to avoid capitalist development, jump out of capitalism, or skip over it, by some means other than the class struggle on the basis and within the limits of capitalism.

All these principles of Marxism have been proved and explained in minute detail in general and with regard to Russia in particular. It follows from these principles that the idea of seeking salvation for the working class in anything save the further development of capitalism is *reactionary*. In countries like Russia, the working class suffers not so much from capitalism as from the lack of capitalist development. The working class is therefore undoubtedly interested in the widest, freest and speediest development of capitalism. The removal of all the remnants of the old order which are hampering the wide, free and speedy development of capitalism is of *absolute advantage* to the working class. The bourgeois revolution is precisely a revolution which most resolutely sweeps away the survivals of the past, the remnants of serfdom (which include not only autocracy but monarchy as well); it is a revolution which most fully guarantees the widest, freest and speediest development of capitalism.

Therefore, the *bourgeois* revolution is in the *highest degree advantageous to the proletariat*. The bourgeois revolution is *absolutely* necessary for the interests of the proletariat. The more complete, determined and consistent the bourgeois revolution is, the more secure will the proletarian struggle against the bourgeoisie and for socialism become. Such a conclusion may appear new, strange or even paradoxical only to those who are ignorant of the rudiments of scientific socialism. And from this conclusion, among other things, follows the postulate that, *in a certain sense,* the bourgeois revolution is more *advantageous* to the proletariat than it is to the bourgeoisie. This postulate is undoubtedly correct in the following sense: It is to the advantage of the bourgeoisie to rely on certain remnants of the past which are against the proletariat, for instance, on a monarchy, a standing army, etc. It is to the advantage of the bourgeoisie if the bourgeois revolution does not too resolutely sweep away the remnants of the past, but leaves some—i.e., if this revolution is not fully consistent, if it does not proceed to its logical conclusion, and if it is not determined and ruthless. Social Democrats often express this idea somewhat differently by stating that the bourgeoisie betrays itself, that the bourgeoisie betrays the cause of liberty, that the bourgeoisie is incapable of being consistently democratic. It is to the advantage of the bourgeoisie if the necessary bourgeois-democratic changes take place more slowly, more gradually, more cautiously and with less determination, by means of reforms and not by means of revolution; if these changes spare the "venerable" institution of feudalism (such as monarchy); if these reforms develop as little as possible the revolutionary initiative and the energy of the common people (i.e., the peasantry and especially the workers), for otherwise it will be easier for the workers, as the French say, "to pass the rifle from one shoulder to the other," to turn the guns which the bourgeois revolution will place in their hands—the liberty which the revolution will bring, the democratic institutions which will spring up on the ground that will be cleared of feudalism—against the bourgeoisie.

On the other hand, it is more advantageous for the working class if the necessary bourgeois-democratic changes take place in the form of revolution and not reform, for the latter is the road of delay, procrastination, of painfully slow decomposition of the putrid parts of the national organism. It is the proletariat and the peasantry that suffer first and most of all from this putrefaction. The revolutionary way is one of quick amputation, least painful to the proletariat, the way of direct amputation of the decomposing parts, the way of fewest concessions to and least consideration for the monarchy and the disgusting, vile contaminating institutions which correspond to it. (*The Two Tactics of Social Democracy in the Democratic Revolution,* July, 1905, *Selected Works,* III, 73–76.)

It is particularly important to advance the fundamental demands with every attempt to establish a provisional revolutionary government in order to show to the whole of the people, even to the most ignorant masses, in brief formulas, in clear and sharp outlines, the aims of this government and its national tasks.

In our opinion, it is possible to point to *six* such basic points which must become the political banner and the immediate program of any revolutionary government, which must enlist the sympathies of the people for the government and upon which the whole revolutionary energy of the people must be concentrated as upon its most urgent task.

The six points are these: (1) a national constituent assembly, (2) arming of the people, (3) political liberty, (4) complete freedom for the oppressed and disfranchised nationalities, (5) an eight-hour working day and (6) peasant revolutionary committees. Of course, this is only an approximate list, only *titles,* designations of a whole series of changes that are required immediately in order to achieve this democratic republic. We do not claim that the list is complete. We merely want to explain clearly what we think of the importance of certain basic tasks. The revolutionary government must strive to rely on the support of the masses of the people, on the masses of the working class and peasantry; unless it does this it will not be able to maintain itself. Without the revolutionary activity of the people it will be nil, worse than nil. It is our business to forewarn the people against the adventurous character of high-sounding but absurd promises (like immediate "socialization," which is not understood even by those who talk about it), while at the same time advocating changes that can really be made at the moment and that are really necessary for strengthening the cause of the revolution. The revolutionary government must arouse the "people" and *organize* the people's revolutionary activity. Complete freedom for oppressed nationalities, i.e., the recognition not only of their cultural rights but also of their right to political self-determination; the introduction of urgent measures for the protection of the working class (an eight-hour day as the first in the series of these measures); and, lastly, the guarantee of serious measures, uninfluenced by considerations for the landowners' greed, in favor of the masses of the peasantry—such, in our opinion, are the chief points which must be especially emphasized by every revolutionary government. We shall not discuss the first three points; they are too obvious to require comment. We shall not discuss the necessity for bringing about reforms even in a small territory, for instance, one recaptured from tsarism; the practical fulfillment is a thousand times more important than manifestos, and, of course, a thousand times more difficult. We merely want to call attention to the fact that it is necessary immediately to spread by every possible means a correct idea of our national and imminent tasks. It is necessary to know how to approach the people—in the true sense of the word—not only with a general call to fight (this is sufficient in a period before the formation of the revolutionary government), but also with a direct call for the immediate fulfillment of the main democratic reforms to be immediately and independently carried out. (*The Revolutionary Army and the Revolutionary Government,* July, 1905, *Selected Works,* III, 316 f.)

8. FREEDOM

"Freedom" is a grand word, even though under the banner of free trade the most predatory wars were conducted, and under the banner of free labor the toilers were robbed. The modern use of the term "freedom of criticism" contains the same inherent falsehood. Those who are really convinced that they have advanced science would demand, not freedom for the new views to continue side by side with the old, but the substitution of the new views for the old. The cry, "Long live freedom of criticism," that is heard today, too strongly calls to mind the fable of the empty barrel.[18] (*What Is To Be Done?* 1902, *Selected Works,* II, 33.)

---

[18]The allusion is to Krylov's fable, "Two Barrels," the moral of which runs: "He who never stops shouting about his own achievements is probably good for nothing."—*Ed.*

The[19] Social Democrats are out, first and foremost, to win *political liberty*. They need political liberty in order to unite all the Russian workers in broad and open associations for the struggle for a new and better order of society, for a socialist society.

What is political liberty?

To understand this, the peasant must begin by comparing his present state of freedom with serfdom. Under serfdom a peasant could not even marry without the landowner's permission. Today the peasant is free to marry without anyone's permission. Under serfdom the peasant had to work for his landowner on the days fixed by the latter's bailiff. Today the peasant is free to choose the employer he will work for, the days he will work and for what wages. Under serfdom the peasant could not leave his village without the landowner's permission. Today the peasant is free to go wherever he pleases—if the *mir* allows him to go, if he is not in arrears with his taxes, if he can get a passport, and if the governor or the police do not forbid migrations. This means that even today the peasant is not quite free to go where he pleases, that he does not possess complete freedom of movement: the peasant is still a semiserf. Presently we shall explain in detail why the Russian peasant is still a semiserf and what he must do to change his condition.

Under serfdom the peasant had no right to acquire property without the landlord's permission and could not buy land. Today the peasant is free to acquire any kind of property (but even today he is not free to leave the *mir* or to dispose of his land as he pleases). Under serfdom the peasant could be flogged by the landowner. Today the peasant cannot be flogged by the landowner, although he is still liable to corporal punishment.

This freedom is called *civil* liberty—freedom in family matters, in private matters, in matters of property. The peasant and the

---

[19] The following passages (pp. 81–89) are selected from *To the Rural Poor; An Explanation for the Peasants of What the Social Democrats Want*, April 1903. Only volume and page from *Selected Works* are acknowledged in the text.— *Ed.*

worker are free (although not quite free) to arrange their family life and their private business as they please, to dispose of their labor (choose their employer) and of their property.

But neither the Russian workers nor the Russian people as a whole are yet free to settle their *national* affairs as they please. Just as the peasants used to be the serfs of individual landowners, so the people as a whole is the serf of the government officials. The Russian people have not the right to choose their officials, nor the right to elect representatives to legislate for the whole country. The Russian people have not even the right to meet to discuss *state* affairs. We cannot even print newspapers or books, we cannot even speak to all and for all on matters of the state unless we get permission from the officials who have been put in authority over us without our consent, just as the landowner used to appoint his bailiffs without the consent of the peasants!

Just as the peasants used to be the slaves of the landowners, so the Russian people are still the slaves of the officials. Just as the peasants under serfdom were deprived of civil liberty, so the Russian people are still deprived of *political* liberty. Political liberty means the freedom of the people to settle affairs relating to the people as a whole, to the state. Political liberty means the right of the people to elect deputies to represent them in a parliament. All laws should be discussed and passed, all taxes and dues should be fixed only by such a parliament elected by the whole people. Political liberty means the right of the people to choose their own officials, to call any meeting they please for the discussion of all the affairs of state, to publish whatever papers and books they please, without having to ask for permission.

All the other European peoples won political liberty for themselves long ago. Only in Turkey and in Russia are the people still politically the slaves of the sultan's government or the government of the autocratic tsar. The tsar's autocracy means the unlimited power of the tsar. The people play no part in the constitution of the state or in the administration of the state. All the laws are made and all the officials are appointed by the tsar alone, by his personal, unlimited, autocratic authority. But of course the tsar *cannot* know all that goes on in the country. The tsar simply endorses the will of a few score of the biggest and most important officials. However much he may want to, one man cannot govern an enormous country like Russia. It is not the tsar that governs Russia; to say "autocracy is government by one man" is merely uttering a phrase. Russia is governed by a handful of the richest and most highborn officials. The tsar learns only what this handful is pleased to tell him. The tsar is quite powerless to go against the will of this handful of nobles of high rank. The tsar himself is a landowner and one of the nobility; from his earliest childhood he has been surrounded by these highborn people, and only by them. It was they who brought him up and educated him. What he knows of the rest of the Russian people is only what these noble gentry know, what these rich landowners and the few very rich merchants who are received at the tsar's court know.

In every *volost* office you will find the same picture hanging on the wall: it depicts the tsar, Alexander III (the father of the present tsar), speaking to the *volost* headmen who have come to his coronation. The tsar is saying to them: *"Obey your marshals of the nobility."* And the present tsar, Nicholas II, has repeated these words. This means that the tsars themselves admit they can only govern the country with the aid of the nobility and through the nobility. We must firmly remember these words of the tsar about the peasants having to obey the gentry. We must clearly realize that those who depict the tsarist government as the best government are liars. In other countries . . . the government is elected; but it is the rich who are elected, and they govern unjustly and oppress the poor. In Russia the government is not elected; an autocratic tsar governs the country. The tsar stands above everyone, above rich and poor. The tsar, they tell us, is just to everyone, to the poor and rich alike.

Such talk is mere humbug. Every Russian knows the kind of justice that is dispensed by our government. Everyone knows whether a plain workingman or a peasant laborer can become a member of the State Council. In all other European countries, factory workers and farmhands are members of the parliament, and they can freely speak to all the people about the miserable condition of the workers and call upon the workers to unite and to fight for better conditions. And no one dare stop these speeches of the people's representatives, no policeman dare lay a finger on them.

Russia has no representative government, and it is not merely the rich and the highborn who govern her, but the worst of these. She is governed by those who are best at intriguing at the tsar's court, who are cleverest at mischief-making, who carry lies and slanders to the tsar, who flatter him and toady to him. They govern in secret; the people do not know and cannot know what new laws are being prepared, what wars are being hatched, what new taxes are being introduced, which officials are being rewarded and for what services, and which are being dismissed. In no country is there such a multitude of officials as in Russia. The officials tower above the voiceless people like a dense forest —a mere workingman can never make his way through this forest, can never obtain justice. No complaint against the bribery, the robbery or the violence of the officials is ever brought to light; every complaint is smothered in official red tape. The voice of an isolated man can never reach the people; it is lost in the dense thickets, it is stifled in the police torture chamber. An army of officials, who were never elected by the people and who are not responsible to the people, has woven a thick web, and men and women are struggling in this web like flies.

The tsarist autocracy is an autocracy of officials. The tsarist autocracy means the feudal dependence of the people upon the officials and especially upon the police. The tsarist autocracy is police autocracy.

This is why the workers come out into the streets with banners bearing the inscriptions: "Down with the autocracy!" "Long live political liberty!" This is why the tens of millions of the village poor must support and take up this battle cry of the urban workers. Like them, regardless of all persecution, of all the enemy's threats and violence, and undeterred by the first reverses, the farm laborers and the poor peasants must come forward for a decisive struggle for the freedom of the whole of the Russian people and demand first of all the *convocation of the representatives of the people.* Let the people themselves throughout the length and breadth of Russia elect their deputies. Let these deputies form a supreme assembly, which will introduce representative government in Russia, free the people from serfdom to the officials and the police, secure for the people the right to meet freely, to speak freely, and to have a free press.

This is what the Social Democrats want first and foremost. This is the meaning of their first demand, the *demand for political liberty.*

We know that political liberty, free elections to the parliament, freedom of meetings, freedom of the press will not deliver the working people from poverty and oppression at one stroke. There is no recipe for delivering the poor of town and country at one stroke from the burden of working for the rich. The working people have no one to place their hopes in and no one to rely upon *but themselves.* No one will free the workingman from poverty *unless he frees himself.* And to free themselves the workers of the whole country, of the whole of Russia, must unite to form one association, one party. But millions of workers cannot unite if the autocratic police government forbids all meetings, all working class newspapers, the election of workers' deputies. To unite they must have the right to form any association they please, they must have the right to organize, they must have political liberty.

Political liberty will not deliver the working people from poverty all at once, *but it will give the workers a weapon with which to fight poverty.* There is no other means and there can be no other means of fighting poverty except the *unification of the workers.* But millions of people cannot unite unless there is *political liberty. (Selected Works,* II, 245–250.)

The Social Democrats fight for the liberation of all the toilers from robbery, oppression and injustice. To become free, the working class must first of all become united. And to become united it must have freedom to unite, it must have the right to unite, it must have *political liberty*. . . . Autocratic government means making the people the serfs of the officials and of the police. Political liberty is therefore needed by the whole of the people, except for a handful of courtiers and a few money-bags and high dignitaries who are received at court. But it is the workers and the peasants who most of all need political liberty. The rich can purchase freedom for themselves from the tyranny and caprices of the officials and of the police. The rich can make their complaints heard in the highest places. And this being so, the police and the officials take fewer liberties with the rich than with the poor. The workers and the peasants have no money with which to bribe the police or the officials, they have no one to complain to, they are not in a position to sue them in court. The workers and the peasants will never rid themselves of the extortions, the whims or the insults of the police and the officials as long there is no *representative government, as long as there is no national assembly of deputies*. It is only such a national assembly of deputies that can free the people from serfdom to the officials. Every intelligent peasant must stand for the Social Democrats, who first and foremost demand of the tsarist government that a *national assembly of deputies be convened*. The deputies must be elected by all, irrespective of "estate," irrespective of wealth and poverty. The elections must be free, without any interference on the part of the officials; they must be carried out under the supervision of the people's delegates and not of police officers. . . . Under such conditions, the representatives of the people will be able to discuss all the needs of the people and introduce a better state of affairs in Russia.

The Social Democrats demand that the police be deprived of the power to imprison anyone without trial. The officials must be severely punished for arbitrarily arresting anyone. To prevent them from violating the law, the officials must be chosen by the people, and everyone must have the right to sue any official before a court without first having to ask for permission. What is the use of complaining about the police to the *zemsky nachalnik,* or about the *zemsky nachalnik* to the governor? Of course, the *zemsky nachalnik* will always protect the police with his authority, and the governor will always protect the *zemsky nachalnik,* and the plaintiff runs a fair chance of being punished himself, of being put into prison or deported to Siberia. Only when everyone in Russia (as has long been the case in other countries) has the right to complain to the national assembly, to the elected courts, and to speak freely of his needs, to write about them in the newspapers—only then will the officials feel that they have someone to be afraid of.

The Russian people are still the serfs of the officials. Without the permission of the officials the people cannot call meetings, they cannot print books or newspapers! Is this not serfdom? If meetings cannot be freely called, or books freely printed, how can one obtain redress against the officials or against the rich? Of course, the officials suppress every book and every utterance that tells the truth about the people's poverty. The present book, too, has to be printed by the Social Democratic party secretly and circulated secretly: anyone who is found in possession of this book will see no end of courts and prisons. But the Social Democratic workers are not afraid of this: they print more and more and give the people more and more truthful books to read. And no prisons, no persecution can stop the fight for the people's liberty! (*Selected Works,* II, 278–279.)

The Social Democrats demand that the people have complete freedom to move from place to place and to choose their occupations. What does this mean, this *freedom to move from place to place?* It means that the peasant must be free to go where he pleases, to move wherever he wants, to choose for himself the village or the town he prefers, without having to ask for permission. It means that passports must be abolished in Russia, too (in foreign countries passports were abolished long ago), that no police officer, no *zemsky nachalnik* must be allowed to stop any peasant from settling down or working wherever he pleases. The Russian peasant is still the serf of the officials to such an extent that he is not free to move to a town or free to settle in a new district. The minister issues orders that the governors should not allow *unauthorized* settlement! The governor knows better than the peasant what place is good for the peasant! Is this not serfdom, I ask you? Is it not an insult to the people when every miserable profligate nobleman is allowed to order grown-up farmers about? (*Selected Works,* II, 280.)

The Social Democrats further demand that everyone have the unrestricted right to belong to whatever denomination he pleases. Of the European countries, Russia and Turkey are the only ones which have retained these shameful laws against persons belonging to any other than the officially sanctioned religion, the laws against schismatics, dissenters and Jews. These laws either directly forbid the practice of a certain religion or forbid preaching it, or deprive those who belong to it of certain rights. All these laws are as unjust, as arbitrary and as shameful as can be. Everyone must be perfectly free not only to belong to whatever religion he pleases, but *he must also be free to preach his religion and to change his religion.* (*Selected Works,* II, 284.)

The peasants seem to have forgotten that all the best land and the factories have been seized by the rich, by the landowners and the bourgeoisie precisely for the purpose of starving the people into working for the property owners. The peasants forget that the rich class is defended not only by the sermons of the priests, but also by the tsarist government with its masses of bureaucrats and soldiers. The tsarist government has reminded the peasants of all this. It brutally showed the peasants what state authority is, whose servant and whose protector it is. We must remind the peasants of this lesson again and again, and then they will easily understand why it is necessary to *change the constitution of the state* and why we need *political liberty.* Peasant insurrections will have a conscious aim when larger and larger numbers of people understand all this, when every peasant who can read and write and who thinks for himself becomes familiar with *the three principal demands* which must be fought for first of all. The first demand is that a *national assembly of deputies* be convened *with the aim of establishing a popular representative government in Russia instead of the present autocratic government.* The second demand is that *everyone be free to publish any book or newspaper he pleases.* The third demand is that *the complete equality of rights of the peasants with the other estates be recognized by law and that elected peasant committees be convened, with the primary aim of abolishing all forms of feudal bondage.* (*Selected Works,* II, 307.)

But the doctrines of Social Democracy cannot be taught from books alone; every instance, every case of oppression and injustice we encounter must be used to illustate these doctrines. Social Democracy is the doctrine of struggle against every form of oppression, against every form of robbery and injustice. A true Social Democrat is one who knows the causes of oppression and who, *all his life, fights every cause of oppression.* (*Selected Works,* II, 308.)

All political liberties secured on the basis of the present, i.e., capitalist, relations of production are bourgeois liberties. The demand for political liberties expresses first of all the interests of the bourgeoisie. Its representatives were the first to put forward this demand. Its supporters have everywhere used the liberties they acquired like masters, and have reduced them to moderate and exact bourgeois doses, combining them with the suppression of the revolutionary proletariat by methods most refined in peacetime and brutally cruel in times of storm.

But only the Narodnik rebels, anarchists and economists could deduce from this that the struggle for liberty must be rejected or degraded. These intellectual philistine doctrines could be foisted on the proletariat only for a time and against its will. The proletariat always instinctively realized that it needed political liberty more than anyone else, in spite of the fact that its immediate effect would be to strengthen and organize the bourgeoisie. The proletariat seeks its salvation not by avoiding the class struggle, but by developing it, by extending its scope, its own class consciousness, organization and determination. The Social Democrat who debases the tasks of the political struggle becomes transformed from a tribune of the people into a trade union secretary. The Social Democrat who debases the proletarian tasks in a democratic bourgeois revolution becomes transformed from a leader of the people's revolution into a mere leader of a free labor union.

. . . .

We Marxists must know that there is not, nor can there be, any other path to real freedom for the proletariat and the peasantry than the path of bourgeois freedom and bourgeois progress. We must not forget that there is not, nor can there be at the present time, any other means of bringing socialism nearer than by complete political liberty, a democratic republic, a revolutionary democratic dictatorship of the proletariat and the peasantry. Being the representatives of the advanced and of the only revolutionary class, revolutionary without reservations, doubts and retrospection, we must present to the whole of the people the tasks of a democratic revolution as widely and as boldly as possible, and display the maximum of initiative in so doing. The degradation of these tasks, theoretically, is tantamount to making a caricature of Marxism, tantamount to a philistine distortion of it.

. . . .

At the head of the whole of the people, and particularly of the peasantry—for complete freedom, for a consistent democratic revolution, for a republic! At the head of all the toilers and the exploited—for socialism! Such must in practice be the policy of the revolutionary proletariat, such is the class slogan which must permeate and determine the solution of every tactical question, and every practical step of the workers' party during the revolution. (*The Two Tactics of Social Democracy in the Democratic Revolution,* July, 1905, *Selected Works,* III, 120 f., 122, 124.)

9. God and Morality

It is not true that god is a complex of ideas which arouse and organize social sentiments. This . . . conceals the material origin of ideas. God is (from the historical and practical standpoint) primarily a complex of ideas begotten by the crass submissiveness of man, by external nature and by class oppression—ideas which tend to *perpetuate* this submissiveness, to *deaden the force* of the class struggle. There was a time in history when, despite this origin and this true meaning of the idea of god, the struggle of democracy and the proletariat took the form of a struggle of *one religious idea against another.*

But this time, too, has long since passed.

Now, both in Europe and in Russia, *every* advocacy or justification of the idea of god, even the most subtle, even the best-intentioned, is a justification of reaction. (*Letter to Gorky,* December, 1913, *Selected Works,* XI, 679.)

Yes, of course we are violating the treaty; we have violated it thirty or forty times. (*War and Peace,* March 7, 1918, *Selected Works,* VII, 301.)

In what sense do we repudiate ethics and morality?

In the sense that they were preached by the bourgeoisie, who declared that ethics were God's commandments. We, of course, say that we do not believe in God, and that we know perfectly well that the clergy, the landowners, and the bourgeoisie spoke in the name of God in order to pursue their own exploiters' interests. Or, instead of deducing these ethics from the commandments of morality, from the commandments of God, they deduced them from idealistic or semi-idealistic phrases, which were always very similar to God's commandments.

We repudiate all morality that is taken outside of human, class concepts. We say that this deception, a fraud, which clogs the brains of the workers and peasants in the interests of the landowners and capitalists.

We say that our morality is entirely subordinated to the interests of the class struggle of the proletariat. Our morality is deduced from the class struggle of the proletariat.

.   .   .   .

For the Communist, morality consists entirely of compact united discipline and conscious mass struggle against the exploiters. We do not believe in eternal morality, and we expose all the fables about morality. Morality serves the purpose of helping human society to rise to a higher level and to abolish the exploitation of labor. (*The Tasks of the Youth Leagues,* October 2, 1920, *Selected Works,* IX, 475, 478.)

II

ECONOMICS

1. TAXES

The abolition of indirect taxation, which the Social Democrats demand, would be an enormous relief. Indirect taxes are those taxes which are not assessed on a definite piece of land or farm, but are paid by the people *indirectly,* by paying a higher price for what they buy. The treasury places a tax on sugar, on liquor, on kerosene, on matches and all sorts of articles of consumption; the tax is paid to the treasury by the merchant or by the manufacturer, but, of course, he does not pay it out of his own pocket, but out of the money his customers pay him. The price of liquor, of sugar, of kerosene, of matches is increased, so that every purchaser of a bottle of liquor or of a pound of sugar has to pay the tax in addition to the price of the goods. Out of the fourteen kopeks you pay for a pound of sugar, let us say, about four kopeks constitutes the tax; the sugar manufacturer has already paid the tax to the treasury and is now exacting the sum he has paid from every one of his customers. You see that indirect taxes are taxes on articles of consumption, taxes which are paid by the consumer paying a higher price for the article he buys. It is sometimes said that indirect taxes are the fairest taxes: You pay in the measure in which you buy. But this is not so. Indirect taxes are the most unfair of all taxes, because they are harder for the poor to pay than they are for the rich. The rich man's income is ten times or maybe a hundred times as large as the peasant's or the worker's. But does the rich man require a hundred times as much sugar? Or ten times as much liquor or matches or kerosene? Of course not! At the very most, a rich family will buy three times as much kerosene or liquor or sugar as a poor family. And this means that the rich man will pay a *smaller part* of his income than the poor man. (*To the Rural Poor,* April, 1903, *Selected Works,* II, 281 f.)

2. COMPETITION

Among the absurdities which the bourgeoisie are fond of spreading about socialism is the argument that Socialists deny the importance of competition. As a matter of fact, it is only socialism which, by abolishing classes, and, consequently, by abolishing the enslavement of the masses, for the first time opens the way for competition on a really mass scale. And it is precisely the Soviet organization, in passing from the formal democracy of the bourgeois republic to the real participation of the masses of the toilers in *administration,* that for the first time puts competition on a broad basis. It is much easier to organize this in the political field than in the economic field; but for the success of socialism, it is precisely the latter that is important.

. . . .

We have not yet started on the enormous, difficult but grateful task of organizing competition between communes, of introducing accounting and publicity in the process of the production of bread, clothes and other things, of transforming dry, dead, bureaucratic accounts into living examples, both repulsive and attractive. Under the capitalist mode of production, the significance of individual example, say, the example of some co-operative workshop, would inevitably be exceedingly restricted, and only those who are imbued with petty bourgeois illusions can dream of "correcting" capitalism by the force of example of good institutions. After political power has passed to the proletariat, after the expropriators have been expropriated, the situation radically

changes—as prominent Socialists have repeatedly pointed out—
and force of example for the first time is able to exercise mass
influence. Model communes should and will serve as educators,
teachers, helping to raise the backward communes. The press
must serve as an instrument of socialist construction, give publicity to the successes achieved by the model communes in all their
details, study the causes of these successes, the methods these
communes employ, and, on the other hand, put on the "blacklist"
those communes which persist in the "traditions of capitalism,"
i.e., anarchy, laziness, disorder and profiteering. In capitalist
society, statistics were entirely a matter for "official persons," or
for narrow specialists; we must carry statistics to the masses and
make them popular, so that the toilers themselves may gradually
learn to understand and see how long it is necessary to work,
how much time can be allowed for rest, so that the comparison
of the business results of the various communes may become a
matter of general interest and study, and so that the most outstanding communes may be rewarded immediately (by reducing
the working day to a certain extent, raising wages, placing a larger
amount of cultural or aesthetic facilities, or other values, at their
disposal, etc.). (*The Immediate Tasks of the Soviet Government*,
April, 1918, *Selected Works*, VII, 333, 334 f.)

3. Monopoly

Monopoly manifests itself in five principal forms: (1) cartels,
syndicates and trusts—the concentration of production has reached
a stage which gives rise to these monopolistic combinations of
capitalists; (2) the monopolistic position of the big banks—three,
four or five gigantic banks manipulate the whole economic life
of America, France, Germany; (3) seizure of the sources of
raw material by the trusts and the financial oligarchy (finance
capital is monopolistic industrial capital merged with bank
capital); (4) the (economic) partition of the world by the international cartels *has begun*. Such international cartels, which
command the *entire* world market and divide it "amicably"
among themselves—until war *re*divides it—already number over
one hundred! The export of capital, a highly characteristic phe-

nomenon distinct from the export of commodities under non-monopoly capitalism, is closely connected with the economic and territorial-political partition of the world; (5) the territorial partition of the world (colonies) is *completed*. (*Imperialism and the Split in Socialism*, Fall, 1916, *Selected Works*, XI, 748 f.)

4. LABOR

The raising of the productivity of labor first of all requires that the material basis of large-scale industry shall be assured, viz., the development of the production of fuel, iron, the engineering and chemical industries. . . . Another condition for raising the productivity of labor is, first, the raising of the educational and cultural level of the masses of the population. . . . Secondly, a condition for economic revival is the raising of the discipline of the toilers, their skill, their dexterity, increasing the intensity of labor and improving its organization.

.   .   .   .

The Russian is a bad worker compared with workers of the advanced countries. Nor could it be otherwise under the tsarist regime and in view of the tenacity of the remnants of serfdom. The Soviet government must set this task, in all its scope, before the people: Learn to work. The Taylor system, the last word of capitalism in this respect, like all capitalist progress, is a combination of the subtle brutality of bourgeois exploitation and a number of its greatest scientific achievements in the field of analyzing mechanical motions during work, eliminating superfluous and awkward motions, working out correct methods of work, introducing the best system of accounting and control, etc. The Soviet Republic must at all costs adopt all that is valuable in the achievements of science and technology in this field. The possibility of building socialism will be determined precisely by our success in combining the Soviet government and the Soviet organization of administration with the modern achievements of capitalism. We must organize in Russia the study and teaching of the Taylor system and systematically try it out and adapt it to our purposes. (*The Immediate Tasks of the Soviet Government*, April, 1918, *Selected Works*, VII, 332 f.)

The introduction of compulsory labor service and the raising of labor discipline. The old capitalism, based on free trade and competition, has been greatly undermined by the war throughout Europe.

The war led to the introduction of compulsory labor service for the population in many countries. In actual fact, however, it turned out that compulsory labor service was introduced only for the poor, because the rich could easily evade it. We must introduce compulsory labor service not primarily for the poor, who even without that have brought sufficient sacrifices to the altar of war, but for the rich, who amassed wealth out of the war. It is from this measure that we must start. We must introduce workers' budget-tax books primarily for the rich, in order that it may be seen what share of work each performs for the purpose of saving his country. Supervision will be exercised by the local Soviets.

In regard to the poor, this measure is at present superfluous because they have quite enough work to do as it is; moreover, the trade unions are adopting all measures to increase productivity and to raise labor discipline. (*Speech* . . . , May 18, 1918, *Selected Works,* VII, 381.)

We shall work for the eradication of that accursed law, "every man for himself and the devil take the hindmost," for the eradication of the habit of regarding labor only as something performed under compulsion and justified only when paid for in accordance with certain labor standards. We shall work to inculcate in people the habit, to implant in the everyday life of the masses the law, "all for one and one for all," "from each according to his ability, to each according to his needs," to introduce, gradually but undeviatingly, communist discipline in communist toil. We have dislodged a rock of tremendous weight, the rock of inertia, ignorance and stubborn adherence to the habit of free trade, the free purchase and sale of labor power and human power like any other commodity. We have begun to loosen and to destroy the most ingrained prejudices, the most ancient and deep-rooted habits. In one year, our subbotniks have made tremendous progress. They are still infinitely weak. But that does not daunt us. (*From the First Subbotnik on the Moscow-Kazan Railway to the All-Russian May Day Subbotnik*, May 2, 1920, *Selected Works*, VIII, 245.)

5. ECONOMIC MANAGEMENT

This is the plan for the electrification of Russia. This plan has been thought out by the best agronomists and engineers. We cannot expedite its realization without the help of foreign capital and means of production. But to obtain assistance we must pay for it. . . . In order to enlist the Americans, we must pay them: They are businessmen. And what are we to pay them with? Gold? But we cannot throw gold about. We cannot give raw materials, because we have not yet fed all our own people. When the question arises in the Council of People's Commissars of giving 100,000 poods of grain to the Italians, the People's Commissar of Food gets up and refuses. We are bargaining for every trainload of grain. Without grain we cannot develop foreign trade. What then shall we give? Rubbish? They have enough rubbish of their own. They say, let us trade in grain; but we cannot give grain. We are therefore solving the problem by means of concessions.

.   .   .   .

Concessions are nothing but a new form of war. Europe fought us, and now the war is moving into a new plane. Formerly, the war was conducted in the field in which the imperialists were infinitely stronger, the military field. If you count the number of guns and machine guns they have and the number we have, the number of soldiers their governments can mobilize and the number our government can mobilize, we undoubtedly ought to have been crushed in a fortnight. Nevertheless, we held our own in this field, and we undertake to continue the fight and are passing to an economic war. It is definitely stated that side by side with the concession land, the concession square of territory, there will be our square, and then again their square; we shall learn from them how to organize model enterprises by placing our own side by side with theirs. If we are incapable of doing that, it is not worth talking about anything. To procure the last word in technology in the matter of equipment at the present time is not an easy task, and we have to learn, learn it in practice; for this is not a thing to be got from schools, universities or courses. And that is why we are granting concessions on the checkerboard system: Come and learn on the spot.

Economically, we have a vast deal to gain from concessions. Of course, when settlements are created, they will bring capitalist customs with them, they will demoralize the peasantry. But watch must be kept, we must put up our communist influence in opposition at every step. This also is a kind of war, the military rivalry of two methods, two formations, two kinds of economy—communist and capitalist. We shall prove that we are the stronger.

As long as capitalism and socialism exist, we cannot live in peace: In the end, one or the other will triumph—a funeral dirge will be sung either over the Soviet Republic or over world capitalism. This is a respite in war. The capitalists will seek pretexts for fighting. If they accept the proposal and agree to concessions, it will be harder for them. On the one hand, we shall have the best conditions in the event of war; on the other hand, those who want to go to war will not agree to concessions. The existence of concessions is an economic and political argument against war. The states that might war on us will not war on us if they take concessions. From the point of view of the danger of a collision between capitalism and bolshevism, it must be said that concessions are a continuation of the war, but in a different sphere. (*Speech* . . . , November 26, 1920, *Selected Works*, VIII, 294, 295 f., 297.)

We shall achieve nothing by the old methods; but we shall achieve victory by the methods of propaganda, agitation and organized influence which we have learned, and shall so bring it about that not only will decrees be adopted, institutions created and documents written—it is not enough to send orders flying all over the country—but also that, by spring, the fields will be sown better than before, that a definite improvement will be achieved in the husbandry of the small peasant—let it be even the most elementary (the more cautious we are the better)—but it must be achieved at all costs on a mass scale.

.   .   .   .

In the matter of fuel we have achieved a very important success in the shape of the hydraulic method of extracting peat. Peat is a fuel we possess in very large quantities, but which we were unable to utilize because hitherto the work had to be performed under intolerable conditions. And this new method will enable us to overcome the fuel shortage, one of the greatest dangers on our economic front. . . . We possess vast deposits of peat, but we cannot utilize them because we cannot send people to work under such inhuman conditions. The capitalist system could send people to work under such inhuman conditions. In the capitalist state people would be driven to work there by hunger, but in the socialist state we cannot consign people to such inhuman work, and nobody will go voluntarily. . . . We must introduce more machines everywhere, we must resort to machine technique as widely as possible. The extraction of peat by the hydraulic method . . . makes it possible to extract fuel in vast quantities and to eliminate the need for trained workers, since even untrained workers can work under this method.

.   .   .   .

There can be no question but that we have learned politics. We cannot be misled here; here we have a basis. But things are bad as far as economic matters are concerned. Henceforward, the best politics will be less politics. Let us have more engineers and agronomists; let us learn from them, keep a check on their work, make our congresses and conferences not meeting-holding bodies, but bodies for testing our economic achievements, bodies in which we can really learn the business of economic development.

.   .   .   .

We must adopt a definite plan. Of course, it will be a plan only to a first approximation. This Party program will not be as unchangeable as our real Party program, which can be changed only by Party congresses. No, this program will be improved, elaborated, perfected and modified every day, in every workshop and in every volost. We need it as a first draft, which will be submitted to the whole of Russia as a great economic plan designed for a period of not less than ten years and which will indicate how Russia is to be placed on the real economic basis which is required for communism.

.   .   .   .

The capitalists in Russia may return and may grow stronger than we are. This must be clearly realized. This must serve as the mainspring of our work and the condition and criterion of our actual success. As long as we live in a small-peasant country, there is a surer economic basis for capitalism in Russia than for communism. This must be borne in mind. Anyone who has carefully observed life in the countryside, as compared with life in the towns, knows that we have not torn up the roots of capitalism and have not undermined the foundation, the basis of the internal enemy. This foundation depends on small-scale production, and there is only one way of undermining it, namely, to place the economy of the country, including agriculture, on a new technical basis, the technical basis of modern large-scale production. And it is only in electricity that we have such a basis.

Communism is the Soviet power plus the electrification of the whole country. Otherwise the country will remain a small-peasant country, and that we must clearly realize. We are weaker than capitalism, not only on the world scale but also within the country. Everybody knows that. We have realized it, and we shall see to it that the economic basis is transformed from a small-peasant basis into a large-scale industrial basis. Only when the country has been electrified, when industry, agriculture and transport have been placed on the technical basis of modern large-scale industry, only then shall we be finally victorious.

.   .   .   .

We must see to it that every factory and every electric power station shall become a center of enlightenment, and if Russia becomes covered by a dense network of electric power stations and powerful technical installations, our communist economic development will become a model for a future socialist Europe and Asia. (*The Work of the Council of People's Commissars*, December 22, 1920, *Selected Works*, VIII, 265, 270, 274, 275, 276 f.)

February 2–7, 1920, i.e., more than a year ago, a session of the All-Russian Central Executive Committee was held which adopted a resolution on electrification. In this resolution we read:

> Side by side with the immediate, essential, unpostponable and urgent tasks in the regulation of transport, the elimination of the fuel and food crises, the combating of epidemics and the organization of disciplined armies of labor, it has for the first time become possible for Soviet Russia to proceed to more systematic economic construction, to the scientific elaboration and the consistent realization of a state plan for the whole national economy. . . .

Is that not clear? "The scientific elaboration of a state plan for the whole national economy." Can one fail to understand these words, this decision of our highest government authority?

. . . .

Let us glance at Germany. There a similar work has been performed by a certain scientist, Ballod. He has drawn up a scientific plan for the socialist reconstruction of the whole national economy of Germany. In capitalist Germany this plan hung fire, remained a piece of journalism, the work of an isolated individual. Ours was a commission given by the state. We mobilized hundreds of experts, and in ten months (of course, not in two months, as was originally indicated) we obtained a single economic plan, scientifically constructed. We are legitimately entitled to be proud of this work; only we must *understand how* to utilize this plan, and it is precisely the failure to understand *this* that we now have to combat. (*A Single Economic Plan,* February, 1921, *Selected Works,* VIII, 300, 302 f.)

The moderate and cautious application of the concessions policy will undoubtedly help us quickly (to a certain, not very large, degree) to improve the state of industry and the conditions of the workers and peasants—of course, at the cost of certain sacrifices, the surrender to the capitalist of tens and tens of millions of poods of valuable products. The measure and the conditions that will make concessions advantageous and not dangerous to us are determined by the relation of forces, they are decided by struggle; for concessions are also a form of struggle, they are the continuation of the class struggle in another form, and under no circumstances are they the substitution of class peace for class war. Practice will determine the methods of struggle. (*The Collapse of the Second International,* April 21, 1921, *Selected Works,* IX, 182.)

6. Soviet Reality

Are successes *really* being achieved by the big factories, the agricultural communes, Committees of Poor Peasants and local Councils of National Economy in the building of the new *economy?* What sort of successes? Are they proved? Is there not some fiction, boastfulness, promises by intellectuals ("being organized," "a plan has been drawn up," "exerting efforts," "now pledge ourselves," "improvements beyond doubt" and other charlatan plans, in the drawing up of which "we" are past masters) in these reports? How were these successes achieved? How can they be extended? (*The Character of Our Newspapers,* September, 1918, *Selected Works,* IX, 504.)

Compared with the advanced countries, it was easier for the Russians to *start* the great proletarian revolution, but it will be more difficult for them to *continue* it and carry it to complete victory, in the sense of organizing complete socialist society. (*The Third International and Its Place in History,* April 15, 1919, *Selected Works,* X, 34.)

It is evident from our Party program . . . that our state is a workers' state with bureaucratic distortions. And we should have stuck this sad—what shall I call it, label?—on it. Here you have, then, the reality of the transition. Well, the state has in practice taken this form; does that mean that the trade unions have nothing to protect, that we can dispense with them in the protection of the material and spiritual interests of the entirely organized proletariat? No. That is an entirely wrong argument theoretically. . . . Our present state is such that the entirely organized proletariat must protect itself, and we must utilize these workers' organizations for the purpose of protecting the workers from their own state and in order that the workers may protect our state. *(The Trade Unions, the Present Situations, and the Mistakes of Comrade Trotsky,* January 19, 1921, *Selected Works,* IX, 9.)

We must have the courage to look the bitter truth straight in the face. The Party is sick. The Party is shaking with fever. The whole question is: Has the sickness affected only the "feverish higher ranks," and perhaps only the Moscow higher ranks, or has it affected the whole body?

.   .   .   .

In speaking of the discussion of December 30, 1920, I must correct another mistake I made. I said: "Our state is not really a workers' state, but a workers' and peasants' state." Comrade Bukharin immediately exclaimed: "What kind of state?" And in reply I referred him to the Eighth Congress of Soviets, which had just closed. Reading the report of that discussion now, I realize that I was wrong and Comrade Bukharin was right. I should have said: "A workers' state is an abstraction. Actually we have a workers' state—with this peculiarity, firstly, that it is not the working class population that predominates in the country but the peasant population, and, secondly, it is a workers' state with bureaucratic distortions."

.   .   .   .

Up to now our platform has been: Don't defend the excesses of bureaucracy, rectify them. The fight against bureaucracy is a long and arduous one. Excesses can and must be rectified at once. It is not those who point to harmful excesses and strive to rectify them that undermine the prestige of the military workers and the appointees, but those who resist this rectification. . . . Now we have added to our platform the following: We must combat the ideological confusion and those *unsound* elements of the opposition who go to the lengths of repudiating all "militarization of economy," of repudiating not only the "method of appointing," which has been the prevailing method up to now, but all "appointments"; for in the last analysis this means repudiating the leading role of the *Party* in relation to the non-Party masses. We must combat the syndicalist deviation, which will kill the Party if the latter is not completely cured of it.

Undoubtedly, the capitalists of the Entente will try to take advantage of our Party's sickness to organize a new invasion; and the Socialist Revolutionaries will take advantage of it for the purpose of organizing conspiracies and rebellions. But we do not fear this because we shall all unite as one man, not fearing to admit the disease but recognizing that it demands from all of us greater discipline, greater endurance, greater firmness at every post. The Party will not be weaker but stronger by the time the Tenth Congress of the Russian Communist party meets in March, and after the congress. (*The Party Crisis,* January 19, 1921, *Selected Works,* IX, 28, 33, 38 f.)

The essence of the peculiar "war communism" was that practically we took all the surplus grain—and sometimes not only surplus grain, but part of the grain the peasant required for food —for the purpose of meeting the requirements of the army and of sustaining the workers. Most often we took the grain on loan, for paper money. Had we not done that we would have been unable to vanquish the landowners and the capitalists in a ruined small-peasant country. And the fact that we were victorious (in spite of the assistance our exploiters obtained from the most powerful countries of the world) shows not only what miracles of heroism the workers and peasants are capable of in the struggle for their emancipation; it also shows the role of lackeys of the bourgeoisie that the Mensheviks, Socialist Revolutionaries and Kautsky and Company played when they *blamed us* for this "war communism." It should be put to our credit.

.   .   .   .

Capitalism is evil compared with socialism. Capitalism is good compared with medievalism, compared with small production, compared with bureaucracy, which is connected with the dispersed character of the small producers. Inasmuch as we are as yet unable to pass directly from small production to socialism, capitalism is inevitable to a certain degree as the elemental product of small production and exchange, and we must utilize capitalism (and, in particular, direct it into the channels of state capitalism) as the intermediary link between small production and socialism, as a means, a path, a method of raising the productive forces.

Take the question of bureaucracy and glance at it from the economic aspect. On May 5, 1918, bureaucracy was not within our field of vision. Six months after the October Revolution, after we had smashed the old, bureaucratic apparatus from top to bottom, we did not yet feel this evil.

Another year passed. At the Eighth Congress of the Russian Communist party (March 18–23, 1919), a new Party program was adopted, and in this program—not fearing to recognize an evil, but desiring to reveal it, to expose it, to pillory it, to rouse the idea and will, energy and action to combat it—we straightforwardly spoke of *"a partial revival of bureaucracy in the Soviet system."*

Another two years passed. In the spring of 1921, after the Eighth Congress of Soviets (December, 1920), which discussed the question of bureaucracy, after the Tenth Congress of the Russian Communist party (March, 1921), which summed up the controversies that were closely connected with the analysis of bureaucracy, we see *this* evil confronting us more clearly, more distinctly and more menacingly. What are the economic roots of bureaucracy? . . . It is the fragmented and dispersed character of small production, its proverty, lack of culture, absence of roads, illiteracy, absence of *exchange* between agriculture and industry, the absence of connection and interaction between them. *(The Food Tax,* April 21, 1921, *Selected Works,* IX, 178, 186–188.)

The Soviet laws are very good laws because they provide everyone with the opportunity of fighting against bureaucracy and red tape, an opportunity which is not provided for the workers and peasants in any capitalist state. But does anybody take advantage of this opportunity? Hardly anybody does! Not only the peasants, but an enormous percentage of the Communists do not know how to take advantage of the Soviet laws to combat red tape and bureaucracy, or such a truly Russian phenomenon as bribery. What hinders the fight against this phenomenon? Our laws? Our propaganda? On the contrary! We have any number of laws! Why have we achieved no success in this struggle? Because it cannot be waged by propaganda alone. It can be waged only if the masses of the people assist in it. No less than half our Communists are incapable of fighting, not to speak of those who hinder the fight. It is true that 99 per cent of you are Communists, and you know that we are performing an operation on these latter Communists, an operation which is being performed by the Party Purging Commission, and there is hope that we shall remove a hundred thousand or so of them. Some say two hundred thousand, and I like that figure much better.

I hope very much that we shall expel a hundred thousand to two hundred thousand Communists who have "attached" themselves to the Party and who are not only unable to fight against red tape and bribery, but even hinder the fight.

.   .   .   .

In my opinion, three principal enemies now confront one, irrespective of one's departmental function; three tasks confront the political educator, if he is a Communist, and most of the political educators are. The three principal enemies that confront him are the following: the first enemy—communist vanity; the second enemy—illiteracy; and the third enemy—bribery. (*The Tasks of the Political Education Departments*, October, 1921, *Selected Works*, IX, 271, 273.)

There was a character in Russian life—Oblomov. He was always lolling on his bed and mentally drawing up plans. That was a long time ago. Since then Russia has passed through three revolutions; but the Oblomovs have remained, for there were Oblomovs not only among the landowners but also among the peasants, and not only among the peasants but among the intellectuals, and not only among the intellectuals but also among the workers and Communists. It is sufficient to watch us at our meetings, at our work on commissions, to be able to say that *the old Oblomov has remained, and it will be necessary to give him a good washing and cleaning, a good rubbing and drubbing to make a man of him.*

Our worst internal enemy is the Communist who occupies a responsible (or not responsible) Soviet post and enjoys universal respect as a conscientious man. "He is not much of a musician, but he never touches a drop." He has not learned to fight against red tape, he is unable to fight against it, he shields it. *We must rid ourselves of this enemy, and with the aid of all class-conscious workers and peasants we shall get at him. The whole mass of non-party workers and peasants will follow the lead of the vanguard of the Communist party in the fight against this enemy and this inefficiency and Oblomovism. There can be no vacillation whatever on this score.*

. . . .

No effort is made to take care of the kopeks that are put in their charge, no effort is made to make the kopek grow into two kopeks; but they draw up plans affecting billions and even trillions of Soviet rubles. It is against this evil that we are waging our struggle. *(The International and Internal Position of the Soviet Republic,* March 6, 1922, *Selected Works,* IX, 316 f., 318, 319.)

It is easier to win power in a revolutionary epoch than to know how to use this power properly. *(On the Significance of Militant Materialism,* March 12, 1922, *Selected Works,* XI, 73.)

The capitalist was able to supply things. He did it badly, he did it exorbitantly, he insulted and robbed us. The simple workers and peasants who do not argue about communism because they do not know what sort of thing it is know this.

"But the capitalist was able to supply things—are you? You are not able to do so." This is what we heard last spring, not always clearly, but it served as the sub-soil of the whole of the crisis last spring. They said: "You are excellent people; but you cannot perform the economic work you have undertaken to do." This is the simple and withering criticism which the peasantry, and through the peasantry a number of strata of workers, directed against the Communist party last year.

During the past year we showed quite clearly that we cannot do business. This is the fundamental lesson.

. . . .

We, and I particularly, because of my position, hear a lot of sentimental, communist lies, "communlies," every day, and sometimes we get mortally sick of them.

. . . .

The economic power in the hands of the proletarian state of Russia is quite adequate to assure the transition to communism. What then is lacking? That is clear; what is lacking is culture among that stratum of the Communists who perform the work of administration. But if we take Moscow, with its 4,700 responsible Communists, and if we take that huge bureaucratic machine, that huge pile, we must ask: Who is leading whom? I doubt very much whether it could be said that the Communists were guiding this pile. To tell the truth, it is not they who are leading; they are being led. Here something happened that is similar to what we were told in our history lessons when we were children: Sometimes one nation conquers another; the nation that conquered is the conqueror and the nation that is vanquished is the conquered nation. This is simple and intelligible to all. But what becomes of the culture of these nations? Here things are not so simple. If the conquering nation is more cultured than the vanquished nation, the former imposes its culture upon the latter; but if the opposite is the case, the vanquished nation imposes its culture upon the conqueror. Has something like this happened in the capital of the Russian Social Federated Soviet Republic? And have the 4,700 Communists (nearly a whole army division, and all of them the very best) become subjected to an alien culture? It is true that one may get the impression that, in this case, the vanquished enjoy a high level of culture. But this is not the case at all. Their culture is on a miserably low and insignificant level. Nevertheless, it is higher than ours. Miserable and meager as it is, it is higher than that of our responsible Communist administrators, for the latter lack the ability to administer.

We have eighteen People's Commissariats, of these not less than fifteen are useless. (*Political Report of the Central Committee of the 11th Congress of the Russian Communist Party* [Bolsheviks], March 27, 1922, *Selected Works,* IX, 333, 334, 346, 348 f., 367.)

We have bureaucrats, not only in the Soviet institutions, but also in the Party institutions.

.   .   .   .

The Russian found consolation for the bleak bureaucratic realities at home in unusually bold theoretical constructions, and that is why these unusually bold theoretical constructions assumed an unusually one-sided character among us. Among us, theoretical audacity in general constructions lived side by side with astonishing timidity in regard to some very minor reform in office routine. A great universal agrarian revolution was worked out with an audacity unprecedented in any other country, and at the same time the imagination was lacking to work out a tenth-rate reform in office routine. (*Better Fewer, But Better,* March 2, 1923, *Selected Works,* IX, 394, 396 f.)

7. NEW ECONOMIC POLICY

In essence, the small farmer can be satisfied with two things. First of all, there must be a certain amount of freedom of turnover, of freedom for the small, private proprietor; and secondly, commodities and products must be provided. What is the use of freedom of turnover if there is nothing to turn over, freedom to trade if there is nothing to trade in? . . . What is freedom of turnover? Freedom of turnover is freedom to trade, and freedom to trade means going back to capitalism. Freedom of turnover and freedom to trade mean commodity exchange between individual, small proprietors. All of us who have learned at least the ABC of Marxism know that this turnover and freedom to trade inevitably lead to the division of the commodity producers into owners of capital and owners of labor power, a division into capitalists and wage workers. . . . The question arises, can the Communist party recognize, adopt free trade? Are there no irreconcilable contradictions here? To this we must reply that, of course, the practical solution of this problem is an extremely difficult one.

.   .   .   .

Can it be done, theoretically speaking; can we, to a certain extent, restore freedom to trade, freedom for capitalism to the small farmer, without at the same time cutting at the roots of the political power of the proletariat? Can it be done? It can, for the question is one of degree. If we were able to place at least a small quantity of goods in the hands of the state, in the hands of the proletariat which possesses political power, and to put these goods into circulation, we would, as a state, add economic power to political power. By putting these goods into circulation we would stimulate small farming, which at the present time is frightfully crushed under the burden of the severe conditions of war and ruin, and under the burden of the impossibility of expanding small farming. As long as he remains small, the small farmer must have a stimulus, an impetus, something to rouse him with respect to his economic base, i.e., small, individual farming. We cannot get away from local free turnover in this case. If this turnover gives the state a minimum quantity of grain sufficient to meet the requirements of the cities, of the factories, of industry, in exchange for manufactured goods, then economic turnover will be restored in such a way that state power will remain in the hands of the proletariat and become stronger. The peasantry demands a practical demonstration of the ability of the workers who own the factories, the works, industry, to organize exchange with it. (*The Tax in Kind*, March 15, 1921, *Selected Works*, IX, 111, 112.)

We must foster "proper" trade, trade that does not evade state control; it is to our advantage to develop this sort of trade. But profiteering, taken in its political and economic sense, *cannot* be distinguished from "proper" trade. Free trade is capitalism; capitalism is profiteering. It would be ridiculous to close our eyes to this.

What should we do? Declare profiteering to be unpunishable?

No. We must revise and redraft all the laws on profiteering, and declare all *thieving* and every direct or indirect, open or concealed *evasion of state control, supervision and accounting* to be a punishable offense (and in fact prosecute it with trebled severity). It is precisely by presenting the question in this way . . . that we shall succeed in directing the inevitable, and to a certain extent necessary, development of capitalism into the channels of *state* capitalism. (*The Food Tax,* April 21, 1921, *Selected Works,* IX, 194.)

The task of socialism is to abolish classes. In the front ranks of the exploiting class we find the big landowners and the capitalist manufacturers. In regard to them, the work of destruction is fairly easy; it can be completed within a few months, and sometimes within a few weeks or days. We in Russia have expropriated our exploiters, the big landowners as well as the capitalists.

. . . .

But, in addition to this class of exploiters, there is in nearly all other capitalist countries, with the exception, perhaps, of England, the class of small producers and small farmers. The principal problem of the revolution now is the struggle against these two classes. In order to rid ourselves of them we must adopt methods other than those employed against the big landowners and capitalists. We could simply expropriate and expel the two latter classes, and this is what we did. But we cannot act in this way toward the two last capitalist classes, the small producers and the petty bourgeoisie, which exist in all countries. In most capitalist countries these classes constitute a very considerable minority, approximately from 30 to 45 per cent of the population. If to them we add the petty bourgeois elements of the working class, we shall get even more than 50 per cent. These cannot be expropriated or expelled; other methods of struggle must be adopted in this case. From the international point of view, if we envisage the international revolution as a single process, the significance of the period into which we are now entering in Russia in essence is that we must now find a practical solution for the problem of the attitude the proletariat should adopt toward this last capitalist class in Russia. All Marxists have solved this problem properly and easily in theory. But theory and practice are two different things; solving a problem in theory is not the same thing as solving it in practice. We know definitely that we have made serious mistakes. From the international point of view, the fact that we are now trying to determine the attitude that the proletariat in power should adopt toward the last capitalist class, toward the deepest foundations of capitalism, the small proprietor, the small producer, is a sign of great progress. This problem now confronts us in a practical manner.

. . . .

The tax in kind means free trade. After having paid the tax in kind, the peasant will have the right freely to exchange the remainder of his grain. This freedom of exchange means freedom for capitalism. We say this openly and emphasize it. We do not conceal it in the least. Things would go very hard with us if we attempted to conceal it. Free trade means freedom for capitalism, but at the same time it means a new form of capitalism. It means that we are re-creating capitalism to a certain extent. We are doing this quite openly. It is state capitalism. But state capitalism in a society in which power belongs to capital and state capitalism in a proletarian state are two different concepts. In a capitalist state, state capitalism is recognized by the state and is controlled by it for the benefit of the bourgeoisie, and in opposition to the interest of the proletariat. In the proletarian state, the same thing is done for the benefit of the working class, for the purpose of withstanding the (as yet strong) bourgeoisie and of fighting it. It goes without saying that we must grant the foreign bourgeoisie, foreign capital, concessions. Without the slightest denationalization, we shall lease mines, forests and oil wells to foreign capitalists, and receive in exchange manufactured goods, machinery, etc., and thus restore our own industry. (*The Tactics of the Russian Communist Party* [Bolsheviks], July 5, 1921, *Selected Works*, IX, 229, 231, 237 f.)

The New Economic Policy . . . means transition to the restoration of capitalism to a considerable degree. To what degree we do not know. Concessions to foreign capitalists (it is true that we have granted only a very few, particularly compared with the number of offers we have made), leasing enterprises to private capitalists—this is the direct restoration of capitalism, and it is connected with the very roots of the New Economic Policy. . . .

.   .   .   .

If capitalism gains, industrial production will grow, and the proletariat will also grow. The capitalists will gain from our policy and will create an industrial proletariat, which in our country, owing to the war and the desperate poverty and ruin, has become declassed, i.e., dislodged from its class groove, and has ceased to be a proletariat. The proletariat is the class which is engaged in the production of material values in large-scale capitalist industrial enterprises. Since large-scale capitalist industry has been destroyed, since the factories and works are at a standstill, the proletariat has disappeared. Sometimes it was considered to exist officially, but it was not bound together by economic roots.

The restoration of capitalism will mean the restoration of the proletarian class, engaged in the production of socially useful material values, engaged in large factories employing machinery, and not engaged in profiteering, not in the making of cigarette lighters for sale and in other "work" that is not very useful, but quite inevitable when our industry is in a state of ruin.

The whole question is: Who will get there first? If the capitalists succeed in organizing first, they will drive away the Communists, and that will be the end of it. We must look at these things soberly: Who will win? Or else the proletarian state, relying on the peasantry, will prove capable of keeping the bridle on messieurs the capitalists in order to direct capitalism along state grooves and to create a capitalism that will be subordinate to the state and serve the state.

.   .   .   .

We must not calculate on a directly communist transition. We must build on the basis of the peasant's personal incentive. We are told, "The personal incentive of the peasant means restoring private property." But we have never interfered with the private ownership of articles of consumption and of tools

as far as the peasant is concerned. We abolished the private ownership of land; the peasant has carried on husbandry without
the private ownership of land, for example, on rented land.
This system has existed in very many countries. There is nothing
economically impossible about it. The difficulty lies in creating
personal incentive. We must give every specialist an incentive
to become interested in the development of production.

Have we been able to do that? No, we have not. . . . We say
that every important branch of national economy must be built
up on the principle of personal incentive: collective discussion,
but individual responsibility. We suffer at every step from our
inability to apply this principle.

.   .   .   .

Manage, all of you! The capitalists will be by your side, and
so will the foreign capitalists, concessionaires and leaseholders;
they will knock hundreds of per cent of profit out of you, they
will enrich themselves by your side. Let them. Meanwhile you
will learn from them the art of management, and only when you
do that will you be able to build up a communist republic.
Because of the necessity of learning quickly, any slowing down
would be a great crime. And we must accept this tuition, this
severe, stern, and sometimes even cruel tuition, because there
is no other path open to us.

.   .   .   .

Can we continue showing the people what we want to build?
No. Even the simplest worker will begin to sneer at us and say:
"What's the use of your keeping on showing us what you want
to build? Show us that you can build. If you can't build, your
way is not ours and you can go to hell!" And he will be right.
(*The New Economic Policy and the Tasks of the Political Education Departments,* October 17, 1921, *Selected Works,* IX, 260,
261 f., 265, 267, 269.)

By the spring of 1921, it became clear that we had suffered
defeat in our attempt to adopt the socialist principles of production and distribution by the tactics of "direct assault," i.e., by
the shortest, quickest and most direct route. The political situa-

tion in the spring of 1921 revealed to us that retreat to the position of state capitalism, the substitution of "siege" tactics for "direct assault" tactics was inevitable on a number of economic questions.

.   .   .   .

Do not be afraid of admitting defeat. Learn from defeat. Do over again more thoroughly, more carefully, and more systematically what has been done badly. If we agreed with the point of view that, like the surrender of positions, admission of defeat gives rise to despondency and relaxation of effort in the struggle, we should have to say that revolutionaries who give way to such despondency are not worth a damn.

The revival of economic life—and this is what we must have at all costs—increased productivity, which we must also have at all costs: These we are beginning to obtain as a result of the partial reversion to the system of state capitalism. (*The New Economic Policy*, October 29, 1921, *Selected Works*, IX, 286, 288.)

Since the spring of 1921, in place of this [direct, communist] approach, plan, method or system of action, we are adopting (we have not yet "adopted" but are still "adopting," and we have not yet fully appreciated this) a totally different method, a reformist type of method: not to *break up* the old socio-economic system—trade, small production, small proprietorship, capitalism—but to *revive* trade, small proprietorship, capitalism, while cautiously and gradually getting the upper hand over it, or creating the possibility of subjecting it to state regulation, *only in proportion* to the extent of its revival.

This is quite a different approach to the problem.

Compared with the previous revolutionary approach, this is a reformist approach. (Revolution is a transformation which breaks the foundations and roots of the old and does not remodel it cautiously, slowly, gradually, trying to break as little as possible.)

.   .   .   .

The greatest danger—perhaps the only danger—that confronts a genuine revolutionary is exaggeration of revolutionariness, forgetting the limits and conditions in which revolutionary methods are appropriate and can be successfully employed. Genuine revolutionaries have most often broken their necks when they began to write "revolution" with a capital R, to elevate "revolution" to something almost divine, to lose their heads, to lose the ability in the coolest and most sober manner to reflect, to weigh up and to ascertain at what moment, under what circumstances and in which sphere it is necessary to act in a revolutionary manner, and when it is necessary to adopt reformist action. Genuine revolutionaries will perish (not that they will be defeated from outside, but that their internal affairs will collapse) only if—and they certainly will if they do—they lose their sobriety of outlook and take it into their heads that "the great, victorious, world revolution" can and must solve all problems in a revolutionary manner under all circumstances and in all spheres of action.

Whoever "takes such a thing into his head" must perish, because he invents something stupid in connection with a fundamental problem; and in the midst of fierce war (and revolution is the fiercest sort of war) the penalty for stupidity is defeat.

Why does it follow that "the great, victorious, world revolution" can and must employ only revolutionary methods? It does not follow at all. It is absolutely untrue, as is clear from purely theoretical propositions if we do not depart from Marxism. That it is untrue is proved also by the experience of our revolution. Theoretically: Engels said that stupid things are done in time of revolution as at any other time, and he was right.

. . . .

At the present moment the link . . . is the revival of internal *trade* under proper state regulation (direction). Trade—this is the "link" in the historical chain of events, in the transitional forms of our socialist construction in 1921–22, which we, the proletarian state, we, the leading Communist party, *must "grasp with all our might."* If we "grasp" this link with sufficient force *now* we shall certainly control the *whole* chain in the very near future. Unless we do it, we shall not control the whole chain, we shall not create the foundation for socialist socio-economic relations.

Communism and trade? That may sound strange. It seems to be something disjointed, incongruous, remote. But if we ponder over it from the point of view of *economics,* we shall find that the one is not more remote from the other than communism is from small-peasant, patriarchal agriculture.

.   .   .   .

Trade is the only possible economic link between the scores of millions of small farmers and large-scale industry *if . . . if* there is not alongside these farmers an excellently equipped large-scale machine industry with a network of electric cables, an industry so well-equipped technically, and having its organizational "superstructures" and accompanying accessories, as to be able to supply the small farmers with the best products in large quantities, more quickly and cheaper than before. On a world scale this "if" *has already been achieved.* This condition already exists; but a country—and one of the most backward capitalist countries at that—standing alone, having tried directly and at one stroke to realize, to put into practice, to organize practically the *new* links between industry and agriculture, failed to achieve this task by "direct assault," and must now try to achieve it by a number of slow, gradual and cautious "siege" operations. (*The Importance of Gold Now and After the Complete Victory of Socialism,* November 5, 1921, *Selected Works,* IX, 296 f., 299 f.)

8. RETURN TO CAPITALISM

We must build up our whole organization in such a way that there shall be no one at the head of our commercial enterprises who has no experience in this field. Very often we find at the head of our institutions a Communist, an admittedly conscientious comrade, tried and tested in the struggle for communism, who has suffered imprisonment for the cause and for that reason was put at the head of a state trust. But he does not know how to trade. He has all the undoubted qualities of a Communist, but the merchant cheats him, and does it excellently. It is a mistake to put a most worthy, excellent Communist, whose loyalty no one but a madman would doubt, in a place that should be occupied by a smart, conscientious salesman who could cope with his work ever so much better than the most loyal Communist. (*The International and Internal Position of the Soviet Republic,* March 6, 1922, *Selected Works,* IX, 317.)

The turn toward the New Economic Policy was decided on at the last [Party] congress with extraordinary unanimity, with even greater unanimity than other questions in our Party (which, it must be admitted, is generally distinguished for its unanimity) have been decided. This unanimity showed that the need for a new approach to socialist economics had fully matured. People who differed on many questions and who appraised the situation from different points of view unanimously and very quickly, without any wavering, agreed that we lacked a real approach to socialist economy, to building its foundation, and that the only way of finding this approach was the New Economic Policy.

.   .   .   .

Our New Economic Policy is the application by us Communists of commercial methods, of capitalist methods.

.   .   .   .

There is something we must now do in economics: We must withstand the competition of the simple shop assistant, of the simple capitalist, of the merchant who will go to the peasant without arguing about communism. Just imagine, he will not begin to argue about communism but will argue in this way: "Since it is necessary to supply things, to trade properly, to be able to build, I will build at a high price, and the Communists will perhaps build at a higher price, perhaps ten times higher." This is the kind of agitation that is now the essence of the matter; herein lies the root of economics.

.   .   .   .

The Communist, the revolutionary who has made the greatest revolution in the world . . . must learn from an ordinary salesman who has had ten years' commercial experience and knows the business, whereas he, the responsible Communist and loyal revolutionary, not only does not know the business but does not realize that he does not know it.

.   .   .   .

Here the "last fight" is impending; here there are no political or any other detours that we can make because this is an examination in competition with private capital. Either we pass this examination in competition with private capital or we suffer utter defeat.

.   .   .   .

But you will not find what we are discussing in those old books. Those books deal with the state capitalism that exists under capitalism. Not a single book has been written about the state capitalism that exists under communism. It did not even occur to Marx to write a word about this subject, and he died without leaving a single precise quotation or irrefutable instruction on it. That is why we must get out of the difficulty entirely by our own efforts.

.   .   .   .

A situation in which the proletariat, the revolutionary vanguard, possesses sufficient political power, with state capitalism existing alongside it, is absolutely unprecedented in history. The crux of the question lies in our understanding that this is the capitalism which we can and must permit, which we can and must put within certain limits; for this capitalism is necessary for the broad masses of the peasantry and for private capital, which must trade in such a way as to satisfy the needs of the peasantry. Things must be arranged in such a way as to enable the ordinary operation of capitalist economy and capitalist turnover to proceed, because this is necessary for the people, and without it existence is impossible. (*Political Report of the Central Committee to the 11th Congress of the Russian Communist Party* [Bolsheviks], March 27, 1922, *Selected Works,* IX, 328, 332 f., 335–338.)

We . . . lack sufficient civilization to enable us to pass directly to socialism, although we have the political requisites for this. (*Better Fewer, But Better,* March 2, 1923, *Selected Works,* IX, 400.)

III

THE AGRARIAN QUESTION

Having established the fact that the production and employment of agricultural machinery in post-reform agriculture in Russia is developing with extreme rapidity, we must now examine the question as to the social and economic significance of this phenomenon. From what has been said above in regard to the economics of peasant and landowner farming, the following postulates must be deduced: On the one hand, it is precisely capitalism which is the factor that gives rise to and spreads the employment of machinery in agriculture; on the other hand, the application of machinery in agriculture bears a capitalist character, i.e., it leads to the establishment of capitalist relationships and to the further development of these relationships.

. . . .

To proceed. Machines lead to the concentration of production and to the introduction of capitalist co-operation in agriculture. The introduction of machinery calls, on the one hand, for the investment of large amounts of capital, and consequently only big farmers are able to acquire it; on the other hand, the employment of machinery pays only when an enormous quantity of goods is turned out: The expansion of production becomes a necessity with the introduction of machinery. The spread of reaping machines, steam threshers, etc., therefore, indicates the concentration of agricultural production (and we shall indeed see later on that the district of Russian agriculture in which the employment of machinery is particularly widespread is distinguished for the great size of its farms).

The results of the application of machinery in agriculture confirm what has been said and reveal all the typical features of capitalist progress, with all the contradictions peculiar to it. Machines, to an enormous degree, increase the productivity of labor in agriculture, which, until the present epoch, has remained almost untouched by the process of social development. Hence the mere fact that the employment of machinery in Russian agriculture is increasing is sufficient to reveal how unsound is Mr. N——on's assertion that there is "absolute stagnation" (*Outlines*) in the production of grain in Russia, and even that there is a "diminution in the productivity" of agricultural labor. Later on we will return to this assertion which contradicts generally established facts and which Mr. N——on made only for the purpose of idealizing pre-capitalist conditions. Here we will merely observe that it would be a mistake to imagine that concentration in agriculture only takes place in the form of extensive expansion of cultivated areas (as Mr. N——on does); as a matter of fact, concentration in agricultural production manifests itself in the most diverse forms, corresponding to the forms of merchant farming. The concentration of production is inseparably connected with wide co-operation between the workers employed on the farm. Above we saw an example of a large estate on which *hundreds* of reaping machines were employed simultaneously for the purpose of harvesting the grain.

Machines *create* a home market for capitalism: first, a market for means of production (for the products of the engineering industry, mining industry, etc., etc.), and second, a market for labor power.

. . . .

We note the extreme inconsistency in the attitude of the Narodniki toward the question of the employment of machinery in agriculture. To admit the usefulness and progressive character of the employment of machinery, to defend all measures directed toward developing and facilitating it, and at the same time to ignore the fact that machinery in Russian agriculture is employed in a capitalistic manner means to sink to the point of view of the

small and big agrarians. And our Narodniki do ignore the capitalist character of the employment of agricultural machinery and
improved implements and do not even attempt to analyze what
type of peasant and landowner introduce machines on their
farms. Mr. V. V. angrily calls Mr. V. Chernayev "a representative
of capitalistic technique." Perhaps Mr. V. Chernayev or some
other official in the ministry of agriculture is to blame for the
fact that machinery in Russia is employed capitalistically! In
spite of the grandiloquent promise "not to depart from the facts"
(*Outlines,* Chap. XIV), Mr. N——on preferred to ignore the fact
that it is precisely capitalism that has developed the utilization
of machinery in our agriculture, and he invented the diverting
theory according to which exchange reduces the productivity of
labor in agriculture! It is neither possible, nor is there any need to
criticize this theory without any analysis of the facts. We will limit
ourselves to giving a small sample of Mr. N——on's reasoning.

> If the productivity of labor in Russia had doubled, the price of a
> quarter of wheat would now be, not twelve rubles, but six, and
> that is all there is to say about it.

Not all, by any means, most worthy economist. "In Russia"
(as indeed in commodity society everywhere), only individual
employers adopt a higher technique and only gradually is it
adopted by the rest. "In Russia," only the rural entrepreneurs
are in a position to improve their technique. "In Russia," this
progress of the rural enterpreneur, small and big, is inseparably
connected with the ruin of the peasantry and the creation of a
rural proletariat. Therefore, if the higher level of techniques of
farming employed by rural entrepreneurs became socially necessary (and only under such circumstances would the price be
reduced by half), this would mean that almost the whole of
agriculture had passed into the hands of capitalists; it would
mean the complete proletarianization of millions of peasants; it
would mean an enormous growth in the non-agricultural population and an increase in the number of factories. (In order that
the productivity of labor in our agriculture may be doubled, an
enormous development is required in the engineering industry,

the mining industry, steam transport, the construction of a mass of new types of farm buildings, granaries, warehouses, canals, etc., etc.) Mr. N——on here repeats the little error that he usually commits in his reasoning: He skips the consecutive steps that are necessary in the development of capitalism; he skips over the intricate complex of socio-economic changes which inevitably accompany the development of capitalism, and then he mourns and weeps over the danger of capitalist "drastic changes."

. . . .

Agricultural capitalism for the first time has put an end to the age-old stagnation in our agriculture and given a tremendous impetus to the transformation of its techniques and to the development of the productive forces of social labor. A few decades of capitalist "change" have done more than whole centuries of preceding history. Monotonous, routine, natural, self-sufficing economy has given way to diversified forms of commercial agriculture; primitive agricultural implements have begun to give way to perfected implements and machines; the immobility of ancient systems of husbandry has been undermined by new methods of agriculture. All these changes are inseparably linked with the above-mentioned phenomenon of specialization in agriculture. By its very nature, capitalism in agriculture (as in industry) cannot develop evenly: In one place (in one country, in one district, on a certain farm) it pushes to the front one side of agriculture, in another place it pushes to the front another, etc. In one case it changes the techniques of certain agricultural operations, in other cases it changes other operations and breaks them away from patriarchal peasant economy and from the patriarchal labor rent system. In view of the fact that the whole of this process takes place under the guidance of the capricious demands of the market, which are not always known to the producer, capitalist agriculture in each separate case (not infrequently in each separate district, sometimes even in each separate country) becomes more and more one-sided compared with previous agriculture; but, taken as a whole, it becomes immeasurably more many-sided and rational than patriarchal agriculture. The rise of special forms of commercial agriculture makes capitalist crises possible and inevitable in agriculture in the event of capitalist overproduction, but these crises (like capitalist crises in general) give a still more powerful impetus to the development of world production and to the socialization of labor.[1]

Thirdly, capitalism for the first time has created in Russia large-scale agricultural production based on the employment of machinery and the wide co-operation of workers. Before capitalism, the production of agricultural products was carried on in an invariable, miserable, petty form, when the peasant worked for himself as well as when he worked for the landowner, and the "commune" character of agriculture was totally unable to put an end to this enormous fragmentation of production. Inseparably connected with the fragmentation of production was the isolation of the producers themselves.[2] Tied to their allotment, to their tiny "commune," they were sharply isolated even from the peasants in the neighboring village commune by the various

---

[1]West European romanticists and Russian Narodniki lay strong emphasis on this process, on the one-sidedness of capitalist agriculture, on the instability and crises created by capitalism, and on these grounds they deny the progressive character of capitalist progress, as compared with pre-capitalist stagnation.

[2]Hence, in spite of the difference in the forms of landownership, the same thing can be applied to the Russian peasant as was said about the French small peasant by Marx: "The peasants who farm their own small holdings form the majority of the French population. Throughout the country, they live in almost identical conditions, but enter very little into relationships one with another. Their mode of production isolates them instead of bringing them into mutual contact. The isolation is intensified by the inadequacy of the means of communication in France and by the poverty of the peasants. Their farms are so small that there is practically no scope for a division of labor, no opportunity for scientific agriculture. Among the peasantry, therefore, there can be no multiplicity of development, no differentiation of talents, no wealth of social relationships. Each family is almost self-sufficient, producing on its own plot of land the greater part of its requirements, and thus providing itself with the necessities of life through an interchange with nature rather than by means of intercourse with society. Here is a small plot of land with a peasant farmer and his family; there is another plot of land, another peasant with his wife and children. A score or two of these atoms make up a village, and a few score of villages make up a department. In this way, the great mass of the French nation is formed by the simple addition of like entities, much as a sack of potatoes consists of a lot of potatoes huddled in a sack." *Der achtzehnte Brumaire des Louis Bonaparte* (Hamburg, 1885), pp. 98–99.

categories to which they respectively belonged (former landowners' peasants, former state peasants, etc.), by the different
sizes of their land holdings, by differences in the conditions under
which they were emancipated (and these conditions were sometimes determined by the individual characters of the landowners
and their caprices). Capitalism for the first time has broken
down these purely medieval obstacles—and has done a very good
thing in doing so. Already, the differences between the various
categories of peasants—the difference in their categories according to the size of their allotment holdings—are proving to be
incomparably less important than the economic differences within
each category and within each village commune. Capitalism destroys local isolation and insularity, and in place of the petty
medieval division among the farmers it introduces division on a
large scale, throughout the whole nation, dividing them into
classes which occupy different positions in the general system
of capitalist economy.[3] Formerly, the very conditions of production determined that the masses of tillers of the soil would be
tied down to their place of residence; but the rise of various
forms and various districts of commercial and capitalist agriculture could not but give rise to the migration of enormous
masses of the population over the whole country. And without
the mobility of the population (as has already been observed
above) the development of its intelligence and initiative is impossible. (*The Development of Capitalism in Russia,* 1898, *Selected Works,* III, 146, 148 f., 153 f., 173–175.)

The Unity Congress of the Russian Social Democratic Labor
party[4] accepted the principle of "municipalization" in its agrarian
program. Municipalization means peasant ownership of allot-

---

[3]The need for union and amalgamation in capitalist society has not dimin-
ished but, on the contrary, has enormously increased. However, it is absolutely
absurd to use the old measures to satisfy this need of the new society. This
new society now demands, firstly, that the union not be local, according to
estate and category; and, secondly, that its starting point be the difference in
position and interest that has been created by capitalism and the disintegration of the peasantry.

[4]The Unity Congress of the Russian Social Democratic Labor party was held
April 10–25 (April 23–May 8), 1905, in Stockholm.

ment land and the leasing to the peasants of the landowner estates that are to be transferred to the zemstvos. This, in essence, is something midway between the real agrarian revolution and Cadet agrarian reform. The peasants will not accept such a plan. They will either demand one simple division of the land or its complete transfer to the people. Municipalization would be a serious democratic reform only in the event of a complete democratic revolution—if a republican regime were established and if government officials were elected by the people. We proposed to the Congress that it should at least link municipalization with these conditions, but the Congress rejected our proposals. And without these conditions, municipalization, as a liberal bureaucratic reform, will give the peasants something very different from what they require, and at the same time it will give new strength, new influence to bourgeois antiproletarian elements which dominate the zemstvos, for it puts the distribution of the land fund practically into their hands. We must explain this point to the broad masses of the workers and peasants. (*An Appeal to the Party* . . . , May, 1906, *Selected Works*, III, 469–470.)

Let[5] us take the Stolypin program, which is supported by the right wing landowners and by the Octobrists. It is frankly a landowners' program. Yet can it be said that it is reactionary also in the economic sense, i.e., that it precludes, or tries to preclude, the development of capitalism, to prevent a bourgeois agrarian evolution? Not at all. On the contrary, the famous agrarian legislation introduced by Stolypin under Article 87 is thoroughly impregnated with the purely bourgeois spirit. There can be no doubt that this follows the line of capitalist evolution, facilitates and pushes forward this evolution, hastens the expropriation of the peasantry, the breakup of the village commune and the creation of a peasant bourgeoisie. Without a doubt, this legislation is progressive in the scientific economic sense.

---

[5]The following passages (pp. 127–139) are selected from *The Agrarian Program of Social Democracy in the First Russian Revolution, 1905–1907*, December, 1907. Only volume and page from *Selected Works* are acknowledged in the text.

But does this mean that Social Democrats should "support" this legislation? Not at all. Such might be the reasoning only of vulgar Marxism, the seeds of which are so persistently sown by Plekhanov and the Mensheviks who sing, shout, appeal and proclaim: We must support the bourgeoisie in its struggle against the old order of things. No. In order to facilitate the development of the productive forces (the highest criterion of social progress), we must give our support not to bourgeois evolution of the landowner type, but to bourgeois evolution of the peasant type. The former implies the utmost preservation of bondage and serfdom—remodelled in a bourgeois fashion—the least rapid development of the productive forces and the retarded development of capitalism; it implies infinitely greater misery and suffering, exploitation and oppression for the large masses of the peasantry and also, consequently, for the proletariat. The second type implies the most rapid development of the productive forces and the best conditions of existence for the mass of the peasantry possible under the commodity system of production. Social Democratic tactics in the Russian bourgeois revolution are not determined by the task of supporting the liberal bourgeoisie, as the opportunists think, but by the task of supporting the struggling peasantry. (*Selected Works,* III, 184–185.)

In the draft issued by the "Emancipation of Labor" group in 1885, the agrarian program was outlined as follows:

> A radical revision of our agrarian relations, i.e., of the conditions of buying out the land and allotting it to the peasant communes. The granting of the right to abandon their allotment and to leave the commune to those peasants who may find it advantageous to do so, etc.

This is all. The mistake in this program is not one of principle or wrong partial demands. No. Its principles are correct, while the only partial demand it raises (the right to abandon allotments) is so incontestable that it has now been carried out by Stolypin's special legislation. The mistake in this program lies in its abstract character, the absence of any concrete view on the subject. Properly speaking, this is not a program but a Marxian declaration in the most general terms. (*Selected Works*, III, 197.)

The present agrarian program of the Social Democratic party which was adopted at the Stockholm Congress marked a great step forward in comparison with the preceding one in one important respect, viz., by recognizing the confiscation of the landowners' estates, the Social Democratic party resolutely started on the path of recognizing the peasant agrarian revolution. This idea is definitely expressed in the following words of the program: " . . . supporting the revolutionary action of the peasantry up to and including the confiscation of the landowners' estates." In the course of the discussion at the Stockholm Congress, one of the reporters, Plekhanov, who together with John proposed this program, spoke definitely of the necessity of ceasing to be afraid of a "peasant agrarian revolution."

One would have thought that this admission—that our bourgeois revolution, in the domain of agrarian relations, must be regarded as a "peasant agrarian revolution"—would remove the extreme differences of opinion among Social Democrats on the question of the agrarian program. Actually, however, differences arose over the question as to whether Social Democrats should support the division of the landowners' estates among the peasants as private property, or advocate the municipalization of the landowners' estates, or the nationalization of all the land. (*Selected Works*, III, 200.)

The present agrarian program of the Russian Social Democratic Labor Party demands that the confiscated lands be transformed into public property (in a special form, i.e., the nationalization of forests, waters and colonization reserves, and the municipalization of privately owned lands), at least in the event of the "victorious development of the revolution." In the event of "unfavorable conditions," the principle of dividing the landowners' estates among the peasants as private property is adopted. In all cases, the property rights of the peasants and small holders to their present holdings are generally recognized. Consequently, the program provides for a dual system of land tenure in a reformed bourgeois Russia: private ownership of land

and (at least in the event of the victorious development of the revolution) public ownership in the form of municipalization and nationalization. (*Selected Works*, III, 201.)

If the demand for the confiscation of all the landowners' estates was proved to be historically correct—and such is undoubtedly the case—it implied that the wide development of capitalism calls for new agrarian relationships, that the nascent capitalism on the landowners' estates can and must be sacrificed to the wide and free development of capitalism on the basis of a rejuvenated small production system. To accept the demand for the confiscation of the landowners' estates is to accept the possibility and the necessity of the rejuvenation of small farming under capitalism.

Is this admissible? Is it not an adventure to support small agriculture under capitalism? Is not the rejuvenation of small agriculture a vain dream? Is it not a demagogic "trap for the peasants," a *Bauernfang?* Such, no doubt, were the misgivings of some comrades. But they were mistaken. The rejuvenation of small agriculture is possible even under capitalism if the historical task is to fight against the pre-capitalist order. In this way small agriculture was rejuvenated in America, where the slave owning latifundia were broken up in a revolutionary manner and the conditions were created for the rapid and unhindered development of capitalism. In the Russian revolution the struggle for the land is nothing more nor less than a struggle for the rejuvenated path of capitalist development. The consistent slogan of such a rejuvenation is: nationalization of the land. To exclude peasant allotments from this slogan is economically reactionary (we shall deal with the politically reactionary aspect separately). The "divisionists" are skipping the historical task of the present revolution, for they assume that the very things for which the mass struggle of the peasants has only just begun have already been achieved. Instead of stimulating the process of rejuvenation, instead of explaining to the peasantry what the conditions for consistent rejuvenation are, they are already cutting out a dressing gown for the appeased, rejuvenated farmer.[6] (*Selected Works*, III, 234.)

Nationalization means transforming the whole of the land into the property of the state. Property of the state means that the state is entitled to draw the rent from it and lay down general rules governing the possession and use of the land for the whole country. Under nationalization such general rules include absolute prohibition of any sort of intermediary, i.e., the prohibition of subletting or transferring land to anyone except the actual tiller, and so on. Furthermore, if the state in question is really a democratic state (not in the Menshevik sense, *à la* Novosedsky), state ownership of the land does not mean that the land cannot be placed at the disposal of the local and regional authorities within the limits of the general laws of the country. On the contrary, that is exactly what it implies. As I have already pointed out in my pamphlet, *A Revision of the Agrarian Program of the Workers' Party*, this is exactly what our minimum program demands when it calls for the self-determination of nations, for wide regional local government and so on. Hence, the drafting of the regulations governing the allotment or distribution of land among individual persons, associations, etc., according to the requirements of local conditions must necessarily be left to the jurisdiction of the local organs of the state, i.e., to the local government authorities.

---

[6]The advocates of division frequently cite the words of Marx: "The free ownership of the self-employing farmer is evidently the most normal form of landed property for small-scale production. . . . The ownership of the soil is as necessary for the complete development of this mode of production as the ownership of the instrument is for the free development of handicraft production." (*Capital*, Vol. III, chap. xlvii, sec. v.) From this it merely follows that the complete triumph of free peasant agriculture may call for private ownership of land. But present day small-scale agriculture is not free. State ownership of land is "an instrument in the hands of the landowner rather than of the peasant, an instrument for extracting labor rent rather than an instrument of free labor of the peasant." The abolition of all forms of feudal landownership and the creation of the conditions under which the peasants will be free to settle where they please are essential for the promotion of free, small-scale agriculture.

If any misunderstanding could arise on all these points, it must have been due either to a failure to understand the differences in the terms: ownership, possession, disposal and use, or to demagogical flirting with provincialism and federalism.[7] The difference between municipalization and nationalization is not the apportionment of rights as between the central and provincial authorities, and still less the "bureaucracy" of the central authority—only quite ignorant people can think and talk like that—but that under municipalization, private ownership is retained for one category of land, whereas under nationalization it is entirely abolished. (*Selected Works,* III, 247–249.)

The agrarian question is the basis of the bourgeois revolution in Russia and determines the national peculiarity of this revolution.

The essence of this question is the struggle of the peasantry for the abolition of the landed gentry and the remnants of serfdom in the agricultural system of Russia, and also, consequently, in all her social and political institutions.

Ten and a half million peasant households in European Russia own together 75,000,000 dessiatins of land. Thirty thousand, chiefly noble but also partly "common," landowners each own 500 dessiatins and over—a total of 70,000,000 dessiatins. Such is the main background of the picture. These are the main reasons for the predominance of feudal landowners in the agri-

---

[7]We observe this kind of flirting on the part of Maslov. . . . In an article in *Obrazovaniye,* 1907, No. 3, he writes: "Perhaps, in some localities, the peasants would agree to divide their lands; but the refusal of the peasants in a single large region (e.g., Poland) to allow their lands to be divided would suffice to reduce the proposal to nationalize the whole of the land to absurdity." This is a sample of vulgar argumentation in which there is no trace of thought, but simply empty phraseology. The "refusal" of a region, which occupies an exceptional position, to divide the land cannot alter the general program nor make it absurd: Certain territories may "refuse" to municipalize the land. This is not the important thing. What is important is the fact that in a united capitalist state, private ownership of land and nationalization on a large scale cannot exist side by side. One of these two systems will have to get the upper hand. It is the business of the workers' party to advocate the superior system, that which facilitates the rapid development of the forces of production and freedom to wage the class struggle.

cultural system of Russia and, consequently, in the Russian state and in the whole of Russian life generally. The owners of the latifundia are feudal landowners in the economic sense of the term: the basis of their landed property was created by the history of serfdom, the history of land grabbing by the nobility through the centuries. The basis of their present methods of farming is the system of labor rent, i.e., a direct survival of *barshchina;* it implies cultivation of the land with the implements of the peasants and by the virtual enslavement of the small tillers in an endless variety of ways: winter hiring, yearly leases, sharecropping, labor rent, bondage for debts, bondage for *"otrezki,"* for the use of forests, meadows, water and so on and so forth, *ad infinitum.* Capitalist development in Russia during the last half century has made such strides that the retention of serfdom in agriculture has become absolutely impossible, and its abolition has assumed the forms of a violent crisis, a nationwide revolution. However, the abolition of serfdom in a bourgeois country is possible in two ways.

Serfdom may be abolished by the gradual transformation of the landowners' feudal latifundia into *Junker*-bourgeois estates by transforming the masses of the peasants into landless peasants and farm hands, by forcibly keeping the masses down to the pauper standard of living, by the rise of small groups of *Grossbauern,* i.e., rich bourgeois peasants who inevitably spring up under capitalism from among the peasantry. The Black Hundred landowners and Stolypin, their minister, have chosen this very path. They realized that it would be impossible to clear the path for the development of Russia without forcibly breaking up the rusty medieval forms of landownership. And they boldly set out to break these up in the interests of the landowners. They abandoned the sympathy which only recently prevailed among the bureaucracy and the landlords for the semifeudal commune. They evaded all the "constitutional" laws in order to break up the village communes by force. They gave the kulaks *carte blanche* to rob the peasant masses, to break up the old system of landownership, to ruin thousands of peasant farmers; they handed over the medieval village to be "sacked and plundered" by those who had rubles in their purses. They cannot act otherwise if they are to retain their class rule, for they have realized the necessity of adapting themselves to capitalist development and not of fighting against it. And in order to preserve their rule they can find no other allies against the masses of the peasants than the "commoners," the Razuvayevs and Kolupayevs. They had no other alternative than to shout to these Kolupayevs: *"Enrichissez-vous!"*—get rich! We shall create opportunities for you to make a hundred rubles for every one you invest if only you will help us to save the basis of our power under the new conditions! This path of development, if it is to be traveled successfully, calls for wholesale, systematic, unbridled violence against the peasant masses and against the proletariat. And the landowner counterrevolution is hastening to organize this violence all along the line.

The other path of development we have designated as the American path, in contradistinction to the former, which we designated the Prussian path. It, too, necessitates the forcible breaking up of the old system of landownership, for only the stupid philistines of Russian liberalism can dream of the possibility of a painless, peaceful solution of the exceedingly acute crisis in Russia.

But this indispensable and inevitable breaking up may be carried out in the interests of the peasant masses and not of the landowner gang. A mass of free farmers may serve as the basis for the development of capitalism without any landowner farming whatsoever, for taken as a whole the latter form of farming is economically reactionary, whereas the elements of free farming were created among the peasantry by the preceding economic history of the country. If capitalist development proceeds along this course it should develop infinitely more broadly, more freely and more rapidly as the result of the tremendous growth of the home market and the rise in the standard of living, the energy, initiative and culture of the whole of the population. And the gigantic colonization reserves of Russia, the utilization of which is greatly hampered by the feudal oppression of the mass of the peasantry in Russia proper, as well as by the feudal-bureaucratic handling of the agrarian policy—these reserves will provide the economic foundation for the tremendous expansion of agriculture and increase of production both in volume and in scope.

Such a path of development calls for much more than the mere abolition of the landed gentry. For the rule of the feudal landowners through the centuries has put its mark upon all forms of landownership in the country, upon the peasant allotments as well as the holdings of the settlers in the relatively free border lands. The whole of the colonization policy of the autocracy is permeated with the Asiatic interference of a die-hard bureaucracy, which hampered the free settlement of the immigrants, introduced terrible confusion to the new agrarian relationships and contaminated the border regions with the virus of the feudal bureaucracy of central Russia. Not only is the landed gentry in Russia a medieval institution, but so also is the peasant allotment system. The latter is in a terrible tangle. It splits up the peasantry into thousands of small units, medieval groups, social categories. It reflects the medieval history of reckless interference in the relationships of the peasants by both the central government and the local authorities. It confines the peasants, as in a ghetto, in petty medieval associations of a fiscal, tax-extorting character, in associations for the ownership of allotted land, i.e., in the village communes. And Russia's economic development is actually pulling the peasantry out of this medieval environment, on the one hand, by giving rise to the leasing and abandonment of allotments and, on the other hand, by creating the system of farming by the free farmers of the future (or by the future *Grossbauern* of a *Junker* Russia) out of the fragments of the most diversified forms of landownership: privately owned allotments, rented allotments, purchased property, land rented from the landowner, land rented from the state and so on.

In order to establish really free farming in Russia it is necessary to "disenclose" all the lands, those of the landowners as well as the allotments. The whole system of medieval landownership must be broken up, and all lands must be made equal for the free farmers upon a free soil. The greatest possible facilities must be created for the exchange of holdings, for the free choice of settlements, for rounding off holdings, for the creation of free, new associations, instead of the musty, tax-extorting village commune. The whole land must be "cleared" of all medievalism.

The expression of this economic necessity is the nationalization of the land, the abolition of private ownership of land and the transfer of all the land to the property of the state, which will mark a complete rupture with the traditions of serfdom in the countryside. It is this economic necessity that has turned the mass of Russian peasants into supporters of land nationalization. The mass of small holders and tillers declared themselves for nationalization at the congresses of the Peasant League in 1905, in the First Duma in 1906, and in the Second Duma in 1907, i.e., during the whole of the first period of the revolution. They did not do so because the "commune" has infected them with certain special "germs," certain special, non-bourgeois "labor principles." On the contrary, they did so because life has urged them to seek emancipation from the medieval commune and the medieval allotments. They did not do so because they wanted to or could build up socialist agriculture, but because they wanted and now want to, because they could and can now build up real, bourgeois, small agriculture, i.e., agriculture purged to the utmost of all the traditions of serfdom.

Thus, it was neither chance nor the influence of this or that doctrine (as some short-sighted people think) that determined this peculiar attitude of the classes struggling in the Russian revolution toward the question of private ownership of land. This peculiar attitude is to be explained by the conditions of the development of capitalism in Russia and the requirements of capitalism at this stage of its development. All the Black Hundred landowners, all the counterrevolutionary bourgeoisie (including the Octobrists and the Cadets), stand for private ownership of land. The whole of the peasantry and the whole of the proletariat are opposed to private ownership of land. The reformist way of creating a *Junker*-bourgeois Russia necessarily presupposes the preservation of the foundations of the old system of landownership and a slow adaptation to capitalism, which would be painful for the masses of the population. The revolutionary way of really overthrowing the old order inevitably demands, as its economic basis, the destruction of all old forms of landownership together with all the old political institutions of Russia. The experience of the first period of the Russian revolution has conclusively proved that it can be victorious only as a peasant agrarian revolution and that the latter cannot completely fulfil its historic mission unless the land is nationalized.

Certainly, Social Democracy, as the party of the international proletariat, the party which has set itself worldwide socialist aims, cannot identify itself with any epoch of any bourgeois revolution, nor can it bind its destiny with this or that outcome of this or that bourgeois revolution. No matter what the outcome may be, we must remain an independent, purely proletarian party which consistently leads the toiling masses to their great socialist goal. We cannot, therefore, undertake to guarantee that any of the gains of the bourgeois revolution will be permanent, because impermanence and inherent contradiction are immanent features of *all* the gains of bourgeois revolutions as such. The "invention" of "guarantees against restoration" can only be the fruit of illogical thinking. We have but one task: to rally the proletariat for the socialist revolution, to support every fight against the old order in the most resolute way, to fight for the best possible conditions for the proletariat in the developing bourgeois society. And it inevitably follows from all this that our Social Democratic program in the Russian bourgeois revolution can *only* be the nationalization of the land. Like every other *part* of our program we must connect it with definite forms and a definite degree of political reforms, because the extent of the political and agrarian revolution cannot but be identical. Like every other part of our program, we must isolate it strictly from petty bourgeois illusions, from intelligentsia-bureaucratic babble about "scales," from the reactionary literature in favor of strengthening the village commune or of equal land tenure. The interests of the proletariat do not demand that special slogans, "plans" or "systems" be invented for this or that bourgeois revolution, they only demand that the objective conditions for this revolution shall be *consistently* expressed and these objective, economically unavoidable conditions be purged of illusion and utopia. The nationalization of the land is not only the sole means for completely liquidating medievalism in agriculture, but is also the best form of agrarian relationships conceivable under capitalism.

Three circumstances temporarily diverted the Russian Social Democrats from this correct agrarian program. First, P. Maslov, the initiator of "municipalization" in Russia, "revised" the theory of Marx, repudiated the theory of absolute rent, revived the semi-decayed bourgeois doctrines of the law of diminishing fertility, its connection with the theory of rent, etc. The negation of absolute rent is tantamount to denying that private land-ownership has any economic significance under capitalism and, consequently, it inevitably leads to the distortion of the Marxian view on nationalization. Secondly, not perceiving the *beginning* of the peasant revolution, Russian Social Democrats could not but regard its possibilities with caution, because, for the revolution to be victorious, a number of especially favorable conditions and an especially favorable sweep of the revolutionary class consciousness, energy and initiative of the masses are required. Not having had any *experience,* and holding that it is impossible to invent *bourgeois* movements, the Russian Marxists naturally could not, *before the revolution,* present a correct agrarian program. But even *after* the revolution had begun, they committed the following mistake: Instead of *applying* the theory of Marx to the peculiar conditions prevailing in Russia (our theory is not a dogma, Marx and Engels always taught, but a *guide to action*), they uncritically repeated the conclusions drawn from the application of Marx's theory to foreign conditions, to a *different* epoch. (*Selected Works,* III, 278–284.)

Thirdly, the municipalization program obviously reflects the mistaken tactical line of Menshevism in the Russian bourgeois revolution: the failure to understand that only a "coalition between the proletariat and the peasantry" can guarantee its vic-

tory; the failure to understand the leading role of the proletariat
in the bourgeois revolution; the striving to push the proletariat
aside, to adapt it to an incomplete outcome of the revolution,
to convert it from a leader into an auxiliary (actually into a
laborer and servant) of the liberal bourgeoisie. . . .

The fight against the "passion" for petty bourgeois socialism
must result, not in the diminution, but in the increase of the
sweep of the revolution and of its tasks as determined by the
proletariat. We must not encourage "regionalism," no matter
how strong it may be among the backward strata of the petty
bourgeoisie or the privileged peasantry (cossacks), nor encourage
the isolation of the different nationalities—no, we must explain
to the peasantry the importance of unity if victory is to be
achieved, we must advance slogans that will widen the movement, not narrow it, that will place the responsibility for the
incomplete bourgeois revolution on the backwardness of the
bourgeoisie and not on the lack of understanding of the proletariat. We must not "adapt" our program to "local" democracy;
we must not invent rural "municipal socialism," which is absurd
and impossible under a non-democratic central government, we
must not make petty bourgeois, socialist reformism fit in with
the bourgeois revolution, but must concentrate the attention of
the masses on the actual conditions of the victory of the revolution as a bourgeois revolution, on the need for achieving not
only local, but "central," democracy, i.e., the democratization of
the central government in order to achieve complete victory—
and not only democracy in general, but the most complete,
highest form of democracy, for otherwise the peasant agrarian
revolution in Russia will become *utopian* in the scientific sense
of the word. (*Selected Works,* III, 285.)

We will now sum up what has been said about the essence of
the agrarian question and the agrarian crisis in Russia at the
end of the nineteenth century.

What is the essence of this crisis? M. Shanin, in his pamphlet,
Municipalization or Distribution (Vilna, 1907), insists that our
agricultural crisis is an agronomic crisis and that its deepest roots

lie in the necessity of raising the technological level of agriculture, which is incredibly low in Russia, in the necessity of
adopting a higher system of farming, etc.

This opinion is wrong because it is too abstract. Undoubtedly,
it is necessary to adopt a superior system of farming, but, in
the first place, this superior system was adopted in Russia after
1861. However slow progress may be, it cannot be denied that
both landowner and peasant farmers, as represented by the
wealthy minority, have adopted grass sowing, are employing
improved implements, are more systematically and carefully
manuring their land, etc. And since this slow progress in agricultural techniques has been a general process since 1861, it is
obvious that this in itself does not explain the universally admitted intensification of the agricultural crisis at the end of the
nineteenth century. Secondly, both "solutions" of the agrarian
problem that have been proposed—the Stolypin proposal to
solve it *from above,* by preserving the landed gentry and finally
destroying the village commune by allowing it to be plundered
by the kulaks, and the peasant (trudovik) proposal to solve
it *from below,* by abolishing the landed gentry and by nation-
alizing all the land—both these solutions, each in its own way,
facilitate the adoption of superior techniques; both are in line
with agronomic progress. The only difference between them is
that one bases this progress on the acceleration of the process
of squeezing the poor peasants out of agriculture, and the other
bases it on the acceleration of the process of abolishing the labor
rent system by destroying the feudal latifundia. It is an undoubted fact that the poor peasants "manage" their land extremely badly. It is also beyond doubt that if their land is
handed over to be plundered by a handful of rich peasants,
agriculture will be raised to a higher level. But it is also an
undoubted fact that landowner land, cultivated by means of
the labor rent system and bondage, is also badly cultivated, *even
worse than are the allotments.* (The reader will recall the figures
quoted above: 54 poods per dessiatin on allotment land, 66 poods
per dessiatin on landowner farms, 50 poods per dessiatin under
the share-cropping system and 45 poods per dessiatin on land

rented by the year by peasants.) The labor rent system of land-owner farming means the preservation of incredibly obsolete methods of land cultivation, it means the perpetuation of barbarism in agriculture and in social life. Undoubtedly, therefore, if the labor rent system is torn up by the roots, i.e., if the landed gentry is completely abolished (without compensation), then agriculture will be raised to a higher level.

Consequently, the essence of the agrarian question and of the agrarian crisis is not the removal of the obstacles to raising agriculture to a higher level, but *how* these obstacles are to be removed, which class is to remove them and by what methods.

And it is absolutely necessary to remove these obstacles to the development of the productive forces of the country—necessary not only in the subjective sense of the word, but also in the objective sense, i.e., this removal is inevitable, and no power on earth can prevent it.

The mistake M. Shanin makes, and which many writers on the agrarian question make, is that he took the correct postulate regarding the necessity of raising the level of agricultural techniques in too abstract a manner and failed to take into consideration the peculiar form in which the feudal and capitalist features of agriculture in Russia are interwoven. The principal and fundamental obstacles to the development of the productive forces in Russian agriculture are the survivals of serfdom, i.e., primarily the labor rent system and bondage, then come the serf dues, the state of inequality of the peasantry before the law, their degradation in relation to the higher social classes, etc., etc. The abolition of these survivals of serfdom has long become an economic necessity, and the crisis in agriculture at the end of the nineteenth century became so extraordinarily acute precisely because the liberation of Russia from medievalism has been too long drawn out, because the labor rent system and bondage have "lived" too long. They began to die out after 1861 so slowly that the new organism must rid itself of them quickly by violent means.

What is this new organism of Russian agriculture? Above we tried to show in particular detail what this is, because the economists in the liberal Narodnik camp have particularly wrong ideas on this subject. The new economic organism, which is emerging from the shell of serfdom in Russia, is commercial agriculture and capitalism. In so far as it is not conducted on the labor rent system or on the system of holding the allotment peasant in bondage, the economics of landowner farming clearly reveal capitalist features. The economics of peasant farming—in so far as we are able to see what is going on in the village communes in spite of the official equality of allotment land-ownership—also reveal purely capitalist features everywhere. Commercial agriculture is steadily growing in Russia in spite of all obstacles, and this commercial agriculture is inevitably becoming transformed into capitalist agriculture, although the forms this transformation is taking vary rather considerably in the various districts.

What is meant by the violent abolition of the medieval shell which has become necessary for the further free development of the new economic organism? By that is meant the abolition of medieval landownership. In Russia, right up to the present time, both the landed gentry and, to a considerable extent, peasant landownership, are still medieval. We have seen how the new economic conditions are breaking down the framework and obstacles of medieval landownership, how it is compelling the poor peasant to let his ancient allotment, how it is compelling the rich peasant to build up a relatively large farm out of the fragments of different lands: allotments, purchased land and land rented from the landowner. On landowner land also, the division of land into land worked by peasants in payment for rent, land rented to the peasants on annual leases and land farmed by the landowner himself indicates that the new economic system is being built up outside of the framework of the old medieval system of landownership.

This system of landownership can be abolished at one stroke by a determined rupture with the past. The nationalization of the land would be such a measure, which all the representatives of the peasantry have indeed demanded, more or less consistently, in the period between 1905 and 1907. The abolition of private ownership of land does not by any means change the bourgeois foundations of commercial and capitalist agriculture. There is nothing more erroneous than the opinion that the nationalization of the land has something in common with socialism, or even with the equal right to the use of the land. Socialism, as is well known, means the abolition of commodity production. Nationalization, however, means converting the land into the property of the state, and such a conversion does not in the least affect private enterprise on the land. Whether the land is private property or whether it is in the "possession" of the whole country, of the whole nation, makes no difference in so far as the economic system on the land is concerned, nor does it make any difference whatever to the (capitalist) economic system of the rich muzhik whether he buys land "in perpetuity," rents land from the landowner or the state, or whether he "gathers up" allotment land abandoned by bankrupt peasants. If exchange remains, it is ridiculous to talk of socialism. And the exchange of agricultural products and means of production does not depend upon the form of landownership at all. (I am explaining here only the economic significance of nationalization and not advocating it as a program. However, I advocated this elsewhere.)

In regard to equality, we have already shown above how this is applied in practice in the distribution of allotment land. We have seen that within the village commune, allotment land is distributed fairly equally and operates only slightly to the advantage of the rich. But only a small trace is left of this equality in the long run, owing to the fact that the poor peasants are obliged to let their land and that the rented land is concentrated in the hands of the rich peasants. Clearly, equality of landownership is unable to remove the inequality in the actual use of the land as long as there is inequality in property among owners and a system of exchange which aggravates this inequality.

The economic significance of nationalization does not by any means lie where it is very often sought. It does not lie in the fight against bourgeois relationships (as Marx long ago pointed out, nationalization is one of the most consistent bourgeois measures), but in the fight against feudal relationships. The multiplicity of forms of medieval landownership hampers economic development: the system of dividing the population into estates hampers trade; the disharmony between the old system of landownership and the new system of economy gives rise to acute contradictions; owing to the retention of the latifundia, the landowners prolong the existence of the labor rent system; the peasants are confined to a ghetto, to allotment landownership, the framework of which life is breaking down at every step. Nationalization will sweep away all medieval relations in landownership entirely, will remove all artificial barriers on the land and make the land really free—for whom? For all citizens? Nothing of the kind. The horseless peasant (three and a quarter million households), as we have seen, is free to let his allotment. The land becomes free—for the *master*, for the one who really wants and is really *able* to cultivate it according to the requirements of modern economic conditions in general and the requirements of the world market in particular. Nationalization would accelerate the death of serfdom and the development of purely capitalist farming on land that has been completely cleared of all medievalism. This is the real historical significance of nationalization in Russia as it developed at the end of the nineteenth century.

The other—objectively not impossible—way of clearing landownership for capitalism is, as we have seen, to accelerate the plunder of the village commune by the rich and to consolidate private landownership among the wealthy peasants. This way leaves the principal source of labor rent and bondage untouched; the landowners' latifundia are left intact. Obviously, this way of clearing the ground for capitalism guarantees the free development of the productive forces to a much smaller degree than the first-mentioned way. As long as the latifundia remain intact, the preservation of the bonded peasant, the sharecropper, the annual renting of small plots of land, the cultivation of the "squires'" land with the implements of the peasants, i.e., the preservation of the most backward culture and of all that oriental barbarism that is called patriarchal rural life, are inevitable.

The two methods of "solving" the agrarian question in developing bourgeois Russia correspond to two paths of development of capitalism in agriculture. I call these two paths the Prussian path and the American path. The first is characterized by the fact that medieval relationships in landownership are not liquidated at one stroke; they gradually adapt themselves to capitalism, and for this reason capitalism retains semifeudal features for a long time. Prussian landlordism was not crushed by the bourgeois revolution; it survived and became the basis of *Junker* economy, which is capitalist at bottom, but which still keeps the rural population in a certain degree of dependence, as for example the *Gesindeordnung*, etc. As a consequence, the social and political domination of the *Junker* was strengthened for many decades after 1848, and the development of the productive forces of German agriculture proceeded very much more slowly than in America. On the contrary, in America it was not the slave economy of the large landowners that served as the basis of capitalist agriculture (the Civil War crushed the slave estates), but the free economy of the free farmer working on free land, land free from all medieval fetters, free from serfdom and feudalism on the one hand, and free from the fetters of private ownership of land on the other. Land was given away in America out of an enormous land fund, at a nominal price, and it is only on a new, completely capitalist base that private ownership of land has now developed there.

Both these paths of capitalist development became clearly marked in Russia after 1861. The progress of landowner economy cannot be doubted, but the slowness of this progress is not accidental; it is inevitable as long as the survivals of serfdom are preserved. There is no doubt also that the freer the peasantry is, the less it is oppressed by the remnants of serfdom (in the south, for example, all these favorable conditions exist), and finally, the better the peasants, taken as a whole, are provided with land, the greater will be the disintegration among the peasantry and the more rapid will be the process of the formation of a class of rural capitalist farmers. The whole question of the future development of the country can be reduced to this: Which of the two paths of development will ultimately prevail, and, correspondingly, which class will carry through the necessary and inevitable change—the old landowner or the free peasant farmer?

Some people in Russia think that nationalization of the land means that the land will be removed from the sphere of commerce. This, undoubtedly, is the point of view of the majority of the progressive peasants and ideologists of the peasantry. But this view is radically wrong. The very opposite is the case. Private ownership of land is an obstacle to the investment of capital in land. Therefore, when the free renting of land from the state becomes possible (and this is the essence of nationalization in bourgeois society), the land will be drawn into the sphere of commerce to a *far greater extent* than was the case when private ownership of land prevailed. The possibilities of free investment of capital in land, free competition in agriculture, are much greater under the system of free renting than under the system of private ownership of land. Nationalization of the land is, as it were, large-scale landownership without landowners. And what large-scale landownership in the capitalist development of agriculture means was explained by the profound observations of Marx in his *Theories of Surplus Value.* I have quoted these observations [before] . . . but in view of the importance of the question, I take the liberty of repeating them here.

In the paragraph on the historical conditions of the Ricardian theory of rent (*Theories of Surplus Value,* Vol. II, part 2), Marx says that Ricardo and Anderson "start out from a viewpoint, which is regarded as very strange on the Continent, viz., that landed property, as an obstacle to all application of capital to the land, does not exist at all." At first sight, this would seem to be contradictory because it is precisely in England that feudal landed property is considered to have been completely preserved. But Marx explains that:

> . . . Nowhere in the world has capitalist production dealt so ruthlessly with the traditional relations of agriculture and so adequately molded its conditions and made them subject to itself. England is in this respect the most revolutionary country in all the world. All historically inherited relations—not only the position of the villages but the very villages themselves, not only the inhabitations of the agricultural population but this population itself, not only

the ancient economic centers but the very economy itself—have been ruthlessly swept away where they were in contradiction to the conditions of capitalist production in the countryside or did not correspond to those conditions. The German, for example, finds economic relations determined by the traditional relations of village fields *(Feldmarken),* the position of economic centers and particular conglomerations of the population. The Englishman finds that the historic conditions of agriculture have been progressively created by capital since the end of the fifteenth century. The technical expression customary in the United Kingdom, the "clearing of estates," does not occur in any continental country. But what does this "clearing of estates" mean? It means that, without regard for the local population—which is driven away, for existing villages—which are levelled to the ground, for farm buildings—which are torn down, for the kind of agriculture—which is transformed at a stroke, being converted, for example, from tillage to pasture, all conditions of production, instead of being accepted as they are handed down by tradition, are historically fashioned in the form necessary under the circumstances for the most profitable investment of capital. To that extent, therefore, *no landed property exists;* it allows capital—the farmer—to manage freely since it is only concerned about the money income. A Pomeranian landowner [Marx refers to Rodbertus, whose theory of rent he examined in detail and brilliantly refuted in this work], his mind full of his hereditary estates, economic centers, and the agricultural collegium, is quite likely, therefore, to hold up his hands in horror at Ricardo's "unhistorical" views on the development of agricultural relations. [As a matter of fact,] the English conditions are the only ones in which modern landed property, i.e., landed property modified by capitalist production, has adequately developed. Here the English view [Ricardo's theory of rent] is classical for the modern, i.e., capitalist mode of production.

In England, the release of the land proceeded in revolutionary forms, accompanied by the violent breaking up of peasant landownership. The breakup of the old and obsolete is absolutely inevitable also in Russia, but the nineteenth century (and also the first seven years of the twentieth) did not settle the question as to which class will do this necessary thing and in what form it will be done. We have shown above what the basis of the distribution of land is in Russia at the present time. We have seen that 10.5 million peasant households—having 75,000,000 dessiatins of land—confront 30,000 owners of latifundia of a total area of 70,000,000 dessiatins. One possible outcome of the struggle, which cannot help breaking out on this ground, is that the amount of land owned by tens of millions of households will be almost doubled and the landed properties of the upper 30,000 will disappear. Let us examine this possible outcome from the purely theoretical point of view, from the point of view of the manner in which the agrarian question arose in Russia at the end of the nineteenth century. What would the results of such a change be? From the point of view of agrarian relationships, obviously, that medieval allotment and medieval large-scale landownership would be reshuffled again. The old conditions would be swept away completely. Nothing traditional would be left in agrarian landowning relations. What force would determine agrarian relations? The "principle" of equality? That is what the progressive peasants who are affected by Narodniki ideology are inclined to believe. That is what the Narodnik thinks. But this is an illusion. The "principle" of equality, which in the village commune is recognized by law and hallowed by custom, leads, in fact, to landownership becoming adapted to differences in the amount of property owned. And on the basis of this *economic fact,* which has been confirmed a thousand times by Russian and Western European data, we assert that all hopes placed in equality will be shattered and that the *reshuffling of landownership will be the only durable result.* Would the significance of *such* a result be great? Very great, because no other measure, no other reform, no other change could give such complete guarantees for the rapid, wide and free progress of agricultural techniques in Russia, and for the elimination from our life of all traces of serfdom, social estates and oriental barbarism.

Progress of techniques?—some will ask. But has it not been shown above by means of precise data that landowner farming is on a higher level than peasant farming in regard to the sowing of grass, in regard to the employment of machines, manuring the soil, quality of cattle, etc.? Of course it has been proved, and this fact is beyond a doubt. But it must not be forgotten that all these differences in economic organization, techniques, etc., are summed up in the *yield*. And we have seen that the yield per dessiatin on landowners' land cultivated by the peasants *on the share-cropping and similar . . . systems* is lower than the yield on allotment land. This fact is nearly always forgotten when the agronomic level of landowner and peasant farming in Russia is discussed. Landowner farming is on a higher level *in so far as* it is conducted on capitalist lines. And the whole point is that this "in so far as," at the end of the nineteenth century, meant that the labor rent system was the predominant system of farming in the central districts. *To the extent* that, at the present time, landowners' land is cultivated by the bonded peasant with antiquated implements, methods, etc., *to that extent* large-scale landownership is the principal cause of backwardness and stagnation. The change in the system of landownership that we are discussing would increase the yield of share-cropping and rented lands (at the present time the yield on such lands—cf. figures above—is 50 and 45 poods as compared with 54 poods on allotment land and 66 poods on landowners' farms). Even if the yield was increased *only* to the level of that on allotment land, the progress would be enormous. It goes without saying, of course, that the yield on allotment land would also be increased as a result of the peasant being freed from the yoke of the feudal latifundia and also because the allotment lands, like all the land in the state, would then become free land, equally accessible, not to all citizens, but to citizens owning agricultural capital, i.e., to the farmers.

This conclusion does not by any means emerge from the data concerning the yield we have taken. On the contrary, these data merely serve to illustrate the conclusion that emerges from the *sum total* of data concerning the evolution of Russian landowner and peasant farming. To refute this conclusion it will be necessary to refute the fact that the history of Russian agriculture in the second half of the nineteenth century is the history of the substitution of bourgeois productive relations for feudal relations.

If we keep to the figures of the number of peasant households at the present time, we may get the impression that the agrarian changes we are examining would lead to the land being divided up into extremely small fragments. Just think of it! Thirteen million households for 280 million dessiatins of land! Is this not dividing up the land in a monstrous fashion? To this our reply is: The land is broken up in this extreme fashion *now* because at the *present time* thirteen million farms are working an area of *less* than 280 million dessiatins! Consequently, the change we are interested in would not by any means make things worse in this respect. More than that. We would ask further whether there are any grounds for thinking that, in the event of this change taking place, the number of households will remain unchanged? Usually, those influenced by Narodnik theories, and the peasants, whose thoughts and strivings are concentrated on land and who even dream of converting the industrial workers into small farmers, think it will remain unchanged. Undoubtedly, a certain number of Russian industrial workers at the end of the nineteenth century also adopted the peasant point of view. The question, however, is: Is this point of view *correct?* Does it conform to the *objective* economic conditions and to the progress of economic development? It is sufficient to put this question clearly to enable one to see that the peasant point of view is determined by the obsolete and irrevocable past and not by the growing future. The peasant point of view is *wrong.* It represents the ideology of yesterday, for economic development is, *in fact,* leading not to an increase but to a diminution of the agricultural population.

The change in agrarian relations that we are examining will not and cannot stop this process of diminution of the agricultural population, a process which is common to all countries in which capitalism is developing. I may be asked: How can this change bring about a diminution of the agricultural population, seeing that the land will become freely accessible to all? I would reply to this question with a passage from a speech delivered in the Duma by the peasant deputy (Poltava Guberniya), Mr. Chizhevsky. Speaking in the Duma on June 6, 1906, he said:

The peasants where I come from, the voters who sent us here, calculate as follows: "If we were a little richer and if every one of our families could afford to spend five or six rubles per annum on sugar—in every uyezd where it is possible to grow sugar beets, several sugar refineries would arise in addition to those which already exist." Naturally if these sugar refineries arose, what a demand would arise for laborers if production were intensified! The output of the sugar refineries would increase, etc.

This is a very characteristic admission by a local worker. If one were to ask his opinion on the significance of agrarian reform in general, he would probably give expression to Narodnik views. But since the question has been put not in regard to "opinions" but in regard to the *concrete consequences* of the change, *capitalist truth* would immediately prevail over *Narodnik utopias.* For what the peasants told their deputy, Mr. Chizhevsky, is capitalist truth, the truth of capitalist reality. The increase in the number of sugar refineries and in their productivity would indeed be enormous if some little improvement were brought about in the conditions of life of the masses of small farmers; and it goes without saying that not only the beet sugar industry, but all the manufacturing industries—textile, iron, engineering, building industries, etc., etc.—would receive a powerful impetus and a great demand for "hands" would arise. And this economic necessity would prove to be more powerful than all the beautiful hopes and dreams about equality. Three and a quarter million horseless households will not become "masters" *as a result of any agrarian reform,* not as a result of any change in landownership, not as a result of any "allotment of land." These millions of households (and no small number of one-horse households), as we have seen, *pine away* on their small plots of land, *let their allotments.* An American development of industry would *inevitably* withdraw the majority of these owners, whose position is hopeless in capitalist society, from agriculture, and no "right to the land" would be powerful enough to prevent this. Thirteen million small owners, with the most miserable, wretched and obsolete implements, scratching their allotment and their landowners' land, this is the reality of today—this is *artificial* overpopulation in agriculture, artificial because of the hereditary retention of feudal relations which have long become obsolete and which *could not* be retained for a single day without executions, shootings, punitive expeditions, etc. Any real improvement in the conditions of the masses, a really serious blow to the remnants of serfdom, would *inevitably* put an end to the over-population of the countryside and would, to an enormous degree, accelerate the process (which is taking place slowly even now) of drawing the population from agriculture into industry, would reduce the number of farms from 13,000,000 to a much lower figure, and would lead Russia forward in the American manner and not in the Chinese manner, as is the case now.

The agrarian question in Russia at the end of the nineteenth century has imposed upon the social classes the task: to put an end to antiquated serfdom and to purge landownership, to clear the whole path for capitalism, for the growth of productive forces, for the free and open class struggle. And this very class struggle will determine the manner in which this task will be fulfilled. (*The Agrarian Question in Russia at the End of the Nineteenth Century,* July, 1908, *Selected Works* I, 79–91.)

In Europe there is no serf bondage. There are rich peasants and peasants with medium-sized farms, and there are laborers in Europe, but not millions of utterly ruined, destitute peasants, driven to madness by perennial suffering and hard labor, disfranchised, downtrodden, dependent on the *"barin."*

What is to be done? What is the way out?

There is only one way out: the liberation of the countryside from the oppression of these feudal latifundia, the transfer of those *seventy million* dessiatins of land from the landowners to the peasants, a transfer that must be effected without any compensation.

Only such a solution can make Russia really resemble a European country. Only such a solution will enable the millions of Russian peasants to breathe freely and recover. Only such a solution will make it possible to transform Russia from a country of perennially starving, destitute peasants, crushed by bondage to the landowner, into a country of "European progress"—from a country of illiterate people into a literate country—from a country of backwardness and hopeless stagnation into a country capable of developing and going forward—from a disfranchised country, a country of slaves, into a free country.

And the party of the working class—knowing that without free, democratic institutions there is and there can be no road to socialism—points, as a way out of the blind alley into which the government with its agrarian policy has again led Russia, to the free transfer of all the landowners' estates to the peasants, to the winning of full political liberty by a new revolution. (*The Question of the (General) Agrarian Policy of the Present Government*, June, 1913, *Selected Works*, IV, 240 f.)

DRAFT OF THE RESOLUTION ON THE AGRARIAN QUESTION

Proposed to the First All-Russian Congress
of Peasants' Deputies (June, 1917)

1. All landed estates and privately owned lands, as well as appanages, church lands, etc., must be turned over immediately to the people without compensation.

2. The peasantry must, in an organized manner, through their Soviets of Peasants' Deputies, immediately take over all the lands in their localities for the purpose of their economic exploitation, without, however, in any way prejudicing the final settlement of agrarian relations by the Constituent Assembly or by an All-Russian Council of Soviets, should the people decide to entrust the central power of the state to such a Council of Soviets.

3. Private ownership of land generally must be abolished, i.e., the ownership of the whole land shall be vested solely in the whole people, while the disposal of the land shall be entrusted to the local democratic institutions.

4. The peasants must reject the advice of the capitalists and landowners and of their Provisional Government to come to "an agreement" with the landlords in each locality as to the immediate disposal of the land; the disposal of the land must be determined by the organized will of the majority of the local peasants, and not by an agreement between the majority—i.e., the peasants—and the minority, and an insignificant minority at that—i.e., the landowners.

5. Not only the landowners are resisting, and will continue to resist with every means at their disposal, the transfer of the landed estates to the peasants without compensation, but also the capitalists, who wield tremendous monetary power and exercise great influence on the unenlightened masses through the newspapers, the numerous officials accustomed to the domination of capital, etc. Hence, the transfer without compensation of the landed estates to the peasantry cannot be effected completely or permanently unless the confidence of the peasant masses in the capitalists is undermined, unless a close alliance between the peasantry and the city workers is established, and unless the state power is completely transferred to the Soviets of Workers', Soldiers', Peasants' and other Deputies. Only a state power which is in the hands of such Soviets, and which governs the state not through a police, or a bureaucracy, or a standing army alienated from the people, but through a national, universal and armed militia of workers and peasants, can guarantee the realization of the above-mentioned agrarian reforms, which are being demanded by the entire peasantry.

6. Agricultural wage workers and poor peasants, i.e., such as for the lack of sufficient land, livestock and implements secure their livelihood partly by selling their labor, must make every effort to organize themselves independently into separate Soviets, or into separate groups within the general peasants' Soviets, in order that they may be in a position to defend their interests against the rich peasants who will inevitably strive to form an alliance with the capitalists and landlords.

7. As a result of the war, Russia, like all the other belligerent countries, as well as many neutral countries, is being threatened by economic disruption, disaster and famine because of the lack of hands, coal, iron, etc. Only if the Workers' and Peasants' Deputies assume control and supervision over the production and distribution of goods can the country be saved. It is therefore necessary to proceed immediately to arrange agreements between Soviets of Peasants' Deputies and Soviets of Workers' Deputies regarding the exchange of grain and other rural products for implements, shoes, clothing, etc., without the intermedi-

ary of the capitalists, who must be removed from the management of the factories. With the same purpose in view, the peasants' committees must be encouraged to take over the livestock and implements of the landowners, such livestock and implements to be used in common. Similarly, the transformation of all large private estates into model farms must be encouraged, the land to be cultivated collectively with the aid of the best implements under the direction of agricultural experts and in accordance with the decisions of the local Soviets of Agricultural Workers' Deputies. (*Selected Works,* VI, 349–351.)

The question of the land in its full scope can be settled only by a national constituent assembly.

The most just settlement of the land question is as follows:

1. *The right of private ownership of land shall be abolished in perpetuity:* Land shall not be purchased, sold, leased, mortgaged or otherwise alienated.

All land, whether *state, appanage, tsar's, monasterial, church, factory, primogenitory, private, public, peasant, etc., shall be taken over without compensation* and become the property of the whole people, to be used by those who cultivate it.

Persons who suffer by this property revolution shall be entitled to public support only for a period necessary for adaptation to their new conditions of existence.

2. All mineral wealth, e.g., ore, oil, coal, salt, etc., as well as all forests and waters of state importance, shall be reserved for the exclusive use of the state. Small streams, lakes, woods, etc., shall be reserved for the use of the village communes and shall be administered by the local government bodies.

3. Lands with *highly* developed forms of cultivation, e.g., orchards, plantations, nurseries, hothouses, etc., *shall not be divided up, but shall be transformed into model farms to be cultivated exclusively either by the state or by the village communes,* according to their size and importance.

Urban and village household land, orchards and gardens shall remain in the use of their present owners, the size of such holdings, and the amount of taxation levied for the use thereof, to be determined by law.

4. Stud farms, government and private pedigree stock and poultry farms, etc., shall be confiscated and become the property of the whole people; they shall be run exclusively by the state or by the village communes, according to their size and importance.

The question of compensation is subject to the decision of the Constituent Assembly.

5. All livestock and farm implements of the confiscated lands shall be reserved for the exclusive use of either the state or the village communes, according to their size and importance, and no compensation shall be paid therefor.

The farm implements of peasants possessing little land shall not be subject to confiscation.

6. The right to use the land shall belong to all citizens of the Russian state (without distinction of sex) desiring to cultivate it by their own labor, with the help of their families, or in partnership, and only as long as they are able to cultivate it by their own efforts. The employment of hired labor is prohibited.

In the event of the accidental physical disablement of any member of a village community for a period of two years, the village community shall be obliged to assist him within this period by means of collective cultivation of his land until he is again able to work.

Peasants who, owing to age or ill health, are permanently disabled from personally cultivating the land shall lose their right to the use of it, but, in return, shall receive a pension from the state.

7. Land tenure shall be on an equality basis, i.e., the land shall be distributed among the toilers in conformity with either the labor standard or the consumption standard, as local conditions shall warrant.

There shall be absolutely no restriction as to the forms of land tenure: household, farm, communal or co-operative, as shall be determined in each individual village.

8. All land, when expropriated, shall pass into the land fund

of the people. Its distribution among the toilers shall be controlled by the local and central government bodies, from democratically organized village and city communes, without distinction of social rank, to central oblast government bodies.

The land fund shall be subject to periodical redistribution, in accordance with the growth of population and the increase in the productiveness and efficiency of agriculture.

When the boundaries of land allotments change, the original basis of each allotment must remain unaltered.

The land of lapsed members shall revert to the land fund; preferential right to such land shall belong to the near relatives of the lapsed member, or to persons designated by him.

In the case of land which has reverted to the land fund, the cost of fertilizer and improvements put into the soil, to the extent that they have not been fully exhausted, shall be compensated.

Should the available land fund in a particular district prove inadequate for the needs of the population, the surplus population shall be settled elsewhere.

The state shall take upon itself the organization of resettlement and shall bear the cost thereof, as well as the cost of supplying implements, etc.

Resettlement shall be effected in the following order: first of all, landless peasants desiring to resettle, then members of the village commune of depraved or vicious habits, deserters and so on, and the remainder by lot or by agreement. (*Instructions to the Peasants Concerning the Disposition of the Land, Report and Decree on the Land Question,* October 28, 1917, *Selected Works,* VI, 407 f.)

The proletariat can and must immediately, or at any rate very quickly, deprive the bourgeoisie and the petty bourgeois democrats of *"their" masses,* i.e., of the masses who follow them, *by satisfying their most urgent economic needs in a revolutionary way, i.e., by expropriating the landowners and the bourgeoisie.*

This the bourgeoisie *cannot do,* no matter how "mighty" the state power it possesses.

But this the proletariat *can do* immediately upon seizing the power of the state, for it possesses both the machinery (the Soviets) and the economic means (expropriation of the land-owners and the bourgeoisie) necessary for the purpose.

That is exactly how the Russian proletariat *won the peasantry away* from the Socialist Revolutionaries, doing so literally *within a few hours* after it had seized the state power. For within a few hours after it had gained the victory over the bourgeoisie in Petrograd, the triumphant proletariat promulgated the Decree on the Land, by which it immediately, with revolutionary dis-patch, energy and thoroughness, *satisfied* all the most urgent economic needs of the *majority* of the peasants and completely expropriated the landowners without compensation.

In order to prove to the peasants that it was the desire of the proletarians not to bully them, to order them about, but to assist them and be their friends, the victorious Bolsheviks intro-duced *not one word of their own* into the Decree on the Land, but copied it word for word from the Peasant Instructions (of course the most revolutionary) that had been published by the Socialist Revolutionaries in the Socialist Revolutionary paper.

The Socialist Revolutionaries were enraged, indignant, dis-gusted, and cried out that "the Bolsheviks had stolen their program." But they were only laughed at for their pains. A fine party, indeed, that had to be defeated and driven out of power, in order that all that was revolutionary and advantageous to the toilers in its program might be carried out! (*The Elections to the Constituent Assembly and the Dictatorship of the Proletariat,* December 29, 1919, *Selected Works,* VI, 474 f.)

If any Communist ever dreamed that it would be possible to transform the economic basis, the economic roots of the small farmer within three years, he was, of course, a dreamer; and—it is no use hiding the fact—we have had not a few dreamers in our midst. But there is nothing bad about that. How would it have been possible to start the socialist revolution in a country like this without dreamers? Of course, practice has shown what an enormous part all sorts of experiments and innovations can play in the sphere of collective agriculture. But practice has shown that these experiments, as such, also played a harmful part when people, filled with the best intentions and desires, went into the countryside to organize communes and collectives without the ability to organize, because they lacked collective experience.

The experience of these collective farms merely shows how not to organize: the surrounding peasantry jeer at or gloat over them. You know perfectly well how many examples of this kind there have been. I repeat that this is not surprising, because the transformation of the small farmer, the remolding of his mentality and habits is a work of generations. Only a material base, technology, the employment of tractors and machinery in agriculture on a mass scale, electrification on a mass scale, can solve the problem of the small farmer, make his whole mentality sound, so to speak. This is what would radically, and with enormous rapidity, transform the small peasant. When I say it is a work of generations, I do not mean that it is a work of centuries. You understand perfectly well that to provide tractors and machines, and to electrify an enormous country, must, at all events, take no less than decades. (*The Tax in Kind*, March 15, 1921, *Selected Works*, IX, 110.)

IV

THE STATE

1. THE STATE

"The protection of the economically weak from the economically strong is the first natural task of state interference," continues this very same Mr. Yuzhakov in the very same place [*Russkoye Bogatstvo*, No. 1., 1894], and this is repeated after him in the very same terms by the chronicler of internal affairs in No. 2 of *Russkoye Bogatstvo*. And in order that there may be no doubt that he interprets this philanthropic nonsense[1] in the same way as it is interpreted by his fellow liberal and radical petty bourgeois ideologists in Western Europe, he adds, after what has been quoted above, the following:

> Gladstone's Land Bill, Bismarck's insurance for workers, factory inspection, the idea of our Peasants' Bank, the organization of migration, measures against the kulak—all these are attempts to apply this very principle of state interference for the purpose of protecting the economically weak.

The merit of this lies in its frankness. The author openly declares that he wants to stand on the basis of present social relationships as do Messrs. Gladstone and Bismarck, that he, like them, wants to patch and darn present-day society (bourgeois society—and this is what he, like the Western European adherents of Gladstone and Bismarck, does not understand), and not to fight

---

[1]It is nonsense because the "economically strong" is strong because, among other things, he possesses political power. Without political power he would not be able to maintain the economic rule.

against it. The fact that they regard the state, the organ which has arisen on the soil of present-day society and which protects the interests of the ruling classes in this society, as an instrument of reform, is in complete harmony with this, their fundamental theoretical view. They regard the state as being omnipotent and standing above classes, and expect that it will not only "assist" the toilers, but introduce real and proper order (as Mr. Krivenko informed us). Of course, nothing else could be expected from these purest of philistine ideologists, for one of the most characteristic features of the petty bourgeoisie, and which, incidentally, makes them a reactionary class, is that as a small producer dissociated and isolated by the very conditions of his work, tied down to a definite place and to a definite exploiter, the petty bourgeois is unable to understand the class character of the exploitation and oppression from which he suffers, sometimes not less than the proletarian; he is unable to understand that even the state in bourgeois society cannot but be a class state.[2]

But why is it, most worthy Messrs. "Friends of the People," that up till now—and with particular energy since the passing of the Emancipation Reform—our government has "supported, protected and created" only the bourgeoisie and capitalism? Why is it that this bad behavior on the part of the autocratic and allegedly above-class government has coincided with the historical period during which the internal life of the country is characterized by the development of commodity production, commerce and industry? Why do you think that these last-mentioned changes in internal life came subsequently and that the policy of the goverment came first when, as a matter of fact, these changes took place so deep down in society that the govern-

---

[2]That is why the "friends of the people" are the most out and out reactionaries when they say that the natural task of the state is to protect the economically weak (that is what it *should do* according to their banal, old wives' morality), when the whole history and internal politics of Russia prove that the task of our state is to protect only the feudal landowners and the big bourgeoisie and to punish ruthlessly every attempt on the part of the *economically weak* to stand up for their own interests. That, of course, is its *natural* task, because absolutism and bureaucracy are thoroughly saturated with the feudal bourgeois spirit and because in the economic sphere the bourgeoisie has undivided power and compels the worker to "lie low."

ment did not observe that they were taking place and put innumerable obstacles in their way, when as a matter of fact this very "absolute" government, under other conditions of internal life, "supported, protected and created" another class?

Oh, the "friends of the people" never stop to ask themselves questions like this! All this is materialism, dialectics, "Hegelianism," "mysticism and metaphysics." They think that if they plead with this government nicely enough and humbly enough, it can put everything right. (*What the "Friends of the People" Are and How They Fight Against the Social Democrats,* 1894, *Selected Works,* I, 285–287.)

Turn for help to Engels' book, *The Origin of the Family, Private Property and the State* (1884). This book says that every state in which private ownership of land and the means of production exists, in which capital prevails, however democratic it may be, is a capitalist state, a machine used by the capitalists to keep the working class and the poor peasants in subjection while universal suffrage, a constituent assembly, parliament are merely a form, a sort of promissory note, which does not alter matters in any essential way.

The forms of domination of the state may vary: Capital manifests its power in one way where one form exists, and in another way where another form exists—but essentially the power is in the hands of capital, whether there are voting qualifications or not, or whether the republic is a democratic one or not—in fact, the more democratic it is the cruder and more cynical is the rule of capitalism. One of the most democratic republics in the world is the United States of America, yet nowhere (and those who were there after 1905 probably know it) is the power of capital, the power of a handful of billionaires over the whole of society, so crude and so openly corrupt as in America. Once capital exists it dominates the whole of society, and no democratic republic, no form of franchise can alter the essence of the matter.

The democratic republic and universal suffrage were a great progressive advance on feudalism: they have enabled the proletariat to achieve its present unity and solidarity, to form those firm and disciplined ranks which are waging a systematic struggle against capital. There was nothing even approximately resembling this among the peasant serfs, not to speak of the slaves. The slaves, as we know, revolted, rioted, started civil wars, but they could never create a class-conscious majority and parties to lead the struggle, they could not clearly realize what they were aiming for, and even in the most revolutionary moments of history they were always pawns in the hands of the ruling classes. The bourgeois republic, parliament, universal suffrage all represent great progress from the standpoint of the world development of society. Mankind moved toward capitalism, and it was capitalism alone which, thanks to urban culture, enabled the oppressed class of proletarians to learn to know itself and to create the world working class movement, the millions of workers who are organized all over the world in parties—the Socialist parties which are consciously leading the struggle of the masses. Without parliamentarism, without elections, this development of the working class would have been impossible. That is why all these things have acquired such great importance in the eyes of the broad masses of people. That is why a radical change seems to be so difficult.

.   .   .   .

In reality, as long as there is private property, your state, even if it is a democratic republic, is nothing but a machine used by the capitalists to suppress the workers, and the freer the state, the more clearly is this expressed. Examples of this are Switzerland in Europe and the United States in the Americas. Nowhere does capital rule so cynically and ruthlessly, and nowhere is this so apparent, as in these countries, although they are democratic republics, no matter how finely they are painted and notwithstanding all the talk about labor democracy and the equality of all citizens. The fact is that in Switzerland and America capital dominates, and every attempt of the workers to achieve the slightest real improvement in their condition is immediately met by civil war. There are fewer soldiers, a smaller standing army in these countries—Switzerland has a militia and every Swiss has a gun at home, while in America there was no standing army until quite recently—and so when there is a strike, the bourgeoisie arms, hires soldiery and suppresses the strike; and nowhere is this suppression of the working class movement accompanied by such ruthless severity as in Switzerland and in America; and nowhere does the influence of capital in parliament manifest itself as powerfully as in these countries. The power of capital is everything, the stock exchange is everything, while parliament and elections are marionettes, puppets.... But the eyes of the workers are being opened more and more, and the idea of Soviet government is spreading wider and wider, especially after the bloody carnage through which we have just passed. The necessity for a merciless war on the capitalists is becoming clearer and clearer to the working class.

Whatever forms a republic may assume, even the most democratic republic, if it is a bourgeois republic, if it retains private ownership of land, mills and factories, and if private capital keeps the whole of society in wage slavery, that is, if it does not carry out what is proclaimed in the program of our Party and in the Soviet Constitution, then this state is a machine for the suppression of certain people by others. And we shall place this machine in the hands of the class that is to overthrow the power of capital. We shall reject all the old prejudices about the state meaning universal equality. That is a fraud: As long as there is exploitation, there cannot be equality. (*The State*, July 11, 1919, *Selected Works*, XI, 654 f., 655 f.)

2. DEMOCRACY

"Broad democracy" in Party organization, amidst the gloom of autocracy and the domination of police selection, is nothing more than a *useless and harmful toy*. It is a useless toy because, as a matter of fact, no revolutionary organization has ever practiced *broad* democracy, nor could it, however much it desired to do so. It is a harmful toy because any attempt to practice the "broad democratic principles" will simply facilitate the work of the police in making big raids, it will perpetuate the prevailing primitiveness, divert the thoughts of the practical workers from the

serious and imperative task of training themselves to become professional revolutionaries to that of drawing up detailed "paper"
rules for election systems.

. . . .

The only serious organizational principle the active workers
of our movement can accept is strict secrecy, strict selection of
members and the training of professional revolutionaries. If we
possessed these qualities, something even more than "democracy"
would be guaranteed to us, namely, complete, comradely, mutual
confidence among revolutionaries. And this is absolutely essential
for us because in Russia it is useless to think that democratic
control can serve as a substitute for it. It would be a great mistake
to believe that because it is impossible to establish real "democratic" control, the members of the revolutionary organization
will remain altogether uncontrolled. They have not the time to
think about the toy forms of democracy (democracy within a
close and compact body of comrades in which complete, mutual
confidence prevails), but they have a lively sense of their
responsibility, because they know from experience that an organization of real revolutionaries will stop at nothing to rid itself
of an undesirable member. Moreover, there is a fairly well
developed public opinion in Russian (and international) revolutionary circles which has a long history behind it, and which
sternly and ruthlessly punishes every departure from the duties
of comradeship (and does not "democracy," real and not toy
democracy, form a part of the conception of comradeship?).

. . . .

Those who have carried on practical work in our movement
know how widespead is the "primitive" conception of democracy
among the masses of the students and workers. It is not surprising
that this conception permeates rules of organization and literature. The economists of the Bernstein persuasion included in
their rules the following: "All affairs affecting the interests of
the whole of the union organization shall be decided by a
majority vote of all its members." The economists of the terrorist
persuasion repeat after them: "The decisions of the committee

must be circulated among all the circles and become effective only after this has been done.". . . Observe that this proposal for a widely applied referendum is advanced *in addition* to the demand that *the whole* of the organization be organized on an elective basis! We would not, of course, on this account condemn practical workers who have had too few opportunities for studying the theory and practice of real democratic organization. But when *Rabocheye Dyelo,* which claims to play a leading role, confines itself, under such conditions, to resolutions about broad democratic principles, how else can it be described than as a mere "striving after effect"? (*What Is To Be Done? Burning Questions of Our Movement,* 1902, *Selected Works,* II, 154, 155 f., 157.)

In English parliamentary reports we often find the characteristic word "division." The House "divided" into such and such a majority and minority is the expression used in speaking of taking a vote on an issue. The "division" of our Social Democratic House on the various issues discussed at the Congress presents a picture of the struggle inside the Party, of its shades of opinion and groups, that is *unique and incomparable for its completeness and precision.* To make the picture more striking, to obtain a real *picture,* instead of a heap of disconnected, disjointed and isolated facts, to put an end to the endless and senseless controversies over separate divisions (who voted for whom and who supported whom), I have decided to try to represent *all the basic* types of "division" at our Congress in the form of a *diagram.* This at first will probably seem strange to very many people, but I doubt whether there is any better method that would really generalize and sum up the results in the most complete and accurate way possible. In all cases when the votes were taken by roll call, it can be determined with complete accuracy whether a given delegate voted for or against a given motion; likewise, in certain important cases when the vote was not taken by roll call, the minutes enable us to answer the question with a very great degree of probability, with a sufficient degree of approximation to the truth. If, at the same time, we take into account *all* the divisions by roll call and all the other divisions on issues of any importance (which can be measured by the length and heatedness of the debates), we shall obtain a picture of the struggle inside our Party that will be as objective as is obtainable with the material at our disposal. In doing this, instead of trying to give a photographic representation, i.e., instead of representing every division separately, we shall try to give a picture, i.e., to present all the main *types* of division, and leave out relatively unimportant exceptions and variations which would only serve to confuse the matter. In any case, with the aid of the minutes it will be possible for anyone to check every detail of our picture, to fill it in with individual divisions, in a word, to criticize it not only by arguing, expressing doubt and picking out isolated cases, but by drawing up a *different picture* with the aid of the same material.

In marking on the diagram every delegate who took part in a division, we shall indicate by a special shading the four main groups which we have traced in detail throughout the course of the debates at the Congress, viz.: (1) *Iskra*-ists of the majority, (2) *Iskra*-ists of the minority, (3) center and (4) anti-*Iskra*-ists. We have seen that in a *number of instances* these groups were distinguished by shades of difference in matters of principle, and if anyone objects to the *name* given to each group, which reminds the zigzag lovers too much of *Iskra* and of *Iskra*'s line of policy, we shall remark that it is not the name that matters. Now that the shades of opinion have been traced through *all* the debates at the Congress it is easy to substitute for the Party nicknames that have become established and familiar (but which jar on the ears of certain people) a description of the *essential differences between the groups.* This substitution would result in the following names for the same four groups: (1) consistent revolutionary Social Democrats, (2) minor opportunists, (3) middling opportunists and (4) major opportunists (major, according to our Russian standards). Let us hope that these names will be less shocking to those who for some time have been trying to convince themselves and others that *Iskra*-ist is a name denoting only a "circle" and not a *line of policy. (One Step Forward, One Step Backward,* May, 1904, *Selected Works,* II, 416–418.)

The very position the proletariat occupies as a class compels it to be consistently democratic. The bourgeoisie looks backward, is afraid of democratic progress which threatens to strengthen the proletariat. The proletariat has nothing to lose but its chains, but by means of democracy it has the whole world to win. Therefore, the more consistent the bourgeois revolution is in its democratic reforms, the less will it limit itself to those measures which are advantageous only to the bourgeoisie. The more consistent the bourgeois revolution is, the more does it guarantee the advantages which the proletariat and the peasantry will derive from a democratic revolution.

Marxism teaches the proletarian not to keep aloof from the bourgeois revolution, not to refuse to take part in it, not to allow the leadership of the revolution to be assumed by the bourgeoisie but, on the contrary, to take a most energetic part in it, to fight resolutely for consistent proletarian democracy, to fight to carry the revolution to its completion. We cannot jump out of the bourgeois-democratic boundaries of the Russian revolution, but we can enormously extend those boundaries, and within those boundaries we can and must fight for the interests of the proletariat, for its immediate needs and for the prerequisites for training its forces for the complete victory that is to come.

. . . .

A Social Democrat must never, even for an instant, forget that the proletarian class struggle for socialism against the most democratic and republican bourgeoisie and petty bourgeoisie is inevitable. This is beyond doubt. From this logically follows the absolute necessity of a separate, independent and strictly class party of Social Democracy. From this logically follows the provisional character of our tactics to "strike together" with the bourgeoisie and the duty to carefully watch "our ally, as if he were an enemy," etc. All this is also beyond doubt. But it would be ridiculous and reactionary to deduce from this that we must forget, ignore or neglect those tasks which, although transient and temporary, are vital at the present time. The struggle against autocracy is a temporary and transient task of the Socialists, but to ignore or neglect this task would be tantamount to betraying socialism and rendering a service to reaction. Certainly, the revolutionary-democratic dictatorship of the proletariat and the peasantry is only a transient, provisional task of the Socialists, but to ignore this task in the period of a democratic revolution would be simply reactionary.

Concrete political tasks must be presented in concrete circumstances. All things are relative, all things flow and are subject to change. (*The Two Tactics of Social Democracy in the Democratic Revolution,* July, 1905, *Selected Works,* III, 77, 100.)

Democracy is also a form of state which must disappear when the state disappears, but this will take place only in the process of transition from completely victorious and consolidated socialism to complete communism.

The socialist revolution is not one single act, not one single battle on a single front, but a whole epoch of intensified class conflicts, a long series of battles on all fronts, i.e., battles around all the problems of economics and politics, which can culminate only in the expropriation of the bourgeoisie. It would be a fundamental mistake to suppose that the struggle for democracy can divert the proletariat from the socialist revolution, or obscure, or overshadow it, etc. On the contrary, just as socialism cannot be victorious unless it introduces complete democracy, so the proletariat will be unable to prepare for victory over the bourgeoisie unless it wages a many-sided, consistent and revolutionary struggle for democracy. (*The Socialist Revolution and the Right of Nations to Self-Determination,* March, 1916, *Selected Works,* V, 267 f.)

Nothing in our times can be done without elections; nothing can be done without the masses. And in this era of printing and parliamentarism, it is *impossible* to gain the following of the masses without a widely ramified, systematically managed, well-equipped system of flattery, lies, fraud, juggling with popular catchwords and promising reforms and blessings to the workers right and left—as long as they renounce the revolutionary struggle for the overthrow of the bourgeoisie. (*Imperialism and the Split in Socialism,* Fall, 1916, *Selected Works,* XI, 760.)

We must look forward to the new democracy which is in process of being born and which is already ceasing to be a democracy. For democracy means the rule of the people, whereas the armed people cannot rule over themselves.

The term democracy is not only scientifically incorrect when applied to a Communist party; it has now, since March, 1917, simply become a *blinker* covering the eyes of the revolutionary people and *preventing* them from boldly and freely, on their own initiative, building up the new: the Soviets of Workers', Soldiers' and all other Deputies, as *the sole power* in the state and as the harbinger of the "withering away" of the state in every form. (*The Tasks of the Proletariat in Our Revolution,* April 23, 1917, *Selected Works,* VI, 74.)

What is control? . . . In order to control, one must have power. If this is not understood by the broad masses of the petty bourgeois bloc, we must have the patience to explain it to them, but under no circumstances must we tell them an untruth. And if I obscure this fundamental condition by the demand for control, I tell an untruth and play into the hands of the capitalists and the imperialists. "You may control me if you please, but I shall have the guns. You can have all the control you like," they say. They know that at the present moment the people cannot be denied. Control without power is a petty bourgeois phrase that blocks the march and development of the Russian revolution. (*Report on the Current Situation* . . . , May 7, 1917, *Selected Works,* VI, 91.)

The constitution of the Russian democratic republic must assure:

1. The sovereignty of the people. The supreme power of the

state must be vested entirely in the people's representatives, who shall be elected by the people and be subject to recall at any time, and who shall constitute a single popular assembly, a single chamber.

2. Universal, equal and direct suffrage for all male and female citizens of twenty years of age or over in all elections to the legislative assembly and to the various local government bodies, secret ballot, the right of every voter to be elected to any representative institution, biennial parliaments, payment of people's representatives, proportional representation at all elections, all delegates and elected officials, without exception, to be subject to recall at any time upon the decision of a majority of their electors.

3. Local government on a wide scale; regional government in all localities where the population is specific in composition and is distinguished by specific social conditions; the abolition of all local and provincial authorities appointed by the state.

4. Inviolability of person and domicile.

5. Unhampered freedom of conscience, speech, press, assembly, strikes and organization.

6. Freedom of movement and occupation.

7. Abolition of social distinction and equal rights for all citizens irrespective of sex, creed, race, or nationality.

8. The right of the people to receive instruction in their native tongue in schools established at the expense of the state and local government bodies; the right of every citizen to speak at assemblies in his native language; the use of the native language equally with the state language in all local, public and state institutions; the abolition of an obligatory state language.

9. The right of all nationalities forming part of the state to freely separate and to form independent states. The republic of the Russian people must attract other nations or peoples not by force, but exclusively by their voluntary consent to the creation of a common state. The unity and fraternal alliance of the workers of all countries cannot be reconciled with the direct or indirect exercise of force against other nationalities.

10. The right of all persons to sue any official before an ordinary court of jury.

11. Election by the people of judges and other officials, both civil and military, with the right to recall any of them at any time by decision of a majority of their electors.

12. Replacement of the police and standing army by the universally armed people; manual and nonmanual workers to receive regular wages from the capitalists during time devoted to public service in the national militia.

13. Separation of church from the state and schools from the church; schools to be absolutely secular.

14. Free and compulsory general and technical education (familiarizing the student with the theoretical and practical aspects of the most important branches of industry) for all children of both sexes up to the age of sixteen; education to be closely associated with the performance by children of socially productive labor.

15. Students to be provided with food, clothing and educational supplies at the expense of the state.

16. Education to be entrusted to democratically elected local government bodies; the central government not to be allowed to interfere with the arrangement of the school curriculum, or with the selection of the teaching staffs; teachers to be elected directly by the population itself with the right of the latter to remove undesirable teachers.

As a fundamental condition for the democratization of the economic life of the state, the Russian Social Democratic Labor party demands the abolition of all indirect taxes and the establishment of a progressive tax on incomes and inheritances.

The high level of development of capitalism in the banking business and in the syndicated branches of industry, on the one hand, and the economic disruption caused by the imperialist war, everywhere provoking a demand for state and public control of the production and distribution of all important products, on the other, prompt the Party to demand the nationalization of banks, syndicates (trusts), etc.

In order to safeguard the working class against physical and moral deterioration, and in order to assure the development of its ability to carry on the struggle for emancipation, the Party demands:

1. Limitation of the working day of all wage workers to eight hours, including a break of not less than one hour for meals, where work is continuous. In dangerous and unhealthy industries the working day to be reduced to four to six hours.

2. A weekly uninterrupted rest period of not less than forty-two hours to be established by law for all wage workers of both sexes in all branches of the national economy.

3. Complete prohibition of overtime work.

4. Prohibition of night work (from 8 P.M. to 6 A.M.) in all branches of the national economy with the exception of those in which it is absolutely necessary for technical considerations attested by labor organizations—provided, however, that night work shall not exceed four hours.

5. Prohibition of the employment of children of school age (up to sixteen), restriction of the working day of adolescents (from sixteen to twenty) to four hours, and prohibition of the employment of adolescents on night work, in unhealthy industries and in mines.

6. Prohibition of female labor in all branches of industry injurious to the health of women; prohibition of night work for women; women to be released from work eight weeks before and eight weeks after childbirth, with retention of regular pay during this period and the receipt of free medical and pharmaceutical aid.

7. Establishment of nurseries for infants and small children and rooms for nursing mothers in all works, factories and other enterprises employing women; nursing mothers to be allowed recesses of at least half-hour duration at intervals of not more than three hours; nursing mothers to be provided with material assistance and their working day to be limited to six hours.

8. Full social insurance: (a) for all types of wage labor; (b) against every kind of disability, e.g., sickness, injury, infirmity, old age, occupational disease, childbirth, widowhood, orphanhood and also against unemployment; (c) all insurance institu-

tions to be administered entirely by the insured themselves; (d) the expense of insurance to be born by the capitalists; (e) free medical and pharmaceutical treatment under the control of self-governing sick-benefit societies, the management bodies of which are to be elected by the workers.

9. The establishment of a labor inspectorate elected by the workers' organizations and covering all enterprises employing wage labor, as well as domestic servants; women inspectors to be appointed in enterprises employing female labor.

10. Sanitary laws for the improvement of hygienic conditions and the protection of the life and health of workers in enterprises employing wage labor; questions of hygiene to be entrusted to a sanitary inspectorate elected by the workers.

11. Housing laws to be enacted and housing inspectors elected by the workers' organizations for the purpose of supervising the sanitary condition of living quarters. However, only by the abolition of private ownership of land and the erection of cheap and hygienic dwellings can the housing problem be solved.

12. Industrial courts in all branches of the national economy.

13. Establishment of labor exchanges for the proper organization of the placing of unemployed workers. The labor exchanges must be proletarian class organizations (and not organized on a parity basis), and must be closely associated with the trade unions and other working class organizations and financed by local government bodies. (*Materials Relating to the Revision of the Party Program,* May, 1917, *Selected Works,* VI, 117–122.)

"Constitutional illusion" is the term for a political error which consists in the fact that people believe in the existence of a normal, juridical, regulated and legalized, in brief, "constitutional," system which in fact does not exist at all. It would seem at first glance that in present-day Russia, in this month of August, 1917, when a constitution has not even been drafted, such constitutional illusions are impossible. But that is a profound mistake. In fact, the essential characteristic of the present political situation in Russia is that extremely large numbers of the population are under the sway of constitutional illusions. Unless this is understood, it is impossible to understand anything of the present political situation in Russia. Not even an approach to a correct conception of the tactical tasks in present-day Russia is possible unless prime attention is devoted to a systematic and merciless exposure of constitutional illusions, to laying bare their roots, and to re-establishing a proper political perspective. (*Constitutional Illusions*, August 8, 1917, *Selected Works*, VI, 175.)

At its very inception the Russian revolution created Soviets of Workers', Soldiers' and Peasants' Deputies as the mass organization of the toiling and exploited classes, and as the only organization capable of leading the struggle of these classes for their complete political and economic emancipation.

During the whole of the first period of the Russian revolution the Soviets multiplied, grew and gained in strength. Experience taught them to discard illusions of compromise with the bourgeoisie and the deceptive forms of bourgeois-democratic parliamentarism, and brought them to the practical conclusion that the emancipation of the oppressed classes was impossible unless they abandoned these parliamentary forms and every form of compromise. Such was the October Revolution, which transferred the entire power to the Soviets.

The Constituent Assembly, elected on the basis of lists drawn up prior to the October Revolution, was an expression of the old relation of political forces, which existed when the compromisers and the Cadets were in power. When the people at that time voted for the candidates of the Socialist Revolutionary party, they were not in a position to choose between the right wing Socialist Revolutionaries, the supporters of the bourgeoisie, and the left wing Socialist Revolutionaries, the supporters of socialism. Hence the Constituent Assembly, which was to have been the crown of the bourgeois parliamentary republic, could not but become an obstacle in the path of the October Revolution and the Soviet power.

The October Revolution, by handing the power over to the Soviets and, through the Soviets, to the toiling and exploited classes, aroused the desperate resistance of the exploiters. In the process of crushing this resistance the revolution proved itself to be the beginning of the socialist revolution. The toiling classes learned by experience that the old bourgeois parliamentarism had outlived itself and was entirely incapable of achieving socialism. They learned that not national institutions, but only class institutions (such as the Soviets are) were capable of breaking the resistance of the possessing classes and of laying the foundations of a socialist society. To relinquish at this stage any particle of the power of the Soviets, the Soviet republic won by the people, for the sake of bourgeois parliamentarism and the Constituent Assembly would be a step backward and would mean the complete collapse of the October workers' and peasants' revolution.

Owing to the circumstances mentioned above, the majority in the Constituent Assembly, when it met on January 18, was found to belong to the party of the right wing Socialist Revolutionaries, the party of Kerensky, Avksentyev and Chernov. It was only natural that this party should refuse to discuss the absolutely clear, precise and unambiguous proposal of the supreme organ of the Soviet power, the Central Executive Committee of the Soviets, to approve the program of the Soviet power, to approve the Declaration of the Rights of the Toiling and Exploited People and to recognize the October Revolution and the Soviet power. Thereby the Constituent Assembly severed all ties with the Soviet republic of Russia. The withdrawal from this Constituent Assembly of the factions of the Bolsheviks and the left wing Socialist Revolutionaries, who now patently represent the overwhelming majority in the Soviets and enjoy the confidence of the workers and the majority of the peasants, became inevitable.

The right wing Socialist Revolutionary and Menshevik parties are in fact carrying on outside the walls of the Constituent Assembly a most bitter struggle against the Soviet power, openly calling in their press for its overthrow and characterizing as arbitrary and unlawful the crushing of the resistance of the exploiters by the toiling classes, which is essential in the interests of emancipation from exploitation. They are supporting the saboteurs, the servitors of capital, and are even going to the length of undisguised appeals for terrorism, which indeed certain "unidentified groups" have already begun to practice. It is obvious that under such circumstances the remaining part of the Constituent Assembly would only have served as a screen for the struggle of the counterrevolutionaries to overthrow the Soviet power.

Accordingly, the Central Executive Committee resolves:

The Constituent Assembly is hereby dissolved. (*Draft Decree on the Dissolution of the Constituent Assembly,* January 19, 1918, *Selected Works,* VI, 460–462.)

The Soviet power is a new type of state in which there is no bureaucracy, no police, no standing army, and in which bourgeois democracy is replaced by a new democracy—a democracy which brings to the forefront the vanguard of the toiling masses, turning them into legislators, executives and military guards, and which creates an apparatus capable of re-educating the masses.

In Russia this has barely begun, and badly at that. If we realize what is bad in what we have begun, we shall overcome it. (*Report on Revising the Program and the Name of the Party* ..., March 8, 1918, *Selected Works,* VIII, 318 f.)

The socialist character of Soviet, i.e., *proletarian,* democracy, as concretely applied today, lies first in that the electors are the toiling and exploited masses; the bourgeoisie is excluded. Secondly, it lies in the fact that all bureaucratic formalism and restriction of elections are abolished; the masses themselves determine the order and time of elections, and every elected person is subject to recall. Thirdly, it lies in that the best mass organization of the vanguard of the toilers, i.e., the proletariat engaged in large-scale industry, is created, which enables it to lead the vast masses of the exploited, to draw them into independent political life, to educate them politically by their own experience and in that, for the first time, a start is thus made in teaching the *whole* of the population the art of administration and in their beginning to administer.

Such are the principal distinguishing features of the democracy which is being applied in Russia, which is a higher type of democracy, a rupture with the bourgeois distortion of democracy, its transition to socialist democracy and to the conditions in which the state can begin to wither away. (*On the Party Program,* April, 1918, *Selected Works,* VII, 345 f.)

We Bolsheviks were opposed to the law on the socialization of the land. Yet we signed it because we did not wish to go counter to the will of the majority of the peasantry. The will of the majority is binding on us always, and to oppose the will of the majority is to betray the revolution. (*Speech Delivered to . . . Poor Peasants . . .* , November 8, 1918, *Selected Works,* VIII, 140.)

The "right of assembly" may be taken as an example of the demands of "pure democracy." Every class-conscious worker who has not broken connections with his class will understand at once that it would be absurd to promise the right of assembly to the exploiters in the period and in the circumstances in which the exploiters are resisting their overthrow and are defending their privileges. Neither in England in 1649, nor in France in 1793 did the bourgeoisie, when it was revolutionary, grant the "right of assembly" to the monarchists and nobles who called for the intervention of foreign troops, and who "assembled" for the purpose of organizing attempts at restoration. If the modern bourgeoisie, which became reactionary long ago, demands that the proletariat give it guarantees beforehand that it will give the "right of assembly" to the exploiters—irrespective of the resistance the capitalists put up to their expropriation—the proletariat will only laugh at the hypocrisy of the bourgeoisie.

On the other hand, the workers know perfectly well that even in the most democratic bourgeois republics the "right of assembly" is but an empty phrase because the rich own all the best

public and private buildings and have sufficient leisure to attend
meetings, which are protected by the bourgeois state apparatus.
The proletarians of town and country and the small peasants,
i.e., the overwhelming majority of the population, do not enjoy
either the first, the second or the third of these privileges. As
long as this situation prevails, "equality," i.e., "pure democracy,"
is a sham. In order to achieve real equality, in order to realize
democracy, in part, for the toilers, it is first of all necessary to
deprive the exploiters of all public and luxurious private buildings, it is first of all necessary to give leisure to the toilers and
to have the freedom of their assemblies protected by the armed
workers and not by the sons of the aristocracy or capitalist officers
commanding browbeaten soldiers.

Only after this change has taken place will it be possible,
without mocking at the workers, the toilers and the poor, to
speak of freedom of assembly, of equality. And nobody but the
vanguard of the toilers, viz., the proletariat, which overthrows
the exploiters, the bourgeoisie, can bring about this change.

"Freedom of the press" is another of the principal slogans of
"pure democracy." Here, too, the workers know, and the Socialists of all countries have admitted a million times, that this
freedom is a sham as long as the best printing plants and the
huge stocks of paper are in the possession of the capitalists, and
as long as the press is ruled by capital—which rule manifests
itself the more strikingly, more sharply and more cynically, the
more democracy and the republican system are developed, as,
for example, in America. In order to achieve real equality and
real democracy for the toilers, for the workers and peasants, it is
first of all necessary to deprive capital of the opportunity of
hiring writers, of buying up publishing houses and bribing newspapers, and it is necessary to overthrow the yoke of capital, to
overthrow the exploiters and to suppress their resistance. By
"freedom" the capitalists have always meant the freedom of the
rich to accumulate profits, and the freedom of the workers to
die of starvation. By freedom of the press the capitalists mean
the freedom of the rich to bribe the press, freedom to utilize
wealth for the purposes of fabricating and manipulating so-called

public opinion. Here, too, the champions of "pure democracy" prove in fact to be champions of the filthy and venal system by which the rich control the means for the education of the masses, they prove to be deceivers of the people who, by means of plausible, eloquent and absolutely false phrases, turn the people away from the concrete historical tasks of liberating the press from its bondage to capital. Real freedom and equality will exist under the system which the Communists are building and under which it will be impossible for anyone to enrich himself at another's expense, under which it will be objectively impossible, either directly or indirectly, to subject the press to the power of money, and under which there will be nothing to prevent every toiler (or group of toilers in any number) from having and exercising an equal right to use the public printing plants and public stocks of paper. (*Theses and Report on Bourgeois Democracy and the Dictatorship of the Proletariat,* March 4, 1919, *Selected Works,* VII, 225–227.)

The whole history of bourgeois democracy, particularly in the advanced countries, has transformed the parliamentary tribune into the principal, or one of the principal, arenas of unprecedented fraud, of the financial and political deception of the people, careerism, hypocrisy and the oppression of the toilers. Hence, the burning hatred toward parliaments entertained by the best representatives of the revolutionary proletariat is quite legitimate. That is why the Communist parties and all parties which are affiliated to the Third International—particularly in those cases when they have arisen, not as a result of a split from the old parties and of a prolonged and persistent struggle against them, but as a result of the transition (often nominal) of the old parties to the new position—must adopt an exceptionally strict attitude toward their parliamentary fractions: the latter must be completely subordinated to the control and guidance of the Central Committees of the parties; they must consist mainly of revolutionary workers; the speeches of deputies must be subjected to careful analysis in the Party press and at Party meetings from the point of view of Communist consistency;

deputies must be commissioned to carry on agitational work among the masses, members of these fractions who betray Second International trends must be expelled, etc. (*Theses on the Fundamental Tasks of the Second Congress of the Communist International,* July 4, 1920, *Selected Works,* X, 170 f.)

3. DICTATORSHIP OF THE PROLETARIAT

Such a victory [of the revolution over tsarism] will assume the form of a dictatorship, i.e., it is inevitably bound to rely on military force, on the arming of the masses, on an uprising, and not on institutions established by "lawful" or "peaceful" means. It can only be a dictatorship, for the introduction of the reforms which are urgently and absolutely necessary for the proletariat and the peasantry will call forth the desperate resistance of the landowners, the big bourgeoisie and tsarism. Without a dictatorship it will be impossible to break down that resistance and repel the counterrevolutionary attempts. But of course it will be a democratic, not a socialist, dictatorship. It will not be able (without a series of intermediary stages of revolutionary development) to affect the foundations of capitalism. At best it may bring about a radical redistribution of the land to the advantage of the peasantry, establish consistent and full democracy including the republic, eliminate all the oppressive features of Asiatic bondage, not only of village but also of factory life, lay the foundation for thorough improvement in the position of the workers and raise their standard of living and, last but not least, carry the revolutionary conflagration into Europe. Such a victory will by no means transform our bourgeois revolution into a socialist revolution; the democratic revolution will not extend beyond the scope of bourgeois social and economic relationships. (*The Two Tactics of Social Democracy in the Democratic Revolution,* July, 1905, *Selected Works,* III, 82 f.)

Marx castigated the bourgeois democrats for entertaining "constitutional dreams" in an epoch of revolution and open civil war. The meaning of these words becomes particularly obvious from the article in *Die Neue Rheinische Zeitung* of June 6, 1848. Marx wrote:

> A constituent national assembly must first of all be an active, revolutionary-active assembly. But the Frankfort Assembly is busying itself with school exercises in parliamentarism while allowing the government to act. Let us assume that this learned assembly succeeded after mature consideration in working out the best agenda and the best constitution. But what would be the use of the best agenda and of the best constitution, if the government had in the meantime placed the bayonet on the agenda?

Such is the meaning of the slogan "dictatorship." Hence we can gauge what Marx's attitude would have been toward resolutions which call the "decision to organize a constituent assembly" a decisive victory or which invite us to "remain a party of extreme revolutionary opposition."

Great questions in the life of nations are settled only by force. The reactionary classes are usually themselves the first to resort to violence, to civil war; they are the first to "place the bayonet on the agenda," as Russian autocracy has been doing systematically, consistently, everywhere, all over the country, ever since January 9 [1905]. And since such a situation has arisen, since the bayonet has really taken first place on the political agenda, since the uprising has become necessary and urgent, the constitutional dreams and school exercises in parliamentarism are becoming only a screen for the bourgeois betrayal of the revolution, a screen for the "desertion" of the bourgeoisie from the cause of the revolution. The genuinely revolutionary class must, then, advance precisely the slogan of dictatorship.

On the question of the tasks of this dictatorship Marx had already written in *Die Neue Rheinische Zeitung* as follows:

> The national assembly should have acted dictatorially against all the reactionary attempts of the obsolete governments, and then it would have gained on its side public opinion of such power against which all bayonets and rifle butts would have broken into splinters. . . . But this assembly bores the German people instead of carrying the people with it or being carried away by it.

In the opinion of Marx, the national assembly should have "eliminated from the actually existing regime of Germany everything that contradicted the principle of the sovereignty of the people," then "it should have defended the revolutionary ground on which it rested in order to make the sovereignty of the people, won by the revolution, secure against all attacks."

Thus, the tasks which Marx set before the revolutionary government or the dictatorship in 1848 amounted in substance first of all to *democratic* revolution, i.e., defense against counter-revolution and actual abolition of everything that contradicted the sovereignty of the people. And this is nothing else than revolutionary-democratic dictatorship.

.   .   .   .

Not only a "decision to organize a constituent assembly," but even its actual convocation is insufficient for a decisive victory of the revolution! Even after a partial victory in an armed struggle (the victory of the Berlin workers over the troops on March 18, 1848) an "incomplete" and "unfinished" revolution is possible. What does its final consummation depend on? It depends on the question, to whose hands is the immediate rule transferred? To those of the Petrunkeviches or Rodichevs, that is to say, the Camphausens and the Hansemanns, or of the *people,* i.e., of the workers and the democratic bourgeoisie? In the first case the bourgeoisie will possess power, and the proletariat—"freedom to criticize," "freedom to remain a party of extreme revolutionary opposition." Immediately after victory the bourgeoisie will enter into an alliance with reaction (this would also inevitably happen in Russia, if, for example, the St. Petersburg workers gained only a partial victory in street fighting with the troops and allowed Messrs. Petrunkevich and company to form a government). In the second case a revolutionary-democratic dictatorship, i.e., a complete victory of the revolution, would be possible. (*The Two Tactics of Social Democracy in the Democratic Revolution,* July, 1905, *Selected Works,* III, 126–128.)

The irrefutable experience of history has shown that in the history of revolutionary movements the dictatorship of individ-

ual persons was very often the vehicle, the channel of the dictatorship of the revolutionary classes. Undoubtedly, the dictatorship
of individual persons was compatible with bourgeois democracy.
But at this point in their abuse of the Soviet government, the
bourgeoisie, as well as their petty bourgeois henchmen, always
display remarkable legerdemain: on the one hand, they declare
the Soviet government to be something absurd and anarchistically
savage, and they carefully evade all our historical examples and
theoretical arguments which prove that the Soviets are a higher
form of democracy, and even more, the beginning of the *socialist*
form of democracy; on the other hand, they demand of us a
higher democracy than bourgeois democracy and say: Personal
dictatorship is absolutely incompatible with your Bolshevik (i.e.,
not bourgeois, but *socialist*) Soviet democracy.

These are very poor arguments. If we are not anarchists, we
must admit that the state, i.e., *coercion,* is necessary for the transition from capitalism to socialism. The form of coercion is determined by the degree of development of the given revolutionary
class as well as by special circumstances, such as, for example,
the heritage of a long and reactionary war and the forms of
resistance put up by the bourgeoisie or the petty bourgeoisie.
Hence, there is absolutely no contradiction in principle between
Soviet (i.e., socialist) democracy and the exercise of dictatorial
powers by individual persons. The difference between proletarian
dictatorship and bourgeois dictatorship is that the former strikes
at the exploiting minority in the interests of the exploited
majority, and that it is exercised—also through *individual* persons—not only by the masses of the toilers and exploited, but
also by organizations which are built in such a way as to rouse
among the masses the historical creative spirit. The Soviet organizations are organizations of this kind. (*The Immediate Tasks of
the Soviet Government,* April, 1918, *Selected Works,* VII, 341 f.)

"Dictatorship of the proletariat" . . . means the following:
Only a definite class, namely, the urban and the industrial
workers in general, is able to lead the whole mass of toilers and

exploited in the struggle for the overthrow of the yoke of capital, in the process of this overthrow, in the struggle for holding and consolidating the victory, in the work of creating the new, socialist, social system, and in the whole struggle for the complete abolition of classes. . . . The mistake the "Berne," yellow International commits is that its leaders accept the class struggle and the leading role of the proletariat only in words and are afraid to think it out to its logical conclusion; they are afraid of the very conclusion which particularly terrifies the bourgeoisie and which is absolutely unacceptable to it. They are afraid to admit that the dictatorship of the proletariat is *also* a period of the class struggle, which is inevitable as long as classes exist, and which changes in form, being particularly fierce and particularly characteristic in the first period after the overthrow of capital.

The proletariat does not cease the class struggle after it has captured political power but continues it until classes are abolished. (*A Great Beginning,* June 28, 1919, *Selected Works,* IX, 432.)

The old source of discipline, capital, has been enfeebled; the old source of unity has disappeared. We must create a different kind of discipline, a different source of discipline and unity. Compulsion provokes the indignation, howls and outcries of the bourgeois democrats, who make great play of the words freedom and equality but do not understand that freedom for capital is a crime against the toilers. In our fight against falsehood we introduced labor service and proceeded to unite the toilers, without fearing compulsion. For nowhere has a revolution ever been effected without compulsion, and the proletariat has the right to resort to compulsion in order to maintain itself at all costs. (*Report of the Central Committee at the Ninth Congress of the Russian Communist Party* [Bolsheviks], March 29, 1920, *Selected Works,* VIII, 87.)

The dictatorship of the proletariat was successful because it knew how to combine compulsion with persuasion. The dictatorship of the proletariat does not fear resorting to compulsion, and to the most severe, decisive and ruthless expression of state compulsion; for the advanced class, which was the class most oppressed by capitalism, is entitled to resort to compulsion, because it is doing so in the interests of the toilers and exploited, and because it possesses means of compulsion and persuasion such as were not possessed by any of the former classes, although they had incomparably greater material opportunities for propaganda and agitation than we. (*The Work of the Council of People's Commissars*, December 22, 1920, *Selected Works*, VIII, 257.)

The trade unions are not state organizations, not organizations for coercion, they are educational organizations, organizations that enlist, that train; they are schools, schools of administration, schools of management, schools of communism. They are not the ordinary type of school, for there are no teachers and pupils; what we have is an extremely peculiar combination of what capitalism has left us, and could not but leave us. . . .

The place the trade unions occupy in the system of the dictatorship of the proletariat is, if we may so express it, between the Party and the state power. In the transition to socialism, the dictatorship of the proletariat is inevitable, but this dictatorship is not effected by the organizations which embrace all the industrial workers. . . . The Party, so to speak, absorbs into itself the vanguard of the proletariat, and this vanguard effects the dictatorship of the proletariat. Without a foundation like the trade unions, the dictatorship cannot be effected, state functions cannot be fulfilled. These functions in their turn have to be fulfilled through the medium of a number of special institutions also of a new type, namely, the Soviet apparatus. Wherein lies the peculiarity of the position in regard to the practical conclusions that have to be drawn? It lies in the fact that the trade unions establish connection between the vanguard and the masses, the trade unions by their daily work convince the masses, the masses of the class which alone is capable of carrying us from capitalism to communism. On the other hand, the trade unions are a "reservoir" of state power. This is what the trade unions are in the period of transition from capitalism to communism.

.   .   .   .

We have a complicated system of cogwheels and . . . there cannot be a simple system; for the dictatorship of the proletariat cannot be effected by organizations that embrace the whole of the proletariat. It is impossible to effect the dictatorship without having a number of "transmission belts" from the vanguard to the masses of the advanced class, and from the latter to the masses of the toilers. In Russia these masses are the peasants. These masses do not exist in other countries; but even in the most advanced countries there are non-proletarian, or not purely proletarian, masses. (*The Trade Unions, the Present Situation and the Mistakes of Comrade Trotsky,* December 30, 1920, *Selected Works,* IX, 4 f., 6.)

On the question of the state apparatus we should now draw the conclusion from our past experience that it would be better to go more slowly.

The situation in regard to our state apparatus is so deplorable, not to say outrageous, that we must first of all think very carefully how to eliminate its defects, bearing in mind that the roots of these defects lie in the past, which, although it has been overturned, has not yet been overcome, has not yet passed into a culture of the remote past. I raise the question of culture because in these matters we can regard as achievements only what has been assimilated in culture, in social life, in custom.

.   .   .   .

We must come to our senses in time. We must become highly skeptical of too rapid progress, of boastfulness, etc. We must think of testing the steps forward which we proclaim to the world every hour, which we take every minute and which later prove to be flimsy, superficial and not understood every second. The worst thing of all would be haste. The worst thing of all would be to rely on the assumption that we know anything or on the assumption that we possess any considerable quantity of the elements necessary for building a really new apparatus that would really deserve the name of socialist, Soviet, etc.

No, we have no such apparatus. (*Better Fewer, But Better,* March 2, 1923, *Selected Works,* IX, 387, 388.)

4. BUREAUCRACY

We have been hearing complaints about bureaucracy for a long time; the complaints are undoubtedly well founded. We have done what no other state has done in the fight against bureaucracy. The apparatus which was a thoroughly bureaucratic and bourgeois apparatus of oppression, and which remains such even in the freest of bourgeois republics, we have destroyed to its very foundations.

. . . .

We can fight bureaucracy to the bitter end, to a complete victory, only when the whole population participates in the work of government. In the bourgeois republics not only was this impossible, *but the very law prevented it.* The best of the bourgeois republics, no matter how democratic they may be, have thousands of legislative hindrances which prevent the toilers from participating in the work of government. We have removed these hindrances, but so far we have not managed to get the toiling masses to participate in the work of government. Apart from the law, there is still the level of culture, which you cannot subject to any law. The result of this low cultural level is that the Soviets, which, by virtue of their program, are organs of government *by the toilers,* are in fact organs of government *for the toilers,* by means of the advanced stratum of the proletariat, but not by means of the toiling masses.

Here we are confronted by a problem which cannot be solved except by prolonged education. (*On the Party Program,* March 19, 1919, *Selected Works,* VIII, 352, 353.)

5. REVOLUTION AND STATE[3]

THE STATE AS THE PRODUCT OF THE IRRECONCILABILITY OF CLASS ANTAGONISMS

What is now happening to Marx's doctrine has, in the course of history, often happened to the doctrines of other revolutionary thinkers and leaders of oppressed classes struggling for emancipation. During the lifetime of great revolutionaries, the oppressing classes have visited relentless persecution on them and received their teaching with the most savage hostility, the most furious hatred, the most ruthless campaign of lies and slanders. After their death, attempts are made to turn them into harmless icons, canonize them, and surround their *names* with a certain halo for the "consolation" of the oppressed classes and with the object of duping them, while at the same time emasculating and vulgarizing the *real essence* of their revolutionary theories and blunting their revolutionary edge. (*Selected Works*, VII, 7.)

The state is the product and the manifestations of the *irreconcilability* of class antagonisms. The state arises when, where, and to the extent that the class antagonisms *cannot* be objectively reconciled. And, conversely, the existence of the state proves that the class antagonisms *are* irreconcilable. (*Selected Works*, VII, 8.)

According to Marx, the state could neither arise nor maintain itself if a reconciliation of classes were possible. But with the petty bourgeois and philistine professors and publicists, the state —and this frequently on the strength of benevolent references to Marx!—becomes a conciliator of the classes. According to Marx, the state is an organ of class *domination,* an organ of *oppression* of one class by another; its aim is the creation of "order" which legalizes and perpetuates this oppression by mod-

---

[3]The following passages (pp. 189–209) are selected from *State and Revolution*, 1916–Sept., 1917. Only volume and page from *Selected Works* are acknowledged.

erating the collisions between the classes. But in the opinion of the petty bourgeois politicians, order means reconciliation of the classes and not oppression of one class by another; to moderate collisions does not mean, they say, to deprive the oppressed class of certain definite means and methods of struggle for overthrowing the oppressors, but to practice reconciliation. (*Selected Works,* VII, 9.)

If the state is the product of the irreconcilable character of class antagonisms, if it is a force standing *above* society and "increasingly separating itself from it," then it is clear that the liberation of the oppressed class is impossible, not only without a violent revolution, *but also without the destruction* of the apparatus of state power, which was created by the ruling class and in which this "separation" is embodied. (*Selected Works,* VII, 10.)

SPECIAL BODIES OF ARMED MEN . . .

Society, in the period of civilization, is broken up into antagonistic and, indeed, irreconcilably antagonistic classes, which, if armed in a "self-acting" manner, would come into armed struggle with each other. A state is formed, a special power is created in the form of special bodies of armed men, and every revolution, by shattering the state apparatus, demonstrates to us how the ruling class aims at the restoration of the special bodies of armed men at *its* service, and how the oppressed class tries to create a new organization of this kind, capable of serving not the exploiters, but the exploited. (*Selected Works,* VII, 11 f.)

THE STATE AS AN INSTRUMENT FOR THE EXPLOITATION
OF THE OPPRESSED CLASS

In a democratic republic, "wealth wields its power indirectly, but all the more effectively," first, by means of "direct corruption of the officials" (America); second, by means of "the alliance of the government with the stock exchange" (France and America).

At the present time, imperialism and the domination of the banks have "developed" to an unusually fine art both these methods of defending and asserting the omnipotence of wealth in democratic republics of all descriptions. (*Selected Works,* VII, 14.)

The omnipotence of "wealth" is thus more *secure* in a democratic republic, since it does not depend on the poor political shell of capitalism. A democratic republic is the best possible political shell for capitalism, and therefore, once capital has gained control . . . of this very best shell, it establishes its power so securely, so firmly that *no* change, either of persons, or institutions, or parties, in the bourgeois republic can shake it. (*Selected Works,* VII, 15.)

The "Withering Away" of the State and Violent Revolution

Unlike the anarchist doctrine of the "abolition" of the state, according to Marx the state "withers away." . . . The current popular conception . . . of the "withering away" of the state undoubtedly means a slurring over, if not a negation, of revolution. (*Selected Works,* VII, 17.)

In assuming state power, the proletariat by that very act "puts an end to the state as the state." One is "not accustomed" to reflect on what this really means. . . . These words express succinctly the experience of one of the greatest proletarian revolutions—the Paris Commune of 1871 . . . . (*Selected Works,* VII, 17 f.)

Engels speaks . . . of the destruction of the bourgeois state by the proletarian revolution, while the words about its withering away refer to the remains of *proletarian* statehood *after* the socialist revolution. The bourgeois state does not "wither away," according to Engels, but is "put to an end" by the proletariat in the course of the revolution. What withers away after the revolution is the proletarian state or semistate.

... The state is a "special repressive force." ... It follows from this that the "special repressive force" of the bourgeoisie for the suppression of the proletariat, of the millions of workers by a handful of the rich, must be replaced by a "special repressive force" of the proletariat for the suppression of the bourgeoisie (the dictatorship of the proletariat). It is just this that constitutes the destruction of "the state as the state." It is just this that constitutes the "act" of "the seizure of the means of production in the name of society." And it is obvious that such a substitution of one (proletarian) "special repressive force" for another (bourgeois) "special repressive force" can in no way take place in the form of a "withering away."

As to the "withering away" or, more expressively and colorfully, as to the state "becoming dormant," Engels refers quite clearly and definitely to the period *after* "the seizure of the means of production [by the state] in the name of society," that is, *after* the socialist revolution. We all know that the political form of the "state" at that time is complete democracy. ... When Engels speaks ... of the state "withering away," or "becoming dormant," he speaks of *democracy*. At first sight this seems very strange. But it is "unintelligible" only to one who has not reflected on the fact that democracy is *also* a state and that, consequently, democracy will *also* disappear when the state disappears. The bourgeois state can only be "put to an end" by a revolution. The state in general, *i.e.*, most complete democracy, can only "wither away." *(Selected Works,* VII, 18 f.)

In the same work of Engels, from which every one remembers his argument on the "withering away" of the state, there is also a disquisition on the significance of a violent revolution. *(Selected Works,* VII, 20.)

Here is Engel's argument:

> ... That force, however, plays another role (other than that of a diabolical power) in history, a revolutionary role; that, in the words of Marx, it is the midwife of every old society which is pregnant with the new; that it is the instrument with whose aid social movement forces its way through and shatters the dead, fossilized political forms—of this there is not a word in Herr Dühring. It is only with sighs and groans that he admits the possibility that force will perhaps be necessary for the overthrow of the economic system of exploitation—unfortunately! because all use of force, forsooth, demoralizes the person who uses it. And this in spite of the immense moral and spiritual impetus which has resulted from every victorious revolution! And this in Germany, where a violent collision—which indeed may be forced on the people—would at least have the advantage of wiping out the servility which has permeated the national consciousness as a result of the humiliation of the Thirty Years' War. And this parson's mode of thought—lifeless, insipid and impotent—claims to impose itself on the most revolutionary party which history has known?

How can this panegyric on violent revolution, which Engels insistently brought to the attention of the German Social Democrats between 1878 and 1894, *i.e.,* right to the time of his death, be combined with the theory of the "withering away" of the state to form one doctrine? (*Loc. cit.*)

The teaching of Marx and Engels regarding the inevitability of a violent revolution refers to the bourgeois state. It *cannot* be replaced by the proletarian state (the dictatorship of the proletariat) through "withering away," but, as a general rule, only through a violent revolution. (*Selected Works,* VII, 21.)

The replacement of the bourgeois by the proletarian state is impossible without a violent revolution. The abolition of the proletarian state, *i.e.,* of all states, is only possible through "withering away." (*Loc. cit.*)

EXPERIENCE OF THE PARIS COMMUNE OF 1871:
MARX'S ANALYSIS

The last preface to a new German edition of the *Communist Manifesto* signed by both its authors is dated June 24, 1872. In this preface the authors, Karl Marx and Friedrich Engels, say that the program of the *Communist Manifesto* is now "in places out of date."

> One thing especially [they continue] was proved by the Commune, *viz., that the "working class cannot simply lay hold of the ready-made state machinery and wield it for its own purposes."*

The words within quotation marks in this passage are borrowed by its authors from Marx's book, *The Civil War in France.*

It thus appears that one principal and fundamental lesson of the Paris Commune was considered by Marx and Engels to be of such enormous importance that they introduced it as a vital correction into the *Communist Manifesto. (Selected Works,* VII, 35 f.)

Marx's idea is that the working class must *break up, shatter* the "ready-made state machinery," and not confine itself merely to taking possession of it. *(Selected Works,* VII, 36.)

It is interesting to note two particular points in the passages of Marx quoted. First, he confines his conclusions to the Continent. This was natural in 1871, when England was still the model of a purely capitalist country, but without a military machine and, in large measure, without a bureaucracy. Hence Marx excluded England, where a revolution, even a people's revolution, could be imagined, and was then possible, *without* the preliminary condition of destroying the "ready-made state machinery."

Today, in 1917, in the epoch of the first great imperialist war, this exception made by Marx is no longer valid.... Today, both in England and in America, the "precondition of any real people's revolution" is the *break-up,* the *shattering* of the "ready-made state machinery." . . .

Secondly, particular attention should be given to Marx's extremely profound remark that the destruction of the military and bureaucratic apparatus of the state is "the precondition of any real *people's* revolution." (*Selected Works,* VII, 37.)

WHAT IS TO REPLACE THE SHATTERED STATE MACHINERY?

The commune . . . replaced the shattered state machinery "only" by fuller democracy: abolition of the standing army; all officials to be fully elective and subject to recall. But, as a matter of fact, this "only" signifies a gigantic replacement of one type of institution by others of a fundamentally different order. Here we observe a case of "transformation of quantity into quality": democracy, introduced as fully and consistently as is generally thinkable, is transformed from capitalist democracy into proletarian democracy; from the state (*i.e.,* a special force for the suppression of a particular class) into something which is no longer really the state in the accepted sense of the word.

It is still necessary to suppress the bourgeoisie and crush its resistance. This was particularly necessary for the commune; and one of the reasons for its defeat was that it did not do this with sufficient determination. But the organ of suppression is now the majority of the population, and not a minority, as was always the case under slavery, serfdom, and wage labor. And, once the majority of the people *itself* suppresses its oppressors, a "special force" for suppression is *no longer necessary.* In this sense the state *begins to wither away.* Instead of the special institutions of a privileged minority (privileged officialdom, heads of a standing army), the majority can itself directly fulfil all these functions and the more the discharge of the functions of state power devolves upon the people generally, the less need is there for the existence of this power. (*Selected Works,* VII, 40 f.)

THE DESTRUCTION OF PARLIAMENTARISM

The commune [says Marx] was to be a working, not a parliamentary, body, executive and legislative at the same time . . . . Instead of deciding once in three or six years which member of the ruling class was to represent the people in parliament, universal suffrage was to serve the people, constituted in communes, as individual suffrage serves every other employer in the search for the workmen and managers in his business.

This remarkable criticism of parliamentarism, made in 1871, also belongs to the "forgotten words" of Marxism. (*Selected Works*, VII, 43.)

The way out of parliamentarism is to be found, of course, not in the abolition of the representative institutions and the elective principle, but in the conversion of the representative institutions from mere "talking shops" into working bodies. (*Selected Works*, VII, 44.)

The venal and rotten parliamentarism of bourgeois society is replaced in the commune by institutions in which freedom of opinion and discussion does not degenerate into deception, for the parliamentarians must themselves work, must themselves execute their own laws, must themselves verify their results in actual life, must themselves be directly responsible to their electorate. Representative institutions remain, but parliamentarism as a special system, as a division of labor between the legislative and the executive functions, as a privileged position for the deputies *no longer exists.* Without representative institutions we cannot imagine democracy, not even proletarian democracy; but we can and *must* think of democracy without parliamentarism, if criticism of bourgeois society is not mere empty words. . . . (*Selected Works*, VII, 46.)

There is no trace of utopianism in Marx, in the sense of inventing or imagining a "new" society. No, he studies, as a process of natural history, the *birth* of the new society *from* the old, the forms of transition from the latter to the former. He takes the actual experience of a mass proletarian movement and tries to draw practical lessons from it (*Loc. cit.*).

To destroy officialdom immediately, everywhere, completely— this cannot be thought of. That is a utopia. But to *break up* at once the old bureaucratic machine and to start immediately the construction of a new one which will enable us gradually to reduce all officialdom to naught—this is *no* utopia, it is the experience of the commune, it is the direct and urgent task of the revolutionary proletariat. (*Selected Works,* VII, 47.)

We are not utopians, we do not indulge in "dreams" of how best to do away *immediately* with all administration, with all subordination; these anarchist dreams, based upon a lack of understanding of the task of proletarian dictatorship, are basic- ally foreign to Marxism, and, as a matter of fact, they serve but to put off the socialist revolution until human nature is different. No, we want the socialist revolution with human nature as it is now, with human nature that cannot do without subordination, control, and "managers."

But if there be subordination, it must be to the armed van- guard of all the exploited and the laboring—to the proletariat. The specific "commanding" methods of the state officials can and must begin to be replaced—immediately, within twenty-four hours—by the simple functions of "managers" and bookkeepers, functions which are now already within the capacity of the average city dweller and can well be performed for "working- men's wages."

We organize large-scale production, starting from what capital- ism has already created; we workers *ourselves,* relying on our own experience as workers, establishing a strict, an iron disci- pline, supported by the state power of the armed workers, shall reduce the role of the state officials to that of simply carrying out our instructions as responsible, moderately paid "managers" (of course, with technical knowledge of all sorts, types and de- grees). This is *our* proletarian task, with this we can and must *begin* when carrying through a proletarian revolution. Such a beginning, on the basis of large-scale production, of itself leads to the gradual "withering away" of all bureaucracy, to the gradual creation of a new order, an order without quotation marks, an order which has nothing to do with wage slavery, an order in which the more and more simplified functions of control and accounting will be performed by each in turn, will then become a habit, and will finally die out as *special* functions of a special stratum of the population.

A witty German Social Democrat of the 1870's called the *post office* an example of the socialist system. This is very true. . . . Overthrow the capitalists, crush with the iron hand of the armed workers the resistance of these exploiters, break the bureaucratic machine of the modern state—and you have before you a mechanism of the highest technical equipment, freed of "parasites," capable of being set into motion by the united workers themselves who hire their own technicians, managers, bookkeepers, and pay them *all,* as, indeed, every "state" official, with the usual workers' wage. Here is a concrete, practicable task, immediately realizable. . . .

To organize the *whole* national economy like the postal system, in such a way that the technicians, managers, bookkeepers as well as *all* officials should receive no higher wages than "workingmen's wages," all under the control and leadership of the armed proletariat—this is our immediate aim. This is the kind of state and economic basis we need. This is what will produce the destruction of parliamentarism, while retaining representative institutions. This is what will free the laboring classes from the prostitution of these institutions by the bourgeoisie. (*Selected Works,* VII, 47–49.)

THE ORGANIZATION OF NATIONAL UNITY

Marx agrees with Proudhon in that they both stand for the "destruction" of the contemporary state machinery. This common ground of Marxism with anarchism (both with Proudhon and with Bakunin) neither the opportunists nor the Kautskyists

wish to see, for on this point they have themselves departed
from Marxism.

Marx differs from both Proudhon and Bakunin precisely on
the point of federalism (not to speak of the dictatorship of the
proletariat). Federalism arises, as a principle, from the petty
bourgeois views of anarchism. Marx is a centralist. In the above
quoted observations of his there is no deviation from centralism.
Only people full of petty bourgeois "superstitious faith" in the
state can mistake the destruction of the bourgeois state for the
destruction of centralism. (*Selected Works,* VII, 50 f.)

DESTRUCTION OF THE PARASITE STATE

The utopians busied themselves with the "discovery" of the
political forms under which the socialist reconstruction of society
could take place. The anarchists turned away from the question
of political forms altogether. The opportunists of modern Social
Democracy accepted the bourgeois political forms of a parliamentary, democratic state as the limit which cannot be overstepped;
they broke their foreheads praying before this idol, denouncing
as anarchism every attempt to *destroy* these forms.

Marx deducted from the whole history of socialism and political struggle that the state was bound to disappear, and that the
transitional form of its disappearance (the transition from the
political state to no state) would be the "proletariat organized
as the ruling class." But Marx did not undertake the task of
discovering the political *forms* of this future stage. He limited
himself to an exact observation of French history, its analysis
and the conclusion to which the year 1851 had led, *viz.,* that
matters were moving toward the *destruction* of the bourgeois
machinery of state.

And when the mass revolutionary movement of the proletariat
burst forth, Marx, in spite of the failure of that movement, in
spite of its short life and its patent weakness, began to study what
political forms it had *disclosed.*

The commune is the form "at last discovered" by the proletarian revolution, under which the economic liberation of labor can proceed.

The commune is the first attempt of a proletarian revolution to *break up* the bourgeois state machinery and constitutes the political form, "at last discovered," which can and must *take the place* of the broken machine.

The Russian revolutions of 1905 and 1917, in different surroundings and under different circumstances, continued the work of the commune and confirmed the historic analysis made by the genius of Marx. (*Selected Works,* VII, 53.)

CRITICISM OF THE DRAFT OF THE ERFURT PROGRAM

In the field of economics Engels . . . makes an exceedingly valuable observation which shows how attentively and thoughtfully he followed the changes in modern capitalism, and how he was able, in a measure, to foresee the problems of our own, the imperialist, epoch. Here is the point: touching on the word "planlessness" used in the draft program, as characteristic of capitalism, Engels writes:

> When we pass from joint stock companies to trusts which control and monopolize whole branches of industry, not only private production comes to an end at that point, but also planlessness.

Here we have what is most essential in the theoretical appreciation of the latest phase of capitalism, *i.e.,* imperialism, *viz.,* that capitalism becomes monopoly *capitalism*. This fact must be emphasized because the bourgeois reformist view that monopoly capitalism or state-monopoly capitalism is *no longer* capitalism, but can already be termed "state socialism," or something of that sort, is a very widespread error. The trusts, of course, have not created, do not create now, and cannot create full and complete planning. But, however much of a plan they may create, however closely capitalist magnates may estimate in advance the extent of production on a national and even international scale, and however systematically they may regulate it, we still remain *under capitalism*—capitalism, it is true, in its new stage, but still, unquestionably, capitalism. The "proximity" of *such* capitalism to socialism should serve for the real representatives of the proletariat as an argument proving the nearness, ease, feasibility and urgency of the socialist revolution, and not at all as an argument for tolerating a repudiation of such a revolution or for making capitalism more attractive, in which work all the reformists are engaged. (*Selected Works,* VII, 62 f.)

Engels by no means understands democratic centralism in the bureaucratic sense. . . . Centralism does not, with Engels, in the least exclude such wide local self-government which combines a voluntary defense of the unity of the state by the "communes" and districts with the complete abolition of all bureaucracy and all "commanding" from above. (*Selected Works,* VII, 67.)

Engels, armed with facts, disproves by a telling example the superstition, very widespread especially among the petty bourgeois democracy, that a federal republic necessarily means a greater amount of freedom than a centralized republic. This is not true. It is disproved by the facts cited by Engels regarding the centralized French Republic of 1792–1798 and the federal Swiss Republic. The really democratic centralized republic gave *more* freedom than the federal republic. In other words, the *greatest* amount of local, provincial and other freedom known in history was granted by a *centralized,* and not by a federal, republic. (*Selected Works,* VII, 68.)

ENGELS ON OVERCOMING DEMOCRACY

It is constantly forgotten that the destruction of the state means also the destruction of democracy; that the withering away of the state also means the withering away of democracy.

At first sight such a statement seems exceedingly strange and incomprehensible; indeed, someone may even begin to fear lest we be expecting the advent of such an order of society in which the principle of the subordination of the minority to the majority will not be respected—for is not a democracy just the recognition of this principle?

No, democracy is *not* identical with the subordination of the minority to the majority. Democracy is a *state* recognizing the subordination of the minority to the majority, i.e., an organization for the systematic use of *violence* by one class against the other, by one part of the population against another.

We set ourselves the ultimate aim of destroying the state, i.e., every organized and systematic violence, every use of violence against man in general. We do not expect the advent of an order of society in which the principle of subordination of minority to majority will not be observed. But, striving for socialism, we are convinced that it will develop into communism; that, side by side with this, there will vanish all need for force, for the *subjection* of one man to another, and of one part of the population to another, since people will *grow accustomed* to observing the elementary conditions of social existence *without force and without subjection.*

In order to emphasize this element of habit, Engels speaks of a *new generation,* "reared under new and free social conditions," which "will be able to throw on the scrap heap all this state rubbish"—every kind of state, including even the democratic-republican state. (*Selected Works,* VII, 74 f.)

6. THE ECONOMIC BASE OF THE WITHERING AWAY OF THE STATE

TRANSITION FROM CAPITALISM TO COMMUNISM

Only communism renders the state absolutely unnecessary, for there is *no one* to be suppressed—"no one" in the sense of a *class,* in the sense of a systematic struggle with a definite section of the population. We are not utopians, and we do not in the least deny the possibility and inevitability of excesses on the part of *individual persons,* nor the need to suppress *such* excesses. But, in the first place, no special machinery, no special apparatus of repression is needed for this; this will be done by the armed people itself, as simply and as readily as any crowd of civilized people, even in modern society, parts a pair of combatants or does not allow a woman to be outraged. And, secondly, we know that the fundamental social cause of excesses which consist in violating the rules of social life is the exploitation of the masses, their want and their poverty. With the removal of this chief cause, excesses will inevitably begin to *"wither away."* We do not know how quickly and in what succession, but we know that they will wither away. With their withering away, the state will also *wither away.* (*Selected Works,* VII, 76–83.)

FIRST PHASE OF COMMUNIST SOCIETY

It is this communist society—a society which has just come into the world out of the womb of capitalism, and which, in all respects, bears the stamp of the old society—that Marx terms the "first," or lower, phase of communist society.

The means of production are no longer the private property of individuals. The means of production belong to the whole of society. Every member of society, performing a certain part of socially necessary work, receives a certificate from society to the effect that he has done such and such a quantity of work. According to this certificate, he receives from the public warehouses, where articles of consumption are stored, a corresponding quantity of products. Deducting that proportion of labor which goes to the public fund, every worker, therefore, receives from society as much as he has given it.

"Equality" seems to reign supreme. (*Selected Works,* VII, 83 f.)

"Equal right," says Marx, we indeed have here; but it is *still* a "bourgeois right," which, like every right, *presupposes inequality.* Every right is an application of the *same* measure to *different* people who, in fact, are not the same and are not equal to one another; this is why "equal right" is really a violation of equality, and an injustice. In effect, every man, having done as much social labor as every other, receives an equal share of the social products (with the above-mentioned deductions).

But different people are not alike: one is strong, another is weak; one is married, the other is not; one has more children, another has less, and so on. (*Selected Works,* VII, 84 f.)

The first phase of communism, therefore, still cannot produce justice and equality; differences, and unjust differences, in wealth will still exist, but the *exploitation* of man by man will have become impossible, because it will be impossible to seize as private property the *means of production,* the factories, machines, land, and so on. . . . Marx shows the *course of development* of communist society, which is forced at first to destroy *only* the "injustice" that consists in the means of production having been seized by private individuals, and which *is not capable* of destroying at once the further injustice consisting in the distribution of the articles of consumption "according to work performed" (and not according to need). (*Selected Works,* VII, 85.)

And so, in the first phase of communist society (generally called socialism) "bourgeois right" is *not* abolished in its entirety, but only in part, only in proportion to the economic transformation so far attained, i.e., only in respect of the means of production. "Bourgeois right" recognizes them as the private property of separate individuals. Socialism converts them into common property. *To that extent,* and to that extent alone, does "bourgeois right" disappear.

However, it continues to exist as far as its other part is concerned; it remains in the capacity of regulator (determining factor), distributing the products and allotting labor among the members of society. "He who does not work shall not eat"— this socialist principle is *already* realized; "for an equal quantity of labor, an equal quantity of products"—this socialist principle is also *already* realized. However, this is not yet communism, and this does not abolish "bourgeois right," which gives to unequal individuals, in return for an unequal (in reality unequal) amount of work, an equal quantity of products.

This is a "defect," says Marx, but it is unavoidable during the first phase of communism; for, if we are not to fall into utopianism, we cannot imagine that, having overthrown capitalism, people will at once learn to work for society *without any standards of right;* indeed, the abolition of capitalism *does not immediately lay* the economic foundations for *such* a change.

And there is no other standard yet than that of "bourgeois right." To this extent, therefore, a form of state is still necessary, which, while maintaining public ownership of the means of production, would preserve the equality of labor and equality in the distribution of products.

The state is withering away in so far as there are no longer any capitalists, any classes, and, consequently, no *class* can be suppressed.

But the state has not yet altogether withered away, since there still remains the protection of "bourgeois right" which sanctifies actual inequality. For the complete extinction of the state, complete communism is necessary. (*Selected Works*, VII, 85 f.)

HIGHER PHASE OF COMMUNIST SOCIETY

While the state exists there is no freedom. When there is freedom, there will be no state.

The economic basis for the complete withering away of the state is that high stage of development of communism when the antagonism between mental and physical labor disappears, that is to say, when one of the principal sources of modern *social* inequality disappears—a source, moreover, which it is impossible to remove immediately by the mere conversion of the means of production into public property, by the mere expropriation of the capitalists.

This expropriation will make a gigantic development of the productive forces *possible*. And seeing how incredibly, even now, capitalism *retards* this development, how much progress could be made even on the basis of modern technology at the level it has reached, we have a right to say, with the fullest confidence, that the expropriation of the capitalists will inevitably result in a gigantic development of the productive forces of human society. But how rapidly this development will go forward, how soon it will reach the point of breaking away from the division of labor, of removing the antagonism between mental and physical labor, of transforming work into the "first necessity of life"—this we do not and *cannot* know.

Consequently, we have a right to speak solely of the inevitable withering away of the state, emphasizing the protracted nature of this process and its dependence upon the rapidity of development of the *higher phase* of communism; leaving quite open the question of lengths of time, or the concrete forms of withering away, since material for the solution of such questions is *not available.*

The state will be able to wither away completely when society has realized the rule: "From each according to his ability; to each according to his needs," i.e., when people have become accustomed to observing the fundamental rules of social life, and their labor is so productive, that they voluntarily work *according to their ability.* "The narrow horizon of bourgeois rights," which compels one to calculate, with the hardheartedness of a Shylock, whether he has not worked half an hour more than another, whether he is not getting less pay than another—this narrow horizon will then be left behind. There will then be no need for any exact calculation by society of the quantity of products to be distributed to each of its members; each will take freely "according to his needs." *(Selected Works,* VII, 87 f.)

Until the "higher" phase of communism arrives, the socialists demand the *strictest* control, *by society and by the state,* of the quantity of labor and the quantity of consumption; only this control must *start* with the expropriation of the capitalists, with the control of the workers over the capitalists, and must be carried out, not by a state of bureaucrats, but by a state of *armed workers. (Selected Works,* VII, 89.)

Democracy is of great importance for the working class in its struggle for freedom against the capitalists. But democracy is by no means a limit one may not overstep; it is only one of the stages in the course of development from feudalism to capitalism, and from capitalism to communism.

Democracy means equality. The great significance of the struggle of the proletariat for equality, and the significance of equality as a slogan, are apparent if we correctly interpret it as meaning the abolition of *classes.* But democracy means only *formal* equality. Immediately after the attainment of equality for all members of society *in respect of* the ownership of the means of production, that is, of equality of labor and equality of wages, there will inevitably arise before humanity the question of going further, from formal equality to real equality, i.e., to realizing the rule, "From each according to his ability; to each according to his needs." By what stages, by means of what practical measures humanity will proceed to this higher aim—this we do not and cannot know. But it is important to realize how infinitely mendacious is the usual bourgeois presentation of socialism as something lifeless, petrified, fixed once for all, whereas in reality, it is *only* with socialism that there will commence a rapid, genuine, real mass advance, in which first the *majority* and then the whole of the population will take part—an advance in all domains of social and individual life.

Democracy is a form of the state—one of its varieties. Consequently, like every state, it consists in organized, systematic application of force against human beings. This on the one hand. On the other hand, however, it signifies the formal recognition of the equality of all citizens, the equal right of all to determine the structure and administration of the state. This, in turn, is connected with the fact that, at a certain stage in the development of democracy, it first rallies the proletariat as a revolutionary class against capitalism, and gives it an opportunity to crush, to smash to bits, to wipe off the face of the earth the bourgeois state machinery—even its republican variety: the standing army, the police, and bureaucracy; then it substitutes for all this a *more* democratic, but still a state, machinery in the shape of armed masses of workers, which becomes transformed into universal participation of the people in the militia.

Here "quantity is transformed into quality": *such* a degree of democracy is bound up with the abandonment of the framework of bourgeois society, and the beginning of its socialist reconstruction. If *everyone* really takes part in the administration of the state, capitalism cannot retain its hold. In its turn, capitalism, as it develops, itself creates *prerequisites* for "everyone" *to be able* really to take part in the administration of the state. Among such prerequisites are: universal literacy, already realized in most of the advanced capitalist countries; then the "training and disciplining" of millions of workers by the huge, complex, and socialized apparatus of the post office, the railways, the big factories, large-scale commerce, banking, etc., etc.

With such *economic* prerequisites it is perfectly possible, immediately, within twenty-four hours after the overthrow of the capitalists and bureaucrats, to replace them, in the control of production and distribution, in the business of *control* of labor and products, by the armed workers, by the whole people in arms. (The question of control and accounting must not be confused with the question of the scientifically educated staff of engineers, agronomists and so on. These gentlemen work today, obeying the capitalists; they will work even better tomorrow, obeying the armed workers.)

Accounting and control—these are the *chief* things necessary for the organizing and correct functioning of the *first phase* of communist society. *All* citizens are here transformed into hired employees of the state, which is made up of the armed workers. *All* citizens become employees and workers of *one* national state "syndicate." All that is required is that they should work equally, should regularly do their share of work, and should receive equal pay. The accounting and control necessary for this have been *simplified* by capitalism to the utmost, till they have become the extraordinarily simple operations of watching, recording and issuing receipts, within the reach of anybody who can read and write and knows the first four rules of arithmetic.[4]

When the *majority* of the people begin everywhere to keep such accounts and maintain such control over the capitalists (now converted into employees) and over the intellectual gentry, who still retain capitalist habits, this control will really become

---

[4]When most of the functions of the state are reduced to this accounting and control by the workers themselves, then it ceases to be a "political state," and the "public functions will lose their political character and be transformed into simple administrative functions" (*cf.* Engels' polemic against the anarchists).

universal, general, national; and there will be no way of getting away from it, there will be "nowhere to go."

The whole of society will have become one office and one factory, with equal work and equal pay.

But this "factory" discipline, which the proletariat will extend to the whole of society after the defeat of the capitalists and the overthrow of the exploiters, is by no means our ideal, or our final aim. It is but a *foothold* necessary for the radical cleansing of society of all the hideousness and foulness of capitalist exploitation, *in order to advance further.*

From the moment when all members of society, or even only the overwhelming majority, have learned how to govern the state *themselves,* have taken this business into their own hands, have "established" control over the insignificant minority of capitalists, over the gentry with capitalist leanings, and the workers thoroughly demoralized by capitalism—from this moment the need for any government begins to disappear. The more complete the democracy, the nearer the moment when it begins to be unnecessary. The more democratic the "state" consisting of armed workers, which is "no longer a state in the proper sense of the word," the more rapidly does *every* state begin to wither away.

For when *all* have learned to manage, and independently are actually managing by themselves social production, keeping accounts, controlling the idlers, the gentlefolk, the swindlers and similar "guardians of capitalist traditions," then the escape from this national accounting and control will inevitably become so increasingly difficult, such a rare exception, and will probably be accompanied by such swift and severe punishment (for the armed workers are men of practical life, not sentimental intellectuals, and they will scarcely allow anyone to trifle with them) that very soon the *necessity* of observing the simple, fundamental rules of everyday social life in common will have become a *habit.*

The door will then be wide open for the transition from the first phase of communist society to its higher phase, and along with it to the complete withering away of the state. (*Selected Works,* VII, 91–93.)

7. THE PROLETARIAN REVOLUTION AND RENEGADE KAUTSKY[5]

HOW KAUTSKY TRANSFORMED MARX INTO A COMMON LIBERAL

The title of Kautsky's pamphlet is *The Dictatorship of the Proletariat*. Everybody knows that this is the very essence of Marx's teaching; and, after talking beside the point for a long time, Kautsky was obliged to quote Marx's words on the dictatorship of the proletariat. But the *way* in which he, the "Marxist," did this was simply farcical. Listen:

"This view" (which Kautsky dubs "contempt for democracy") "rests upon a single word of Marx." This is what Kautsky literally says. . . . The same thing is repeated in a still more pointed form, to the effect that the Bolsheviks "opportunely remembered the catchword" (this is literally what he says: *des Wörtchens*) "dictatorship of the proletariat, which Marx once used in 1875 in a letter." This is Marx's "catchword":

> Between capitalist and communist society lies a period of revolutionary transformation from one to the other. There corresponds also to this a political transition period during which the state can be nothing else than the *revolutionary dictatorship of the proletariat*.[6]

To call this celebrated passage of Marx, which sums up all his revolutionary teaching, "a single word" and even a catchword is a mockery of Marxism, is complete renunciation of it. It must not be forgotten that Kautsky knows Marx almost by heart, and, judging by all he has written, he has in his desk, or in his head, a number of pigeonholes in which all that was ever written by Marx is carefully distributed so as to be ready at hand for quotation. Kautsky *cannot but know* that both Marx and Engels, in their letters as well as in their published works, *repeatedly*

---

[5]The following passages (pp. 210–223) are selected from *The Proletarian Revolution and Renegade Kautsky*, 1918. Only volume and page from *Selected Works* are acknowledged.
[6]Karl Marx, *Critique of the Gotha Program*.

spoke about the dictatorship of the proletariat, both before and after the Paris Commune. Kautsky cannot but know that the formula "dictatorship of the proletariat" is but a more historically concrete and more scientifically exact formulation of the proletariat's task to "smash" the bourgeois state machine, about which Marx and Engels, in summing up the experience of the Revolution of 1848, and, still more so, of 1871, spoke *for forty years*, between 1852 and 1891. (*Selected Works*, VII, 119.)

Marx, unfortunately, failed to show us in greater detail how he conceived this dictatorship. [This is a thoroughly mendacious phrase of a renegade, for Marx and Engels gave us quite a number of most precise indications which our "erudite" Marxist has deliberately ignored.] Literally, the word "dictatorship" means the abolition of democracy. But taken literally, this word also means the undivided rule of a single individual unrestricted by any laws —an autocracy, which differs from despotism only in that it is regarded, not as a permanent state institution, but as a transitory emergency measure.

The term "dictatorship of the proletariat," hence, not the dictatorship of a single individual, but of a class, *ipso facto* precludes the possibility that Marx in this connection had in mind "dictatorship" in the literal sense of the term.

He speaks in this connection *not of a form of government,* but of a *state of things,* which must necessarily arise whenever and wherever the proletariat has conquered political power. That Marx did not have in view a form of government is proved by the fact that he was of the opinion that in England and America the transition could take place peacefully, i.e., in a democratic way.

I deliberately quoted this disquisition in full in order that the reader may clearly see the method Kautsky, the "theoretician," employs.

Kautsky chose to approach the question in such a way as to begin with a definition of the word "dictatorship."

Very well. Everybody has the sacred right to approach a subject in whatever way he pleases. One must only distinguish a serious and honest approach to a question from a dishonest one. Any one who wanted to be serious in approaching this question ought to have given *his own definition* of the "word"; then the question would have been put fairly and squarely. But Kautsky does not do that.

"Literally," he writes, "the word 'dictatorship' means the abolition of democracy."

In the first place this is not a definition. If Kautsky wanted to avoid giving a definition of the concept of dictatorship, why did he choose this particular approach to the question?

Secondly, it is obviously wrong. A liberal naturally speaks of "democracy" in general; but a Marxist will never forget to ask: for what class? Everybody knows, for instance (and Kautsky, the "historian," also knows it), that the rebellions of and even the strong ferment among the slaves in antiquity immediately revealed the fact that in essence the state of antiquity was the *dictatorship of the slave owners.* Did this dictatorship abolish democracy *among* and *for* the *slave owners?* Everybody knows that it did not.

The "Marxist," Kautsky, uttered absolute nonsense and an untruth, because he "forgot" the class struggle. . . .

In order to transform Kautsky's liberal and lying assertion into a Marxian and true one, one must say: dictatorship does not necessarily mean the abolition of democracy for the class that exercises dictatorship over other classes; but it certainly does mean the abolition (or very material restriction, which is also a form of abolition) of democracy for that class over which, or against which, the dictatorship is exercised. But however true this assertion may be, it does not give a definition of dictatorship.

Let us examine Kautsky's next sentence:

> But of course, taken literally, this word also means the undivided rule of a single individual unrestricted by any laws.

Like a blind puppy casually sniffing in one direction and then in another, Kautsky accidentally stumbled upon *one* true idea (namely, that dictatorship is power unrestricted by any laws) but he *failed* to give a definition of dictatorship, and, moreover, he uttered an obvious historical falsehood, viz., that dictatorship means the power of a single person. This is not even grammatically correct, since the power of dictatorship can also be exercised by a handful of persons, by an oligarchy, by a class, etc. (*Selected Works,* VII, 120–121.)

Dictatorship is power, based directly upon force, and unrestricted by any laws.

The revolutionary dictatorship of the proletariat is power won and maintained by the violence of the proletariat against the bourgeoisie, power that is unrestricted by any laws. (*Selected Works,* VII, 122.)

Kautsky committed a subterfuge by proclaiming the obvious nonsense that the word dictatorship, in its literal sense, means the dictatorship of a single person, and then, on the strength of this subterfuge, he declared that Marx's words about dictatorship of a class must not be taken literally (but must be taken to mean that dictatorship does not connote revolutionary violence, but merely "the peaceful winning of a majority under bourgeois"—mark you—democracy). (*Selected Works,* VII, 123.)

Kautsky found it necessary to interpret dictatorship as a "state of domination" (this is the literal expression he uses on the very next page . . .), because, then, *revolutionary violence, violent revolution, disappears.* A "state of domination" is a state in which any majority finds itself under a "democracy." Thanks to such a fraudulent trick, *revolution* easily disappears. . . . One cannot do away with the fact that a dictatorship presupposes and means a "state" (very disagreeable to all renegades) of revolutionary violence of one class against another. . . . Monarchy and republic are two different forms of government. Both these forms of government, as well as all transitional forms of government under capitalism, are but so many varieties of the *bourgeois state,* i.e., of the *dictatorship of the bourgeoisie.* (*Selected Works,* VII, 123 f.)

Was there in the seventies of last century anything which

made England and America an exception in regard to what we *are now discussing?* It will be obvious to any one familiar with the requirements of science in the domain of historical problems that such a question must be put. To fail to put it is tantamount to falsifying science, to engaging in sophistry. And the question having been put, there can be no doubt as to the reply: The revolutionary dictatorship of the proletariat is violence against the bourgeoisie; and the necessity for such violence is *particularly* created, as Marx and Engels have repeatedly explained in detail (particularly in *The Civil War in France* and in the preface to it), by the existence of militarism and bureaucracy. But it is precisely these institutions that were nonexistent in England and America in the 1870's, when Marx made his observations (they *do* exist in England and America *now*). . . .

In defining the term "dictatorship," Kautsky tried his utmost to conceal from the reader the fundamental symptom of this concept, namely, revolutionary *violence*. But now the truth has emerged: the point under discussion is the antithesis between *peaceful* and *violent revolutions*.

That is the whole point. (*Selected Works,* VII, 125.)

The Paris Commune was a dictatorship of the proletariat, but it was elected by *universal suffrage,* the bourgeoisie was not deprived of the franchise, i.e., the Commune was elected "democratically." And Kautsky says elatedly:

> The dictatorship of the proletariat, for him [Marx], is a state of things which necessarily follows from pure democracy, if the proletariat represents the overwhelming majority. . . . (*Selected Works,* VII, 126.)

Marx and Engels analyzed the Paris Commune in a most detailed manner and showed that its merit lies in its attempt *to smash, to break up* the "existing state machine." Marx and Engels considered this conclusion to be so important that it was the *only* amendment they made in 1872 to the "obsolete" *Communist Manifesto*. Marx and Engels showed that the Paris Commune abolished the army and the bureaucracy, abolished *parliamentarism,* destroyed "that parasitic excrescence, the state," etc.; but the all-wise Kautsky, donning his night-cap, repeats the fairytale about "pure democracy," which has been told a thousand times by liberal professors. *(Selected Works,* VII, 127.)

Third evasion:

> When we speak of the dictatorship as a form of government we cannot speak of the dictatorship of a class, since a class, as we have already pointed out, can only dominate, but not govern.

It is "organizations" or "parties" that govern! *(Loc. cit.)*

Dictatorship is not a "form of government"; that is ridiculous nonsense. And Marx does not speak of the form of *government,* but of the form or type of *state.* That is something altogether different. It is altogether wrong, also, to say that a class cannot govern. Such an absurdity can only be uttered by a parliamentary cretin who sees nothing but bourgeois parliaments, who has noticed nothing but "ruling parties." Any European country will provide Kautsky with examples of government by a *ruling class,* as, for instance, by the landowners in the Middle Ages, in spite of their insufficient organization. *(Selected Works,* VII, 128.)

Bourgeois and Proletarian Democracy

If we are not to mock at common sense and history, it is obvious that we cannot speak of "pure democracy" so long as different *classes* exist; we can only speak of *class* democracy. *(Selected Works,* VII, 129.)

"Pure democracy" is the mendacious phrase of a liberal who wants to fool the working class. History knows of bourgeois democracy which takes the place of feudalism, and of proletarian democracy which takes the place of bourgeois democracy. *(Loc. cit.)*

Bourgeois democracy, while constituting a great historical advance in comparison with medievalism, nevertheless remains, and cannot but remain, under capitalism, restricted, truncated, false and hypocritical, a paradise for the rich and a trap and a snare and a deception for the exploited, for the poor. (*Selected Works,* VII, 130.)

There is not a single state, however democratic, which does not contain loopholes or limiting clauses in its constitution guaranteeing the bourgeoisie the legal possibility of dispatching troops against the workers, of proclaiming martial law, and so forth, in case of a "disturbance of the peace," i.e., in case the exploited class "disturbs" its position of slavery and tries to behave in a non-slavish manner. Kautsky shamelessly embellishes bourgeois democracy and hushes up, for instance, what the most democratic and republican bourgeoisie of America and Switzerland do against workers on strike. (*Selected Works,* VII, 131.)

The ruling party in a bourgeois democracy extends the protection of minorities only to the other *bourgeois* party, while on all *serious, profound and fundamental* issues, the working class gets martial law and pogroms, instead of the "protection of minorities." *The more developed democracy is, the more imminent is the danger of pogroms or civil war in connection with any profound political divergence which is dangerous for the bourgeoisie.* (*Selected Works,* VII, 132.)

The *more* democracy is developed, the *more* the bourgeois parliaments fall under the control of the stock exchange and the bankers? This, of course, does not mean that we must not use bourgeois parliaments (the Bolsheviks have made better use of them than any other party in the world, for in 1912–1914 we captured the entire workers' representation in the fourth Duma). But it does mean that only a liberal can forget the historical limitations and conventional character of bourgeois parliamentarism as Kautsky does. Even in the most democratic bourgeois states the oppressed masses meet at every step the crying contradiction between the *formal* equality proclaimed by the "democracy" of the capitalists, and the thousand and one *de facto*

limitations and restrictions which make the proletarians *wage
slaves*. It is precisely this contradiction that opens the eyes of
the masses to the rottenness, hypocrisy, and mendacity of capitalism. It is this contradiction which the agitators and propagandists of socialism are constantly showing up to the masses,
in order to prepare them for the revolution. (*Selected Works*,
VII, 133.)

Proletarian democracy, of which the Soviet government constitutes one of the forms, has given a development and expansion
of democracy hitherto unprecedented in the world, precisely for
the vast majority of the population, for the exploited and for
the toilers. (*Loc. cit.*)

Take foreign policy. In no bourgeois state, not even in the
most democratic one, is it carried on openly. In all democratic
countries—France, Switzerland, America or England—the masses
are deceived in an incomparably wider and more subtle manner
than in other countries. The Soviet government, in a revolutionary manner, has torn the veil of mystery from foreign policy. . . .
In the present era of predatory wars and secret treaties for the
"division of spheres of influences" i.e., for the partition of the
world among the capitalist bandits), the subject is one of cardinal
importance, for it is a matter that determines the question of
peace, it is a question of life and death for tens of millions of
people.

Take the organization of the state. Kautsky clutches at all
manner of "trifles" down to the argument that under the Soviet
Constitution elections are "indirect," but he misses the substance
of the thing. He fails to see the *class* nature of the state apparatus, of the machinery of state: Under bourgeois democracy the
capitalists, by a thousand and one tricks—which are more artful
and effective, the more "purely" democracy is developed—keep
the masses away from the work of administration and frustrate
the freedom of the press, the right of assembly, etc. The Soviet
government is the *first* in the world (or, strictly speaking, the
second, because the Paris Commune began to do the same thing)

to *attract* the masses, precisely the *exploited* masses, to the work of administration. For the toiling masses, participation in bourgeois parliaments (which *never decide* the most important questions under bourgeois democracy, because they are decided by the stock exchange and the banks) is hindered by a thousand and one obstacles, and the workers know and feel, see and realize perfectly well that the bourgeois parliaments are alien institutions to them, are an *instrument for the oppression* of the proletariat by the bourgeoisie, are an institution of the hostile class, of the exploiting minority.

The Soviets are the direct organization of the toiling and exploited masses themselves, enabling them to organize and administer the state themselves in every possible way. And it is precisely the vanguard of the toiling and exploited, the urban proletariat, that gains the advantage of this, because it is best organized by the large enterprises; it is much easier for it to elect and to watch elections. The Soviet organization automatically *helps* unite all the toilers and exploited around their vanguard, the proletariat. The old bourgeois apparatus, the bureaucracy, the privileges of wealth, of bourgeois education, of social connections, etc., which are the more varied the more highly bourgeois democracy is developed—all this disappears under the Soviet organization. Freedom of the press ceases to be hypocrisy, because the printing presses and stocks of paper are taken away from the bourgeoisie. The same thing applies to the best buildings, the palaces, the mansions and manor houses. The Soviet government has taken thousands and thousands of these best buildings from the exploiters, and in this way it has made the right of assembly —without which democracy is a fraud—a million times more "democratic." The indirect elections to the non-local Soviets make it easier to hold congresses of Soviets, it makes the *entire* apparatus less costly, more flexible, more accessible to the workers and peasants at a time when life is seething and it is necessary to be able quickly to recall a deputy or to elect him to the General Congress of Soviets.

Proletarian democracy is a million times more democratic than any bourgeois democracy; the Soviet government is a million times more democratic than the most democratic bourgeois republic. (*Selected Works*, VII, 133–135.)

Is there a single country in the world, even among the most democratic bourgeois countries, in which the *average rank and file* worker, the average rank and file *village laborer,* or village semiproletarian generally (i.e., the representative of the oppressed masses, the overwhelming majority of the population), enjoys anything approaching such *liberty* to hold meetings in the best buildings, such *liberty* to use the best printing works and largest stocks of paper, to express his ideas and to protect his interests, such liberty to promote men and women of his own class to administer and to "run" the state as in Soviet Russia? (*Selected Works*, VII, 135.)

In Russia the bureaucratic apparatus has been completely smashed up, not a stone of it has been left unturned; the old judges have all been expelled, the bourgeois has been dispersed— and *far more accessible* representation has been given to the workers and peasants; *their* Soviets have replaced the bureaucrats, or *their* Soviets now control the bureaucrats, and *their* Soviets now elect the judges. This fact alone is enough to cause all the oppressed classes to recognize the Soviet government, i.e., the present form of the dictatorship of the proletariat, as being a million times more democratic than the most democratic bourgeois republic. (*Selected Works,* VII, 136.)

CAN THERE BE EQUALITY BETWEEN THE EXPLOITED AND THE EXPLOITERS?

Kautsky says: "The exploiters always represented only a small minority of the population." This is certainly true. Taking this as the starting point, what should be the argument? One may argue in a Marxian, in a socialist way, taking as a basis the relation between the exploited and the exploiter; or one may argue in a liberal, in a bourgeois-democratic way, taking as a basis the relation between the majority and the minority. If we argue in a Marxian way we must say: The exploiters inevitably transform the state (we are speaking of democracy, i.e., one of the forms of the state) into an instrument for the domination of their class, of the exploiters, over the exploited. Hence, so long as there are exploiters who rule the majority, the exploited, the democratic state must inevitably be democracy for the exploiters. The state of the exploited must fundamentally differ from such a state; it must be democracy for the exploited, and a means of suppressing the exploiters; and the suppression of a class means inequality for this class, its exclusion from "democracy."

If we argue in a liberal way, we must say: The majority decides, the minority submits. Those who do not submit are punished. That is all. Nothing need be said about the class character of the state in general, or about "pure democracy" in particular, because it is irrelevant; for a majority is a majority and a minority is a minority. A pound of flesh is a pound of flesh; and that is all there is to it.

And this is exactly the way Kautsky argues. He says: "Why should the rule of the proletariat assume, and necessarily assume, a form which is incompatible with democracy?". . . The conclusion is:

> A regime which is so strongly rooted in the masses has not the slightest reason for infringing upon democracy. It cannot always dispense with violence in cases when violence is employed to suppress democracy. Violence can only be met with violence. But a regime which knows that it has the support of the masses will employ violence only in order to *protect* democracy and not to *destroy* it. It would be simply committing suicide if it attempted to destroy its own most reliable basis—universal suffrage, that deep source of mighty moral authority. (*Selected Works*, VII, 137 f.)

Why do we need a dictatorship when we have a majority? And Marx and Engels explain: In order to break down the resistance of the bourgeoisie; in order to inspire the reactionaries with fear; in order to maintain the authority of the armed people against the bourgeoisie; in order that the proletariat may forcibly suppress its enemies! *(Selected Works,* VII, 139.)

To assume that in a revolution that is at all profound and serious the issue is decided simply by the relation between the majority and the minority is the acme of stupidity, the stupid prejudice of a common liberal, is the *deception of the masses,* concealing from them a well-established historical truth. This historical truth is that in every profound revolution, the *prolonged, stubborn, desperate* resistance of the exploiters, who for a number of years enjoy important practical advantages over the exploited, is the *rule.* Never ... will the exploiters submit to the decision of the exploited majority without making use of their advantages in a last desperate battle, or in a series of battles.

The transition from capitalism to communism represents an entire historical epoch. Until this epoch has terminated, the exploiters will inevitably cherish the hope of restoration, and this *hope* will be converted into *attempts* at restoration. *(Selected Works,* VII, 140.)

In the wake of the capitalist exploiters will be found the broad masses of the petty bourgeoisie, to whose vacillation and hesitation the historical experience of every country for decades bears witness; one day they march behind the proletariat, the next day they will take fright at the difficulties of the revolution, become panic stricken at the first defeat or semidefeat of the workers; they become irritable, they run about, snivel and rush from one camp to the other. . . . In these circumstances, in the epoch of desperate, acute war, when history is placing the question of the life and death of age-long privilege on the order of the day—at such a time to talk about majority and minority, about pure democracy, about dictatorship being unnecessary, and about equality between the exploiter and the exploited! *(Selected Works,* VII, 141.)

The necessary symptom, the necessary condition of dictatorship is the *forcible* suppression of the exploiters as a class, and, consequently, the *infringement* of "pure democracy," i.e., of equality and freedom, *for that class*. (*Selected Works*, VII, 143.)

The proletariat cannot achieve victory *without breaking the resistance* of the bourgeoisie, *without forcibly suppressing its enemies* . . . where there is "forcible suppressing," where there is no "freedom," *there, of course, is no democracy*. (*Selected Works*, VII, 143 f.*)

THE SOVIETS DARE NOT BECOME STATE ORGANIZATIONS

The Soviets are the Russian form of the proletarian dictatorship. If a Marxian theoretician, writing on the dictatorship of the proletariat, had seriously set to work to study the subject . . . he would first of all have given a general definition of dictatorship, and would then have examined its peculiar national form, the Soviets; he would have given his critique of them as one of the forms of the dictatorship of the proletariat. (*Selected Works*, VII, 145.)

This crux is the question: Should the Soviets aspire to become state organizations . . . *or*, should the Soviets not strive for this, should they refrain from taking political power in their hands, refrain from becoming state organizations and remain the "militant organizations of one class." (*Selected Works*, VII, 146 f.)

Whoever sincerely shares the Marxian view that the state is nothing but a machine for the suppression of one class by another, and who has at all reflected upon this truth, could never have reached the absurd conclusion that the proletarian organizations capable of defeating finance capital must not become transformed into state organizations. . . . Why, indeed, should the proletariat, *"one class,"* be permitted to wage determined war against *capital*, which rules not only over the proletariat, but over the whole people, over the whole of the petty bourgeoisie, over the whole peasantry, but why should this proletariat, this *"one class"* not be permitted to transform its organizations into a state organization? Because the petty bourgeois is *afraid* of the class struggle, and does not carry it to its logical conclusion, to its *main* object. (*Selected Works,* VII, 149.)

From the point of view of practical politics the idea that Soviets are necessary as fighting organizations but must not be transformed into state organizations is infinitely more absurd than from the theoretical point of view. Even in peace time, when there is no revolutionary situation, the mass struggle of the workers against the capitalists—for instance, a mass strike—causes great bitterness on both sides, gives rise to fierce passions in the struggle, to the bougeoisie insisting on remaining "master in its own house," etc. But in the time of revolution, when political life reaches the boiling point, an organization like the Soviets, which embraces *all* workers, *all* industries, *all* the soldiers and *all* the toiling and poorest section of the rural population—such an organization in the course of the struggle, by the simple logic of attack and defense, automatically has to raise the question of power *point blank.* The attempt to take up a middle position and to "reconcile" the proletariat with the bourgeoisie is sheer stupidity and is doomed to miserable failure. (*Selected Works,* VII, 150 f.)

V

NATIONAL QUESTION

1. COLONIZATION

We have shown how erroneous was the theory that links up the question of the foreign market for capitalism with the question of the realization of the product. The fact that capitalism stands in need of a foreign market is explained, not by the impossibility of realizing the product on the home market, but by the fact that capitalism is unable to repeat one and the same process of production in the same magnitude in unchanged conditions (as was the case under the pre-capitalist system), and that it inevitably leads to the unlimited growth of production which overflows the old, narrow limits of previous economic units. In view of the unevenness of development which is a feature of capitalism, one branch of production surpasses the others and strives to extend beyond the boundaries of the old radius of economic relations. Take, for example, the textile industry at the beginning of the post-Reform epoch. Being fairly well developed capitalistically (manufacture, which was beginning to change over to factory production), it was in complete command of the market in central Russia. But the big factories, which sprang up so rapidly, could not be satisfied with the previous dimensions of the market; they began to seek farther afield, among the new population that colonized Novorossia, the Southeast Volga region, North Caucasus, Siberia, etc. The effort on the part of the big factories to stretch out beyond the boundaries of the old markets cannot be doubted. But does that mean that the districts that served as these old markets could not absorb a larger quantity of textile goods? Does it mean that the industrial and central agricultural guberniyas, for example, cannot absorb a larger quantity of manufactured goods? It does not. We know that the disintegration of the peasantry, the growth of commercial agriculture and the increase in the industrial population continued, and still continue, to enlarge the home market even in this old region. But the expansion of the home market is retarded by many circumstances (chiefly by the preservation of obsolete institutions which retard the development of agricultural capitalism), and the manufacturers will not, of course, wait until the other branches of the national economy catch up to the textile industry in their capitalist development. The manufacturers must have a market at once, and if the backwardness of the other branches of industry restricts the market in the old district, they will seek for markets in another district, or in other countries, or in the colonies of the old country.

But what is a colony in the politico-economic sense? ... According to Marx, the main features of this concept are the following: (1) the existence of unoccupied, free land, easily accessible to settlers; (2) the existence of developed world division of labor, a world market, thanks to which the colonies can specialize in the mass production of agricultural products and receive in exchange finished manufactured goods "which, under other circumstances, they would have to manufacture themselves.". . . The southern and eastern outlying regions of European Russia which were colonized in the post-Reform epoch bear these distinctive features and represent, in the economic sense, the colonies of central European Russia. The term colony is still more applicable to the other outlying regions, for example, the Caucasus. The economic "conquest" of the Caucasus by Russia took place much later than its political conquest, and its complete economic subjugation has not been accomplished to this day. In the post-Reform epoch there took place, on the one hand, the intensive colonization of the Caucasus, the extensive plowing up of the land by colonists (particularly in the North Caucasus) who produced wheat, tobacco, etc., for the market, and who attracted masses of rural wage laborers from Russia. On the other hand, the ancient, native *"kustar"* industries were squeezed out by the competition of the manufactured goods brought from Moscow. The ancient gunsmith's craft declined as a result of the competition of Tula and Belgian weapons, the ancient smith's craft declined as a result of the competition of ironware brought from Russia and so also did the crafts of the coppersmith, goldsmith, silversmith, potter, soap boiler, tanner, etc. The kinds of goods produced by all these craftsmen were produced more cheaply in the Russian factories, which sent their goods to the Caucasus. The manufacture of drinking horns and beakers declined as a consequence of the decline of the feudal system in Georgia and, with it, its historical feasts; the sheepskin hat industry declined as a result of the introduction of European clothing in place of Asiatic clothing; the manufacture of wine skins and wine jugs declined because, for the first time, the wine of this district began to be sold, and, in turn, to capture the Russian market, and thus gave rise to the barrel making industry. In this way, Russian capitalism drew the Caucasus into the sphere of world commodity circulation, obliterated its local peculiarities—the remnants of ancient patriarchal isolation—and *created for itself* a market for its goods. A country which was thinly populated at the beginning of the post-Reform epoch, or populated by mountaineers who lived out of the course of world economy and even out of the course of history, was transformed into a land of oil traders, wine merchants, wheat growers and tobacco growers, and M. Coupon ruthlessly divested the proud mountaineer of his picturesque national costume and dressed him in the livery of the European lackey. Simultaneously with the growth of the colonization of the Caucasus and the accelerated growth of its agricultural population there was also a process (concealed by the latter growth) of attraction of the agricultural population into industry. From 1863 to 1897, the urban population of the Caucasus increased from 350,000 to 900,000 (the total population increased by 95 per cent from 1851 to 1897). There is no need for us to add that the same thing has taken place, and is taking place, in Central Asia, Siberia, etc.

Thus, the question naturally arises, where is the border line between the home and the foreign market? To take the political border line of a state would be too mechanical a solution, and would it be a solution? If Central Asia is a home market and Persia is a foreign market, then to which category do Khiva and Bokhara belong? If Siberia is a home market and China a foreign market, then to which category does Manchuria belong? Such questions are not of great importance, however. What is important is that the capitalist system cannot exist and develop without constantly extending its sphere of domination, without colonizing new countries and without drawing ancient, non-capitalist countries into the whirlpool of world economy. And this feature of capitalism has strongly manifested itself and continues to manifest itself in post-Reform Russia.

Hence, the process of the formation of a market for capital has two phases, viz., the development of capitalism in depth, as it were, i.e., the further growth of capitalism in agriculture and in industry in the given, definite and exclusive territory, and the development of capitalism in breadth, i.e., the extension of the sphere of domination of capitalism to new territory. In accordance with the plan of the present work, we have confined ourselves almost exclusively to the first phase of the process, and that is why we think it necessary to lay special emphasis at this point on the fact that the other phase is of extreme importance. Anything like a complete study of the process of colonization of the outlying regions and the expansion of Russian territory from the point of view of capitalist development would require a whole volume in itself. It is sufficient for us to observe here that Russia is in a particularly favorable position compared with other capitalist countries owing to the abundance of free and accessible land for colonization in its outlying regions.[1] Apart from Asiatic Russia, we have in European Russia regions which, owing to their enormous distances and bad means of communication, are economically still weakly connected with Central Russia. Take, for example, the "Far North"—the Archangel Guberniya. This boundless territory and its unlimited natural wealth is still exploited only to a most insignificant degree. One of the principal products of the region, timber, was until recently exported mainly to England. In this respect, therefore, this region of European Russia served as a foreign market for England without being a home market for Russia. The Russian entrepreneurs, of course, envied the English entrepreneurs, and now, since the railway is being extended to Archangel, they are rejoicing in anticipation of the "rise of spirit and enterprising activity in various branches of industry in the region." *The Development of Capitalism in Russia,* 1896–1898, *Selected Works,* I, 250–254.)

2. THE NATIONAL QUESTION

We have included in our draft of the Party program the demand for a republic with a democratic constitution that would, among other things, assure "the recognition of the right of self-

---

[1]The circumstance described in the text has another aspect. The development of capitalism in depth in old, long inhabited territories is retarded by the colonization of the outlying regions. The solution of the contradictions which are a feature of capitalism and which capitalism gives rise to, is temporarily postponed by the fact that capitalism can very easily develop in breadth. For example, the simultaneous existence of the most advanced forms of industry and semi-medieval forms of agriculture undoubtedly is a contradiction. If Russian capitalism were unable to expand beyond the limits of the territory it has occupied since the beginning of the post-Reform period, this contradiction between capitalist large-scale industry and the archaic institutions in rural life (the tying down of the peasant to the land, etc.) would very soon have led to the abolition of these institutions and to the complete clearing of the path of agricultural capitalism in Russia. But the possibility of seeking and finding a market in the outlying regions which are being colonized (for the manufacturer), the possibility of moving to new territories (for the peasants) softens this contradiction and retards its solution. It goes without saying that such a retardation of the growth of capitalism is tantamount to preparing for an even greater and more extensive growth in the near future.

determination to all the nationalities contained in the state."
As many did not find this point in our program sufficiently clear,
we took occasion . . . to explain the meaning of this point
in the following way: The Social Democrats will always combat
every attempt to influence national self-determination by violence
or by any injustice from without. But our unqualified recognition of the struggle for the right of self-determination does
not commit us to supporting every demand for national self-
determination. Social Democracy, as the party of the proletariat,
considers it to be its positive and principal task to advance the
self-determination of the working class within each nationality
rather than the self-determination of peoples and nationalities.
We must always and unconditionally strive to achieve the
closest unity of the proletariat of all nationalities, and only in
isolated and exceptional cases may we advance and actively support demands tending to set up a new class state or to substitute
a loose federal unity for the complete political unity of a state.

. . . .

That program [right of self-determination] does not preclude
the Polish proletariat adopting the slogan of a free and independent Polish republic, even though the probability of its becoming a reality before the introduction of socialism is infinitesi-
mal. The program merely demands that a genuinely socialist
party shall not corrupt proletarian consciousness, or slur over
the class struggle, or seduce the working class by bourgeois-
democratic phrases, or disrupt the unity of the contemporary
political struggle of the proletariat. The whole point lies in
this reservation, for only with this reservation do we recognize
self-determination. It is useless for the Polish Socialist Party to
pretend that they differ from the Russian and German Social
Democrats in that the latter reject the right of self determination,
the right to aspire to a free and independent republic. It is not
this, but the fact that they forget the class point of view, obscure
it by chauvinism and disrupt the unity of the contemporary political struggle, that prevents us from regarding the Polish Socialist
party as a genuine Social Democratic Labor party. This, for
instance, is the way the Polish Socialist party usually formulates

the question: ". . . We can only *weaken* tsarism by wresting
Poland from it, the Russian comrades must overthrow it." Or
again: ". . . after the overthrow of tsarism we would simply take
our fate into our own hands and secede from Russia." See to
what monstrous conclusions this monstrous logic leads, even from
the point of view of the program demand for the restoration of
Poland. *Because* the restoration of Poland is one of the possible
consequences of democratic evolution (but by no means certain,
as long as the bourgeoisie rules), *therefore,* the Polish proletariat
must not fight together with the Russian proletariat to overthrow
tsarism, but "only" to weaken it by wresting Poland from it.
Because Russian tsarism is concluding a closer and closer alliance
with the bourgeoisie and the governments of Germany, Austria,
etc., *therefore,* the Polish proletariat must weaken its alliance with
the proletariat of Russia, Germany, etc., by whose side it is now
fighting against a *common* yoke. This is nothing more nor less
than sacrificing the most vital interests of the proletariat for the
bourgeois-democratic interpretation of national independence.
The disintegration of Russia, which the Polish Socialist party
desires, *in contrast* with our aim of overthrowing tsarism, is and
will remain a hollow phrase as long as economic evolution continues to unite the different parts of a political whole more and
more closely and as long as the bourgeoisie of all countries unites
more and more against its common enemy, the proletariat, and in
support of its common ally, the tsar. But the *split in the proletariat,* which is now suffering under the yoke of tsarism, is the
sad reality, the direct consequence of the error of the Polish
Socialist party, the direct result of its admiration for bourgeois-
democratic formula, (*The National Question in Our Program,*
July, 1903, *Selected Works,* II, 322, 328 f.)

WHAT IS SELF-DETERMINATION OF NATIONS?

Naturally, this is the first question to arise when any attempt
is made to consider what self-determination is, from a Marxist
viewpoint. What is meant by that term? . . . Self determination
of nations is dealt with not only in the Russian program of 1903,
but also in the resolution of the London International Congress
of 1896.

This is not the first time national movements have arisen in Russia, nor are they peculiar to Russia alone. Throughout the world, the period of the final victory of capitalism over feudalism has been linked with national movements. The economic basis of these movements is the fact that in order to achieve complete victory for commodity production the bourgeoisie must capture the home market, must have politically united territories with a population speaking the same language, and all obstacles to the development of this language and to its consolidation in literature must be removed. Language is the most important means of human intercourse. Unity of language and its unimpeded development are most important conditions for genuinely free and extensive commercial intercourse on a scale commensurate with modern capitalism, for a free and broad grouping of the population in all its separate classes and, lastly, for the establishment of close connection between the market and each and every proprietor, big or little, seller and buyer.

Therefore, the tendency of every national movement is toward the formation of *national states,* under which these requirements of modern capitalism are best satisfied. The profoundest economic factors drive toward this goal, and therefore, for the whole of Western Europe, nay, for the entire civilized world, the *typical,* normal state for the capitalist period is the national state.

Consequently, if we want to learn the meaning of self-determination of nations not by juggling with legal definitions, or "inventing" abstract definitions, but by examining the historical and economic conditions of the national movements, we shall inevitably reach the conclusion that self-determination of nations means the political separation of these nations from alien national bodies, the formation of an independent national state.

Later on we shall see still other reasons why it would be incorrect to understand the right to self-determination to mean anything but the right to separate state existence.

.   .   .   .

There is no doubt that the greater part of Asia, the most populous part of the world, consists either of colonies of the "great powers" or of states which are extremely dependent and oppressed as nations. But does this commonly known circumstance in any way shake the undoubted fact that in Asia itself the conditions for the most complete development of commodity production, for the freest, widest and speediest growth of capitalism, have been created only in Japan, *i.e.,* only in an independent national state? This state is a bourgeois state, therefore, it, itself has begun to oppress other nations and to enslave colonies. We cannot say whether Asia will have time before the downfall of capitalism to become crystallized into a system of independent national states, like Europe; but it remains an undisputed fact that capitalism, having awakened Asia, has called forth national movements everywhere in that continent, too; that the tendency of these movements is toward the creation of national states there; that the best conditions for the development of capitalism are ensured precisely by such states.

.   .   .   .

The national state is the rule and the "norm" of capitalism; the heterogeneous nation state represents backwardness, or is an exception. From the standpoint of national relations, the best conditions for the development of capitalism are undoubtedly provided by the national state. This does not mean, of course, that such a state, based on bourgeois relations, could eliminate the exploitation and oppression of nations. It only means that Marxists cannot ignore the powerful *economic* factors that give rise to the aspiration to create national states. It means that "self-determination of nations" in the program of the Marxists *cannot* from a historical-economic point of view, have any other meaning than political self-determination, political independence, the formation of a national state.

.   .   .   .

The categorical demand of Marxist theory in examining any social question is that the question be formulated within *definite* historical limits, and if it refers to a particular country (e.g., the national program for a given country), the specific features that distinguish that country from others within the same historical epoch be taken into account.

What does this categorical demand of Marxism imply as regards the question we are discussing?

First of all, it implies that a strict distinction must be drawn between two periods of capitalism, which differ radically from each other as far as the national movement is concerned. On the one hand, the period of the downfall of feudalism and absolutism, the period of the formation of bourgeois-democratic society and state, when the national movements for the first time become mass movements and in one way or another draw *all* classes of the population into politics by means of the press, participation in representative institutions, etc. On the other hand, we have the period of definitely crystallized capitalist states with a long-established constitutional regime, with a strongly developed antagonism between the proletariat and the bourgeoisie—the period that may be called the eve of the downfall of capitalism.

The typical features of the first period are the awakening of national movements and the drawing of the peasants, the most numerous and the most "sluggish" section of the population, into these movements, in connection with the struggle for political liberty in general and for national rights in particular. The typical features of the second period are the absence of mass bourgeois-democratic movements; the fact that developed capitalism, while bringing the nations that have already been fully drawn into commercial intercourse closer together and causing them to intermingle to an increasing degree, pushes into the forefront the antagonism between internationally united capital and the international labor movement.

Of course, the two periods cannot be separated into watertight compartments; they are connected by numerous transitional links, while the various countries differ from each other in the rapidity of their national development, in national composition and distribution of their population, and so forth. The Marxists of a given country cannot proceed to draw up their national program without taking into account all these general historical and concrete state conditions.

.   .   .   .

In Western, continental Europe, the period of the bourgeois-democratic revolutions embraces a fairly definite portion of time, approximately from 1789 to 1871. This was precisely the period of national movements and the creation of national states. When this period drew to a close Western Europe had been transformed into a settled system of bourgeois states, which, as a general rule, were national uniform states. . . . In Eastern Europe and in Asia the period of bourgeois-democratic revolutions only began in 1905. The revolutions in Russia, Persia, Turkey and China, the wars in the Balkans, such is the chain of world events of *our* period in our "Orient." And only the blind can fail to see in this chain of events the awakening of a *whole series* of bourgeois-democratic national movements, strivings to create nationally independent and nationally uniform states. It is precisely and solely because Russia and the neighboring countries are passing through this period that we require an item in our program on the rights of nations to self-determination.

.   .   .   .

In Austria this revolution began in 1848, and was over in 1867. Since then, for nearly half a century, there has prevailed what on the whole is an established bourgeois constitution on the basis of which a legal workers' party is legally functioning.

Therefore, in the inherent conditions of the development of Austria (*i.e.,* from the standpoint of the development of capitalism in Austria in general, and among its separate nations in particular), there are *no* factors that produce leaps, one of the concomitants of which may be the formation of nationally independent states.

The entirely different relations between the nationalities in Austria and in Russia are particularly important for the question we are concerned with. Not only was Austria for a long time a state in which the Germans were predominant, but the Austrian Germans laid claim to hegemony in the German nation as a whole. This "claim". . . was defeated in the war of 1866. The German nation predominating in Austria found itself *outside the pale* of the independent German state which finally took shape in 1871. On the other hand, the attempt of the Hungarians to create an independent national state collapsed as far back as 1849, under the blows of the Russian army of serfs.

A very peculiar situation was thus created: a striving on the part of the Hungarians and then of the Czechs, not for separation from Austria, but on the contrary, for the preservation of Austria's integrity, precisely in order to preserve national independence, which might have been completely crushed by more rapacious and powerful neighbors! Owing to this peculiar situation, Austria assumed the form of a double-centered (dual) state, and is now being transformed into a triple-centered (triune) state (Germans, Hungarians, Slavs).

Is there anything like this in Russia? Is there in our country a striving of "alien races" for unity with the Great Russians in order to escape a *worse* national oppression?

It suffices to put this question to see that the comparison between Russia and Austria in the question of self-determination of nations is senseless, platitudinous and ignorant.

The peculiar conditions in Russia as regards the national question are just the reverse of those we see in Austria. Russia is a state with a single national center—Great Russia. The Great Russians occupy a vast, uninterrupted stretch of territory, and number about 70,000,000. The specific features of this national state are, first, that "alien races" (which, on the whole, form the majority of the entire population—57 per cent) inhabit the border regions. Second, the oppression of these alien races is much worse than in the neighboring states (and not in the European states alone). Third, in a number of cases the oppressed nationalities inhabiting the border regions have compatriots across the border who enjoy greater national independence (suffice it to mention the Finns, the Swedes, the Poles, the Ukrainians and the Rumanians along the western and southern frontiers of the state). Fourth, the development of capitalism and the general level of culture are often higher in the border regions inhabited by "alien races" than in the center. Lastly, it is precisely in the neighboring Asian states that we observe incipient bourgeois revolutions and national movements, which partly affect the kindred nationalities within the border of Russia.

Thus, it is precisely the concrete, historical specific features of the national question in Russia that make the recognition of the right of nations to self-determination in the present period a matter of special urgency in our country.

. . . .

Let us examine the position of an oppressing nation. Can a nation be free if it oppresses other nations? It cannot. The interests of the freedom of the Great Russian population demand a struggle against such oppression. The long, agelong history of the suppression of the movements of the oppressed nations, the systematic propaganda in favor of such suppression on the part of the "upper" classes, have created enormous obstacles to the cause of freedom of the Great Russian people itself, in the form of prejudices, etc.

The Great Russian Black Hundreds deliberately foster and fan these prejudices. The Great Russian bourgeoisie tolerates them or panders to them. The Great Russian proletariat cannot achieve *its own* aims, cannot clear the road to freedom for itself unless it systematically combats these prejudices.

In Russia, the creation of an independent national state so far remains the privilege of one nation, the Great Russian nation. We, the Great Russian proletarians, defend no privileges, and we do not defend this privilege. In our fight we take the given state as our basis; we unite the workers of all nations in the given state; we cannot vouch for any particular path of national development, we are marching to our class goal by *all* possible paths.

But we cannot advance to that goal unless we combat all nationalism, unless we fight for the equality of the workers of all nations. Whether the Ukraine, for example, is destined to form an independent state is a matter that will be determined by a thousand factors, which cannot be foreseen. Without attempting idle "guesses," we firmly uphold what is beyond doubt: the right of the Ukraine to form such a state. We respect this right; we do not uphold the privileges of the Great Russians over the Ukrainians; we *teach* the masses to recognize that right, and to reject the *state* privileges of any nation.

In the leaps which all nations take in the period of bourgeois revolutions, clashes and struggle over the right to a national state are possible and probable. We proletarians declare in advance that we are *opposed* to Great Russian privileges, and this is what guides our entire propaganda and agitation.

. . . .

To make this question, which has been so confused by the Liberals (and by those who echo them in their simplicity), a little clearer, we shall cite a very simple example. Let us take the question of divorce. The reactionaries are opposed to freedom of divorce; they say that this must be "handled carefully," and loudly declare that it means the "disintegration of the family." The democrats, however, believe that the reactionaries are hypocrites, that, actually, they are defending the omnipotence of the police and the bureaucracy, the privileges of one sex, and the worst kind of oppression of women. They believe that freedom of divorce will not cause the "disintegration" of family ties but, on the contrary, will strengthen them on a democratic basis, which is the only possible and durable basis in civilized society.

To accuse the supporters of freedom of self-determination, i.e., freedom to secede, of encouraging separatism, is as foolish and as hypocritical as accusing the advocates of freedom of divorce of wishing to destroy family ties. Just as in bourgeois society the defenders of privilege and corruption, on which bourgeois marriage rests, oppose freedom of divorce, so, in the capitalist state, repudiation of the right to self-determination, i.e., the right of nations to secede, is tantamount to defending the privileges of the dominating nation and police methods of administration as against democratic methods.

Social Democrats would be equally running counter to proletarian policy and subordinating the workers to the policy of the bourgeoisie if they were to repudiate the right of nations to self-determination, i.e., the right of an oppressed nation to secede, or if they were to support all the national demands of the bourgeoisie of the oppressed nations. It makes no difference to the wage worker whether he is exploited chiefly by the Great Russian bourgeoisie rather than by the non-Russian bourgeoisie, or by the Polish bourgeoisie rather than the Jewish bourgeoisie, etc. The wage worker who understands his class interests is equally indifferent to the state privileges of the Great Russian capitalists and to the promises of the Polish or Ukrainian capitalists to set up an earthly paradise when they obtain state privileges. Capitalism is developing and will continue to develop, in one way or another, both in united heterogeneous states and in separate national states.

In any case the wage laborers will be exploited. And in order to be able to fight successfully against exploitation, the proletariat must be free of nationalism, must be absolutely neutral, so to speak, in the struggle for supremacy that is going on among the bourgeoisie of the various nations. If the proletariat of any one nation gives the slightest support to the privileges of "its" national bourgeoisie, this will inevitably arouse distrust among the proletariat of the other nation; it will weaken the international class solidarity of the workers and divide them, to the delight of the bourgeoisie. And repudiation of the right to self-determination, or secession, inevitably means, in practice, supporting the privileges of the dominating nation.

Karl Marx and Frederick Engels considered that it was the bounden duty of the whole of western European democracy, and still more of Social Democracy, actively to support the demand for the independence of Poland. For the period of the 1840's, and 1860's, the period of the bourgeois revolutions in Austria and Germany, and the period of the Peasant Reform in Russia, this point of view was quite correct and the only one that was consistently democratic and proletarian. So long as the masses of the people in Russia, and in most of the Slavic countries, were still dormant, so long as *there were no* independent, mass, democratic movements in these countries, the *aristocratic* liberation movement in Poland assumed immense, paramount importance from the point of view, not only of Russian, not only of Slavic, but of European democracy as a whole.

While this view of Marx was correct for the 40's, 50's and 60's or for the third quarter of the nineteenth century, it has ceased to be correct in the twentieth century. Independent democratic movements, and even an independent proletarian movement, have arisen in most Slavic countries, even in one of the most backward Slavic countries, Russia. Aristocratic Poland has disappeared, yielding place to capitalist Poland. Under such circumstances Poland could not but lose its *exceptional* revolutionary importance.

The attempt of the Polish Socialist party... to "fix" for all time the point of view Marx held in a *different epoch* was an attempt to use the *letter* of Marxism against the *spirit* of Marxism. Therefore, the Polish Social Democrats were quite right when they attacked the extreme nationalism of the Polish petty bourgeoisie and pointed out that the national question was of secondary importance for Polish workers, when they for the first time created a purely proletarian party in Poland and proclaimed the extremely important principle that the Polish and the Russian workers must maintain the closest alliance in their class struggle.

But did this mean that at the beginning of the twentieth century the International could regard the principle of political self-determination of nations, or the right to secession, as superfluous for eastern Europe and for Asia? This would have been the height of absurdity, and (theoretically) tantamount to admitting that the bourgeois democratic reformation of the Turkish, Russian and Chinese states has been consummated, would have been tantamount (in effect) to opportunism toward despotism.

No. During the period of incipient bourgeois-democratic revolutions in eastern Europe and Asia, during the period of the awakening and intensification of national movements, during the period of formation of independent proletarian parties, the task of these parties in connection with national policy must be twofold: first, to recognize the right to self-determination for all nations, because the bourgeois-democratic reformation is not yet consummated, because working-class democracy consistently, seriously and sincerely . . . fights for equal rights for nations, and, second, to maintain the closest, inseparable alliance in the class struggle of the proletarians of all nations in a given state, throughout all the vicissitudes of its history, irrespective of any reshaping of the frontiers of the individual states by the bourgeoisie.

.   .   .   .

To sum up:

From the point of view of the theory of Marxism in general the question of the right of self-determination presents no difficulties. No one can seriously dispute the London resolution of 1896, or the fact that self-determination implies only the right to secession, or the fact that the formation of independent national states is the tendency of all bourgeois-democratic revolutions.

The difficulty is created to a certain extent by the fact that in Russia the proletariat of both oppressed and oppressing nations are fighting and must fight side by side. The task is to preserve the unity of the class struggle of the proletariat for socialism, to resist all the bourgeois and Black Hundred nationalist influences. Among the oppressed nations the separate organizations of the proletariat as an independent party sometimes leads to such a bitter struggle against the nationalism of the respective nation that the perspective becomes distorted and the nationalism of the oppressing nation is forgotten.

But this distortion of the perspective cannot last long. The experience of the joint struggle of the proletarians of various nations has demonstrated only too plainly that we must formulate political questions . . . from the all-Russian point of view. And in all-Russian politics it is the Cadets and the revolutionary landowners who rule. Their ideas are predominant, their persecution of alien races for "separatism," for their *thinking* about secession, is being preached and practised in the Duma, in the schools, in the churches, in the barracks and in hundreds and thousands of newspapers. It is this Great Russian poison of nationalism that is contaminating the entire all-Russian political atmosphere. It is the misfortune of a nation, which, in subjugating other nations, is strengthening reaction throughout Russia. The memories of 1849 and 1863 form a living political tradition, which, unless great storms sweep the country, threatens to hamper every democratic and *especially* every Social Democratic movement for many decades.

There can be no doubt that, however natural the point of view of certain Marxists of the oppressed nations (whose "misfortune" is sometimes that the masses of the population are blinded by the idea of "their" national liberation) may appear sometimes, *in reality* the objective alignment of class forces in Russia makes refusal to advocate the right of self-determination tantamount to the worst opportunism. . . .

. . . .

Even now, and probably for a fairly long time to come, proletarian democracy must reckon with the nationalism of the Great Russian peasants (not in the sense of making concessions to it, but in the sense of combating it). The awakening of nationalism among the oppressed nations, which became so pronounced after 1905 . . . will inevitably cause the intensification of nationalism among the Great Russian petty bourgeoisie in town and country. The slower the democratization of Russia, the more persistent, brutal and bitter will be national persecution and quarreling among the bourgeoisie of the various nations. The particularly reactionary spirit of the Russian Cadets will at the same time engender (and strengthen) "separatist" tendencies among the various oppressed nationalities which sometimes enjoy far greater freedom in the neighboring states.

Such a state of affairs sets the proletariat of Russia a twofold, or, rather, a two-sided task: first, to fight against all nationalism and, above all, against Great Russian nationalism; to recognize not only complete equality of rights for all nations in general, but also equality of rights as regards forming an independent state, i.e., the right of nations to self-determination, to secession. And second, precisely in the interests of the successful struggle against the nationalism of all nations in *any* form, it sets the task of preserving the unity of the proletarian struggle and of the proletarian organizations, of amalgamating these organizations into an international association, in spite of the bourgeois strivings for national segregation.

Complete equality of rights for all nations; the right of nations to self-determination; the amalgamation of the workers of all nations—this is the national program that Marxism, the experience of the whole world and the experience of Russia, teaches the workers. (*The Right of Nations to Self-Determination,* February–May, 1914 (New York: International Publishers, 1951), pp. 9–64. Compare with *Selected Works,* IV, 249, 250, 251, 253–254, 255–256, 260, 261, 262, 267, 268, 271, 272, 289, 291, 292, 293.)

SELF-DETERMINATION OF NATIONS

The most widespread deception of the people by the bourgeoisie in the present war consists in hiding its predatory aims under an ideology of "national liberation." The English promise freedom to Belgium, the Germans to Poland, etc. As we have seen, this is in reality a war of the oppressors of the majority of the nations of the world for deepening and widening such oppression.

The Socialists cannot reach their great aim without fighting against every form of national oppression. They must therefore unequivocally demand that the Social Democrats of the *oppressing* countries (of the so-called great nations in particular) should recognize and defend the right of the *oppressed* nations to self-determination in the political sense of the word, i.e., the right to political separation. A Socialist of a great nation or a nation possessing colonies who does not defend this right is a chauvinist.

To defend this right does in no way mean to encourage the formation of small states, but on the contrary it leads to a freer, more fearless and therefore wider and more universal formation of larger governments and unions of governments—a phenomenon more advantageous for the masses and more in accord with economic development.

On the other hand, the Socialists of the *oppressed* nations must unequivocally fight for complete unity of the *workers* of both the oppressed and the oppressor nationalities (which also means organizational unity). The idea of a lawful separation between one nationality and the other (the so-called national cultural autonomy) is a reactionary idea.

Imperialism is the period of an increasing oppression of the nations of the whole world by a handful of "great" nations; the struggle for a Socialist international revolution against imperialism is therefore impossible without the recognition of the right of nations to self-determination. "No people oppressing other peoples can be free" (Marx and Engels). No proletariat reconciling itself to the least violation by "its" nation of the rights of other nations can be socialist. (From *Socialism and War*, July–August, 1915. Compare with *The Right of Nations to Self-Determination* (New York: International Publishers, 1951), p. 65.)

The Zimmerwald Manifesto,[2] like the majority of the programs of the Social Democratic parties or their resolutions on tactics, proclaims the right of nations to self-determination. Comrade Parabellum, in Nos. 252 and 523 of the *Berner Tagwacht*,[3] declares the "struggle for the non-existent right to self-determination" to be illusory; this struggle he contrasts with a "revolutionary mass struggle of the proletariat against capitalism," at the same time asserting that "we are against annexations" and against all "national acts of violence."

The arguments in favor of Comrade Parabellum's position reduce themselves to the assertion that all national problems of the present, like those of Alsace-Lorraine, Armenia, etc., are problems of imperialism; that capital has outgrown the framework of national states; that it is impossible to turn the wheel of history backward to the antiquated ideal of national states, etc.

Let us see whether Comrade Parabellum's arguments are correct.

First of all, it is Comrade Parabellum who looks backward and not forward when, at the beginning of his campaign against the acceptance by the working class "of the ideal of a national state," he directs his glance toward England, France, Italy, Germany,

---

[2] The Manifesto adopted at the first international conference of representatives of Socialist parties and groups opposed to the imperialist war of 1914–18 held at Zimmerwald, Switzerland, in 1915. A Left grouping led by Lenin was formed at this conference.

[3] Article by Karl Radek (Parabellum), "Annexations and Social Democracy," in *Berner Tagwacht* (*Berne Guardian*), Nos. 252, 253, Oct. 28–29, 1915.

i.e., countries where the national movement for liberation is a thing of the past, and not toward the Orient, Asia, Africa, the colonies, where this movement is a thing not of the past, but of the present and the future. Suffice it to mention India, China, Persia, Egypt.

Imperialism, further, means that capital has outgrown the framework of national states; it means the widening and sharpening of national oppression on a new historical basis. It follows from this, in contradiction to the conception of Comrade Parabellum, that we must *connect* the revolutionary struggle for socialism with a revolutionary program on the national question.

As to Comrade Parabellum, he, in the name of a socialist revolution, scornfully rejects a consistently revolutionary program in the realm of democracy. This is incorrect. The proletariat cannot become victor save through democracy, i.e., through introducing complete democracy and through combining with every step of its movement democratic demands formulated most vigorously, most decisively. It is senseless to *contrast* the socialist revolution and the revolutionary struggle against capitalism to *one* of the questions of democracy, in this case the national question. On the contrary, we must combine the revolutionary struggle against capitalism with a revolutionary program and revolutionary tactics relative to *all* democratic demands: a republic, a militia, officials elected by the people, equal rights for women, self-determination of nations, etc. While capitalism exists, all these demands are realizable only as an exception, and in an incomplete, distorted form. Basing ourselves on democracy as it already exists, exposing its incompleteness under capitalism, we advocate the overthrow of capitalism, expropriation of the bourgeoisie as a necessary basis both for the abolition of the poverty of the masses and for a complete and manifold realization of all democratic reforms. Some of those reforms will be started prior to the overthrow of the bourgeoisie, others in the process of the overthrow, still others after it has been accomplished. The socialist revolution is by no means a single battle; on the contrary, it is an epoch of a whole series of battles around *all* problems of economic and democratic reforms, which can be completed only by the expropriation of the bourgeoisie. It is for the sake of this final aim that we must formulate in a consistently revolutionary manner every one of our democratic demands. It is quite conceivable that the workers of a certain country may overthrow the bourgeoisie *before* even one fundamental democratic reform has been realized in full. It is entirely inconceivable, however, that the proletariat as a historical class will be able to defeat the bourgeoisie if it is not prepared for this task by being educated in the spirit of the most consistent and determined revolutionary democracy.

Imperialism is the progressing oppression of the nations of the world by a handful of great powers; it is an epoch of wars among them for the widening and strengthening of national oppression; it is the epoch when the masses of the people are deceived by the hypocritical social-patriots, i.e., people who under the pretext of "freedom of nations," "right of nations to self-determination" and "defense of the fatherland" justify and defend the oppression of a majority of the world's nations by the great powers.

This is just why the central point in a program of Social Democrats must be that distinction between oppressing and oppressed nations, since the distinction is the essence of imperialism. ... This distinction is not important from the point of view of bourgeois pacifism, or the petty bourgeois utopia of peaceful competition between independent nations under capitalism, but it is most important from the point of view of the revolutionary struggle against imperialism. From this distinction there follows *our* consistently democratic and revolutionary definition of the "right of nations to self-determination," which is in accord with the general task of the immediate struggle for socialism. It is in the name of this right, and fighting for its unequivocal recognition, that the Social Democrats of the *oppressing* nations must demand the freedom of separation for the oppressed nations, for otherwise recognition of the equal rights of nations and international solidarity of the workers in reality remains an empty phrase, a hypocritical gesture. The Social Democrats of the *oppressed* nations, however, must view as foremost the demand for the unity and the *fusion* of the workers of the oppressed nations with the workers of the oppressing nations, because otherwise those Social Democrats involuntarily become the allies of one or the other national bourgeoisie, which *always* betrays the interest of the people and of democracy, and which in its turn is *always* ready for annexations and for oppressing other nations.

The approach to the national problem by the end of the 60's of the nineteenth century may serve as an instructive example. The petty bourgeois democrats, devoid of every idea concerning the class struggle and the socialist revolution, pictured a utopia of peaceful competition between free and equal nations under capitalism. The Proudhonists "denied" entirely the national question and the right of self-determination of nations and precisely from the point of view of the immediate tasks of a social revolution. Marx scoffed at Proudhonism showing its affinity to chauvinism ("All Europe must sit quietly and obediently on its behind until the masters abolish 'poverty and ignorance' in France; by the denial of the national question, they seem to understand, without being aware of it, the swallowing up of the nations by the exemplary French nation"). Marx demanded the *separation of Ireland* from England, "although after the separation there may come federation," and not from the standpoint of the petty bourgeois utopia of a peaceful capitalism, not from considerations of "justice to Ireland," but from the standpoint of the interests of the revolutionary struggle of the proletariat of the *oppressing*, i.e., *the English, nation* against capitalism. The freedom of *that* nation was cramped and mutilated by the fact that it oppressed another nation. The internationalism of the *English* proletariat would have remained a hypocritical phase were *it* not to demand the separation of Ireland. Marx never was in favor of small states, or of splitting up states, or of the federation principle. Still he considered the separation of an oppressed nation as a step toward federation, consequently not toward a splitting of nations but toward concentration, toward political and economic concentration, but concentration on the basis of democracy. From Comrade Parabellum's standpoint,

Marx must have fought an "illusory" battle when he demanded the separation of Ireland. In reality, however, only this demand was a consistent revolutionary program, only it corresponded to internationalism, only it represented concentration *not* along the lines of imperalism.

The imperialism of our days has brought about a situation where the oppression of nations by the great powers is a common phenomenon. It is precisely the standpoint of struggle against the social patriots of the great power nations that are now waging an imperialist war for the purpose of strengthening the oppression of nations—that are oppressing the majority of nations the world and the majority of the earth's population—it is precisely this standpoint that must become the decisive, cardinal, basic point in the Social Democratic national program.

. . . .

Russia *is* a prison of peoples not only because of the military, feudal character of tsarism, not only because the Great Russian bourgeoisie supports tsarism, but also because the Polish, Lettish, etc., bourgeoisie has sacrificed the freedom of nations and democracy in general for the interests of capitalist expansion. The proletariat of Russia, marching at the head of the people, cannot complete the victorious democratic revolution (which is its immediate task); neither can it fight with its brothers, the proletarians of Europe, for a social revolution, without demanding at once full and *"unreserved"* freedom of separation from Russia for all the nations oppressed by Russia. This we demand not as something independent from our revolutionary struggle for socialism, but because this struggle would remain an idle phrase if it were not linked with a revolutionary approach to all the questions of democracy, including the national question. We demand the freedom of self-determination, i.e., independence, i.e., the freedom of separation for the oppressed nations, not because we dream of an economically atomized world, nor because we cherish the ideal of small states, but on the contrary because we are for large states and for a coming closer, even a fusion of nations, but on a truly democratic, truly internationalist basis, which is *unthinkable* without the freedom of separation. In the same way as Marx in 1869 demanded the separation of Ireland, not for the purpose of splitting England, but for a subsequent free alliance of Ireland with England, not for the sake of "justice to Ireland," but for the interests of the revolutionary struggle of the *English* proletariat, so we at present consider the refusal by the Socialists of Russia to demand freedom of self-determination for the nations, in the sense indicated by us above, as a direct betrayal of democracy, internationalism and socialism. (*The Revolutionary Proletariat and the Right of Nations to Self-Determination*, November, 1915. Compare with *Selected Works*, V, 282–286; 288, and *The Right of Nations to Self-Determination* (New York: International Publishers, 1951), pp. 66–72.)

The right of nations to self-determination means only the right to independence in a political sense, the right to free, political secession from the oppressing nation. Concretely, this political, democratic demand implies complete freedom to carry on agitation in favor of secession, and freedom to settle the question of secession by means of a referendum of the nation that desires to secede. Consequently, this demand is by no means identical with the demand for secession, for partition, for the formation of small states. It is merely the logical expression of the struggle against national oppression in every form. The more closely the democratic system of state approximates to complete freedom of secession, the rarer and weaker will the striving for secession be in practice; for the advantages of large states, both from the point of view of economic progress and from the point of view of the interests of the masses, are beyond doubt, and these advantages increase with the growth of capitalism. The recognition of self-determination is not the same as making federation a principle. One may be a determined opponent of this principle and a partisan of democratic centralism and yet prefer federation to national inequality as the only path toward complete democratic centralism. . . .

The aim of socialism is not only to abolish the present division of mankind into small states and all national isolation; not only to bring the nations closer to each other, but also to merge them. . . .

Just as mankind can achieve the abolition of classes only by passing through the transition period of the dictatorship of the oppressed class, so mankind can achieve the inevitable merging of nations only by passing through the transition period of complete liberation of all the oppressed nations, i.e., their freedom to secede.

.   .   .   .

The proletariat cannot evade the question that is particularly "unpleasant" for the imperialist bourgeoisie, namely, the question of the *frontiers* of a state that is based on national oppression. The proletariat cannot but fight against the forcible retention of the oppressed nations within the boundaries of a given state, and this is exactly what the struggle for the right of self-determination means. The proletariat must demand the right of political secession for the colonies and for the nations that "its own" nation oppresses. Unless it does this, proletarian internationalism will remain a meaningless phrase; mutual confidence and class solidarity between the workers of the oppressing and oppressed nations will be impossible. . . .

The Socialists of the oppressed nations, on the other hand, must particularly fight for and maintain complete, absolute unity (also organizational) between the workers of the oppressed nation and the workers of the oppressing nation. Without such unity it will be impossible to maintain an independent proletarian policy and class solidarity with the proletariat of other countries in the face of all subterfuge, treachery and trickery of the bourgeoisie; for the bourgeoisie of the oppressed nations always converts the slogan of national liberation into a means for deceiving the workers; in internal politics it utilizes these slogans as a means for concluding reactionary agreements with the bourgeoisie of the ruling nation (for instance, the Poles in Austria and Russia, who entered into pacts with reaction in order to oppress the Jews and the Ukrainians); in the realm of foreign politics it strives to enter into pacts with one of the rival imperialist powers for the purpose of achieving its own predatory aims (the policies of the small states in the Balkans, etc.).

The fact that the struggle for national liberation against one imperialist power may, under certain circumstances, be utilized by another great power in its equally imperialist interests should have no more weight in inducing Social Democracy to renounce its recognition of the right of nations to self-determination than the numerous cases of the bourgeoisie utilizing republican slogans for the purpose of political deception and financial robbery, for example, in the Latin countries, have had in inducing them to renounce republicanism. (From *The Socialist Revolution and the Right of Nations to Self-Determination,* January–February, 1916. Compare with *The Right of Nations to Self-Determination* (New York: International Publishers, 1951), pp. 76–78.)

The most difficult but most important task is to merge the class struggle of the workers in the oppressing nations with the class struggle of the workers in the oppressed nations.

. . . .

In Russia—where no less than 57 per cent, i.e., over 100,000,000 of the population, belong to oppressed nations, where those nations mainly inhabit the border provinces, where some of those nations are more cultured than the Great Russians, where the political system is distinguished by its particularly barbarous and medieval character, where the bourgeois-democratic revolution has not yet been completed—the recognition of the right of the nations oppressed by tsarism to free secession from Russia is absolutely obligatory for Social Democracy in the interests of its democratic and socialist tasks. (*The Socialist Revolution and the Right of Nations to Self-Determination,* March, 1916, *Selected Works,* V, 270 f., 271–273, 275, 278.)

It is necessary to explain what annexations mean, and why and how Socialists must fight against them. Not *every* appropriation of "foreign" territory may be described as annexation, for, generally speaking, Socialists are in favor of abolishing frontiers between nations and the formation of larger states; nor may every disturbance of the *status quo* be described as annexation, for this would be extremely reactionary and a mockery of the fundamental concepts of the science of history; nor may every military appropriation of territory be called annexation, for

Socialists cannot repudiate violence and wars in the interests of the majority of the population. The term annexation must be applied only to the appropriation of territory *against the will* of the population of that territory, in other words, the concept "annexation" is inseparably bound up with the concept "self-determination of nations."

.   .   .   .

It is not sufficient for the Socialists in every country to pay lip service to the equality of nations, or to declaim, vow and solemnly declare that they are opposed to annexations. The Socialists in every country must demand immediate and unconditional *freedom of secession* for the colonies and nations that are oppressed by *their* own "fatherland." (*Proposals . . . to the Second Socialist Conference,* April, 1916, *Selected Works,* V, 236, 237.

. . . Marx was in favor of Polish independence in the interests of *European* democracy in its struggle against the power and influence—we may say, against the omnipotence and predominating reactionary influence—of tsarism. That this attitude was correct was most clearly and practically demonstrated in 1849, when the Russian serf army crushed the national liberation and revolutionary-democratic rebellion in Hungary. From that time until Marx's death, and even later, until 1890, when there was a danger that tsarism, allied with France, would wage a reactionary war against a *non-imperialist* but nationally independent Germany, Engels stood first and foremost for a struggle against tsarism. It was for this reason, and exclusively for this reason, that Marx and Engels were opposed to the national movement of the Czechs and South Slavs. A simple comparison with what Marx and Engels wrote in 1848 and 1849 will prove to any one who is interested in Marxism, not merely in order to brush Marxism aside, that Marx and Engels at that time drew a clear and definite *distinction* between "whole reactionary peoples" serving as "Russian outposts" in Europe, and "revolutionary peoples," namely, the Germans, Poles and Magyars. This is a fact. And this fact was indicated *at the time with incontrovertible* truth: in 1848 revolutionary peoples fought for liberty, the principal enemy of which was tsarism, whereas the Czechs, etc., were really reactionary nations, outposts of tsarism.

What does this concrete example, which must be analyzed *concretely* if one wishes to be true to Marxism, imply? Only this: (1) that the interests of the liberation of a number of big and very big nations in Europe stand higher than the interests of the movement for liberation of small nations; (2) that a democratic demand must not be considered in isolation, but on a European —today we should say a world—scale.

Nothing more. There is not a hint in this of repudiation of the elementary socialist principle . . . that no nation can be free if it oppresses other nations. If the concrete situation which confronted Marx in the epoch when tsarist influence was predominant in international politics were to repeat itself, for instance, in such a form that a number of nations were to start a socialist revolution (as a bourgeois-democratic revolution was started in Europe in 1848), while *other* nations serve as the chief bulwarks of bourgeois reaction—then we would have to be in favor of a revolutionary war against the latter, in favor of "crushing" them, in favor of destroying all their outposts, no matter what small national movements arose there. Consequently, we must not discard examples of Marx's tactics—this would mean professing Marxism in words while discarding it in practice —we must anlayze them concretely and draw invaluable lessons from them for the future. The various demands of democracy, including self-determination, are not absolute, but a *small* part of the general democratic (now: general Socialist) *world* movement. Possibly, in individual concrete cases, the part may contradict the whole; if so, it must be rejected. It is possible that the republican movement in one country may be merely an instrument of the clerical or financial-monarchical intrigues of other countries; if so, we must *not* support this particular, concrete movement. But it would be ridiculous on these grounds to delete the demand for a republic from the program of international Social Democracy. (From *The Discussion on Self-Determination Summed Up,* July, 1916. Compare with *The Right of Nations to Self-Determination* (New York: International Publishers, 1951), pp. 103–105.)

As regards the national question, the proletarian party first of all must insist on the promulgation and immediate realization of complete freedom of secession from Russia for all nations and peoples who were oppressed by tsarism, or who were forcibly annexed to, or forcibly retained within, the boundaries of the state. . . .The proletarian party strives to create as large a state as possible, for that is to the advantage of the toilers; it strives to bring about *closer ties* between nations and the *further fusion* of nations; but it desires to achieve this aim not by force, but by a free, fraternal union of the workers and the toiling masses of all nations. (*The Tasks of the Proletariat in Our Revolution,* April 23, 1917, *Selected Works,* VI, 61.)

Why should we, great Russians, who have been oppressing a greater number of nations than any other people, why should we repudiate the right of secession for Poland, the Ukraine, Finland? We are asked to become chauvinist, because by doing so we would ease the position of the Social Democrats in Poland. We do not claim the liberation of Poland because the Polish people dwell between two states which are capable of fighting—they say. But instead of saying that the Polish workers should argue in this way, viz., only those Social Democrats remain democrats who consider that the Polish people ought to be free, for there is no place for chauvinists in the ranks of the Socialist party—the Polish Social Democrats argue that precisely because they find the union with the Russian workers advantageous, they are opposed to Poland's secession. They have a perfect right to do so. But these people do not wish to understand that in order to strengthen internationalism there is no need to reiterate the same words; what we in Russia do is to stress the right of secession for the subject nations, while in Poland we must stress the right of such nations to unite. The right to unite implies the right to secede. We Russians must emphasize the right to secede, while the Poles must emphasize the right to unite.

.   .   .   .

Once upon a time Alexander I and Napoleon traded peoples, once upon a time tsars traded portions of Poland. Are we to continue these tactics of the tsars? This is the repudiation of the tactics of internationalism, this is chauvinism of the worst brand. Suppose Finland does secede, what is there bad about that? Among both peoples, among the proletariat of Norway and that of Sweden, mutual confidence increased after separation. The Swedish landowners wanted to wage war, but the Swedish workers resisted this and said: We shall not go to such a war.

All that the Finns want now is autonomy. We stand for giving Finland complete liberty; that will increase their confidence in Russian democracy, and when they are given the right to secede they will not do so. While Mr. Rodichev goes to Finland to haggle over autonomy, our Finnish comrades come here and say: we must have autonomy. But fire is opened on them from the whole battery and they are told: Wait for the constituent assembly. We, however, say: Any Russian Socialist who denies freedom to Finland is a chauvinist.

We say that frontiers are determined by the will of the population. Russia, don't dare fight over Courland! Germany, withdraw your armies from Courland! This is our solution of the problem of secession. The proletariat cannot resort to violence, for it must not interfere with the freedom of peoples. The slogan, "down with frontiers," will become a true slogan only when the socialist revolution has become a reality, and not a method. Then we shall say: Comrades, come to us. . . .

Now war is an entirely different matter. When necessary, we shall not refuse to wage a revolutionary war. We are not pacifists. . . . But while we have Milyukov, and while he sends Rodichev to Finland, where he shamefully haggles with the Finnish people, we say to the Russian people: Don't dare rape Finland; no nation can be free if it oppresses other nations. In our resolution concerning Borgbjerg, we state: Withdraw your armies and let the nation settle this question itself. But if the Soviet seizes power tomorrow, it will no longer be a "method of socialist revolution"; we shall then say: Germany, withdraw your armies from Poland; Russia, withdraw your armies from Armenia—otherwise, the whole thing will be a deception.

Regarding his oppressed Poland, Comrade Dzerzhinsky tells us that everybody is a chauvinist there. But why does not any Pole tell us what we ought to do with Finland, what we ought to do with the Ukraine? We have been arguing about this question so much, ever since 1903, that it is difficult to say much about it now. Go where you please. . . . He who does not accept this point of view is an annexationist, a chauvinist. We are for the fraternal union of all nations. If there is a Ukrainian republic and a Russian republic, there will be closer contact, greater confidence between the two. If the Ukrainians see that we have a Soviet republic, they will not break away. But if we retain the Milyukov republic, they will break away. When Comrade Pyatakov, contradicting his own views, said that he is opposed to the forcible retention of nations within the frontiers, he really admitted the principle of self-determination. We do not in the least want the peasant in Khiva to live under the Khan of Khiva. By developing our revolution we shall influence the oppressed masses. Agitation among the oppressed masses should be carried on only in this manner.

But any Russian Socialist who does not recognize the freedom of Finland and the Ukraine is bound to degenerate into a chauvinist. And no sophisms, no references to his own "method" will help him to justify himself. (*Speech on the National Question* . . . , May 12, 1917. Compare with *Selected Works,* V, 308, 310–312, and *The Right of Nations to Self-Determination* (New York: International Publishers, 1951), pp. 122–125.)

DECREE ON PEACE

The workers' and peasants' government created by the revolution of November 6–7, 1917, and backed by the Soviets of Workers', Soldiers' and Peasants' Deputies calls upon all the belligerent peoples and their governments to start immediate negotiations for a just and democratic peace.

By a just, or democratic, peace, for which the vast majority of the working and toiling classes of all belligerent countries, exhausted, tormented and racked by the war, are craving, a peace that has been most definitely and insistently demanded by the Russian workers and peasants ever since the overthrow of the tsarist monarchy—by such a peace the government means an immediate peace without annexations (i.e., the seizure of foreign lands or the forcible incorporation of foreign nations) and indemnities.

The government of Russia calls upon all the belligerent nations to conclude such a peace immediately, and expresses its readiness to take the most resolute measures without the least delay, pending the final ratification of the conditions of this peace by plenipotentiary assemblies of the people's representatives of all countries and all nations.

In accordance with the sense of justice of the democracy in general, and of the toiling classes in particular, the government interprets the annexation, or seizure of foreign lands as meaning the incorporation into a large and powerful state of a small or feeble nation without the definitely, clearly and voluntarily expressed consent and wish of that nation, irrespective of the time such forcible incorporation took place, irrespective of the degree of development or backwardness of the nation forcibly annexed to, or forcibly retained within, the frontiers of the given state, and finally, irrespective of whether the nation inhabits Europe or distant, overseas countries.

If any nation whatsoever is forcibly retained within the boundaries of a given state, if, in spite of its expressed desire—no matter whether that desire is expressed in the press, at popular meetings, in party decisions, or in protests and revolts against national oppression—it is not permitted the right to decide the forms of its state existence by a free vote, taken after the complete evacuation of the troops of the incorporating or, generally, of the stronger nation, without the least pressure being brought to bear upon it, such incorporation is annexation, i.e., seizure and coercion. (*Decree on Peace,* November 13, 1917, *Selected Works,* VI, 401 f.)

At the recent conferences on the Ukrainian question, certain comrades accused the writer of "attaching undue importance" to the national question in the Ukraine. The figures for the elections to the Constituent Assembly show that in the Ukraine in November, 1917, the *Ukrainian* Socialist Revolutionaries and

Socialists received the majority (3,400,000 votes plus 500,000, or 3,900,000 votes, as against 1,900,000 votes cast for the *Russian* Socialist Revolutionaries, out of a total of 7,600,000 votes cast in the Ukraine). In the armies on the southwestern and Rumanian fronts the *Ukrainian* Socialists received 30 per cent and 34 per cent of the total vote, respectively, as against 40 per cent and 59 per cent received by the *Russian* Socialist Revolutionaries.

Under such circumstances, to ignore the importance of the national question in the Ukraine—of which Great Russians are frequently guilty (and perhaps Jews not much less frequently than Great Russians) —is a profound and dangerous error. The separation of the Russian and the Ukrainian Socialist Revolutionaries in the Ukraine in 1917 cannot have been a mere accident. It is our duty as internationalists, first, to conduct a particularly energetic campaign against the remnants (at times unconscious) of Great Russian imperialism and chauvinism among the "Russian" Communists, and, secondly, to make concessions on this national question, since, comparatively, it is unimportant (for an internationalist the question of state boundaries is of second-rate, if not of tenth-rate, importance). Other questions are important, such as the fundamental interests of the dictatorship of the proletariat, the unity and discipline of the Red Army fighting against Denikin, the leadership of the proletariat in relation to the peasantry. Whether the Ukraine shall be a separate state or not is a question of far inferior importance. We should not be surprised—or frightened—by the prospect of the workers and peasants of the Ukraine trying various systems, and in the course of several years, say, testing by practical experiment fusion with the Russian Socialist Federal Soviet Republic, secession from it and the formation of an independent Ukrainian Soviet Socialist Republic, various forms of close alliance with the Russian Socialist Federal Soviet Republic, and so on, and so forth. (*The Elections to the Constituent Assembly and the Dictatorship of the Proletariat,* December 29, 1919, *Selected Works,* VI, 480 f.)

At the congress of the Third (Communist) International

I said that the whole world is divided into oppressed nations and dominant nations. The oppressed nations constitute not less than 70 per cent of the population of the earth. The Peace of Versailles has added to them another hundred or hundred and fifty million people.

We are indeed coming forward now not only as the representatives of the proletarians of all countries, but also as the representatives of the oppressed peoples. A journal of the Communist International recently appeared entitled *The Peoples of the East*. The Communist International has issued the following slogan for the peoples of the East: Proletarians of the world and the oppressed peoples, unite! Certain comrades asked: When did the Executive Committee give orders to change slogans? I indeed do not remember it. Of course, from the standpoint of the *Communist Manifesto* this is wrong, but the *Communist Manifesto* was written in entirely different conditions, whereas from the point of view of present-day politics this is correct. (*Speech to Moscow Party Nuclei Secretaries,* November 26, 1920, *Selected Works,* VIII, 292 f.)

3. UNITED STATES

The history of modern civilized America opens with one of those great, really liberating, really revolutionary wars of which there have been so few among the large number of wars of conquest that were caused, like the present imperialist war, by squabbles among kings, landowners and capitalists over the division of seized lands and stolen profits. It was a war of the American people against English robbers who subjected America and held it in colonial slavery as these "civilized" bloodsuckers are even now subjecting and holding in colonial slavery hundreds of millions of people in India, Egypt and in all corners of the world.

Since that time about 150 years have passed. Bourgeois civilization has borne all its luxuriant fruits. By the high level of development of the productive forces of organized human labor, by utilizing machines and all the wonders of modern technic,

America has taken the first place among free and cultured nations. But at the same time America has become one of the foremost countries as regards the depth of the abyss which divides a handful of brazen billionaires who are wallowing in dirt and in luxury on the one hand, and millions of toilers who are always on the verge of starvation. The American people, who gave the world an example of a revolutionary war against feudal subjection, now appears as a new, capitalist wage slave of a handful of billionaires; finds itself playing the role of a hired assassin for the wealthy gang, having strangled the Philippines in 1898 under the pretext of "liberating" them, and strangling the Russian Socialist Republic in 1918 under the pretext of "protecting" it from the Germans.

.   .   .   .

The American billionaires were the richest of all and geographically the most secure. They have profited most of all. They have made all, even the richest countries, their vassals. They have plundered hundreds of billions of dollars. And every dollar is stained with filth: filthy secret pacts between England and her "allies," between Germany and her vassals, pacts on the division of spoils, pacts on mutual "aid" in oppressing the workers and persecuting the Socialist internationalists. Every dollar is stained with the filth of "profitable" military deliveries enriching the rich and despoiling the poor in every country. . . .

.   .   .   .

The beasts of prey of Anglo-French and American imperialism "accuse" us of coming to an "agreement" with German imperialism.

O hypocrites! O scoundrels, who slander the workers' government and shiver from fear of that sympathy which is being shown us by the workers of "their own" countries! But their hypocrisy will be exposed. They pretend not to understand the difference between an agreement made by "Socialists" *with* the bourgeoisie (native or foreign) *against the workers,* against the toilers, and an agreement for the safety of the workers who have defeated their bourgeoisie, with a bourgeoisie on one national color *against* the bourgeoisie of another color for the sake of the utilization by the proletariat of the contradictions between the different groups of the bourgeoisie.

In reality every European knows this difference very well, and the American people particularly, as I shall presently show, have "experienced" it in their own history. There are agreements and agreements, there are *fagots et fagots* as the French say.

When the German imperialist robbers in February, 1918, threw their armies against defenseless, demobilized Russia, which staked its hopes upon the international solidarity of the proletariat before the international revolution had completely ripened, I did not hesitate for a moment to come to a certain "agreement" with the French monarchists. . . . We shook hands with the French monarchist although we knew that each of us would readily hang his "partner." But for a time our interests coincided. To throw back the rapacious advancing Germans *we* made use of the equally rapacious counter interests of the other imperialists, thereby serving the interests of the Russian and the international socialist revolution. In this way we served the interests of the working class of Russia and other countries, we strengthened the proletariat and weakened the bourgeoisie of the whole world, we used the justified practice of maneuvering, necessary in *every* war, of shifting and waiting for the moment when the rapidly growing proletarian revolution in a number of advanced countries had *ripened*.

And despite all the wrathful howling of the sharks of Anglo-French and American imperialism, despite all the calumnies they have showered upon us, despite all the millions spent for bribing the right wing Socialist Revolutionary, Menshevik and other social-patriotic newspapers, *I would not hesitate a single second* to come to the *same kind* of an "agreement" with the German imperialist robbers, should an attack upon Russia by Anglo-French troops demand it. And I know perfectly well that my tactics will meet with the approval of the class-conscious proletariat of Russia, Germany, France, England, America—in a word, of the whole civilized world. Such tactics will lighten the task of Socialist revolution, will hasten its advance, will weaken the international bourgeoisie, will strengthen the position of the working class which is conquering it.

We know that help from you, comrades American workers, will probably not come soon, for the development of the revolution proceeds with a different tempo and in different forms in different countries (and it cannot be otherwise). We know that the European proletarian revolution also may not blaze forth during the next few weeks, no matter how rapidly it has been ripening lately. We stake our chances on the inevitability of the international revolution, but this in no way means that we are so foolish as to stake our chances on the inevitability of the revolution within a *stated* short period. We have seen in our country two great revolutions, in 1905 and in 1917, and we know that revolutions are made neither to order nor by agreement. We know that circumstances brought to the fore *our* Russian detachment of the Socialist proletariat, not by virtue of our merits, but due to the particular backwardness of Russia, and that *before* the outburst of the international revolution there may be several defeats of separate revolutions.

Despite this, we are firmly convinced that we are invincible, because mankind will not break down under the imperialist slaughter, but will overcome it. And the first country which *demolished* the galley chains of imperialist war, was *our* country. We made the greatest of sacrifices in the struggle for the demolition of this chain, but we *broke* it. We are beyond imperialist dependence, we raised before the whole world the banner of struggle for the complete overthrow of imperialism.

We are now as if in a beleaguered fortress until other detachments of the international socialist revolution come to our rescue. But these detachments *exist,* they are *more numerous* than ours, they mature, they grow, they become stronger as the bestialities of imperialism continue. The workers sever connections with their social traitors—the Gomperses, Hendersons, Renaudels, Scheidemanns, Renners. The workers are going slowly, but unswervingly, toward Communist, Bolshevik tactics, toward the proletarian revolution, which is the only one capable of saving perishing culture and perishing mankind.

In a word, we are invincible, because the world proletarian revolution is invincible. (*A Letter to American Workers,* August 20, 1918 (New York: International Publishers, 1934), pp. 9–10, 10–11, 13–15, 21–22.)

An intensification of the struggle between the proletariat and the bourgeoisie may be observed in all the advanced capitalist countries, and the difference in the historical conditions, political regime and forms of the labor movement creates the difference in the manifestations of one and the same tendency. In America and England, where there is complete political liberty, and where live, revolutionary and socialist traditions are completely, or at all events, almost completely lacking among the working class, this intensification is manifested in the intensification of the movement against the trusts, in the extraordinary growth of socialism and in the growing attention being paid to it by the propertied classes, and in the fact that the labor organizations, sometimes the purely industrial organizations [i.e., trade unions], are taking up the systematic and independent proletarian political struggle. (*Inflammable Material in World Politics*, August, 1908, *Selected Works*, IV, 302.)

Legien visited the United States chamber of deputies, called "Congress." The democratic regime of the republic made a favorable impression on the man who was brought up in police-ridden Prussia, and he notes with a pleasure which is quite understandable that the state in America supplies every Congressman not only with a special room furnished according to the last word in comfort, but also with a paid secretary to do a great deal of his work. The simplicity and lack of constraint in the bearing of the Congressmen and of the Speaker differed sharply from what Legien had seen in other European parliaments, especially in Germany. In Europe, a Social Democrat could not even dream of addressing a speech of greeting to a bourgeois parliament at its official session! But in America this was very simple and the title of Social Democrat did not frighten anyone . . . except *that very Social Democrat!*

It was here that the American bourgeois fashion of "killing" unstable Socialists "with kindness," as well as the German opportunish fashion of renouncing socialism to please the "kind," affable and democratic bourgeoisie, was revealed.

Legien's speech of greeting was translated into English (democracy was not a bit frightened by hearing an "alien" language in its parliament), over two hundred Congressmen, each in turn, shook hands with Legien as the "guest" of the republic; the Speaker of Congress thanked him particularly.

> The form and content of my speech of greeting [writes Legien] were favorably commented upon in the Socialist press both of the United States and Germany. Some German editors, however, could not refrain from mentioning that my speech proved once again that it is impossible for a Social Democrat to deliver a Social Democratic speech before a bourgeois audience. . . . Well, if they, these editors, were in my place they would no doubt have delivered a speech against capitalism and in favor of a mass strike, whereas I thought it important to emphasize before that parliament that the Social Democratic and the trade union workers of Germany want peace among nations and desire, through peace, the further development of culture to the highest possible level.

Poor "editors"—Legien has annihilated them with his "statesman"-like speech.

. . . .

The leader of the army of two million German trade unionists, i.e., the Social Democratic trade unions, a member of the Social Democratic faction in the German Reichstag (parliament), delivers a purely liberal bourgeois speech before the supreme assembly of the representatives of capitalist America. Naturally, not a single liberal, not even an Octobrist, would have refused to endorsed the words about "peace" and "culture."

And when the Socialists in Germany remarked that this was not a Social Democratic speech, our "leader" of the wage slaves of capital poured lofty scorn on the Socialists. What are "editors" compared with a "practical politician" and the collector of workers' pennies? Our philistine Narcissus has the same contempt for editors as a police pompadour in a certain country has for the "third element."

They, "these editors," to be sure, would have delivered a speech "against capitalism."

Just think what this quasi-Socialist is mocking at: He is mocking at the idea of a Socialist taking it into his head that he must talk *against* capitalism. Such an idea is utterly foreign to the "statesmen" of German opportunism; they talk in a way that *will not offend* "capitalism." And while disgracing themselves by this flunkeyish renunciation of socialism, they glory in their shame.

Legien does not belong to the man-in-the-street category. He is the representative of an army, or to be more exact, of the officers' corps of the trade-union army. His speech is not an accident or a slip of the tongue, nor is it a solitary escapade or a mistake committed by a provincial German "office clerk" overawed by the kindness of the American capitalists who betray no trace of police arrogance. (*What Should Not Be Imitated in the German Labor Movement,* April, 1914, *Selected Works,* IV, 334 f., 336.)

America, a very rich country, to which all countries are subordinated, cannot buy and sell. . . . Wilson was the idol of philistines and pacifists. . . . Wilson proved to be a fool, and all these illusions were scattered to the winds at the first contact with the shrewd, commercial merchant's policy of capital. . . . The "roots" of Wilson's policy amounted only to the piffle of parsons—petty bourgeois phrases—and the utter failure to understand the class struggle. (*The International Situation and the Fundamental Tasks of the Communist International,* July 19, 1920, *Selected Works,* X, 188.)

Who is Vanderlip? We have not established who he is—but it is known that in the capitalist world telegrams are not dispatched all over the world about ordinary citizens. And when he left us, telegrams were flying all over the world. Well, he related that he had obtained an advantageous concession and began to praise Lenin everywhere. This is rather funny, but allow me to tell you that in this funny situation there is a morsel of politics. When Vanderlip had finished all his negotiations here, he wanted to meet me. I took counsel with the representatives of the appropriate departments and asked whether I ought to receive him. They said, "Let him leave more satisfied." Vanderlip came to see me, we conversed about all these matters, and when he began to relate that he had been in Siberia, that he knows Siberia, that he comes from a worker's family, like the majority of American billionaires, and so on, that they value only practical matters, that only when they see a thing do they believe it, I replied, "Well, you are practical people, if you take a look at the Soviet system you will introduce it in your own country." He stared at me, astonished at the turn the conversation had taken, and said to me in Russian (the whole conversation had been in English), "Perhaps." I asked in surprise where he had got his knowledge of Russian. "Why, I have spent twenty-five years riding through the greater part of the regions of Siberia on horseback." At parting he said: "I shall have to say in America that Mr. Lenin has no horns." I did not at once grasp his meaning, since I understand English badly. "What did you say? Repeat it." He is a lively old fellow—pointing to his temples he said, "No horns." There was an interpreter present who said, "That is just what he says." In America they are convinced that I have horns here, that is to say, the bourgeois say that I am branded by the devil. "And now I shall have to say that there are no horns," said Vanderlip. We parted very amiably. I expressed the hope that on the basis of friendly relations between the two states, not only would the concession be concluded, but mutual economic assistance would develop normally. All in this sort of tone. Then the telegrams were sent flying with stories of Vanderlip, who had arrived from abroad. Vanderlip compared Lenin with Washington and Lincoln. Vanderlip asked for my autographed portrait. I declined. . . . Harding—the man who has been elected President, but who will take office only next March—when the news of the Vanderlip concessions came out, issued an official denial, stating, "I know nothing, I have no relations with the Bolsheviks and have heard nothing about any concessions." This was during the elections, and, for all you know, to confess during elections that you have business with the Bolsheviks may cost you votes. (*Speech* . . . , November 26, 1920, *Selected Works*, VIII, 287 f.)

VI

IMPERIALISM

THE HIGHEST STAGE OF CAPITALISM[1]

1. PREFACE OF JULY 6, 1920

I

As was indicated in the preface to the Russian edition, this pamphlet was written in 1916, with an eye to the tsarist censorship. I am unable to revise the whole text at the present time, nor, perhaps, is this advisable, since the main purpose of the book was and remains: to present, on the basis of the summarized returns of irrefutable bourgeois statistics, and the admissions of bourgeois scholars of all countries, a *general picture* of the world capitalist system in its international relationships at the beginning of the twentieth century—on the eve of the first world imperialist war. (*Selected Works*, V. 7.)

II

In the pamphlet I proved that the war of 1914–18 was imperialistic (that is, an annexationist, predatory, plunderous war) on the

---

[1]The passages from *Imperialism: The Highest Stage of Capitalism*, which Lenin wrote in the spring of 1916, extend from p. 266 to p. 307 of the present selection. Only volume and page of *Selected Works* are acknowledged.

part of both sides; it was a war for the division of the world, for the partition and repartition of colonies, "spheres of influence" of finance capital, etc.

Proof of what was the true social, or rather, the true class character of the war is naturally to be found, not in the diplomatic history of the war, but in any analysis of the *objective* position of the ruling *classes in all* belligerent countries. In order to depict this objective position one must not take examples or isolated data (in view of the extreme complexity of social life it is always quite easy to select any number of examples or separate data to prove any point one desires), but the *whole* of the data concerning the *basis* of economic life in *all* the belligerent countries and the *whole* world.

It is precisely irrefutable summarized data of this kind that I quoted in describing the *partition of the world* in the period of 1876 to 1914 and the distribution of the *railways* all over the world in the period of 1890 to 1913. Railways combine within themselves the basic capitalist industries: coal, iron and steel; and they are the most striking index of the development of international trade and bourgeois-democratic civilization. In the preceding chapters of the book [Imperialism: . . .] I showed how the railways are linked up with large-scale industry, with monopolies, syndicates, cartels, trusts, banks and the financial oligarchy. The uneven distribution of the railways, their uneven development—sums up, as it were, modern world monopolist capitalism. And this summing up proves that imperialist wars are absolutely inevitable under *such* an economic system, *as long as* private property in the means of production exists.

The building of railways seems to be a simple, natural, democratic, cultural and civilizing enterprise; that is what it is in the opinion of bourgeois professors, who are paid to depict capitalist slavery in bright colors, and in the opinion of petty bourgeois philistines. But as a matter of fact the capitalist threads, which in thousands of different intercrossings bind these enterprises with private property in the means of production in general, have converted this work of construction into an instrument for oppressing *a thousand million* people (in the colonies and semi-colonies), that is, more than half the population of the globe, which inhabits the subject countries, as well as the wage slaves of capitalism in the lands of "civilization."

Private property based on the labor of the small proprietor, free competition, democracy, i.e., all the catchwords with which the capitalists and their press deceive the workers and the peasants—are things of the past. Capitalism has grown into a world system of colonial oppression and of the financial strangulation of the overwhelming majority of the people of the world by a handful of "advanced" countries. And this "booty" is shared between two or three powerful world marauders armed to the teeth (America, Great Britain, Japan), who involve the whole world in *their* war over the sharing of *their* booty. (*Selected Works,* V, 7–9.)

III

The Brest-Litovsk Peace Treaty dictated by monarchist Germany, and later on, the much more brutal and despicable Versailles Treaty dictated by the "democratic" republics of America and France and also by "free" England, have rendered very good service to humanity by exposing both the hired coolies of the pen of imperialism and the petty bourgeois reactionaries, although they call themselves pacifists and socialists, who sang praises to "Wilsonism," and who insisted that peace and reform were possible under imperialism.

The tens of millions of dead and maimed left by the war—a war for the purpose of deciding whether the British or German group of financial marauders is to receive the lion's share—and the two "peace treaties," mentioned above, open the eyes of the millions and tens of millions of people who are downtrodden, oppressed, deceived and duped by the bourgeoisie with unprecedented rapidity. Thus, out of the universal ruin caused by the war a worldwide revolutionary crisis is arising which, in spite of the protracted and difficult stages it may have to pass, cannot end in any other way than in a proletarian revolution and in its victory. (*Selected Works,* V, 9.)

The international split of the whole labor movement is now quite evident (Second and Third Internationals). Armed struggle and civil war between the two trends is now a recognized fact: the support given to Kolchak and Denikin in Russia by the Mensheviks and Socialist Revolutionaries against the Bolsheviks; the fight the Scheidemanns, Noskes and company have conducted in conjunction with the bourgeoisie against the Spartacists in Germany; the same thing in Finland, Poland, Hungary, etc. What is the economic basis of this historically important world phenomenon?

Precisely the parasitism and decay of capitalism which are the characteristic features of its highest historical stage of development, i.e., imperialism. As has been shown in this pamphlet, capitalism has now brought to the front a *handful* (less than one-tenth of the inhabitants of the globe; less than one-fifth, if the most "generous" and liberal calculation were made) of very rich and very powerful states which plunder the whole world simply by "clipping coupons." Capital exports produce an income of eight to ten billion francs per annum, according to pre-war prices and pre-war bourgeois statistics. Now, of course, they produce much more than that.

Obviously, out of such enormous *super-profits* (since they are obtained over and above the profits which capitalists squeeze out of the workers of their "home" country) it is quite *possible to bribe* the labor leaders and the upper stratum of the labor aristocracy. And the capitalists of the "advanced" countries are bribing them; they bribe them in a thousand different ways, direct and indirect, overt and covert.

This stratum of bourgeoisified workers, or the "labor aristocracy," who are quite philistine in their mode of life, in the size of their earnings and in their outlook, serves as the principal prop of the Second International, and, in our days, the principal *social* (not military) *prop of the bourgeoisie.* They are the real *agents of the bourgeoisie in the labor movement,* the labor lieutenants of the capitalist class, real channels of reformism and chauvinism. In the civil war between the proletariat and the bourgeoisie they inevitably, and in no small numbers, stand side by side with the bourgeoisie, with the "Versaillese" against the "Communards." (*Selected Works,* V, 11–12.)

Competition becomes transformed into monopoly. The result is immense progress in the socialization of production. In particular, the process of technical invention and improvement becomes socialized.

This is no longer the old type of free competition between manufacturers, scattered and out of touch with one another, and producing for an unknown market. Concentration has reached the point at which it is possible to make an approximate estimate of all sources of raw materials (for example, the iron ore deposits) of a country and even, as we shall see, of several countries, or of the whole world. Not only are such estimates made, but these sources are captured by gigantic monopolist combines. An approximate estimate of the capacity of markets is also made, and the combines divide them up amongst themselves by agreement. Skilled labor is monopolized, the best engineers are engaged; the means of transport are captured: railways in America, shipping companies in Europe and America. Capitalism in its imperialist stage arrives at the threshold of the most complete socialization of production. In spite of themselves, the capitalists are dragged, as it were, into a new social order, a transitional social order from complete free competition to complete socialization. Production becomes social, but appropriation remains private. The social means of production remain the private property of a few. The general framework of formally recognized free competition remains, but the yoke of a few monopolists on the rest of the population becomes a hundred times heavier, more burdensome and intolerable. (*Selected Works,* V, 21 f.)

During the last fifteen or twenty years, especially since the Spanish-American War (1898), and the Anglo-Boer War (1899–1902), the economic and also the political literature of the two hemispheres has more and more often adopted the term "imperialism" in order to define the present era. (*Selected Works,* V, 13.)

2. CONCENTRATION OF PRODUCTION AND MONOPOLIES

The enormous growth of industry and the remarkably rapid process of concentration of production in ever-larger enterprises represent one of the most characteristic features of capitalism. Modern censuses of production give very complete and exact data on this process. (*Selected Works*, V, 14.)

Less than one-hundredth of the total enterprises utilize *more than three-fourths* of the steam and electric power! Two million nine hundred and seventy thousand small enterprises (employing up to five workers), representing 91 per cent of the total, utilize only seven per cent of the steam and electric power. Tens of thousands of large-scale enterprises are everything; millions of small ones are nothing. (*Loc. cit.*)

In another advanced country of modern capitalism, the United States, the growth of the concentration of production is still greater. Here statistics single out industry in the narrow sense of the word and group enterprises according to the value of their annual output. In 1904 large-scale enterprises with an annual output of one million dollars and over numbered 1,900 (out of 216,180, i.e., 0.9 percent). These employed 1,400,000 workers (out of 5,500,000, i.e., 25.6 per cent) and their combined annual output was valued at $5,600,000,000 (out of $14,800,000,000, i.e., 38 per cent.) Five years later, in 1909, the corresponding figures were: large-scale enterprises: 3,060 out of 268,491, i.e., 1.1 per cent; employing: 2,000,000 workers out of 6,600,000, i.e., 30.5 per cent; output: $9,000,000,000 out of $20,700,000,000, i.e., 43.8 per cent.

Almost half the total production of all the enterprises of the country was carried on by a *hundredth part* of those enterprises! These 3,000 giant enterprises embrace 268 branches of industry. From this it can be seen that, at a certain stage of its development, concentration itself, as it were, leads right to monopoly; for a score or so of giant enterprises can easily arrive at an agreement, while on the other hand, the difficulty of competition and the tendency toward monopoly arise from the very dimensions of the enterprises. This transformation of competition into monopoly is one of the most important—if not the most important—phenomena of modern capitalist economy, and we must deal with it in greater detail. But first we must clear up one possible misunderstanding.

American statistics say: 3,000 giant enterprises in 250 branches of industry, as if there were only a dozen large-scale enterprises for each branch of industry.

But this is not the case. Not in every branch of industry are there large-scale enterprises; and moreover, a very important feature of capitalism in its highest stage of development is so-called combined production, that is to say, the grouping in a single enterprise of different branches of industry, which either represent the consecutive stages in the working up of raw materials (for example, the smelting of iron ore into pig iron, the conversion of pig iron into steel and then, perhaps the manufacture steel goods)—or are auxiliary to one another (for example, the utilization of waste or of by-products, the manufacture of packing materials, etc.). (*Selected Works,* V, 15 f.)

Fifty years ago, when Marx was writing *Capital,* free competition appeared to most economists to be a "natural law." Official science tried, by a conspiracy of silence, to kill the works of Marx, which by a theoretical and historical analysis of capitalism showed that free competition gives rise to the concentration of production, which, in turn, at a certain stage of development, leads to monopoly. Today, monopoly has become a fact. The economists are writing mountains of books in which they describe the diverse manifestations of monopoly, and continue to declare in chorus that "Marxism is refuted." But facts are stubborn things, as the English proverb says, and they have to be reckoned with, whether we like it or not. The facts show that differences between capitalist countries, e.g., in the matter of protection or free trade, only give rise to insignificant variation in the form of monopolies or in the moment of their appearance; and that the rise of monopolies, as the result of the concentration of production, is a general and fundamental law of the present stage of development of capitalism. (*Selected Works*, V, 17 f.)

Cartels come to an agreement on the conditions of sale, terms of payment, etc. They divide the markets among themselves. They fix the quantity of goods to be produced. They fix prices. They divide the profits among the various enterprises, etc. (*Selected Works*, V, 19.)

American statistics divide all industrial enterprises into three categories, according to whether they belong to individuals, to private firms or to corporations. These latter in 1904 comprised 23.6 per cent, and in 1909, 25.9 per cent (i.e., more than one-fourth of the total industrial enterprises in the country). These employed in 1904, 70.6 per cent, and in 1909, 75.6 per cent (i.e., more than three-fourths) of the total wage earners. Their output amounted at these two dates to $10,900,000,000 and to $16,300,000,000, i.e., to 73.7 per cent and 79 per cent of the total respectively.

Not infrequently cartels and trusts concentrate in their hands seven- or eight-tenths of the total output of a given branch of industry. (*Selected Works*, V, 19 f.)

The famous Standard Oil Company in the United States was founded in 1900:[2]

> It has an authorized capital of $150,000,000. It issued $100,000,000 common and $106,000,000 preferred stock. From 1900 to 1907 the following dividends were paid on this stock: 48, 48, 45, 44, 36, 40, 40, 40 per cent, in the respective years, i.e., in all, $367,000,000. From 1882 to 1907, out of a total net profits to the amount of $889,000,000, $606,000,000 were distributed in dividends, and the rest went to reserve capital. . . . (*Selected Works*, V, 20.)

. . . The development of capitalism has arrived at a stage when, although commodity production still "reigns" and continues to be regarded as the basis of economic life, it has in reality been

---

[2]Holding company was formed in 1899 to replace trust agreement of 1882.

undermined and the big profits go to the "geniuses" of financial manipulation. At the basis of these swindles and manipulations lies socialized production; but the immense progress of humanity, which achieved this socialization, goes to benefit the speculators. (*Selected Works*, V, 23.)

The statement that cartels can abolish crises is a fable spread by bourgeois economists who at all costs desire to place capitalism in a favorable light. On the the contrary, when monopoly appears in *certain* branches of industry, it increases and intensifies the anarchy inherent in capitalist production *as a whole*. The disparity between the development of agriculture and that of industry, which is characteristic of capitalism, is increased. The privileged position of the most highly cartelized industry, socalled *heavy* industry, especially coal and iron, causes "a still greater lack of concerted organization" in other branches of production. (*Selected Works*, V. 25.)

Crises of every kind—economic crises more frequently, but not only these—in their turn increase very considerably the tendency toward concentration and monopoly. (*Loc. cit.*)

3. THE BANKS AND THEIR NEW ROLE

The principal and primary function of banks is to serve as an intermediary in the making of payments. In doing so they transform inactive money capital into active capital, that is, into capital producing a profit; they collect all kinds of money revenues and place them at the disposal of the capitalist class.

As banking develops and becomes concentrated in a small number of establishments the banks become transformed, and instead of being modest intermediaries they become powerful monopolies having at their command almost the whole of the money capital of all the capitalists and small businessmen and also a large part of the means of production and of the sources of raw materials of the given country and in a number of countries. The transformation of numerous modest intermediaries into a handful of monopolists represents one of the fundamental processes in the transformation of capitalism into capitalist imperialism. (*Selected Works,* V, 27.)

Large-scale enterprises, especially the banks, not only completely absorb small ones, but also "join" them to themselves, subordinate them, bring them into their "own" group or *concern* (to use the technical term) by having "holdings" in their capital, by purchasing or exchanging shares, by controlling them through a system of credits, etc., etc. (*Selected Works,* V, 28.)

... We will quote an example of the "holding" system.

The Deutsche Bank group [in Germany] is one of the biggest, if not the biggest banking group. In order to trace the main threads which connect all the banks in this group, it is necessary to distinguish between holdings of the first, second and third degree, or what amounts to the same thing, between dependence (of the lesser establishments on the Deutsche Bank) in the first, second and third degree. We then obtain the following picture:

THE DEUTSCHE BANK PARTICIPATES:

	PERMANENTLY	FOR AN INDEFINITE PERIOD	OCCASIONALLY	TOTAL
1st degree	in 17 banks	in 5 banks	in 8 banks	in 30 banks
2nd degree	of which 9 participate in 34 others		of which 5 participate in 14 others	of which 14 participate in 48 others
3rd degree	of which 4 participate in 7 others		of which 2 participate in 2 others	of which 6 participate in 9 others

Included in the eight banks dependent on the Deutsche Bank in the "first degree," "occasionally," there are three foreign banks: one Austrian, the Wiener Bankverein, and two Russian, the Siberian Commercial Bank and the Russian Bank for Foreign Trade. Altogether, the Deutsche Bank group comprises, directly and indirectly, partially and totally, no less than 87 banks; and the capital—its own and others which it controls—is estimated at between two and three billion marks.

It is obvious that a bank which stands at the head of such a group, and which enters into agreement with a half dozen other banks only slightly smaller than itself for the purpose of conducting big and profitable operations like floating state loans, is no longer a mere "intermediary" but a combine of a handful of monopolists. (*Selected Works*, V, 29.)

... The concentration of capital and the growth of their turnover is radically changing the significance of the banks. Scattered capitalists are transformed into a single collective capitalist. When carrying the current accounts of a few capitalists, the banks, as it were, transact a purely technical and exclusively auxiliary operation. When, however, these operations grow to enormous dimensions we find that a handful of monopolists control all the operations, both commercial and industrial, of the whole of capitalist society. They can, by means of their banking connections, by running current accounts and transacting other financial operations, first *ascertain exactly* the position of the various capitalists, then *control* them, influence them by restricting or enlarging, facilitating or hindering their credits, and finally they can *entirely determine* their fate, determine their income, deprive them of capital, or, on the other hand, permit them to increase their capital rapidly and to enormous dimensions, etc. (*Selected Works*, V, 31.)

Germany is *governed* by not more than three hundred magnates of capital, and the number of these is constantly diminishing. At all events, banks in all capitalist countries, no matter what the law in regard to them may be, greatly intensify and accelerate the process of concentration of capital and the formation of monopolies.

The banking system, Marx wrote half a century ago in *Capital*, "presents indeed the form of common bookkeeping and distribution of means of production on a social scale, but only the form." ... Figures ... on the growth of bank capital, on the increase in the number of the branches and offices of the biggest banks, the increase in the number of their accounts, etc., present a concrete picture of this "common bookkeeping" of the *whole* capitalist class;

and not only of the capitalists, for the banks collect, even though temporarily, all kinds of financial revenues of small business men, office clerks, and of a small upper stratum of the working class. It is "common distribution of means of production" that, from the formal point of view, grows out of the development of modern banks, the most important of which, numbering from three to six in France, and from six to eight in Germany, control billions and billions. In point of fact, however, the distribution of means of production is by no means "common," but private, i.e., it conforms to the interests of big capital, and primarily, of very big monopoly capital, which operates in conditions in which the masses of the population live in want, in which the whole development of agriculture hopelessly lags behind the development of industry, and within industry itself the "heavy industries" exact tribute from all other branches of industry.

The savings banks and post offices are beginning to compete with the banks in the matter of socializing capitalist economy; they are more "decentralized," i.e., their influence extends to a greater number of localities, to more remote places, to wider sections of the population. (*Selected Works*, V, 33 f.)

As they pay interest at the rate of four per cent and $4\frac{1}{4}$ per cent on deposits, the savings banks must seek "profitable" investments for their capital, they must deal in bills, mortgages, etc. The boundaries between the banks and the savings banks "become more and more obliterated." (*Selected Works*, V, 34.)

The billions entrusted to the savings banks are in the final analysis actually controlled by *these very same* bank magnates, while, on the other hand, state monopoly in capitalist society is nothing more than a means of increasing and guaranteeing the income of millionaires on the verge of bankruptcy in one branch of industry or another.

The change from the old type of capitalism, in which free competition predominated, to the new capitalism, in which monopoly reigns, is expressed, among other things, by a decrease in the importance of the stock exchange. (*Selected Works* V, 35.)

The old capitalism, the capitalism of free competition, and its indispensable regulator, the stock exchange, are passing away. A new capitalism has come to take its place, which bears obvious features of something transitory, which is a mixture of free competition and monopoly. The question naturally arises: to *what* is this new, "transitory" capitalism leading? But the bourgeois scholars are afraid to raise this question.

> Thirty years ago, employers, freely competing against one another, performed nine-tenths of the work connected with their businesses other than manual labor. At the present time, nine-tenths of this business "brain work" is performed by *officials*. Banking is in the forefront of this evolution.

This admission ... brings us once again to the question as to what this new capitalism, capitalism in its imperialist stage, is leading to.

Among the few banks which remain at the head of all capitalist economy as a result of the process of concentration, there is naturally to be observed an increasingly marked tendency toward monopolist agreements, toward a *bank trust*. In America, there are not nine, but *two* big banks, those of the billionaires Rockefeller and Morgan, which control a capital of eleven billion marks. (*Selected Works*, V, 35 f.)

The close ties that exist between the banks and industry are the very things that bring out most strikingly the new role of the banks. When a bank discounts a bill for an industrial firm, opens a current account for it, etc., these operations, taken separately, do not in the least diminish the independence of the industrial firm, and the bank plays no other part than that of a modest intermediary. But when such operations are multiplied and become an established practice, when the bank "collects" in its own hands enormous amounts of capital, when the running of a current account for the firm in question enables the bank—and this is what happens—to become better informed of the economic position of the client, then the result is that the industrial capitalist becomes more completely dependent on the bank.

At the same time a very close personal union is established between the banks and the biggest industrial and commercial enterprises: the merging of one with another through the acquisition of shares, through the appointment of bank directors to the supervisory boards (or boards of directors) of industrial and commercial enterprises, and *vice versa*. (*Selected Works,* V, 36 f.)

The old struggle between big and small capital is being resumed on a new and higher stage of development. It stands to reason that undertakings, financed by big banks handling billions, can accelerate technical progress in a way that cannot possibly be compared with the past. The banks, for example, set up special technical research societies, and only "friendly" industrial enterprises benefit from their work. (*Selected Works,* V, 39 f.)

The old capitalism has had its day. The new capitalism represents a transition toward something. It is hopeless, of course, to seek for "firm principles and a concrete aim" for the purpose of "reconciling" monopoly with free competition. The admission of the practical men has quite a different ring from the official praises of the charms of "organized" capitalism sung by its apologists. . . . (*Selected Works,* V, 40.)

The beginning of the twentieth century marks the turning point from the old capitalism to the new, from the domination of capital in general to the domination of finance capital. (*Selected Works,* V, 41.)

4. FINANCE CAPITAL AND FINANCIAL OLIGARCHY

The concentration of production; the monopoly arising therefrom; the merging or coalescense of banking with industry—this is the history of the rise of finance capital and what gives the term "finance capital" its content. (*Selected Works,* V, 42.)

Experience shows that it is sufficient to own 40 per cent of the shares of a company in order to direct its affairs, since a certain number of small, scattered shareholders find it impossible, in practice, to attend general meetings, etc. The "democratization" of the ownership of shares, from which the bourgeois sophists and opportunist "would-be" Social Democrats expect (or declare that they expect) the "democratization of capital," the strengthening of the role and significance of small-scale production, etc., is, in fact, one of the ways of increasing the power of financial oligarchy. Incidentally this is why, in the more advanced, or in the older and more "experienced" capitalist countries, the law allows the issue of shares of very small denomination. In Germany, it is not permitted by the law to issue shares of less value than one thousand marks, and the magnates of German finance look with an envious eye at England, where the issue of one-pound shares is permitted. Siemens, one of the biggest industrialists and "financial kings" in Germany, told the Reichstag on June 7, 1900, that "the one-pound share is the basis of British imperialism." (*Selected Works*, V, 43 f.)

But the "holding system" not only serves to increase enormously the power of the monopolists; it also enables them to resort with impunity to all sorts of shady tricks to cheat the public, for the directors of the parent company are not legally responsible for the subsidiary companies, which are supposed to be "independent," and *through the medium* of which they can "pull off" *anything*. (*Selected Works*, V, 44.)

As an example of an important monopolist company widely employing this system,—reference is made to the famous General Electric Company (Allgemeine Elektrizitäts Gesellschaft—A.E.G.). . . . In 1912, it was calculated that this company held shares in from *175 to 200* other companies, controlling them, of course, and thus having control of a total capital of *1,500,000,000 marks!*

All rules of control, the publication of balance sheets, the drawing up of balance sheets according to a definite form, the public auditing of accounts, etc., the things about which well-intentioned professors and officials—that is, those imbued with the good intention of defending and embellishing capitalism—discourse to the public, are of no avail. For private property is sacred, and no one can be prohibited from buying, selling, exchanging or mortgaging shares, etc. (*Selected Works*, V, 45.)

Finance capital, concentrated in a few hands and exercising a virtual monopoly, exacts enormous and ever-increasing profits from organizing a network of companies, issue of stock, state loans, etc., tightens the grip of financial oligarchies and levies tribute upon the whole of society for the benefit of monopolists. (*Selected Works*, V, 47.)

Speculation in land situated in the suburbs of rapidly growing towns is a particularly profitable operation for finance capital. The monopoly of the banks merges here with the monopoly of ground rent and with monopoly in the means of communication, since the increase in the value of the land and the possibility of selling it profitably in allotments, etc., is mainly dependent on good means of communication with the center of the town; and these means of communication are in the hands of large companies which are connected by means of the holding system and by the distribution of positions on the directorates, with the interested banks. (*Selected Works*, V, 50.)

A monopoly, once it is formed and controls thousands of millions, inevitably penetrates into *every* sphere of public life, regardless of the form of government and all other "details." In the economic literature of Germany one usually comes across the servile praise of the integrity of the Prussian bureaucracy, and allusions to the French Panama scandal and to political corruption in America. But the fact is that *even* the bourgeois literature devoted to German banking matters constantly has to go far beyond the field of purely banking operations and to speak, for instance, of "the attraction of the banks" in reference to the increasing frequency with which public officials take employment with the banks. (*Selected Works*, V, 51 f.)

It is characteristic of capitalism in general that the ownership of capital is separated from the application of capital to production, that money capital is separated from industrial or productive capital, and that the rentier, who lives entirely on income obtained from money capital, is separated from the entrepreneur and from all who are directly concerned in the management of capital. Imperialism, or the domination of finance capital, is that highest stage of capitalism in which this separation reaches vast proportions. The supremacy of finance capital over all other forms of capital means the predominance of the rentier and of the financial oligarchy; it means the crystallization of a small number of financially "powerful" states from among all the rest. The extent to which this process is going on may be judged from the statistics on emissions, i.e., the issue of all kinds of securities. (*Selected Works,* V, 53.)

We . . . see standing out in sharp relief four of the richest capitalist countries, each of which controls securities to amounts ranging from 100 to 150 billion francs. Two of these countries, England and France, are the oldest capitalist countries, and, as we shall see, possess the most colonies; the other two, the United States and Germany, are in the front rank as regards rapidity of development and the degree of extension of capitalist monopolies in industry. Together, these four countries own 479,000,000,000 francs, that is, nearly 80 per cent of the world's finance capital. Thus, in one way or another, nearly the whole world is more or less the debtor to and tributary of these four international banker countries, the four "pillars" of world finance capital. (*Selected Works,* V, 55.)

5. THE EXPORT OF CAPITAL

Under the old capitalism, when free competition prevailed, the export of *goods* was the most typical feature. Under modern capitalism, when monopolies prevail, the export of *capital* has become the typical feature.

Capitalism is commodity production at the highest stage of development, when labor power itself becomes a commodity.

The growth of internal exchange, and particularly of international exchange, is the characteristic distinguishing feature of capitalism. The uneven and spasmodic character of the development of individual enterprises, of individual branches of industry and individual countries, is inevitable under the capitalist system. England became a capitalist country before any other, and in the middle of the nineteenth century, having adopted free trade, claimed to be the "workshop of the world," the great purveyor of manufactured goods to all countries, which in exchange were to keep her supplied with raw materials. But in the last quarter of the nineteenth century, *this* monopoly was already undermined. Other countries, protecting themselves by tariff walls, had developed into independent capitalist states. On the threshold of the twentieth century, we see a new type of monopoly coming into existence. Firstly, there are monopolist capitalist combines in all advanced capitalist countries; secondly, a few rich countries, in which the accumulation of capital reaches gigantic proportions, occupy a monopolist position. An enormous "superabundance of capital" has accumulated in the advanced countries.

It goes without saying that if capitalism could develop agriculture, which today lags far behind industry everywhere, if it could raise the standard of living of the masses, who are everywhere still poverty-stricken and underfed, in spite of the amazing advance in technical knowledge, there could be no talk of a superabundance of capital. This "argument" the petty bourgeois critics of capitalism advance on every occasion. But if capitalism did these things it would not be capitalism; for uneven development and wretched conditions of the masses are fundamental and inevitable conditions and premises of this mode of production. As long as capitalism remains what it is, surplus capital will never be utilized for the purpose of raising the standard of living of the masses in a given country, for this would mean a decline in profits for the capitalists; it will be used for the purpose of increasing those profits by exporting capital abroad to the backward countries. In these backward countries profits are usually high, for capital is scarce, the price of land is relatively low, wages are low, raw materials are cheap. The possibility of exporting capital is created by the fact that numerous backward countries have been drawn into international capitalist intercourse; main railways have either been built or are being built there; the elementary conditions for industrial development have been created, etc. The necessity for exporting capital arises from the fact that in a few countries capitalism has become "over-ripe" and (owing to the backward state of agriculture and the impoverished state of the masses) capital cannot find "profitable" investment. . . .

. . . The export of capital reached formidable dimensions only in the beginning of the twentieth century. Before the war the capital invested abroad by the three principal countries amounted to between 175,000,000,000 and 200,000,000,000 francs. At the modest rate of 5 per cent, this sum should have brought in from 8 to 10 billions a year. This provided a solid basis for imperialist oppression and the exploitation of most of the countries and nations of the world; a solid basis for the capitalist parasitism of a handful of wealthy states!

How is this capital invested abroad distributed among the various countries? *Where* does it go? . . .

The principal spheres of investment of British capital are the British colonies, which are very large also in America (for example, Canada) not to mention Asia, etc. In this case, enormous exports of capital are bound up with the possession of enormous colonies, of the importance of which for imperialism we shall speak later. In regard to France, the situation is quite different. French capital exports are invested mainly in Europe, particularly in Russia (at least ten billion francs). This is mainly *loan* capital, in the form of government loans and not investments in industrial undertakings. Unlike British colonial imperialism, French imperialism might be termed usury imperialism. In regard to Germany, we have a third type; the German colonies are inconsiderable, and German capital invested abroad is divided fairly evenly between Europe and America.

The export of capital greatly affects and accelerates the development of capitalism in those countries to which it is exported.

While, therefore, the export of capital may tend to a certain extent to arrest development in the countries exporting capital, it can only do so by expanding and deepening the further development of capitalism throughout the world. (*Selected Works,* V, 56–59.)

Finance capital has created the epoch of monopolies, and monopolies introduce everywhere monopolist methods: the utilization of "connections" for profitable transactions takes the place of competition on the open market. The most usual thing is to stipulate that part of the loan that is granted shall be spent on purchases in the country of issue, particularly on orders for war materials, or for ships, etc. In the course of the last two decades (1890–1910), France often resorted to this method. The export of capital abroad thus becomes a means for encouraging the export of commodities. (*Selected Works,* V, 59.)

Finance capital, almost literally, one might say, spreads its net over all countries of the world. Banks founded in the colonies, or their branches, play an important part in these operations. German imperialists look with envy on the "old" colonizing nations which are "well established" in this respect. In 1904, Great Britain had 50 colonial banks with 2,279 branches (in 1910 there were 72 banks with 5,449 branches); France had 20 with 136 branches; Holland 16 with 68 branches; and Germany had a "mere" 13 with 70 branches. The American capitalists, in their turn, are jealous of the English and German: "In South America," they complained in 1915, "five German banks have forty branches and five English banks have seventy branches. . . . England and Germany have invested in Argentina, Brazil and Uruguay in the last twenty-five years approximately four thousand million dollars, and as a result enjoy together 46 per cent of the total trade of these three countries."

The capital exporting countries have divided the world among themselves in the figurative sense of the term. But finance capital has also led to the *actual* division of the world.

6. The Division of the World Among Capitalist Combines

Monopolist capitalist combines — cartels, syndicates, trusts — divide among themselves, first of all, the whole internal market of a country, and impose their control, more or less completely, upon the industry of that country. But under capitalism the home market is inevitably bound up with the foreign market. Capitalism long ago created a world market. As the export of capital increased, and as the foreign and colonial relations and the "spheres of influence" of the big monopolist combines expanded, things "naturally" gravitated toward an international agreement among these combines, and toward the formation of international cartels.

This is a new stage of world concentration of capital and production, incomparably higher than the preceding stages. Let us see how this super-monopoly develops.

The electrical industry is the most typical of the modern technical achievements of capitalism of the *end* of the nineteenth and beginning of the twentieth centuries. This industry has developed most in the two most advanced of the new capitalist countries, the United States and Germany. (*Selected Works,* V, 61.)

After 1900, concentration in Germany proceeded by leaps and bounds. Up to 1900 there had been seven or eight "groups" in the electrical industry. Each was formed of several companies (altogether there were twenty-eight) and each was supported by from two to eleven banks. Between 1908 and 1912 all the groups were merged into two, or possibly one. (*Selected Works,* V, 61 f.)

But concentration in Europe was a part of the process of concentration in America. . . . (*Selected Works,* V, 62.)

In 1907, the German and American trusts concluded an agreement by which they divided the world between themselves. Competition between them ceased. The American General Electric

Company "got" the United States and Canada. The A.E.G. [the German concern] "got" Germany, Austria, Russia, Holland, Denmark, Switzerland, Turkey and the Balkans. Special agreements, naturally secret, were concluded regarding the penetration of "subsidiary" companies into new branches of industry, into "new" countries formally not yet allotted. The two trusts were to exchange inventions and experiments.

It is easy to understand how difficult competition has become against this trust, which is practically worldwide, which controls a capital of several billion, and has its "branches," agencies, representatives, connections, etc., in every corner of the world. But the division of the world between two powerful trusts does not remove the possibility of *redivision,* if the relation of forces changes as a result of uneven development, war, bankruptcy, etc.

The oil industry provides an instructive example of attempts at such a redivision, or rather of a struggle for redivision.

> The world oil market— . . . is even today divided in the main between two great financial groups—Rockefeller's American Standard Oil Co., and the controlling interests of the Russian oil fields in Baku, Rothschild and Nobel. The two groups are in close alliance. But for several years, five enemies have been threatening their monopoly:
>
> (1) The exhaustion of the American oil wells; (2) the competition of the firm of Mantashev of Baku; (3) the Austrian wells; (4) the Rumanian wells; (5) the overseas oilfields, particularly in the Dutch colonies (the extremely rich firms, Samuel and Shell, also connected with British capital). The three last groups are connected with the great German banks, principally, the Deutsche Bank. These banks independently and systematically developed the oil industry in Rumania, in order to have a foothold of their "own." In 1907, 185,000,000 francs of foreign capital were invested in the Rumanian oil industry, of which 74,000,000 came from Germany.

A struggle began, which in economic literature is fittingly called "the struggle for the division of the world." On one side, the Rockefeller trust, wishing to conquer *everything,* formed a subsidiary company *right in* Holland, and bought up oil wells in the Dutch Indies, in order to strike at its principal enemy, the

Anglo-Dutch Shell trust. On the other side, the Deutsche Bank and the other German banks aimed at "retaining" Rumania "for themselves" and at uniting it with Russia against Rockefeller. The latter controlled far more capital and an excellent system of oil transport and distribution. The struggle had to end, and did end in 1907, with the utter defeat of the Deutsche Bank, which was confronted with the alternative: either to liquidate its oil business and lose millions, or to submit. It chose to submit, and concluded a very disadvantageous agreement with the American trust. The Deutsche Bank agreed "not to attempt anything which might injure American interests." Provision was made, however, for the annulment of the agreement in the event of Germany establishing a state oil monopoly.

Then the "comedy of oil" began. One of the German finance kings, von Gwinner, a director of the Deutsche Bank, began through his private secretary, Stauss, a campaign *for* a state oil monopoly. The gigantic machine of the big German bank and all its wide "connections" were set in motion. The press bubbled over with "patriotic" indignation against the "yoke" of the American trust, and, on March 15, 1911, the Reichstag by an almost unanimous vote, adopted a motion asking the government to introduce a bill for the establishment of an oil monopoly. The government seized upon this "popular" idea, and the game of the Deutsche Bank, which hoped to cheat its American partner and improve its business by a state monopoly, appeared to have been won. The German oil magnates saw visions of wonderful profits, which would not be less than those of the Russian sugar refiners. . . . But, firstly, the big German banks quarrelled among themselves over the division of the spoils. The Disconto-Gesellschaft exposed the covetous aims of the Deutsche Bank; secondly, the government took fright at the prospect of a struggle with Rockefeller; it was doubtful whether Germany could be sure of obtaining oil from other sources. (The Rumanian output was small.) Thirdly, just at that time the 1913 credits of a billion marks were voted for Germany's war preparations. The project of the oil monopoly was postponed. The Rockefeller trust came out of the struggle, for the time being, victorious. (*Selected Works,* V, 63–65.)

In mercantile shipping, the tremendous development of concentration has ended also in the division of the world. In Germany two powerful companies have raised themselves to first rank, the Hamburg-Amerika Line and the Norddeutscher Lloyd, each having a capital of 200,000,000 marks (in stocks and bonds) and possessing 185 to 189 million marks worth of shipping tonnage. On the other side, in America, on January 1, 1903, the Morgan trust, the International Mercantile Marine Co., was formed which united nine British and American steamship companies, and which controlled a capital of 120,000,000 dollars. As early as 1903, the German giants and the Anglo-American trust concluded an agreement and divided the world in accordance with the division of profits. The German companies undertook not to compete in the Anglo-American traffic. The ports were carefully "allotted" to each; a joint committee of control was set up, etc. This contract was concluded for twenty years, with the prudent provision for its annulment in the event of war. (*Selected Works*, V, 66.)

The epoch of modern capitalism shows us that certain relations are established between capitalist alliances, *based* on the economic division of the world; while parallel with this fact and in connection with it, certain relations are established between political alliances, between states, on the basis of the territorial division of the world, of the struggle for colonies, of the "struggle for economic territory." (*Selected Works*, V, 68.)

7. THE DIVISION OF THE WORLD AMONG THE GREAT POWERS

Hobson, in his work on imperialism, marks the years 1884-1900 as the period of the intensification of the colonial "expansion" of the chief European states. According to his estimate, Great Britain during these years acquired 3,700,000 square miles of territory with a population of 57,000,000; France acquired 3,600,000 square miles with a population of 36,500,000; Germany 1,000,000 square miles with a population of 16,700,000; Belgium 900,000 square miles with 30,000,000 inhabitants; Portugal 800,000 square miles with 9,000,000 inhabitants. The quest for colonies by all the capitalist states at the end of the nineteenth century and particularly since the 1880's is a commonly known fact in the history of diplomacy and of foreign affairs.

When free competition in Great Britain was at its zenith, i.e., between 1840 and 1860, the leading British bourgeois politicians were opposed to colonial policy and were of the opinion that the liberation of the colonies and their complete separation from Britain was inevitable and desirable.... Disraeli, a statesman generally inclined toward imperialism, declared: "The colonies are millstones round our necks." But at the end of the nineteenth century the heroes of the hour in England were Cecil Rhodes and Joseph Chamberlain, open advocates of imperialism, who applied the imperialist policy in the most cynical manner.

It is not without interest to observe that even at that time these leading British bourgeois politicians fully appreciated the connection between what might be called the purely economic and the politico-social roots of modern imperialism. Chamberlain advocated imperialism by calling it a "true, wise and economical policy," and he pointed particularly to the German, American and Belgian competition which Great Britain was encountering in the world market. Salvation lies in monopolies, said the capitalists as they formed cartels, syndicates and trusts. Salvation lies in monopolies, echoed the political leaders of the bourgeoisie, hastening to appropriate the parts of the world not yet shared out. The journalist, Stead, relates the following remarks uttered by his close friend Cecil Rhodes, in 1895, regarding his imperialist ideas:

> I was in the East End of London yesterday and attended a meeting of the unemployed. I listened to the wild speeches, which were just a cry for "bread," "bread," "bread," and on my way home I pondered over the scene and I became more than ever convinced of the importance of imperialism.... My cherished idea is a solution for the social problem, i.e., in order to save the 40,000,000 inhabitants of the United Kingdom from a bloody civil war, we colonial statesmen must acquire new lands to settle the surplus

population, to provide new markets for the goods produced by them in the factories and mines. The Empire, as I have always said, is a bread and butter question. If you want to avoid civil war, you must become imperialists.

This is what Cecil Rhodes, millionaire, king of finance, the man who was mainly responsible for the Boer War, said in 1895. His defense of imperialism is just crude and cynical, but in substance it does not differ from the "theory" advocated by Messrs. Maslov, Südekum, Potresov, David and the founder of Russian Marxism [Plekhanov] and others. Cecil Rhodes was a somewhat more honest social chauvinist. (*Selected Works*, V, 70–72.)

. . . The unevenness in the rate of expansion of colonial possessions is very marked. If, for instance, we compare France, Germany and Japan, which do not differ very much in area and population, we will see that the first has annexed almost three times as much colonial territory as the other two combined. In regard to finance capital, also, France, at the beginning of the period we are considering, was perhaps several times richer than Germany and Japan put together. In addition to, and on the basis of, purely economic causes, geographical conditions and other factors also affect the dimensions of colonial possessions. However strong the process of levelling the world, of levelling the economic and living conditions in different countries, may have been in the past decades as a result of the pressure of large-scale industry, exchange and finance capital, great differences still remain; and among the six powers, we see, firstly, young capitalist powers (America, Germany, Japan) which progressed very rapidly; secondly, countries with an old capitalist development (France and Great Britain), which, of late, have made much slower progress than the previously mentioned countries, and, thirdly, a country (Russia) which is economically most backward, in which modern capitalist imperialism is enmeshed, so to speak, in a particularly close network of pre-capitalist relations. Alongside the colonial possessions of these great powers, we have placed the small colonies of the small states, which are, so to speak, the next possible and probable objects of a new colonial "shareout." Most of these little states are able to retain their colonies only because of the conflicting interests, frictions, etc., among the big powers, which prevent them from coming to an agreement in regard to the division of the spoils. The "semicolonial states" provide an example of the transitional forms which are to be found in all spheres of nature and society. Finance capital is such a great, it may be said, such a decisive force in all economic and international relations, that it is capable of subordinating to itself, and actually does subordinate to itself, even states enjoying complete political independence. We shall shortly see examples of this. Naturally, however, finance capital finds it most "convenient," and is able to extract the greatest profit from a subordination which involves the loss of the political independence of the subjected countries and peoples. In this connection, the semicolonial countries provide a typical example of the "middle stage." It is natural that the struggle for these semi-dependent countries should have become particularly bitter during the period of finance capital, when the rest of the world had already been divided up.

Colonial policy and imperialism existed before this latest stage of capitalism, and even before capitalism. Rome, founded on slavery, pursued a colonial policy and achieved imperialism. But "general" arguments about imperialism, which ignore, or put into the background the fundamental difference of socio-economic systems, inevitably degenerate into absolutely empty banalities, or into grandiloquent comparisons like "Greater Rome and Greater Britain." Even the colonial policy of capitalism in its *previous* stages is essentially different from the colonial policy of finance capital.

The principal feature of modern capitalism is the domination of monopolist combines of the big capitalists. These monopolies are most firmly established when *all* the sources of raw material are controlled by the one group. And we have seen with what zeal the international capitalist combines exert every effort to make it impossible for their rivals to compete with them; for example, by buying up mineral lands, oil fields, etc. Colonial possession alone gives complete guarantee of success to the monopolies against all the risks of the struggle with competitors, including the risk that the latter will defend themselves by means of a law establishing a state monopoly. The more capitalism is developed, the more the need for raw materials is felt, the more bitter competition becomes, and the more feverishly the hunt for raw materials proceeds throughout the whole world, the more desperate becomes the struggle for the acquisition of colonies. (*Selected Works,* V, 73–75.)

Finance capital is not only interested in the already known sources of raw materials; it is also interested in potential sources of raw materials, because present-day technical development is extremely rapid, and because land which is useless today may be made fertile tomorrow if new methods are applied (to devise these new methods a big bank can equip a whole expedition of engineers, agricultural experts, etc.), and large amounts of capital are invested. This also applies to prospecting for minerals, to new methods of working up and utilizing raw materials, etc., etc. Hence, the inevitable striving of finance capital to extend its economic territory and even its territory in general. In the same way that the trusts capitalize their property by estimating it at two or three times its values, taking into account its "potential" (and not present) returns, and the further results of monopoly, so finance capital strives to seize the largest possible amount of land of all kinds and in any place it can, and by any means, counting on the possibilities of finding raw materials there, and fearing to be left behind in the insensate struggle for the last available scraps of undivided territory, or for the repartition of that which has been already divided. (*Selected Works,* V, 76 f.)

The necessity of exporting capital also gives an impetus to the conquest of colonies, for in the colonial market it is easier to eliminate competition, to make sure of orders, to strengthen the necessary "connections," etc., by monopolistic methods (and sometimes it is the only possible way) .

The non-economic superstructure which grows up on the basis of finance capital, its politics and its ideology, stimulates the striving for colonial conquest. "Finance capital does not want liberty, it wants domination," as Hilferding very truly says. (*Selected Works*, V, 77.)

Since we are speaking of colonial policy in the period of capitalist imperialism, it must be observed that finance capital and its corresponding foreign policy, which reduces itself to the struggle of the great powers for the economic and political division of the world, give rise to a number of *transitional* forms of national dependence. The division of the world into two main groups—of colony-owning countries on the one hand and colonies on the other—is not the only typical feature of this period; there is also a variety of forms of dependent countries; countries which, officially, are politically independent, but which are, in fact, enmeshed in the net of financial and diplomatic dependence. We have already referred to one form of dependence—the semi-colony. Another example is provided by Argentina.

"South America, and especially Argentina," writes Schulze-Gaevernitz in his work on British imperialism, "is so dependent financially on London that it ought to be described as almost a British commercial colony." (*Selected Works*, V, 77 f.)

A somewhat different form of financial and diplomatic dependence, accompanied by political independence, is presented by Portugal. Portugal is an independent sovereign state. In actual fact, however, for more than two hundred years, since the war of the Spanish Succession (1700–14), it has been a British protectorate. Great Britain has protected Portugal and her colonies in order to fortify her own positions in the fight against her rivals, Spain and France. In return she has received commercial advantages, preferential import of goods, and, above all, of capital into Portugal and the Portuguese colonies, the right to use the ports and islands of Portugal, her telegraph cables, etc. Relations of this kind have always existed between big and little states. But during the period of capitalist imperialism they become a general system, they form part of the process of "dividing the world"; they become a link in the chain of operations of world finance capital. (*Selected Works,* V, 78 f.)

8. Imperialism as a Special Stage of Capitalism

We must now try to sum up and put together what has been said above on the subject of imperialism. Imperialism emerged as the development and direct continuation of the fundamental attributes of capitalism in general. But capitalism only became capitalist imperialism at a definite and very high stage of its development, when certain of its fundamental attributes began to be transformed into their opposites, when the features of a period of transition from capitalism to a higher social and economic system began to take shape and reveal themselves all along the line. Economically, the main thing in this process is the substitution of capitalist monopolies for capitalist free competition. Free competition is the fundamental attribute of capitalism and of commodity production generally. Monopoly is exactly the opposite of free competition; but we have seen the latter being transformed into monopoly before our very eyes, creating large-scale industry and eliminating small industry, replacing large-scale industry by still larger-scale industry, finally leading to such a concentration of production and capital that monopoly has been and is the result: cartels, syndicates and trusts, and merging with them, the capital of a dozen or so banks manipulating thousands of millions. At the same time monopoly, which has grown out of free competition, does not abolish the latter, but exists over it and alongside of it, and thereby gives rise to a number of very acute, intense antagonisms, friction and conflicts. Monopoly is the transition from capitalism to a higher system.

If it were necessary to give the briefest possible definition of imperialism, we should have to say that imperialism is the monopoly stage of capitalism. Such a definition would include what is most important, for, on the one hand, finance capital is the bank capital of a few big monopolist banks, merged with the capital of the monopolist combines of manufacturers; and, on the other hand, the division of the world is the transition from a colonial policy which has extended without hindrance to territories unoccupied by any capitalist power, to a colonial policy of monopolistic possession of the territory of the world which has been completely divided up.

But very brief definitions, although convenient, for they sum up the main points, are nevertheless inadequate, because very important features of the phenomenon that has to be defined have to be especially deduced. And so, without forgetting the conditional and relative value of all definitions, which can never include all the concatenations of a phenomenon in its complete development, we must give a definition of imperialism that will embrace the following five essential features:

1. The concentration of production and capital developed to such a high stage that it created monopolies which play a decisive role in economic life.

2. The merging of bank capital with industrial capital, and the creation, on the basis of this "finance capital," of a "financial oligarchy."

3. The export of capital, which has become extremely important as distinguished from the export of commodities.

4. The formation of international capitalist monopolies which share the world among themselves.

5. The territorial division of the whole world among the greatest capitalist powers is completed.

Imperialism is capitalism in that stage of development in which the dominance of monopolies and finance capital has established itself; in which the export of capital has acquired pronounced importance; in which the division of the world among the international trusts has begun; in which the division of all territories of the globe among the great capitalist powers has been completed. (*Selected Works*, V, 80 f.)

Capitalism is growing with the greatest rapidity in the colonies and in overseas countries. Among the latter, *new* imperialist powers are emerging (e.g., Japan). The struggle of world imperialism is becoming more acute. The tribute levied by finance capital on the most profitable colonial and overseas enterprises is increasing. In sharing out this "booty," an exceptionally large part goes to countries which, as far as the development of productive forces is concerned, do not always stand at the top of the list. . . .

About 80 per cent of the total existing railways are concentrated in the hands of the five great powers. But the concentration of the *ownership* of these railways, of finance capital, is much greater still: French and English millionaires, for example, own an enormous amount of stocks and bonds in American, Russian and other railways.

Thanks to her colonies, Great Britain has increased the length of "her" railways by 100,000 kilometres, four times as much as Germany. And yet, it is well known that the development of productive forces in Germany, and especially the development of the coal and iron industries, has been much more rapid during this period than in England—not to mention France and Russia. In 1892, Germany produced 4,900,000 tons of pig iron and Great Britain produced 6,800,000 tons; in 1912, Germany, produced 17,600,000 tons and Great Britain 9,000,000 tons. Germany, therefore, had an overwhelming superiority over England in this respect. We ask, is there *under capitalism* any means of removing the disparity between the development of productive forces and the accumulation of capital on the one side, and the division of colonies and "spheres of influence" for finance capital on the other side—other than by resorting to war? (*Selected Works,* V, 89 f.)

9. THE PARASITISM AND DECAY OF CAPITALISM

As we have seen, the most deep-rooted economic foundation of imperialism is monopoly. This is capitalist monopoly, i.e., monopoly which has grown out of capitalism and exists in the general environment of capitalism, commodity production and competition, and remains in permanent and insoluble contradiction to this general environment. Nevertheless, like all monopoly, this capitalist monopoly inevitably gives rise to a tendency to stagnation and decay. As monopoly prices become fixed, even temporarily, so the stimulus to technical and, consequently, to all progress, disappears to a certain extent, and to that extent, also, the *economic* possibility arises of deliberately retarding technical progress. For instance, in America, a certain Mr. Owens invented a machine which revolutionized the manufacture of bottles. The German bottle manufacturing cartel purchased Owens' patent, but pigeonholed it, refrained from utilizing it. Certainly, monopoly under capitalism can never completely, and for a long period of time, eliminate competition in the world market (and this, by the by, is one of the reasons why the theory of ultra-imperialism is so absurd). Certainly the possibility of reducing cost of production and increasing profits by introducing technical improvements operates in the direction of change. Nevertheless, the *tendency* to stagnation and decay, which is the feature of monopoly, continues, and in certain branches of industry, in certain countries, for certain periods of time, it becomes predominant.

The monopoly of ownership of very extensive, rich or well situated colonies, operates in the same direction.

Further, imperialism is an immense accumulation of money capital in a few countries, which, as we have seen, amounts to 100–150 billion francs in various securities. Hence the extraordinary growth of a class, or rather of a category, of *stockholders (rentiers)*, i.e., people who live by "clipping coupons," who take no part whatever in production, whose profession is idleness. The export of capital, one of the most essential economic bases of imperialism, still more completely isolates the *stockholders* from production and sets the seal of parasitism on the whole country that lives by the exploitation of the labor of several overseas countries and colonies. (*Selected Works,* V, 91 f.)

The income of the stockholders is *five times greater* than the income obtained from the foreign trade of the greatest "trading" country in the world. This is the essence of imperialism and imperialist parasitism.

For that reason the term, "rentier state", or usurer state, is passing into current use in the economic literature that deals with imperialism. The world has become divided into a handful of usurer states on the one side, and a vast majority of debtor states on the other. (*Selected Works*, V, 92 f.)

The rentier state is a state of parasitic, decaying capitalism, and this circumstance cannot fail to influence all the social-political conditions of the countries affected generally, and the two fundamental trends in the working class movement, in particular. To demonstrate this in the clearest possible manner we will quote Hobson, who will be regarded as a more "reliable" witness, since he cannot be suspected of leanings toward "orthodox Marxism"; moreover, he is an Englishman who is very well acquainted with the situation in the country which is richest in colonies, in finance capital, and in imperialist experience.

With the Boer War fresh in his mind, Hobson describes the connection between imperialism and the interests of the "financiers," the growing profits from contracts, etc., and writes:

> While the directors of this definitely parasitic policy are capitalists, the same motives appeal to special classes of the workers. In many towns, most important trades are dependent upon government employment or contracts; the imperialism of the metal and ship-building centers is attributable in no small degree to this fact. (*Selected Works*, V, 93 f.)

In speaking of the British working class, the bourgeois student of "British imperialism at the beginning of the twentieth century" is obliged to distinguish systematically between the *"upper stratum"* of the workers and the *"lower stratum of the proletariat proper."* The upper stratum furnishes the main body of members of co-operatives, of trade unions, of sporting clubs and of numerous religious sects. The electoral system, which in Great Britain is still *"sufficiently restricted to exclude the lower stratum of the proletariat proper,"* is adapted to their level!! In order to present the condition of the British working class in the best possible light, only this upper stratum—which constitues only a *minority* of the proletariat—is generally spoken of. For instance, "the problem of unemployment is mainly a London problem and that of the lower proletarian stratum, *which is of little political moment* for politicians." It would be better to say: which is of little political moment for the bourgeois politicians and the "socialist" opportunists.

Another special feature of imperialism, which is connected with the facts we are describing, is the decline in emigration from imperialist countries, and the increase in immigration into these countries from the backward countries where lower wages are paid. (*Selected Works*, V, 96 f.)

The distinctive feature of the present situation is the prevalence of economic and political conditions which could not but increase the irreconcilability between opportunism and the general and vital interests of the working class movement. Embryonic imperialism has grown into a dominant system; capitalist monopolies occupy first place in economics and politics; the division of the world has been completed. On the other hand, instead of an undisputed monopoly by Great Britain, we see a few imperialist powers contending for the right to share in this monopoly, and this struggle is characteristic of the whole period of the beginning of the twentieth century. Opportunism, therefore, cannot now triumph in the working class movement of any country for decades as it did in England in the second half of the nineteenth century. But, in a number of countries it has grown ripe, over-ripe and rotten, and has become completely merged with bourgeois policy in the form of "social chauvinism." (*Selected Works*, V, 99.)

10. The Critique of Imperialism

By the critique of imperialism, in the broad sense of the term, we mean the attitude toward imperialist policy of the different classes of society as part of their general ideology.

The enormous dimensions of finance capital concentrated in a few hands and creating an extremely extensive and close network of ties and relationships which subordinate not only the small and medium, but also even the very small capitalists and small masters, on the one hand, and the intense struggle waged against other national state groups of financiers for the division of the world and domination over other countries, on the other hand, cause the wholesale transition of the possessing classes to the side of imperialism. The signs of the times are a "general" enthusiasm regarding its prospects, a passionate defense of imperialism, and every possible embellishment of its real nature. The imperialist ideology also penetrates the working class. There is no Chinese Wall between it and the other classes. The leaders of the so-called Social Democratic party of Germany are today justly called "social imperialists," that is, socialists in words and imperialists in deeds; but as early as 1902, Hobson noted the existence of "Fabian imperialists" who belonged to the opportunist Fabian Society in England.

Bourgeois scholars and publicists usually come out in defense of imperialism in a somewhat veiled form, and obscure its complete domination and its profound roots; they strive to concentrate attention on partial and secondary details and do their very best to distract attention from the main issue by means of ridiculous schemes for "reform," such as police supervision of the trusts and banks, etc. Less frequently, cynical and frank imperialists speak out and are bold enough to admit the absurdity of the idea of reforming the fundamental features of imperialism. (*Selected Works,* V, 100 f.)

The question as to whether it is possible to reform the basis of imperialism, whether to go forward to the accentuation and deepening of the antagonisms which it engenders, or backward, toward allaying these antagonisms, is a fundamental question in the critique of imperialism. As a consequence of the fact that the political features of imperialism are reaction all along the line, and increased national oppression, resulting from the oppression of the financial oligarchy and the elimination of free competition, a petty bourgeois-democratic opposition has been rising against imperialism in almost all imperialist countries since the beginning of the twentieth century. (*Selected Works,* V, 101 f.)

Let us consider India, Indo-China and China. It is known that these three colonial and semicolonial countries, inhabited by six to seven hundred million human beings, are subjected to the exploitation of the finance capital of several imperialist states: Great Britain, France, Japan, the U.S.A., etc. We will assume that these imperialist countries form alliances against one another in order to protect and extend their possessions, their interests and their "spheres of influence" in these Asiatic states; these alliances will be "inter-imperialist," or "ultra-imperialist" alliances. We will assure that *all* the imperialist countries conclude an alliance for the "peaceful" division of these parts of Asia; this alliance would be an alliance of "internationally united finance capital." As a matter of fact, alliances of this kind have been made in the twentieth century, notably with regard to China. We ask, is it "conceivable," assuming that the capitalist system remains intact—and this is precisely the assumption that Kautsky does make—that such alliances would be more than temporary, that they would eliminate friction, conflicts and struggle in all and every possible form?

This question need only be stated clearly enough to make it impossible for any other reply to be given than that in the negative; for there can be *no* other conceivable basis under capitalism for the division of spheres of influence, of interests, of colonies, etc., than a calculation of the *strength* of the participants in the division, their general economic, financial, military strength, etc. And the strength of these participants in the division does not change to an equal degree, for under capitalism the development of different undertakings, trusts, branches of industry or countries cannot be *even*. Half a century ago, Germany was a miserable, insignificant country, as far as its capitalist strength was concerned, compared with the strength of England at that time. Japan was similarly insignificant compared with Russia. Is it "conceivable" that in ten or twenty years' time the relative strength of the imperialist powers will have remained *un*changed? Absolutely inconceivable.

Therefore, in the realities of the capitalist system, and not in the banal philistine fantasies of English parsons, or of the German "Marxist," Kautsky, "inter-imperialist" or "ultra-imperialist" alliances, no matter what form they may assume, whether of one imperialist coalition against another, or of a general alliance embracing *all* the imperialist powers, are *inevitably* nothing more than a "truce" in periods between wars. Peaceful alliances prepare the ground for wars, and in their turn grow out of wars; the one is the condition for the other, giving rise to alternating forms of peaceful and non-peaceful struggle out of *one and the same* basis of imperialist connections and the relations between economics and world politics. (*Selected Works*, V, 109 f.)

Imperialism is the epoch of finance capital and of monopolies, which introduce everywhere the striving for domination, not for freedom. The result of these tendencies is reaction all along the line, whatever the political system, and an extreme intensification of existing antagonisms in this domain also. Particularly acute becomes the yoke of national oppression and the striving for annexations, i.e., the violation of national independence (for annexation is nothing but the violation of the right of nations to self-determination). (*Selected Works*, V, 111.)

It is not only in newly opened up countries, but also in the old, that imperialism is leading to annexation, to increased national oppression, and, consequently, also to increasing resistance. (*Selected Works*, V, 112.)

11. THE PLACE OF IMPERIALISM IN HISTORY

We have seen that the economic quintessence of imperialism is monopoly capitalism. This very fact determines its place in history, for monopoly that grew up on the basis of free competition, and precisely out of free competition, is the transition from the capitalist system to a higher social-economic order. We must take special note of the four principal forms of monopoly, or the four principal manifestations of monopoly capitalism, which are characteristic of the epoch under review.

Firstly, monopoly arose out of the concentration of production at a very advanced stage of development. This refers to the monopolist capitalist combines, cartels, syndicates and trusts. We have seen the important part that these play in modern economic life. At the beginning of the twentieth century, monopolies acquired complete supremacy in the advanced countries. And although the first steps toward the formation of the cartels were first taken by countries enjoying the protection of high tariffs (Germany, America), Great Britain, with her system of free trade, was not far behind in revealing the same basic phenomenon, namely, the birth of monopoly out of the concentration of production.

Secondly, monopolies have accelerated the capture of the most important sources of raw materials, especially for the coal and iron industries, which are the basic and most highly cartelized industries in capitalist society. The monopoly of the most important sources of raw materials has enormously increased the power of big capital, and has sharpened the antagonism between cartelized and non-cartelized industry.

Thirdly, monopoly has sprung from the banks. The banks have developed from modest intermediary enterprises into the monopolists of finance capital. Some three or five of the biggest banks in each of the foremost capitalist countries have achieved the "personal union" of industrial and bank capital, and have concentrated in their hands the disposal of thousands upon thousands of millions which form the greater part of the capital and income of entire countries. A financial oligarchy, which throws a close net of relations of dependence over all the economic and political institutions of contemporary bourgeois society without exception—such is the most striking manifestation of this monopoly.

Fourthly, monopoly has grown out of colonial policy. To the numerous "old" motives of colonial policy, finance capital has added the struggle for the sources of raw materials, for the export of capital, for "spheres of influence," i.e., for spheres for profitable deals, concessions, monopolist profits and so on; in fine, for economic territory in general. When the colonies of the European powers in Africa, for instance, comprised only one-tenth of that territory (as was the case in 1876), colonial policy was able to develop by methods other than those of monopoly—by the "free grabbing" of territories, so to speak. But when nine-tenths of Africa had been seized (approximately by 1900), when the whole world had been divided up, there was inevitably ushered in a period of colonial monopoly and, consequently, a period of particularly intense struggle for the division and the redivision of the world.

The extent to which monopolist capital has intensified all the contradictions of capitalism is generally known. It is sufficient to mention the high cost of living and the oppression of the cartels. This intensification of contradictions constitutes the most powerful driving force of the transitional period of history, which began from the time of the definite victory of world finance capital.

Monopolies, oligarchy, the striving for domination instead of the striving for liberty, the exploitation of an increasing number of small or weak nations by an extremely small group of the richest or most powerful nations—all these have given birth to those distinctive characteristics of imperialism which compel us to define it as parasitic or decaying capitalism. More and more prominently there emerges, as one of the tendencies of imperialism, the creation of the stockholding state, the usurer state, in which the bourgeoisie lives on the proceeds of capital exports and by "clipping coupons." It would be a mistake to believe that this tendency to decay precludes the possibility of the rapid growth of capitalism. It does not. In the epoch of imperialism, certain branches of industry, certain strata of the bourgeoisie and certain countries betray, to a more or less degree, one or other of these tendencies. On the whole, capitalism is growing far more rapidly than before. But this growth is not only becoming more and more uneven in general; its unevenness also manifests itself, in particular, in the decay of the countries which are richest in capital (such as England). (*Selected Works*, V, 114–116.)

In its turn, this finance capital which has grown so rapidly is not unwilling (precisely because it has grown so quickly) to pass on to a more "tranquil" possession of colonies which have to be seized—and not only by peaceful methods—from richer nations. In the United States, economic development in the last decades has been even more rapid than in Germany, and *for this very reason* the parasitic character of modern American capitalism has stood out with particular prominence. On the other hand, a comparison of, say, the republican American bourgeoisie with the monarchist Japanese or German bourgeoisie shows that the most pronounced political distinctions diminish to an extreme degree in the epoch of imperialism—not because they are unimportant in general, but because in all these cases we are discussing a bourgeoisie which has definite features of parasitism.

The receipt of high monopoly profits by the capitalists in one of the numerous branches of industry, in one of numerous countries, etc., makes it economically possible for them to corrupt certain sections of the working class, and for a time a fairly considerable minority, and win them to the side of the bourgeoisie of a given industry or nation against all the others. The intensification of antagonisms between imperialist nations for the division of the world increases this striving. And so there is created that bond between imperialism and opportunism, which revealed itself first and most clearly in England, owing to the fact that certain features of imperialist development were observable there much earlier than in other countries. (*Selected Works*, V, 116 f.)

From all that has been said in this book on the economic nature of imperialism, it follows that we must define it as capitalism in transition, or, more precisely, as moribund capitalism. It is very instructive in this respect to note that the bourgeois economists, in describing modern capitalism, frequently employ terms like "interlocking," "absence of isolation," etc.; "in conformity with their functions and course of development," banks are "not purely private business enterprises; they are more and more outgrowing the sphere of purely private business regulation." And this very Riesser, who uttered the words just quoted, declares with all seriousness that the "prophecy" of the Marxists concerning "socialization" has "not come true"!

What then does this word "interlocking" express? It merely expresses the most striking feature of the process going on before our eyes. It shows that the observer counts the separate trees, but cannot see the wood. It slavishly copies the superficial, the fortuitous, the chaotic. It reveals the observer as one who is overwhelmed by the mass of raw material and is utterly incapable of appreciating its meaning and importance. Ownership of shares and relations between owners of private property "interlock in a haphazard way." But the underlying factor of this interlocking, its very base, is the changing social relations of production. When a big enterprise assumes gigantic proportions, and, on the basis of exact computation of mass data, organizes according to plan the supply of primary raw materials to the extent of two-thirds or three-fourths of all that is necessary for tens of millions of people; when the raw materials are transported to the most suitable place of production, sometimes hundreds or thousands of miles away, in a systematic and organized manner; when a single center directs all the successive stages of work right up to the manufacture of numerous varieties of finished articles; when these products are distributed according to a single plan among tens and hundreds of millions of consumers (as in the case of the distribution of oil in America and Germany by the American "oil trust")—then it becomes evident that we have socialization of production, and not mere "interlocking"; that private economic relations and private property relations constitute a shell which is no longer suitable for its contents, a shell which must inevitably begin to decay if its destruction be delayed by artificial means; a shell which may continue in a state of decay for a fairly long period (particularly if the cure of the opportunist abscess is protracted), but which will inevitably be removed. (*Selected Works*, V, 117–119.)

Imperialism is a specific historical stage of capitalism. Its specific character is threefold: Imperialism is (1) monopoly capitalism, (2) parasitic or decaying capitalism, (3) moribund capitalism. The substitution of monopoly for free competition is the fundamental economic feature, the *quintessence* of imperialism.

The Roman proletarian lived at the expense of society. Modern society lives at the expense of the modern proletarian. Marx specially stressed this profound observation of Sismondi. Imperialism somewhat changes the situation. A privileged upper stratum of the proletariat in the imperialist countries lives partly at the expense of hundreds of millions of members of uncivilized nations.

.   .   .   .

Imperialism is the rule *not* of industrial capital but of finance capital, the striving to annex *not* agrarian countries particularly, but *every kind* of country.

.   .   .   .

There is the tendency of the bourgeoisie and the opportunists to convert a handful of very rich and privileged nations into "eternal" parasites on the body of the rest of mankind, to "rest on the laurels" of the exploitation of Negroes, Hindus, etc., keeping them in subjection with the aid of the excellent technique of extermination provided by modern militarism. On the other hand, there is the tendency of the *masses,* who are more oppressed than ever and who bear the whole brunt of imperialist wars, to cast off this yoke and to overthrow the bourgeoisie. It is in the struggle between these two tendencies that the history of the labor movement will inevitably develop from now on. (*Imperialism and the Split in Socialism,* Fall, 1916, *Selected Works,* XI, 748, 749 f., 750, 759.)

World imperialism must fall when the revolutionary onslaught of the exploited and oppressed workers in each country, overcoming the resistance of the petty bourgeois elements and the influence of the small upper stratum of the labor aristocracy, will unite with the revolutionary onslaught of hundreds of millions of people who up to now have stood outside of history and have been regarded merely as the object of history. (*The International Situation and the Fundamental Tasks of the Communist International,* July 19, 1920, *Selected Works,* X, 197.)

The characteristic feature of imperialism is that the whole

world . . . is at present divided into a large number of oppressed nations and an insignificant number of oppressing nations possessing colossal wealth and powerful military forces. The overwhelming majority of the population of the world, numbering more than a billion, in all probability a billion and a quarter, if we take the total population of the world at one and three-quarter billion, i.e., about 70 per cent of the population of the world, belongs to the oppressed nations, which are either in a state of direct colonial dependence or belong to the outlying colonial states such as Persia, Turkey and China, or else, after being conquered by the armies of a big imperialist power, have been forced into dependence upon it by treaties. This distinction, the idea of dividing the nations into oppressing and oppressed nations, runs like a thread through all the theses. (*The Report of the Commission on the National and Colonial Question at the Second Congress of the Communist International,* July 26, 1920, *Selected Works,* X, 239 f.)

VII

ORGANIZATION

To establish and consolidate the Party means establishing and consolidating unity among all Russian Social Democrats, and for the reasons indicated above, such unity cannot be brought about by decree; it cannot be brought about by, let us say, a meeting of representatives passing a resolution. Definite work must be done to bring it about. In the first place, it is necessary to bring about unity of ideas which will remove the differences of opinion and confusion that—we will be frank—reign among Russian Social Democrats at the present time. This unity of ideas must be fortified by a unified Party program. Secondly, an organization must be set up especially for the purpose of maintaining contact among all the centers of the movement, for supplying complete and timely information about the movement, and for regularly distributing the periodical press to all parts of Russia. Only when we have built such an organization, only when we have created a Russian socialist mailing system, will the permanent existence of the Party be assured, only then will it become a real factor and, consequently, a mighty political force. To the first half of this task, i.e., creating a common literature, consistent in principle and capable of ideologically uniting revolutionary Social Democracy, we intend to devote our efforts, for we regard this as one of the pressing tasks of the present day movement and a necessary preliminary measure toward the resumption of Party activity.

As we have already said, the intellectual unity of Russian Social Democrats has still to be established, and in order to achieve this it is necessary, in our opinion, to have an open and thorough discussion of the fundamental principles and tactical questions raised by the present day economists, Bernsteinists and "critics." Before we can unite, and in order that we may unite, we must first of all firmly and definitely draw the lines of demarcation. Otherwise, our unity will be merely a fictitious unity, which will conceal the prevailing confusion and prevent its complete elimination. Naturally, therefore, we do not intend to utilize our publication merely as a storehouse for various views. On the contrary, we shall conduct it along the lines of a strictly defined tendency. This tendency can be expressed by the word Marxism, and there is hardly need to add that we stand for the consistent development of the ideas of Marx and Engels, and utterly reject the half-way, vague and opportunistic emendations which have now become so fashionable as a result of the *legerdemain* of Ed. Bernstein, P. Struve and many others. But while discussing all questions from our own definite point of view, we shall not rule out of our columns polemics between comrades. Open polemics within the sight and hearing of all Russian Social Democrats and class conscious workers are necessary and desirable, in order to explain the profound differences that exist, to obtain a comprehensive discussion of disputed questions, and to combat the extremes into which the representatives, not only of various views, but also of various localities or various "crafts" in the revolutionary movement inevitably fall. As has already been stated, we also consider one of the drawbacks of the present-day movement to be the absence of open polemics among those holding avowedly differing views, an effort to conceal the differences that exist over extremely serious questions.

.   .   .   .

"Push out the framework and broaden the content of our propaganda, agitational and organizational activity"—these words uttered by P. B. Axelrod must serve as our slogan defining the activities of Russian Social Democrats in the immediate future, and we adopt this slogan in the program of our organ.

We appeal not only to Socialists and class-conscious workers; we also call upon all those who are oppressed by the present political system. We place the columns of our publication at their disposal in order that they may expose all the abominations of the Russian autocracy.

Those who regard Social Democracy as an organization serving exclusively the spontaneous struggle of the proletariat may remain satisfied with merely local agitation and "pure and simple" labor literature. We do not regard Social Democracy in this way; we regard it as a revolutionary party, inseparably linked up with the labor movement and directed against absolutism. Only when organized in such a party will the proletariat—the most revolutionary class in modern Russia—be in a position to fulfill the historical task that confronts it, namely, to unite under its banner all the democratic elements in the country and to crown the stubborn fight waged by a number of generations that have perished in the past, with the final triumph over the hated regime. (*Declaration by the Editorial Board of "Iskra,"* September, 1900, *Selected Works,* II, 6 f., 7 f.)

"Organize!" is the appeal *Rabochaya Mysl* repeats to the workers in a thousand different sharps and flats, and this appeal is taken up by all the adherents of the Economist tendency. We, of course, wholly endorse this appeal but we unconditionally add to it: Organize not only in benefit societies, strike funds and workers' circles, but organize also in a political party, organize for the determined struggle against the autocratic government, and against the whole of capitalist society. Unless the proletariat organizes in this way, it will never rise to the heights of class-conscious struggle; unless the workers organize in this way, the labor movement is doomed to impotence. Merely with the aid of funds and circles and benefit societies, the working class will never be able to fulfill its great historic mission: to emancipate itself and the whole of the Russian people from political and economic slavery. Not a single class in history has achieved power without producing its political leaders, its prominent representatives able to organize a movement and lead it.

Organization. This is one of the sorest questions confronting us. In this respect, we lag considerably behind the old workers in the Russian revolutionary movement. We must frankly admit this defect, and exert all our efforts to devise methods of greater secrecy in our work, to conduct systematic propaganda explaining the proper methods of conducting the work, proper methods of deceiving the police and of avoiding their snares. We must train people who will devote to the revolution not only their spare evenings, but the whole of their lives; we must build up an organization large enough to be able to introduce strict division of labor in the various forms of our work. . . . With regard to the question of tactics, we intend to confine ourselves here to the following: Social Democracy does not tie its hands, it does not restrict its activities to some preconceived plan or method of political struggle; it recognizes all methods of struggle, as long as they correspond to the forces at the disposal of the Party and facilitate the achievement of the greatest results possible under the given conditions.

If we have a strongly organized party, a single strike may grow into a political demonstration, into a political victory over the government. If we have a strongly organized party, a rebellion in a single locality may flare up into a victorious revolution. We must bear in mind that the fight against the government for certain demands, the gain of certain concessions, are merely slight skirmishes with the enemy, slight skirmishes of outposts, but that the decisive battle still lies ahead. (*The Urgent Tasks of Our Movement,* December, 1900, *Selected Works* II, 13 f.)

In our opinion, the starting point of all our activities, the first practical step toward creating the organization we desire, the threat that will guide us in unswervingly developing, deepening and expanding that organization, is the establishment of an all-Russian political newspaper. A paper is what we need above all; without it we cannot systematically carry on that extensive and theoretically sound propaganda and agitation which is the principal and constant duty of the Social Democrats in general, and the essential task of the present moment in particular, when interest in politics and in questions of socialism has been aroused among the widest sections of the population. Never before has the need been so strongly felt for supplementing individual agitation in the form of personal influence, local leaflets, pamphlets, etc., with general and regularly conducted agitation, such as can be carried on only with the assistance of a periodical press. It would hardly be an exaggeration to say that the frequency and regularity of publication (and distribution) of the paper would serve as an exact measure of the extent to which that primary and most essential branch of our military activities has been firmly established. Moreover, the paper must be an all-Russian paper. Unless we are able to exercise united influence upon the population and upon the government with the aid of the printed word, it will be utopian to think of combining other more complex, difficult, but more determined forms of exercising influence. Our movement, intellectually, as well as practically and organizationally, suffers most of all from being scattered, from the fact that the vast majority of Social Democrats are almost entirely immersed in purely local work, which narrows their horizon, limits their activities and affects their conspiratorial skill and training. It is in this state of disintegration that we must seek the deepest roots of the instability and vacillation to which I referred above. The *first step* toward removing this defect, and transforming several local movements into a united all-Russian movement, is the establishment of a national all-Russian newspaper. Finally, it is a *political* paper we need. Without a political organ, a political movement deserving that name is inconceivable in modern Europe. Without such a paper it will be absolutely impossible to fulfill our task, namely, to concentrate all the elements of political discontent and protest, and with them fertilize the revolutionary movement of the proletariat.

. . . .

But the role of a paper is not confined solely to the spreading of ideas, to political education and to attracting political allies. A paper is not merely a collective propagandist and collective agitator, it is also a collective organizer. In this respect, it can be compared to the scaffolding erected around a building in construction; it marks the contours of the structure and facilitates communication between the builders, permitting them to distribute the work and to view the common results achieved by their organized labor. With the aid of, and around, a paper, there will automatically develop an organization that will engage, not only in local activities, but also in regular, general work; it will teach its members carefully to watch political events, to estimate their importance and their influence on the various sections of the population, and to devise suitable methods of influencing these events through the revolutionary party. The mere technical problem of procuring a regular supply of material for the newspaper and its regular distribution will make it necessary to create a network of agents of a united party, who will be in close contact with each other, will be acquainted with the general situation, will be accustomed to fulfilling the detailed functions of the national (all-Russian) work, and who will test their strength in the organization of various kinds of revolutionary activities. This network of agents[1] will form the skeleton of the organization we need, namely, one that is sufficiently large to embrace the whole country; sufficiently wide and many-sided to effect a strict and detailed division of labor; sufficiently tried and tempered unswervingly to carry out its own work under all circumstances, at all "turns" and in unexpected contingencies; sufficiently flexible to be able to avoid open battle against the overwhelming and concentrated forces of the enemy, and yet able to take advantage of the clumsiness of the enemy and attack him at a time and place where he least expects attack. (*Where To Begin,* May, 1901, *Selected Works,* II, 19 f., 21 f.)

I[2] recall a conversation I once had with a fairly consistent

---

[1] It is understood, of course, that these agents can act successfully only if they work in close conjunction with the local committees (groups or circles) of our party. Indeed, the whole plan we have sketched can be carried out only with the most active support of the committees, which have already made more than one attempt to achieve a united party, and which, I am certain, sooner or later, and in one form or another, will achieve that unity.

[2] The following passages (pp. 315–326) are taken from *What Is To Be Done? Burning Questions of Our Movement.* Written during January and February, 1902, the book was revised in 1908.—*Ed.*

economist, with whom I had not been previously acquainted. We were discussing the pamphlet *Who Will Make the Political Revolution?* and we were very soon agreed that the principal defect in that brochure was that it ignored the question of organization. We were beginning to think that we were in complete agreement with each other—but as the conversation proceeded, it became clear that we were talking of different things. My interlocutor accused the author of the brochure just mentioned of ignoring strike funds, mutual aid societies, etc.; whereas I had in mind an organization of revolutionaries as an essential factor in "making" the political revolution. After that became clear, I hardly remember a single question of importance upon which I was in agreement with that economist! (*Selected Works,* II, 126.)

The organizations of revolutionaries must consist first and foremost of people whose profession is that of a revolutionary (that is why I speak of organizations of *revolutionaries,* meaning revolutionary Social Democrats). In view of this common feature of the members of such an organization, *all distinctions as between workers and intellectuals,* and certainly distinctions of trade and profession, must be obliterated. Such an organization must of necessity be not too extensive and as secret as possible. (*Selected Works,* II, 127.)

A small, compact core, consisting of reliable, experienced and hardened workers, with responsible agents in the principal districts and connected by all the rules of strict secrecy with the organizations of revolutionaries, can, with the wide support of the masses and without an elaborate organization, perform *all* the functions of a trade union organization. (*Selected Works,* II, 133.)

If we begin with the solid foundation of a strong organization of revolutionaries, we can guarantee the stability of the movement as a whole and carry out the aims of both Social Democracy and of trade unionism. (*Selected Works,* II, 134.)

I assert that it is far more difficult to catch a dozen wise men than it is to catch a hundred fools. And this position I shall defend no matter how much you instigate the crowd against me for my "anti-democratic" views, etc. As I have already said, by "wise men," in connection with organization, I mean *professional revolutionaries,* irrespective of whether they are trained from among students or workingmen. I assert: (1) that no movement can be durable without a stable organization of leaders to maintain continuity; (2) that the more widely the masses are spontaneously drawn into the struggle and form the basis of the movement and participate in it, the more necessary is it to have such an organization, and the more stable must it be (for it is much easier for demagogues to sidetrack the more backward sections of the masses); (3) that the organization must consist chiefly of persons engaged in revolutionary activities as a profession; (4) that in a country with an autocratic government, the more we *restrict* the membership of this organization to persons who are engaged in revolutionary activities as a profession and who have been professionally trained in the art of combating the political police, the more difficult will it be to catch the organization, and (5) the *wider* will be the circle of men and women of the working class or of other classes of society able to join the movement and perform active work in it. (*Selected Works,* II, 138 f.)

It is possible to have a mass *organization* when the maintenance of strict secrecy is essential. We can never give a mass organization that degree of secrecy which is essential for the persistent and continuous struggle against the government. But to concentrate all secret functions in the hands of as small a number of professional revolutionaries as possible does not mean that the latter will "do the thinking for all" and that the crowd will not take an active part in the *movement.* On the contrary, the crowd will advance from its ranks increasing numbers of professional revolutionaries, for it will know that it is not enough for a few students and workingmen, waging economic war, to gather together and form a "committee," but that it takes years to train professional revolutionaries; the crowd will "think" not of primitive ways but of training professional revolutionaries. The centralization of the secret functions of the *organization* does not mean the centralization of all the functions of the *movement*. The active participation of the broad masses in the dissemination of illegal literature will not diminish because a dozen professional revolutionaries centralize the secret part of the work; on the contrary, it will *increase tenfold*. Only in this way will the reading of illegal literature, the contribution to illegal literature, and to some extent even the distribution of illegal literature *almost cease to be secret work,* for the police will soon come to realize the folly and futility of setting the whole judicial and administrative machine into motion to intercept every copy of a publication that is being distributed by the thousands. This applies not only to the press, but to every function of the movement, even to demonstrations. The active and widespread participation of the masses will not suffer; on the contrary, it will benefit by the fact that a "dozen" experienced revolutionaries, no less professionally trained than the police, will centralize all the secret side of the work. (*Selected Works,* II, 139 f.)

Lack of specialization is one of our most serious technical defects, about which B——v justly and bitterly complains. The smaller each separate "operation" in our common cause will be, the more people we shall find capable of carrying out such operations (people, who, in the majority of cases, are not capable of becoming professional revolutionaries), the more difficult will it be for the police to "catch" all these "detail workers," and the more difficult will it be for them to frame up, out of an arrest for some petty affair, a "case" that would justify the government's expenditure on the "secret service.". . .

In order to unite all these tiny factions into one whole, in order, in breaking up functions, to avoid breaking up the movement, and in order to imbue those who carry out these minute functions with the conviction that their work is necessary and important—for without this they will never do the work[3]— it is necessary to have a strong organization of tried revolutionaries. The more secret such an organization would be, the stronger and more widespread would be the confidence of the masses in the Party, and, as we know, in time of war, it is not only of great importance to imbue one's own army with confidence in its own strength, it is important also to convince the enemy and all *neutral* elements of this strength; friendly neutrality may sometimes decide the issue. If such an organization existed on a firm theoretical basis, and possessed a Social Democratic journal, we would have no reason to fear that the movement would be diverted from its path by the numerous "outside" elements that are attracted to it. (On the contrary, it is precisely at the present time, when primitive methods prevail among us, that many Social Democrats are observed to gravitate toward the *Credo,* and only imagine that they are Social Democrats.) In a word, specialization necessarily presupposes centralization, and in its turn imperatively calls for it. (*Selected Works,* II, 143 f.)

In order to be fully prepared for his task, the working class

---

[3] I recall the story a comrade related to me of a factory inspector, who, desiring to help, and while in fact helping Social Democracy, bitterly complained that he did not know whether the "information" he sent reached the proper revolutionary quarter; he did not know how much his help was really required, and what possibilities there were for utilizing his small services. Every practical worker, of course, knows of more than one case, similar to this, of our primitiveness depriving us of allies. And these services, each "small" in itself, but incalculable when taken together, could be rendered to us by office employees and officials, not only in factories, but in the postal service, on the railways, in the customs, among the nobility, among the clergy and every other walk of life, including even the police service and the courts! Had we a real party, a real militant organization of revolutionaries, we would not put the question bluntly to every one of these "abettors," we would not hasten in every single case to bring them right into the very heart of our "illegality," but on the contrary, we would husband them very carefully and would train people especially for such functions, bearing in mind the fact that many students could be of much greater service to the Party as "abettors"—officials—than as "short-term" revolutionaries. But, I repeat, only an organization that is already established and has no lack of active forces would have the right to apply such tactics.

revolutionary must also become a professional revolutionary. Hence B———v is wrong when he says that as the worker is engaged for eleven and a half hours a day in the factory, therefore, the brunt of all the other revolutionary functions (apart from agitation) *"must necessarily* fall mainly upon the shoulders of an extremely small intellectual force." It need not "necessarily" be so. It is so because we are backward, because we do not recognize our duty to assist every capable worker to become a *professional* agitator, organizer, propagandist, literature distributor, etc., etc. In this respect, we waste our strength in a positively shameful manner; we lack the ability to husband that which should be tended and reared with special care. Look at the Germans: they have a hundred times more forces than we have. But they understand perfectly well that the "average" does not too frequently promote really capable agitators, etc., from its ranks. Hence they immediately try to place every capable workingman in such conditions as will enable him to develop and apply his abilities to the utmost: he is made a professional agitator, he is encouraged to widen the field of his activity, to spread it from one factory to the whole of his trade, from one locality to the whole country. He acquires experience and dexterity in his profession, his outlook becomes wider, his knowledge increases, he observes the prominent political leaders from other localities and other parties, he strives to rise to their level and combine within himself the knowledge of working class environment and freshness of socialist convictions with professional skill, without which the proletariat *cannot* carry on a stubborn struggle with the excellently trained enemy. Only in this way can men of the stamp of Bebel and Auer be promoted from the ranks of the working class. But what takes place automatically to a very large degree in a politically free country must in Russia be done deliberately and systematically by our organizations. A workingman agitator who is at all talented and "promising" *must not be left* to work eleven hours a day in a factory. We must arrange that he be maintained by the Party, that he may in due time go underground, that he change the place of his activity, otherwise he will not enlarge his experience, he will not widen his outlook and will not be able to stay in the fight against the police for at least a few years. As the spontaneous rise of the working class masses becomes wider and deeper, they not only promote from their ranks an increasing number of talented agitators, but also of talented organizers, propagandists and "practical workers" in the best sense of the term (of whom there are so few among our intelligentsia who, in the majority of cases, are somewhat careless and sluggish in their habits, so characteristic of Russians). When we have detachments of specially trained working class revolutionaries who have gone through long years of preparation (and, of course, revolutionaries "of all arms"), no political police in the world will be able to contend against them, for these detachments of men absolutely devoted and loyal to the revolution will themselves enjoy the absolute confidence and devotion of the broad masses of the workers. The *sin* we commit is that we do not sufficiently "stimulate" the workers to take this path, "common" to them and to the "intellectuals," of professional revolutionary training, and that we too frequently drag them back by our silly speeches about what "can be understood" by the masses of the workers, by the "average workers," etc. (*Selected Works*, II, 146–148.)

The magnificient organization that the revolutionaries had in the 1870's, and which should serve us all as a model, was not formed by the Narodovolists but by the adherents of *Zemlya i Volya*, who split up into Chernoperedelists and Narodovolists. Consequently, to regard a militant revolutionary organization as something specifically Narodovolist is absurd both historically and logically, because no revolutionary tendency, if it seriously thinks of fighting, can dispense with such an organization. But the mistake the Narodovolists committed was not that they strove to recruit to their organization all the discontented and to hurl this organization into the decisive battle against the autocracy; on the contrary, that was their great historical merit. Their mistake was that they relied on a theory which in substance was not a revolutionary theory at all, and they either did not know how, or circumstances did not permit them, to link up their movement inseparably with the class struggle that went on within developing capitalist society. And only a gross failure to understand Marxism (or an "understanding" of it in the spirit of Struve-ism) could prompt the opinion that the rise of a mass, spontaneous labor movement *relieves* us of the duty of creating as good an organization of revolutionaries as *Zemlya i Volya* had in its time, and even an incomparably better one. On the contrary, this movement *imposes* this duty upon us, because the spontaneous struggle of the proletariat will not become a genuine "class struggle" until it is led by a strong organization of revolutionaries. . . .

We have always protested, and will, of course, continue to protest against *restricting* the political struggle to conspiracies. But this does not, of course, mean that we deny the need for a strong revolutionary organization. . . . We must build an organization so strong as to be able to "resort to rebellion" and to "every other form of attack" in order to "deliver a smashing blow against absolutism." According to its *form,* a strong revolutionary organization of that kind in an autocratic country may also be described as a "conspirative" organization, because the French word *conspiration* means in Russian "conspiracy," and we must have the utmost conspiracy[4] for an organization of that kind. Secrecy is such a necessary condition for an organization that all the other conditions (number and selection of members, functions, etc.) must all be subordinated to it. It would be extremely naive indeed, therefore, to fear the accusation that we Social Democrats desire to create a conspirative organization. (*Selected Works,* II, 149–151.)

A well-organized secret apparatus requires professionally well-

---

[4]The Russian word for conspiracy is *zagovor,* which means "conspiracy" or "plot." But the word *conspiratsiya,* conspiracy, in Russian revolutionary literature usually means "secrecy." Hence, a conspirative organization would be a secret organization, but would not necessarily engage in plots. Except in this case, when it was important to bring out the play of words, the word *conspiratsiya* has been rendered throughout the text as "secrecy," and the word "conspirative" has been used only where the word *zagovor* was used in the text. . . .

trained revolutionaries and proper division of labor, but neither of these requirements can be met by separate local organizations, no matter how strong they may be at any given moment. Not only are the general interests of our movement as a whole (training of the workers in consistent socialist and political principles) *better served by non-local newspapers,* but so also are even specifically local interests. This may seem paradoxical at first sight, but it has been proved up to the hilt by two and a half years of experience. . . . Everyone will agree that if all the local forces that were engaged in the publication of these thirty issues of newspapers had worked on a single newspaper, they could easily have published sixty if not a hundred numbers and, consequently, would have more fully expressed all the specifically local features of the movement. True, it is not an easy matter to attain such a high degree of organization, but we must realize the need for it. Every local circle must think about it, and *work actively* to achieve it, without waiting to be pushed on from outside; and we must stop being tempted by the easiness and closer proximity of a local newspaper which, as our revolutionary experience has shown, proves to a large extent to be illusory. (*Selected Works* II, 160.)

Unless we build up strong political organizations in the localities—even an excellently organized all-Russian newspaper will be of no avail. Absolutely true. But the whole point is that *there is no other way of training* strong political organizations except through the medium of an all-Russian newspaper. The author missed the most important statement *Iskra* made *before it proceeded* to explain its "plan"; that it was necessary "to call for the establishment of a revolutionary organization, capable of combining all the forces and leading the movement *not only in name* but in deed, i.e., *an organization that will be ready at any moment to support every protest and every outbreak,* and to utilize these for the purpose of increasing and strengthening the military forces required for decisive battle." After the February and March events, everyone will agree with this in principle, continues *Iskra,* but we do not need a solution of this problem in principle; *what we need is a practical solution of it;* we must immediately bring forward a definite plan of construction in order that everyone may set to work to build *from every side.* And now we are again being dragged away from a practical solution toward something that is correct in principle, indisputable and great, but absolutely inadequate and absolutely incomprehensible to the broad masses of workers, namely, to "build up strong political organizations"! (*Selected Works,* II, 171.)

The mere function of distributing a newspaper will help to establish *real* contacts (that is, if it is a newspaper worthy of the name, i.e., if it is issued regularly, not once a month like a magazine, but four times a month). At the present time, communication between cities on revolutionary business is an extreme rarity, and at all events the exception rather than the rule. If we had a newspaper, however, such communication would become the rule and would secure not only the distribution of the newspaper, of course, but also (and what is more important) an interchange of experience, material, forces and resources. The scope of organizational work would immediately become ever so much wider, and the success of a single locality would serve as a standing encouragement to further perfection and a desire to utilize the experience gained by comrades working in other parts of the country. Local work would become far richer and more varied than it is now: political and economic exposures gathered from all over Russia would provide mental food for the workers of all trades and in all *stages of development,* would provide material and occasion for talks and readings on the most diverse subjects, which indeed will be suggested by hints in the legal press, by conversations in society and by "shamefaced" government communications. Every outbreak, every demonstration, would be weighed and discussed in all its aspects all over Russia; it would stimulate a desire to catch up with the rest, a desire to excel (we Socialists do not by any means reject all rivalry or all "competition"!) and consciously to prepare for what at first appeared to spring up spontaneously, a desire to take advantage of the favorable conditions in a given district or at a given moment for modifying the plan of attack, etc. At the same time, this revival of local work would render superfluous that desperate, "convulsive" exertion of *all* efforts and the risking of *all* men which every single demonstration or the publication of every single number of a local newspaper now entails. In the first place, the police would find it much more difficut to dig down to the "roots" because they would not know in what district to seek for them. Secondly, regular common work would train our people to regulate the force of a *given* attack in accordance with the strength of the forces of the given local detachment of the army (at the present no one ever thinks of doing that, because in nine cases out of ten these attacks occur spontaneously), and would facilitate the "transport" from one place to another, not only of literature, but also of revolutionary forces.

In a great many cases, these forces at the present time shed their blood in the cause of restricted local work, but under the circumstances we are discussing, occasion would constantly arise for transferring a capable agitator or organizer from one end of the country to the other. Beginning with short journeys on Party business at the Party's expense, our people would become accustomed to being maintained by the Party, would become professional revolutionaries and would train themselves to become real political leaders.

And if indeed we succeeded in reaching a point when all, or at least a considerable majority, of the local committees, local groups and circles actively took up work for the common cause we could, in the not distant future, establish a daily newspaper that would be regularly distributed in tens of thousands of copies over the whole of Russia. This newspaper would become a part of an enormous pair of smith's bellows that would blow every spark of class struggle and popular indignation into a general conflagration. Around what is in itself a very innocent and very small, but a regular and *common cause,* in the full sense of the word, an army of tried warriors would systematically gather and receive their training. On the ladders and scaffolding of this general organizational structure there would soon ascend Social Democratic Zhelyabovs from among our revolutionaries and Russian Bebels from among our workers who would take their place at the head of the mobilized army and rouse the whole people to settle accounts with the shame and the curse of Russia.

That is what we ought to be dreaming about! (*Selected Works,* II, 178–180.)

Comrade Trotsky completely misinterpreted the main idea of my book *What Is To Be Done?* when he said that the Party is not a conspirative organization (many others raised this objection). He forgot that in my book I propose a number of types of organizations, from the most secret and most exclusive to comparatively broad and "free" (*loose*) organizations. He forgot that the Party must be only the vanguard, the leader of the vast masses of the working class, the whole (or nearly the whole) of which works "under the control and guidance" of the Party organizations, but which does not and should not, as a whole, join the "Party." (*Speech . . .*, August 15, 1903, *Selected Works,* II, 360.)

I proposed that a Party member be regarded as one who adheres to the Party program, gives material support to the Party and belongs to one of the organizations of the Party. Martov, however, thought it sufficient if, in addition to the first two conditions, a member worked under the control of one of the Party organizations. I insisted on my formula and pointed out that we could not adopt any other definition of a member of the Party without abandoning the principle of centralism. To regard a person who does not belong to any Party organization as a member of the Party meant opposition to all control by the Party. Martov was introducing a new principle entirely opposed to the principles of *Iskra.* Martov's formula stretched the boundaries of the Party. He argued that our party must become a party of the masses. He left the door wide open for every kind of opportunist and stretched the boundaries of the Party until they became quite blurred. In the conditions in which we have to work this is very dangerous, because it would make it very difficult to draw a line between a revolutionary and an idle talker; this makes it necessary for us to restrict the concept of the Party. Martov's mistake was that he left the door of the Party wide open for every scamp, while it had become apparent that even at the congress fully a third were mere intriguers. Martov on this occasion acted as an opportunist. The formula he proposed introduced a false note into the rules: Every Party member must be under the control of an organization in such a way that the Central Committee may be able to reach him. The formula I proposed gave a stimulus to organization. Comrade Martov cheapened the concept of the Party, while I thought that it must be placed on a high, very high plane. (*Report . . .*, October 27, 1903, *Selected Works*, II, 373.)

The[5] Organization Committee drew up a very elaborate set of standing orders (formalistic and bureaucratic, those would say who now use these words to conceal their political flabbiness) for the Second Congress, got it passed by all the committees and, at last, sanctioned it, one of the provisions being that contained in point eighteen: "All the decisions of the Congress and all the elections carried out by it are the decisions of the Party and are binding on all the organizations of the Party. They cannot be appealed against by anyone on any pretext and can only be revoked or modified by the next congress of the Party." These words, which were adopted in silence at the time as something self-evident, look innocent enough by themselves, do they not? But how strange they sound today—like a verdict pronounced against the "minority"! Why was this point included? Was it just for the sake of formality? By no means. The provision seemed necessary, and was in fact necessary, because the Party consisted of a number of isolated and independent groups, which could be expected to refuse to recognize the Congress. This provision expressed the *good will* of all revolutionaries (there is a great deal of irrelevant talk about it today, because the term

---

[5]The following passages (pp. 317–332) are taken from *One Step Forward, Two Steps Back; The Crisis in Our Party* (February–May, 1904).

"good" is euphemistically applied to what really deserves the epithet capricious). It was equivalent to a *word of honor,* mutually pledged by all Russian Social Democrats. It was intended as a guarantee that the tremendous labors, dangers and expense entailed by the Congress would not be wasted, and that the Congress would not be turned into a farce. It qualified beforehand every refusal to recognize the decisions of and the *elections* at the Congress as a *breach of faith.* (*Selected Works,* II, 412.)

There has been much talk about the "*accidental*" character of the majority at our congress. The diagram clearly shows that in *a certain sense,* but only in that sense, the majority may be called accidental, viz., in the sense that the withdrawal of the seven most opportunist delegates of the "*right wing*" was *accidental.* To the extent that this withdrawal was accidental, *to that extent* (but no more) our majority was also accidental. A glance at the diagram will show better than long arguments on whose side those seven would have been and *ought to have been.* But the question must be asked: How far was the withdrawal of these seven accidental? This is the question that those who talk freely about the accidental character of the majority do not like to ask themselves. Certainly, the question is a very unpleasant one for them. Was it an accident that the most ardent representatives of the *right* wing, and not the *left* wing, of our party withdrew? Was it an accident that the *opportunists* withdrew, and not the consistent *revolutionary Social Democrats?* Is this "accidental" withdrawal in any way connected with the struggle against the opportunist wing which was carried on the whole time the Congress was in session, and which our diagram so strikingly illustrates?

It is sufficient to ask these questions, which are unpleasant for the minority, to realize what fact all this talk about the accidental character of the majority is intended to *conceal.* It is the unquestionable and incontrovertible fact that *the minority was composed of those members of our party who are most inclined toward opportunism.* The elements that comprised the minority were those that *were least steady in theory, least stable in matters of principle.* It was from the *right wing* of the Party that the minority was formed. The division into a majority and a minority is the direct and inevitable continuation of that division of Social Democracy into a revolutionary wing and opportunist wing, into a Mountain and a Gironde, which made its appearance, not yesterday, and not only in the Russian working-class party, and which, no doubt, will not disappear tomorrow. (*Selected Works,* II, 423 f.)

All these "dreadful catchwords" about Jacobinism and the rest express absolutely nothing more than *opportunism.* A Jacobin who is inseparably linked with the *organization* of the proletariat which is *conscious* of its class interests, is a *revolutionary Social Democrat.* A Girondist, longing for professors and high school boys, afraid of the dictatorship of the proletariat and sighing about the absolute value of democratic demands, is an *opportunist.* It is only opportunists who can still be of the opinion that conspirative organizations are a danger at a time when the idea of narrowing the political fight down to a conspiracy has been refuted thousands of times in literature, has been refuted and crowded out by life, when the cardinal importance of mass political agitation has been made clear and chewed over to the point of nausea. The real source of this fear of conspiracy, of Blanquism, is not to be found in any feature that may have revealed itself in the practical movement (as Bernstein and company have long and vainly been trying to show), but in the Girondist timidity of the bourgeois intellectual whose mentality is so often revealed among the Social Democrats of today. Nothing can be more comical than these efforts of the new *Iskra* to utter a *new word* (that has been uttered hundreds of times) of warning against the tactics of the French revolutionary conspirators of the 1840's and 1860's. In the next number of *Iskra,* the Girondists of contemporary Social Democracy will probably point out to us a group of French conspirators of the 1840's for whom the importance of political agitation among the working masses, the importance of the workers' press, as the principal means by which the Party influences the class, was an

A B C that had long ago been learned and forgotten. (*Selected Works*, II, 433 f.)

It is precisely the factory, which some seem to regard as a bogey, that is the highest form of capitalist operation which has brought together and disciplined the proletariat, taught it to organize and placed it at the head of all other sections of the toiling and exploited population. It is precisely Marxism, as the ideology of the proletariat trained by capitalism, that has been teaching unstable intellectuals to distinguish between the factory as an instrument of exploitation (discipline based on the fear of starvation) and as a factor in organization (discipline based on collective work, united under conditions of technically highly developed production). The discipline and organization, which it is so difficult for the bourgeois intellectual to acquire, are easily acquired by the proletarian precisely because of the factory "school" he goes through. Mortal fear of this school and complete inability to understand its importance as an organizing force are characteristic of ways of thinking which reflect a petty bourgeois mode of life and which give rise to that anarchism which the German Social Democrats have called *Edelanarchismus,* i.e., the anarchism of a "noble" gentleman, or gentleman's anarchism, as I would call it. The Russian nihilist is particularly susceptible to this kind of gentleman's anarchism. He thinks of the Party organization as a monstrous "factory" and of the subordination of the part to the majority as "serfdom"; division of labor under the leadership of a center evokes from him tragicomical cries under people being turned into "wheels and screws" (the most outrageous form of this transformation is considered to be the conversion of an editor into a contributor); mention of the organizational rules of the Party calls forth a contemptuous grimace and the disdainful remark (intended for the "formalists") that one can very well dispense with rules altogether. (*Selected Works,* II, 442 f.)

Gentleman's anarchism is unable to understand that formal rules are needed precisely to make the substitution of the wide

Party link for the narrow circle link possible. There was no need, and it was impossible, to establish formal links inside the circle or between the circles, because the circles were kept together by personal friendships and a confidence which had not to be accounted for and for which no reasons had to be given. The Party link cannot and must not rest on either the one or the other; it must be founded on *formal,* "bureaucratically" (from the point of view of the undisciplined intellectual) worded rules, strict adherence to which alone can safeguard us from the willfulness and the caprices of the circle spirit, from the circle wrangling that goes by the name of the free "process" of the ideological struggle. *(Selected Works,* II, 444.)

The only attempt to *analyze* the conception of bureaucracy seems to be contained in the distinction drawn by the new *Iskra* between "formally *democratic* and formally *bureaucratic* principles." This distinction (which, unfortunately, has remained as undeveloped and unexplained as the allusion to the non-*Iskra*-ists) contains a grain of truth. Bureaucracy *versus* democracy is the same thing as centralism *versus* autonomism; it is the organizational principle of revolutionary political democracy as opposed to the organizational principle of the opportunists of Social Democracy. The latter want to proceed from the bottom upward and, consequently, wherever possible and to the extent that it is possible, they support autonomism and "democracy," which may (by the overly zealous) be carried as far as anarchism. The former proceed from the top and advocate the extension of the rights and powers of the center in respect of the parts. *(Selected Works,* II, 447 f.)

It will now be fully apparent to those who remember the debate on point one that the mistake committed by Comrade Martov and Comrade Axelrod ... *inevitably* leads, when developed and deepened, to organizational opportunism. Comrade Martov's initial idea, self-registration of Party members, is nothing else than false "democracy," the idea of building the Party from the bottom upward. My idea, on the other hand, is "bureaucratic" in the sense that the Party is built from the top downward, from the Party Congress to the individual Party organizations. (*Selected Works,* II, 456 f.)

Neither the decrepit rule of Russian tsarism, nor the senile rule of international capital will be able to withstand this army. It will close its ranks more tightly than ever, in spite of all zigzags and steps backward, in spite of all the opportunist phrases of the Girondists of modern Social Democracy, in spite of the smug praise of out-of-date circle spirit, in spite of all the tinsel and fuss of *intellectul* anarchism. (*Selected Works,* II, 466.)

In its struggle for power, the proletariat has no weapon other than organization. Divided by the rule of anarchic competition in the bourgeois world, ground down by slave labor for capital, constantly thrust back to the "lower depths" of utter destitution, savagery and degneration, the proletariat can become, and will inevitably become, an invincible force only when its ideological unity around the principles of Marxism is consolidated by the material unity of an organization, which unites millions of toilers in the army of the working class.

The slogan "organize!" which the adherents of the majority wanted to issue in a definitely formulated form at the Second Congress must now be put into effect immediately. If we fail to take the initiative and boldly form new organizations, we shall have to give up all claims to the role of vanguard. If we stop helplessly at the limits, forms and the framework of the committees, groups, meetings and circles that we have already reached, we shall thereby prove our incompetence. Thousands of circles are now springing up everywhere without our aid, without any definite program or purpose, simply under the influence of events. The Social Democrats must strive to establish and maintain direct contact with the greatest possible number of these circles to assist them, to enlighten them from their own store of knowledge and experience, to animate them with their revolutionary initiative. Let all such circles, except the consciously non-Social Democratic ones, either directly join the Party or *become associated with the Party.* In the latter case we must not demand that they accept our program, or that they enter into obligatory organizational relations with us; the revolutionary sentiment alone, the mere desire to help in the struggle against the autocracy, is sufficient—if Social Democrats go to them and energetically present our views—to transform these circles, under pressure of events, at first into democratic assistants of the Social Democratic Labor party and then into staunch members of it. (*New Tasks and New Forces*, March, 1905, *Selected Works*, III, 438 f.)

It requires no effort to join the Party "under the control of one of the Party organizations"—for this formula is an empty phrase, and always has been from the Second to the Third Congress. But to create a widespread network of a variety of Party organizations, from exclusive and secret organizations to the widest and most public possible—for this, persistent, prolonged and intelligent organizational work is required; and this is the work that now devolves upon our central committee and even more so upon the local committees. It will be the committees who will have to confirm the affiliation to the Party of the largest number of organizations, and in doing this they will have to avoid all unnecessary red tape and captiousness; they will have always and incessantly to urge upon the workers the necessity of creating as large a number of the most diverse labor organizations to affiliate to our party as possible. (*The Third Congress*, May, 1905, *Selected Works*, III, 442 f.)

First on the order of the day is the prolonged task of training, organizing and welding together the class conscious masses of the proletariat. Then, as a task subordinated to this, it is necessary to extend the work of organization to the peasantry and the army, especially in the form of literary propaganda and agitation, and in this our main attention must be given to the socialist education of the proletarian and the semiproletarian elements among the peasantry and in the army. (*Draft Resolution on the Present Situation and the Tasks of the Party*, January, 1909, *Selected Works*, IV, 16.)

The recent All-Russian Conference of the Russian Social Democratic Labor party led the Party on to the high road and apparently marks the turning point in the development of the Russian labor movement after the victory of the counterrevolution. The decisions of the conference, published in a special "Communication" issued by the Central Committee of our party, have been confirmed by the Central Committee, and, therefore, pending the next congress, stand as the decisions of the whole Party. These decisions give a very definite answer to the question concerning the causes and the significance of the crisis, as well as the means of overcoming it. By working in the spirit of the resolutions of this conference, by striving to make *all* Party workers clearly and fully realize the present tasks of the Party, our organizations will succeed in strengthening and consolidating their forces for united and effective revolutionary Social Democratic work.

The main cause of the Party crisis is indicated in the preamble of the resolution on organization. This main cause is the purging of the Party of the vacillating intellectual and petty bourgeois elements who joined the labor movement mainly in the hope of an early triumph of the bourgeois democratic revolution, and were not able to withstand the period of reaction. Their instability was revealed both in theory ("retreat from revolutionary Marxism": the resolution on the present situation) and in tactics (the "curtailment of slogans"), as well as in the domain of the organizational policy of the Party. The class-conscious workers repelled this instability and came out resolutely against the liquidators; they began to take the management as well as the leadership of the party organizations into their own hands. The reason this basic nucleus of our party was unable to overcome the elements of disintegration and of crisis at one stroke was not only that the task was a great and difficult one amidst the triumph of the counterrevolution, but also that a certain indifference toward the Party was displayed in the ranks of those workers who, although revolutionary minded, were not sufficiently class-conscious. It is precisely to the class-conscious workers of Russia that the decisions of the conference are addressed in the first place—as decisions representing the crystalized opinion of Social Democracy concerning the means of fighting disintegration and vacillations.

To strengthen the illegal Party organization, to create Party nuclei in all spheres of work, to create in the first instance "purely Party committees consisting of workers, even if their number be small, in each industrial enterprise," to concentrate the leading functions in the hands of leaders of the Social Democratic movement from the ranks of the workers themselves—such is the task today. And, of course, the task of these nuclei and committees must be to utilize all the semilegal and, as far as possible, legal organizations, to maintain the "closest contact with the masses," and to direct the work in such a way that Social Democracy responds to all the needs of the masses. Every nucleus and every Party workers' committee must become a "base for agitation, propaganda and practical organizational work among the masses," i.e., they must go where the masses are and try at every step to push the consciousness of the latter in the direction of socialism, linking up every specific question with the general tasks of the proletariat, transforming every organizational undertaking into the cause of *class* consolidation, thus winning by their energy and ideological influence (not by their rank and title, of course) the leading role in all the proletarian legal organizations. Even if these nuclei and committees be very few in number at times, they will be linked together by Party tradition, Party organization and a definite class program, and even two or three Social Democratic members of the Party will be able, instead of becoming dissolved in the amorphous legal organization, to pursue their party line under all conditions and circumstances and in all kinds of situations, to influence their environment in the spirit of the whole Party, and not allow themselves to be swamped by this environment. (*On the High Road,* February, 1909, *Selected Works,* IV, 3 f., 10 f.)

One view on unity may place in the forefront the "reconciliation" of "given persons, groups and institutions." The identity of their views on Party work, on the policy of that work, is a matter of secondary importance. Differences of opinion must be hushed up, their causes, their significance, their objective conditions should not be elucidated. The principal thing is to "reconcile" persons and groups. If they do not agree upon the carrying out of a common policy, that policy must be interpreted in such a way as to be acceptable to all. Live and let live. This is philistine "conciliationism," which inevitably leads to narrow-circle diplomacy. To "stop up" the source of disagreement, to hush it up, to "adjust conflicts" at all costs, to neutralize the conflicting trends—it is to this that the main attention of such "conciliationism" is directed. In circumstances in which the illegal Party requires a base abroad for its operations, this narrow-circle diplomacy opens wide the doors to "persons, groups and institutions" which play the part of "honest brokers" in all kinds of attempts at "conciliation" and "neutralization."

. . . .

There is another view on this unity, viz., that a number of profound objective causes, long ago, independently of the manner in which the "given persons, groups and institutions" (submitted to the plenum and at the plenum) were constituted, began to bring about and are steadily continuing to bring about changes in the two old and principal Russian factions among the Social Democrats, changes that create—sometimes in spite of the will and even consciousness of some one of the "given persons, groups and institutions"—ideological and organizational bases for unity. These objective causes are rooted in the peculiarities of the present period of bourgeois development in Russia, the period of bourgeois counterrevolution and attempts by the autocracy to reorganize itself on the model of a bourgeois monarchy. These objective conditions simultaneously cause changes that are indissolubly linked up with one another, changes in the character of the labor movement, in the composition, type and features of the proletarian Social Democratic vanguard, as well as changes in the ideological and political tasks of the Social Democratic movement. Therefore, that bourgeois influence over the proletariat which creates liquidationism (semiliberalism which likes to be regarded as a part of Social Democracy) and otzovism (semi-anarchism, which likes to be regarded as a part of Social Democracy) is not an accident, nor evil intention, stupidity or error on the part of some individual, but the inevitable result of the action of these objective causes, and the superstructure of the entire labor movement of present-day Russia, which is inseparable from the "basis." The realization of the danger of the un-Social Democratic nature and of the harmfulness to the labor movement of both these deviations brings about a *rapprochement* between the elements of various factions and paves the way to Party unity "in spite of all obstacles."

From this point of view the unification of the Party may proceed slowly, with difficulties, vacillations, waverings, relapses, but it cannot but proceed. From this point of view the process of unification does not necessarily take place among the *"given persons, groups and institutions,"* but irrespective of the given persons, subordinating them to itself, rejecting those of the "given" persons who do not understand or who do not want to understand the requirements of objective development, putting forward and attracting new persons, who do not belong to the "given" set, effecting changes, reshufflings and regroupings within the old factions, tendencies, divisions. From this point of view, unity is inseparable from its ideological foundation, it can grow only on the basis of an ideological *rapprochement,* it is connected with the appearance, development and growth of such deviations as liquidationism and otzovism, not by the casual ties of this or that controversy or this or that literary struggle, but by an internal, indissoluble tie such as that which binds cause and effect. (*Notes of a Publicist,* June, 1910, *Selected Works,* IV, 41, 43 f.)

Recognizing that the experience of the last three years has undoubtedly confirmed the basic propositions of the resolution on the organizational question passed by the [Party] conference in December, 1908, and being of the opinion that on the basis of the incipient revival of the labor movement a further development of the organizational forms of Party work becomes possible along the same path, i.e., along the path of setting up illegal Social Democratic nuclei surrounded by the widest possible network of legally existing labor societies of all kinds:

The conference is of the opinion:

1. That the illegal Party organizations must take a most active part in the leadership of the *economic struggle* (strikes, strike committees, etc.), and that co-operation in this field is necessary between the illegal Party nuclei and the trade unions, especially Social Democratic nuclei in the trade unions and also the individual comrades who are active in the trade union movement;

2. That it is desirable, in conformity with the local conditions, to combine the Social Democratic nuclei in the trade unions, which are organized on an industrial basis, with the Party nuclei which are built up on a territorial basis;

3. That it is necessary to display the greatest possible initiative in organizing Social Democratic work in legally existing societies: trade unions, reading rooms, libraries, all kinds of workers' recreation societies, in distributing trade union journals and in guiding the trade union press in the spirit of Marxism, in utilizing the Duma speeches of the Social Democrats, in training lecturers for legal meetings from among the workers, in setting up (in connection with the elections to the Fourth Duma) workers' and other electoral committees according to districts, streets, etc., in Social Democratic agitation in connection with the municipal elections, etc.;

4. That strenuous efforts must be made to strengthen and increase the number of illegal Party nuclei, to discover new and most flexible organizational forms for these nuclei, to create and consolidate the leading illegal Party organizations in every town and to propagate such forms of mass illegal organizations as "labor exchanges," Party meetings at factories, etc.;

5. That it is desirable to draw the propaganda circles into everyday *practical* work: distribution of illegal Social Democratic and legally published Marxian literature, etc.;

6. That it is necessary to bear in mind that systematic literary Social Democratic agitation and especially an illegal Party newspaper, appearing regularly and frequently, can assume great importance in the matter of establishing organizational contacts among the various illegal nuclei as well as among the various Social Democratic nuclei in the legally existing workers' societies.

(*Resolutions of the Prague Conference of the Russian Social Democratic Labor Party,* January, 1912, *Selected Works,* IV, 152–154.)

Take the modern army. It is one of the good examples of organization. This organization is good only because it is *flexible* and is able at the same time to give to millions of people a *single will.* Today these millions are living in their homes in various parts of the country; tomorrow a call for mobilization is issued, and they gather at the appointed centers. Today they lie in the trenches, sometimes for months at a stretch; tomorrow they are led to the attack in another formation. Today they perform miracles hiding from bullets and shrapnel; tomorrow they perform miracles in open combat. Today their forward detachments place mines under the ground; tomorrow they move forward scores of miles, according to the advice of flyers above ground. When, in the pursuit of one aim, animated by one will, millions change the forms of their intercourse and their actions, change the place and the method of their activities, change their tools and weapons in accordance with changing conditions and the requirements of the struggle—this is organization.

The same holds true for the working class struggle against the bourgeoisie. Today there is no revolutionary situation, the conditions that cause ferment among the masses or heighten their activities do not exist; today you are given a ballot— take it. Learn how to organize in order to be able to use it as a weapon against your enemies and not as a means of getting soft parliamentary jobs for men who cling to their seats in fear of having to go to prison. Tomorrow, you are deprived of the ballot, you are given a rifle and a splendid quick firing gun constructed according to the last word of engineering technique —take this weapon of death and destruction, do not listen to the sentimental whiners who are afraid of war. Much has been left in the world that *must* be destroyed by fire and steel in order that the emancipation of the working class may be achieved. And if anger and desperation grow among the masses, if a revolutionary situation arises, prepare to create new organizations and *utilize* these useful weapons of death and destruction *against your* government and *your* bourgeoisie. (*The Collapse of the Second International,* June, 1915, *Selected Works,* V, 214 f.)

During the year under review the current daily work of the Central Committee was conducted by the two bodies elected by the Plenum of the Central Committee: the Organization Bureau of the Central Committee and the Political Bureau of the Central Committee. In order to achieve harmony and consistency in the decisions of these bodies, the Secretary acted as a member of both. The practice established was that the main function of the Organization Bureau was to distribute the forces of the Party, while the function of the Political Bureau was to deal with political questions. It goes without saying that this distinction is to a certain extent artificial: it is obvious that no policy is practicable that does not find expression in appointments and transferring people from one post to another. Consequently, every organizational question assumes a political significance. (*Report of the Central Committee at the Ninth Congress of the Russian Communist Party* (Bolsheviks), March 29, 1920, *Selected Works,* VIII, p 76.)

The parties affiliated to the Communist International must be built up on the principle of democratic *centralism.* In the present epoch of acute civil war the Communist party will be able to perform its duty only if it is organized in the most centralized manner, only if iron discipline bordering on military discipline prevails in it, and if its party center is a powerful organ of authority, enjoying wide powers and the general confidence of the members of the Party....

Every party that wishes to affiliate to the Communist International must render selflessly devoted assistance to every Soviet republic in its struggle against counterrevolutionary forces. The Communist parties must carry on persistent propaganda urging upon the workers to refuse to transport war materials for the enemies of the Soviet republics; and they must carry on legal or illegal propaganda among the armed forces that are sent to strangle the workers' republics, etc.

. . . .

All the decisions of the congresses of the Communist International, as well as the decisions of its executive committee, are binding upon all parties affiliated to the Communist International. . . . Needless to say, in all their work the Communist International and its executive committee must take into account the great diversity of conditions under which the various parties have to fight and operate, and they should adopt universally binding decisions only on questions on which such decisions can be adopted. (*The Conditions of Affiliation to the Communist International*, July, 1920, *Selected Works*, X, 204 f.)

Our party is a government party, and the decision the Party congress arrives at will be binding for the whole republic. (*The Tax in Kind*, March 15, 1921, *Selected Works*, IX, 112.)

The gains of the revolution cannot now be what they were before. Their character inevitably changes in accordance with the transition from the war front to the economic front, the transition to the New Economic Policy, to the conditions demanding, first of all, increased productivity of labor, increased labor discipline. At such a time the principal gains of the revolution are internal gains, not striking, not outstanding, not immediately visible improvements in labor, the organization of labor, results of labor; improvements in the sense that a fight is waged against the influence of the petty bourgeois and petty bourgeois, anarchist element which corrupts the proletariat and the Party. In order to achieve such an improvement the Party must be purged of elements which have become isolated from the masses (and, needless to say, of elements which disgrace the Party in the eyes of the masses). . . . In appraising persons, in determining our attitude to those who have "attached themselves" to us, to those who have become "commissarized" and "bureaucratized," the suggestions of the nonparty proletarian masses, and in many cases of the non-party peasant masses, are extremely valuable. The toiling masses have a fine instinct for the difference between honest and devoted Communists and those who arouse a revulsion of feeling in one who obtains his bread by the sweat of his brow, who enjoys no privileges and who has no "open door to the chief."

Purging the Party with the aid of the suggestions of the non-party toilers is a great thing. It will give us important results. It will make the Party a much stronger vanguard of the class than it was before; it will make it a vanguard that is more strongly linked with the class, more capable of leading it to victory amidst great difficulties and dangers. (*Purging the Party,* September 20, 1921, *Selected Works,* IX, 253 f.)

At the Third Congress [of the Communist International] in 1921 we adopted a resolution on the organizational structure of the Communist parties and on the methods and content of their work. The resolution is an excellent one, but it is almost thoroughly Russian, that is to say, everything is taken from Russian conditions. This is the good side of the resolution, but it is also its bad side. It is its bad side because I am sure that hardly a single foreigner is able to read it—I read the resolution over again before deciding to say this. In the first place it is too long; it has fifty or more points. Usually, foreigners are unable to read things of this length. Secondly, even if they will read it, no foreigner will understand it precisely because it is too Russian. Not that it is written in Russian—it has been excellently translated in all languages—but it is thoroughly permeated with the Russian spirit. And thirdly, if as an exception some foreigner is able to understand it, he cannot carry it out. This is its third defect. (*Five Years of the Russian Revolution and the Prospects of the World Revolution,* November 13, 1922, *Selected Works,* X, 332.)

Everyone knows that big disagreements sometimes grow out of very small, at first even insignificant, differences. Everyone knows that an insignificant bruise, or even a scratch, which everyone has had scores of times in the course of his life, may develop into a very dangerous and sometimes even fatal disease *if* it begins to fester, *if* blood poisoning sets in. This is what happens in all, even purely personal conflicts. This is what also happens in politics.

Every difference, even an insignificant one, may become politically dangerous if it is likely to grow into a split, the kind of split which is capable of shaking and destroying the whole political edifice.

.   .   .   .

If there are radical and profound disagreements on principle, do they not justify the sharpest and most factional pronouncements? If it is necessary to say something new and not understand, does not that sometimes justify even a split?

Of course it does, if the disagreements are really extremely profound and if the wrong direction of the policy of the Party, or of the working class, cannot be rectified in any other way. (*Once Again the Trade Unions; The Present Situation and the Mistakes of Trotsky and Bukharin,* January, 1921, *Selected Works,* IX, 45, 51.)

A deviation is not yet a finished trend. A deviation is something that can be rectified. People have just wandered somewhat from the path, or are beginning to wander from the path, but they can still be put right. This, in my opinion, is what the Russian word *uklon* means. This emphasizes the fact that there is nothing here that is final yet, that the matter can be easily rectified; it is a desire to warn and to raise the question in all its scope and on principle. (*Party Unity and the Anarcho-Syndicalist Deviation,* March 16, 1921, *Selected Works,* IX, 126.)

The waverers are many, we are few. The waverers are disunited, we are united. . . . The waverers do not know what they want. . . . We know what we want.

And that is why we shall win. (*The Food Tax,* April 21, 1921, *Selected Works,* IX, 200.)

VIII

REVOLUTION

Only an armed people can serve as a real bulwark of popular liberty. And the sooner the proletariat succeeds in arming itself, and the longer it maintains its martial position of striker and revolutionary, the sooner will the army begin to waver, the soldiers will at last begin to understand what they are doing, they will go over to the side of the people against the monsters, against the tyrants, against the murderers of defenseless workers and of their wives and children. No matter what the outcome of the present uprising in St. Petersburg may be, it will, in any case, be the first step to a wider, more conscious, better prepared uprising.

. . . .

The immediate arming of the workers and of all citizens in general, the preparation and organization of the revolutionary forces for overthrowing the government authorities and institutions—this is the practical basis on which all revolutionaries can and must unite to strike a common blow. (*The Beginning of the Revolution in Russia,* January, 1905, *Selected Works,* III, 291.)

A people's revolution cannot be ordered; that is correct. We cannot but praise Martynov and the author of the editorial in number 62 of *Iskra* for knowing this truth ("and generally speaking, what is the use of our party talking about preparing for an uprising?"—asks Martynov's loyal comrade-in-arms, or disciple, in that article, waging war on the "utopians"). But if the situation is ripe for a popular uprising, in view of the fact that the revolution in social relationships *has already taken place,* and if we have prepared for it, we can order an uprising. We shall try to make this clear to the new *Iskra*-ists by a simple example. Is it possible to order the labor movement? No, it is not, for it is composed of thousands of separate acts that grow out of the revolution in social relationships. Is it possible to order a strike? It is possible, in spite of the fact—just imagine, Comrade Martynov—*in spite* of the fact that every strike is a result of the change in social relationships. When is it possible to order a strike? When the organization or group that calls the strike has influence among *the masses* of the workers affected and is able accurately to judge the moment when the dissatisfaction and irritation among the masses of workers are rising. Do you understand now what the crux of the matter is, Comrade Martynov and Comrade "leader-writer" of number 62 of *Iskra?* If you do understand, then please take the trouble to compare an uprising with a people's revolution. "A people's revolution cannot be ordered in advance." An uprising can be so ordered, if those who order it have influence among the masses and can correctly judge the moment for calling it. (*Two Tactics,* February, 1905, *Selected Works,* III, 298.)

Have you ever considered, gentlemen, what the real social forces that determine the "sweep of the revolution" are? Let us leave aside the forces of foreign politics, of international combinations, which have turned out favorably for us at the present time, but which we leave out of our discussion, and quite rightly so, in so far as we are discussing the internal forces of Russia. Look at the internal social forces. Against the revolution are rallied the autocracy, the court, the police, the government officials, the army and a handful of the higher aristocracy. The deeper the indignation of the people becomes, the less reliable become the troops and the more the government officials begin to waver. Moreover, the bourgeoisie, on the whole, is now in favor of the revolution, makes zealous speeches about liberty, and more and more frequently talks in the name of the people, and even in the name of the revolution. But we Marxists all know from our theories and from daily and hourly observations of our liberals, Zemstvo councillors and followers of *Osvobozhdeniye* that the bourgeoisie is inconsistent, selfish and cowardly in its support of the revolution. The bourgeoisie, in the mass, will inevitably turn toward counterrevolution, toward autocracy, against the revolution and against the people; as soon as its narrow selfish interests are met it "deserts" consistent democracy (*it is already deserting it!*). There remain the "people," that is, the proletariat and the peasantry. The proletariat alone is capable of marching reliably to the end, for its goal lies far beyond the democratic revolution. That is why the proletariat fights in the front ranks for the republic and contemptuously rejects silly and unworthy advice to take care not to frighten the bourgeoisie. The peasantry consists of a great number of semiproletarian as well as petty bourgeois elements. This causes it also to waver and compels the proletariat to close its ranks in a strictly class party. But the instability of the peasantry differs radically from the instability of the bourgeoisie, for at the present time the peasantry is interested not so much in the absolute preservation of private property as in the confiscation of the landowners' land, one of the principal forms of private property. While this does not cause the peasantry to become socialist or cease to be petty bourgeois, it may cause them to become wholehearted and most radical adherents of the democratic revolution. The peasantry will inevitably become such if only the progress of revolutionary events, which is enlightening it, is not interrupted too soon by the treachery of the bourgeoisie and the defeat of the proletariat. Subject to this condition, the peasantry will inevitably become a bulwark of the revolution and the republic, for only a completely victorious revolution can give the peasantry *everything* in the sphere of agrarian reforms—*everything* that the peasants desire, of which they dream, and of which they truly stand in need (not for the abolition of capitalism as the "Socialist Revolutionaries" imagine, but) in order to raise themselves out of the mire of semi-serfdom, out of the gloom of oppression and servitude, in order to improve their conditions of life as far as it is possible to improve them under commodity production.

Moreover, the peasantry is drawn to the revolution not only by the prospect of a radical agrarian reform but by its general and permanent interests. Even in its fight against the proletariat, the peasantry stands in need of democracy, for only a democratic system is capable of exactly expressing its interests and of ensuring its predominance as the mass and the majority. The more enlightened the peasantry becomes (and since the Japanese War it is becoming enlightened at a much more rapid pace than those who are accustomed to measuring enlightenment by the school standard suspect), the more consistent and determined will it be in its support of the complete democratic revolution; for, unlike the bourgeoisie, it has nothing to fear from the supremacy of the people, but, on the contrary, can only gain by it. The democratic republic will become the ideal of the peasantry as soon as it frees itself from its naive monarchism because the conscious monarchism of the bourgeois brokers (with an upper chamber, etc.,) implies for the peasantry the same disfranchisement and the same ignorance and oppression as it suffers from today, only slightly polished with the varnish of European constitutionalism.

That is why the bourgeoisie as a class naturally and inevitably strives to come under the wing of the Liberal Monarchist party, while the peasantry, in the mass, strives to come under the leadership of the Revolutionary and Republican party. That is why the bourgeoisie is incapable of carrying the democratic revolution to its ultimate conclusion, while the peasantry is capable of carrying the revolution to the end; and we must exert all our efforts to help it to do so.

.   .   .   .

The proletariat must carry out to the end the democratic revolution, and in this unite to itself the mass of the peasantry in order to crush by force the resistance of the autocracy and to paralyze the instability of the bourgeoisie. The proletariat must accom-

*plish the socialist revolution and in this unite to itself the mass
of the semiproletarian elements of the population in order to
crush by force the resistance of the bourgeoisie and to paralyze
the instability of the peasantry and petty bourgeoisie.*

. . . .

Perhaps the most striking expression of this difference between
the intellectual opportunist wing and the proletarian revolutionary wing of the Party was the question: *Dürfen wir siegen?* "Dare
we win?" Is it permissible for us to win? Would not such victory
be dangerous to us? Ought we to win? This at first sight strange
question was raised, however, and had to be raised, because the
opportunists were afraid of victory, were frightening the proletariat away from it, were prophesying various evils that would
result from it, were scoffing at the slogans which directly called
for victory.

The same fundamental division between the intellectual-op-
portunist trend and the proletarian-revolutionary trend exists
also among us, with the very important difference, however, that
here we are faced with the question of a democratic revolution
and not of a socialist revolution. The question "Dare we win?"
absurd as it may seem at first sight, has also been raised here. It
was raised by Martynov in his *Two Dictatorships,* in which he
prophesied dire misfortune if we make effective preparations for
and successfully carry out an uprising.

. . . .

Although Kautsky, for instance, now tries to wax ironical
about our disputes concerning a provisional revolutionary government, and says that it is like dividing the bear's skin before the
bear is killed, this irony only proves that even intelligent and
revolutionary Social Democrats miss the point when they talk
about something they know only by hearsay. German Social
Democracy is a long way from killing its bear (carrying out a
socialist revolution) but the dispute as to whether we "dare"
kill our bear was of enormous importance from the point of
view of principles and of practical politics. Russian Social Democrats are not yet by any means strong enough to "kill their bear"
(to carry out a democratic revolution) but the question as to

whether we "dare" kill it is of extreme importance for the whole future of Russia and for the future of Russian Social Democracy. An army cannot be energetically and successfully recruited and guided unless we are sure that we "dare" win.

. . . .

Revolutions are the locomotives of history, said Marx. Revolutions are the festivals of the oppressed and the exploited. At no other time are the masses of the people in a position to come forward so actively as creators of a new social order as at a time of revolution. At such times the people are capable of performing miracles, if judged by a narrow philistine scale of gradual progress. But the leaders of the revolutionary parties must also, at such a time, present their tasks in a wider and bolder fashion, so that their slogan may always be in advance of the revolutionary initiative of the masses, serve them as a beacon and reveal to them our democratic and socialist ideal in all its magnitude and splendor, indicate the shortest, the most direct route to complete, absolute and final victory. (*The Two Tactics of Social Democracy in the Democratic Revolution,* July, 1905, *Selected Works,* III, 107–111, 117 f., 122 f.)

The organized force of the tsarist government will crush the insurgents group by group if the movement continues to spread as slowly and sporadically from town to town and from district to district as it has been doing up to now. But united, these outbursts can converge into a mighty torrent of revolutionary flame which no power on earth will be able to withstand. And this unity is approaching, approaching by thousands of ways we do not know or even suspect. These separate outbursts and encounters are teaching the people what revolution is, and it is our business, therefore, never to lag behind the tasks of the moment, to be able to point to the next, the higher stage of the struggle, to derive experience and lessons from the past and the present, more boldly and widely to urge the workers and peasants to advance still further forward to the complete victory of the people, to the complete destruction of the autocratic gang which is now fighting with the desperation of the doomed.

Social Democracy did not advance the slogan of insurrection in a rash moment. It has always fought, and will continue to fight, against revolutionary phrase mongering, it will always demand a sober estimation of forces and an analysis of the given situation. Social Democracy has been talking about preparing for an uprising ever since 1902, and has never confused this work of preparation with the senseless fomenting of riots which, if brought about artificially, would merely result in a waste of forces. And only now, after January 22, has the slogan of an uprising been advanced by the workers' party as an immediate slogan, has the necessity for an uprising and the necessity of the task of preparing for it been recognized. The autocracy itself has made this slogan the practical slogan of the labor movement. The autocracy has given the first wide and mass lessons in civil war. This war has begun and is being conducted on a wider and wider front and in an increasingly intensified form. We have only to generalize its lessons, to explain the great significance of the words "civil war," to draw the practical precepts from the separate encounters in this war, to organize our forces and prepare directly and immediately all that is necessary for a real war.
(*The Struggle of the Proletariat and the Servility of the Bourgeoisie,* July, 1905, *Selected Works,* III, 304 f., 306.)

The units of the revolutionary army are springing up out of the army itself.

The task of these units is to proclaim insurrection: to give the masses the military leadership, as necessary in civil war as in any other war; to create cases for an open struggle of the whole of the people; to start uprisings in neighboring districts; to safeguard complete political liberty, if only in a small part of the territory of the state at first; to start the revolutionary reconstruction of the decayed autocratic system; to develop to its farthest limit the revolutionary creative activity of the masses who take but a small part in this activity in time of peace, but who come to the forefront in revolutionary epochs. Only by carrying out these new tasks, only by putting them forward boldly and broadly, will the units of the revolutionary army be able to win complete victory, to serve as the support for *revolutionary government*. And a revolutionary government is as essential and necessary at the present stage of the popular uprising as a revolutionary army. The revolutionary army is required for the military struggle and the military leadership of the masses of the people against the remnants of the military forces of the autocracy. The revolutionary army is needed because great historical questions can be solved only by violence, and the organization of violence in the modern struggle is a military organization.

. . . .

A revolutionary army and a revolutionary government are two sides of the same coin. They are two institutions equally necessary for the success of the uprising and for the consolidation of its results. They are two slogans which must be advanced and explained as the only consistent revolutionary slogans. (*The Revolutionary Army and the Revolutionary Government,* July, 1905, *Selected Works,* III, 312 f., 317.)

We must clearly and resolutely point out the necessity for an uprising in the present state of affairs; we must directly call for insurrection (without, of course, fixing the date beforehand), and call for the immediate organization of a revolutionary army. Only a very bold and wide organization of such an army can serve as a prologue to the insurrection. Only insurrection can guarantee the victory of the revolution and, of course, those who know the local conditions will always warm against attempts at premature insurrection. The real organization of real, popular, local government can take place only as the epilogue of a victorious insurrection. (*The Boycott of the Bulygin Duma and the Insurrection,* August, 1905, *Selected Works,* III, 327.)

Unlike the petty bourgeois Socialist Revolutionaries, we lay the main emphasis *at the present time* on the revolutionary-democratic aspect of the peasant uprising and the special organization of the rural proletariat into a class party. The crux of the question now is not the projects of "Black Redistribution" or nationalization, but to make the peasants conscious of the necessity of securing the *revolutionary* breakup of the old order and of their breaking it up. That is why the Socialist Revolutionaries are so keen on "nationalization," etc., while we are keen on *revolutionary peasant committees*. We say that without the latter all reforms are reduced to naught. It is only with them and by leaning for support on them that the *victory of the peasant rising will become possible*.

We must assist the peasant uprising in every way, including the confiscation of the land, but certainly not *including all sorts of petty bourgeois projects*. We support the peasant movement insofar as it is revolutionary and democratic. We are making ready (making ready at once, immediately) to fight it insofar as it becomes reactionary and antiproletarian. The whole essence of Marxism lies in that double task, which only those who do not understand Marxism can vulgarize or compress into one simple task.

Let us take a concrete example. Let us assume that the peasant uprising is victorious. The revolutionary peasant committees and the provisional revolutionary government (partly relying on these very committees) are able to carry out the confiscation of large property. We stand for confiscation, we have declared that already. But to whom shall we recommend that the confiscated land be given? We have not tied our hands on this question, and never shall do so. . . . The resolution of the Third Congress speaks first of *"purging the revolutionary-democratic content of the peasant movement of all reactionary admixtures,"* and, secondly, of the necessity *"in all cases and under all circumstances of independently organizing the rural proletariat."* Such are our directives. There will always be reactionary admixtures in the peasant movement, and we declare war on them in advance. Class antagonism between the rural proletariat and the peasant bourgeoisie is inevitable, and we reveal it in advance, explain it *and prepare for the struggle on the basis of it*. One of the immediate causes of such a struggle may very likely be the question: To whom shall the confiscated land be given, and how? We do not gloss over that question, we do not promise equal distribution, "socialization," etc. What we say is this: This is a question we shall fight out later on, we shall fight again, on a new field and with other allies. Then, we shall certainly be with the rural proletariat, with the whole of the working class *against* the peasant bourgeoisie. Practically, this may mean the transfer of the land to the class of petty peasant proprietors—wherever the big estates based on bondage and servitude still prevail, where there are as yet no material prerequisites for large-scale socialist production; it may mean nationalization—provided the democratic revolution is completely victorious; or the big capitalist estates may be transferred to *workers' associations,* for, from the democratic revolution we shall at once, according to the degree of our strength, the strength of the class conscious and organized proletariat, begin to pass over to the socialist revolution. We stand for continuous revolution.

. . . .

We shall with all our might help the whole of the peasantry to make the democratic revolution *in order that* it may be *easier* for us, the party of the proletariat, to pass on, as quickly as possible, to the new and higher task—the socialist revolution. We do not promise harmony, equality, "socialization" as a result of the victory of the present peasant uprising—on the contrary, we "promise" a new struggle, new inequality, a new revolution, toward which we are striving. Our doctrine is not as "sweet" as the tales of the Socialist Revolutionaries, but let whoever wants to be fed entirely on sweets join the Socialist Revolutionaries. (*The Attitude of Social Democracy toward the Peasant Movement,* September, 1905, *Selected Works,* III, 144 f., 146.)

To the Marxist, the peasant movement is precisely a democratic and not a socialist movement. In Russia, just as was the case in other countries, it is a necessary companion of the democratic revolution, which is bourgeois in its social and economic content. It is not in the least directed against the foundations of the bourgeois order, against commodity production, against capital. On the contrary, it is directed against the old, serf precapitalist relationships in the rural districts and against the landed gentry, which is the mainstay of all the remnants of serf-dom. Therefore, the complete victory of this peasant movement will not abolish capitalism; on the contrary, it will create a broader foundation for its development, and will hasten and intensify purely capitalist development. A complete victory of the peasant uprising can only create a stronghold for a democratic bourgeois republic within which a clear-cut proletarian struggle against the bourgeoisie will for the first time develop. (*Petty Bourgeois and Proletarian Socialism*, November, 1905, *Selected Works*, III, 150.)

The inexorable logic of the situation that has developed since December, 1905, proves that the strike is subordinate to the uprising. Whether we like it or not, and all "directives" notwithstanding, the acute revolutionary situation is bound to convert a demonstration into a strike, a protest into a fight, a strike into an uprising. Of course, an uprising can flare up as an armed mass struggle only provided it is actively supported by one or another section of the army. Therefore, a strike of the troops, their refusal to shoot at the people, can undoubtedly in certain cases lead to the victory of a merely peaceful strike. But there is hardly any need to prove that such cases would be but single episodes in an exceptionally successful uprising, and there is only one way to increase the number of such episodes, to make them possible, and that is: successful preparation for an uprising, the display of energy and strength in the first insurgent actions, demoralization of the troops by desperately daring attacks or by the desertion of a large section of the army, etc.

.   .   .   .

It remains for us to consider the question of the moment to be chosen for an uprising. The tender love displayed by right wing Social Democrats for the Cadet Duma caused the former to demand immediate action. This idea ended in a solemn fiasco. The attitude taken up by the masses of the working class and urban population shows that the gravity of the situation is appreciated or apprehended. Of course, it is expected that the struggle will be not for the Duma, but for the overthrow of the old government. The delay is due to the general mood prevailing, to the desire to prepare for a really decisive and desperate struggle, the desire to achieve co-ordinated action.

It is possible, and perhaps most probable, that the new struggle will break out in the same elemental way, and just as unexpectedly, as the previous ones have done, as a result of a rise in temper and of one of the inevitable explosions. If things take that turn, if it becomes evident that such a course of development is inevitable, we shall not have to decide the question of the time for action; our task will then be to increase our agitation tenfold and to organize work on the lines already indicated.

However, events may demand that we provide leaders and appoint the time for action. If that be the case we shall counsel an all-Russian action, a strike and an uprising at the end of the summer, or at the beginning of the autumn, by the middle or the end of August. The important thing would be to take advantage of the building season in the towns and the time when the summer work on the land comes to an end. If it were possible to secure agreement among *all* the influential revolutionary organizations and unions as to the time for action, the possibility of carrying it out at the time stated would not be precluded. The simultaneous beginning of the struggle over the whole of Russia would be a great advantage. Even if the government learned the time fixed for the strike it would in all probability have no harmful effect, because it would not be a plot or a military attack which must be made suddenly. The army all over Russia would probably be most demoralized if it were kept in suspense for weeks and weeks in expectation of the imminent outbreak of the struggle, if the troops were kept under arms, and if agitation were carried on with increasing vigor simultaneously by all organizations and the mass of "non-party" revolutionaries. (*The Dissolution of the Duma and the Tasks of the Proletariat,* July, 1906, *Selected Works,* III, 375 f., 383 f.)

From strike and demonstrations to isolated barricades. From isolated barricades to the mass erection of barricades and street fighting against the troops. Over the heads of the organizations, the mass proletarian struggle passed from a strike to an uprising. This is the greatest historical achievement of the Russian revolution, and like all previous achievements, it was obtained at the price of enormous sacrifices. The movement was raised from a general political strike to a higher level. It compelled reaction to go *to extremes* in its resistance and so brought nearer the moment when the revolution will also go to extremes in the application of methods, of attack. The reaction *cannot do more* than bombard barricades, houses and street crowds. But the revolution can go ever so much further than the Moscow fighting units went; it can grow ever so much wider and deeper. And the revolution has made great progress since December, 1905. The base of the revolutionary crisis has become immeasurably broader —the blade must now be sharpened to a keener edge.

The proletariat sensed the change in the objective conditions of the struggle and the need for a transition from the strike to an uprising sooner than its leaders. As is always the case, practice marched ahead of theory. A peaceful strike and demonstrations immediately ceased to satisfy the workers; they asked: What is to be done next? And they demanded more resolute action. The instructions to set up barricades reached the districts exceedingly late, when barricades were already being erected in the center. The masses of the workers set to work, *but were not satisfied even with this. They* demanded to know: What is to be done next? They demanded active measures. In December, 1905, we, the leaders of the Social Democratic proletariat, behaved like a commander-in-chief who had arranged the disposition of his troops in such an absurd way that most of them remained out of action. The masses of the workers demanded but failed to obtain instructions for resolute mass action.

.   .   .   .

The time has come when we must at last openly and publicly admit that political strikes are insufficient; we must carry on the widest agitation among the masses in favor of an armed uprising and make no attempt to obscure this question by talk about "preliminary stages," or by throwing a veil over it. To conceal from the masses the necessity for a desperate, sanguinary war of extermination as the immediate task of future revolutionary action means deceiving both ourselves and the people.

. . . .

December, 1905, confirmed another of Marx's profound postulates, which the opportunists have forgotten, viz., that rebellion is an art, and that the principal rule of this art is that a desperately bold and irrevocably determined offensive must be waged. We have not sufficiently assimilated this truth. We have not sufficiently learned, nor have we taught the masses this art and this rule of attacking at all costs. We must make up for this with all our energy. It is not enough to take sides in the question of political slogans; we must take sides also in the question of an armed uprising. Those who are opposed to armed uprising, those who do not prepare for it, must be ruthlessly cast out of the ranks of the supporters of the revolution and sent back to the ranks of its enemies, of the traitors or cowards; for the day is approaching when the force of events and conditions of the struggle will compel us to separate enemies from friends according to this principle. We must not preach passivity, nor advocate "waiting" until the troops "come over." No! We must proclaim from the housetops the need for a bold offensive and armed attack, the necessity at such times of exterminating the persons in command of the enemy and of a most energetic fight for the wavering troops.

. . . .

Military technique has made new progress recently. The Japanese War produced the hand grenade. The small-arms factories have placed automatic rifles on the market. Both these weapons are already being successfully used in the Russian revolution, but to an inadequate extent. We can and must take advantage of improvements in technique, teach the workers' units to make bombs in large quantities, help them and our fighting units to obtain supplies of explosives, fuses and automatic rifles. (*The Lessons of the Moscow Uprising*, September, 1906, *Selected Works*, 347 f., 351, 352 f.)

How did the uprising of 1905 *grow*? In the first place, mass strikes, demonstrations and meetings caused the clashes between the crowd and the police and military forces to become more frequent. Secondly, the mass strikes roused the peasantry to a number of partial, sporadic, semispontaneous uprisings. Thirdly, the mass strikes very rapidly spread to the army and navy, causing clashes on an economic basis . . . and then insurrections. Fourthly, counterrevolution *itself* started civil war by means of pogroms, the beating up of democrats, etc. (*The Revolutionary Revival,* June, 1912, *Selected Works,* IV, 160.)

We revolutionary Social Democrats regard the attempts at uprising as the *beginning of the uprising of the masses,* as an unsuccessful, untimely, incorrect beginning; but we know that the *masses learn* how to rise successfully only from the experience of unsuccessful uprisings, just as the Russian workers, by a series of unsuccessful and sometimes particularly unsuccessful political strikes in 1901–04, learned to organize the successful strike of October 1905. (*The Present Situation in the Russian Social Democratic Labor Party,* November, 1912, *Selected Works,* IV, 181.)

A Marxist cannot have any doubt that a revolution is impossible without a revolutionary situation; furthermore, not every revolutionary situation leads to revolution. What, generally speaking, are the symptoms of a revolutionary situation? We shall certainly not be mistaken if we point to the following three main symptoms: (1) when it is impossible for the ruling classes to maintain their rule in an unchanged form; when there is a crisis, in one form or another, among the "upper classes," a crisis in the policy of the ruling class which causes fissures, through which the discontent and indignation of the oppressed classes burst forth. Usually, for a revolution to break out it is not enough for the "lower classes to refuse" to live in the old way; it is necessary also that the "upper classes should be unable" to live in the old way; (2) when the want and suffering of the oppressed classes have become more acute than usual; (3) when, as a consequence of the above causes, there is a considerable increase in the activity of the masses, who in "peace time" quietly allow themselves to be robbed, but who in turbulent times are drawn both by the circumstances of the crisis and by the *"upper classes" themselves* into independent historical action.

Without these objective changes, which are not only independent of the will of separate groups and parties, but even of separate classes, a revolution, as a general rule, is impossible. The sum total of all these objective changes is called a revolutionary situation. This situation existed in 1905 in Russia and in all epochs of revolution in the West; but it also existed in the 1860's in Germany, and in 1859–61 and 1879–80 in Russia, although no revolution occurred in these cases. Why? Because not every revolutionary situation gives rise to revolution; revolution arises only out of such a situation when, to the above mentioned objective changes, a subjective change is added, namely, the ability of the revolutionary *class* to carry out revolutionary mass actions *strong* enough to break (or to undermine) the old government, which never, not even in a period of crisis, "falls," if it is not "dropped." (*The Collapse of the Second International,* June, 1905, *Selected Works,* V, 174.)

It was only natural that the revolutionary crisis should have broken out *first* in tsarist Russia, where disorganization was most monstrous and the proletariat most revolutionary (not by virtue of any specific qualities, but because of the vivid traditions of 1905). Here the crisis was hastened by the series of severe defeats suffered by Russia and her allies. These defeats entirely disjointed the old machinery of government and the old order and roused against them the anger of *all* classes of the population; they incensed the army, wiped out a vast number of its old diehard-noble and rotten-bureaucratic commanding staff, and replaced it by a young, fresh commanding staff consisting principally of bourgeois and petty bourgeois. (*Letters from Afar; First Letter; The First Stage of the First Revolution,* March 20, 1917, *Selected Works,* VI, 7.)

The basic question in any revolution is that of state power.

Unless this question is understood, there can be no intelligent participation in the revolution, let alone guidance of the revolution.

The striking feature of our revolution is that it has established a *dual power.* . . . In what does this dual power consist? In the fact that side by side with the Provisional Government, the government of the *bourgeoisie,* there has developed *another* government, weak and embryonic as yet, but undoubtedly an actually existing and growing government—the Soviets of Workers' and Soldiers' Deputies.

What is the class composition of this other government? It consists of the proletariat and the peasantry (clad in army uniform). What is the political nature of this government? It is a revolutionary dictatorship, i..e, a power based on outright revolutionary seizure, on the direct initiative of the masses from below, and not on a *law* made by a centralized government. It is an entirely different power from that of the ordinary type of parliamentary bourgeois democratic republic which has hitherto prevailed in the advanced countries of Europe and America. This circumstance is often forgotten, often not reflected on, yet it is the crux of the matter. This power is of exactly the *same type* as the Paris Commune of 1871. Its fundamental characteristics are: (1) The source of power is not a law previously discussed and passed by parliament, but the direct initiative of the masses from below, in their localities—outright "seizure," to use a popular expression; (2) the direct arming of the whole people in place of the police and the army, which are institutions separated from the people and opposed to the people; order in the state under such a power is maintained by the armed workers and peasants themselves, by the armed people itself; (3) officials and bureaucrats are either displaced by the direct rule of the people or at least placed under special control; they not only become elected officials, but are also *subject to recall* at the first demand of the people; they are reduced to the position of simple agents. (*A Dual Power,* April 22, 1917, *Selected Works,* VI, 27 f.)

The main peculiarity of our revolution, a peculiarity urgently requiring the most thoughtful analysis, is the *dual power* which was established in the very first days of the triumph of the revolution.

. . . .

The second peculiarity of the Russian revolution, a highly important one, is the circumstance that the Petrograd Soviet of Soldiers' and Workers' Deputies, which, everything goes to show, enjoys the confidence of most of the local Soviets, is *voluntarily* transferring the power of the state, is voluntarily surrendering its own supremacy, to the bourgeoisie and its Provisional Government; and, having entered into an agreement to support the latter, is limiting its own function to that of an observer supervising the convocation of the Constituent Assembly (the date of which has not yet even been announced by the Provisional Government).

This extremely peculiar circumstance, unparalleled in history in such a form, has led to the *interlocking of two dictatorships:* the dictatorship of the bourgeoisie (for the Provisional Government of Lvov and company, is a dictatorship, i.e., a power based not on law, nor on the previously expressed will of the people, but on seizure by force, accomplished by a definite class, namely, the bourgeoisie) and the dictatorship of the proletariat and peasantry (the Soviet of Workers' and Soldiers' Deputies).

There is not the slightest doubt that such an "interlocking" cannot last long. Two powers cannot exist in a state. One of them is bound to give way.

. . . .

From the point of view of science and practical politics, one of the chief symptoms of *every* real revolution is the rapid, sudden and sharp increase in the number of "ordinary citizens" who begin to participate actively, independently and vigorously in political life and in *the organization of the state.* (*The Tasks of the Proletariat in Our Revolution; Draft of a Platform for the Proletarian Party; A Peculiar Dual Power and Its Class Significance,* April 23, 1917, *Selected Works,* VI, 47–49.)

Marxism demands an extremely precise and objectively verifiable analysis of the interrelation of classes and of the concrete peculiarities of each historical moment. We Bolsheviks have always tried faithfully to fulfil this demand, since it is absolutely imperative for a scientific foundation of politics.

"Our teaching is not a dogma, but a guide to action," Marx and Engels used to say; and they ridiculed, and rightly ridiculed, the learning and repetition by rote of "formulas" which at best are capable of giving only an outline of *general* tasks that are necessarily liable to be modified by the *concrete* economic and political conditions of each particular phase of the historical process.

.   .   .   .

When analyzing any given situation, a Marxist must proceed *not from the possible,* but from the actual.

.   .   .   .

Many things are possible. . . . But it would be equally mistaken to forget *reality.* (*Letters on Tactics, First Letters,* April, 1917, *Selected Works,* VI, 32, 35, 36.)

One of the most vicious and probably most widespread distortions of Marxism practiced by the prevailing "Socialist" parties consists in the opportunist lie that preparations for insurrection and generally the treatment of insurrection as an art are "Blanquism.". . . Marxists are accused of Blanquism for regarding insurrection as an art! Can there be a more flagrant distortion of the truth, when not a single Marxist will deny that it was Marx who expressed himself on this score in the most definite, precise and categorical manner; that it was Marx who called insurrection precisely an *art,* saying that it must be treated as an art, that the first success must be *gained* and that one must proceed from success to success, never ceasing the offensive against the enemy, taking every advantage of his confusion, etc., etc.?

To be successful, insurrection must rely not upon conspiracy and not upon a party, but upon the advanced class. That is the first point. Insurrection must rely upon the revolutionary spirit of the people. That is the second point. Insurrection must rely upon the *crucial moment* in the history of the growing revolution, when the activity of the advanced ranks of the people is

at its height, and when the *vacillations* in the ranks of the enemies and in the ranks of the *weak, half-hearted and irresolute
friends of the revolution* are strongest. That is the third point.
And these three factors in the attitude toward insurrection distinguish *Marxism from Blanquism.*

But when these factors are operating it is a betrayal of Marxism and a betrayal of the revolution to refuse to regard insurrection as an *art.*

.   .   .   .

All the objective conditions for a successful insurrection exist.
We have the advantage of a situation in which *only* our success
in the insurrection can put an end to that most painful thing
on earth, vacillation, which has worn the people out; a situation
in which *only* the success of our insurrection can foil the game
of a separate peace directed against the revolution by publicly
proposing a fuller, juster and earlier peace *to the benefit* of the
revolution.

Finally, our party alone can save Petrograd by a successful
insurrection; for our proposal for peace is rejected, if we do not
secure even an armistice, then *we* shall become "defensists," we
shall place ourselves *at the head of the war parties,* we shall be
the *"war party"* par excellence, and we shall fight the war in a
truly revolutionary manner. We shall take all the bread and
shoes away from the capitalists. We shall leave them only crusts,
we shall dress them in bast shoes. We shall send all the bread
and shoes to the front.

And we shall save Petrograd.

The resources, both material and spiritual, for a truly revolutionary war in Russia are still immense; the chances are a hundred to one that the Germans will grant us at least an armistice.
And to secure an armistice now would in itself mean beating
the *whole world.*

Having recognized that an insurrection on the part of the
workers of Petrograd and Moscow is absolutely necessary in
order to save the revolution and in order to save Russia from
being "separately" divided up among the imperialists of both
coalitions, we must, first, adapt our political tactics at the Con-

ference to the conditions of the growing insurrection, and secondly, we must show that our acceptance of the idea of Marx that insurrection must be regarded as an art is not merely a verbal acceptance. (*Marxism and Insurrection,* September 27, 1917, *Selected Works,* VI, 218 f, 221 f.)

Let us see what the representative and founder of proletarian revolutionary tactics, Karl Marx, says about the lessons of history on this question:

> Now, insurrection is an art quite as much as war or any other, and subject to certain rules of procedure, which, when neglected, will produce the ruin of the party neglecting them. Those rules, logical deductions from the nature of the parties and the circumstances one has to deal with in such a case, are so plain and simple that the short experience of 1848 had made the Germans pretty well acquainted with them. Firstly, never play with insurrection unless you are fully prepared to face the consequences of your play. Insurrection is a calculus with very definite magnitudes the value of which may change every day; the forces opposed to you have all the advantage of organization, discipline and habitual authority [Marx is referring to the most "difficult" case of insurrection, viz., against an old and "firmly established" power, against an army that has not become disintegrated by the influence of the revolution and the vacillations of the government];[1] unless you bring strong odds against them you are defeated and ruined. Secondly, the insurrection career once entered upon, act with the greatest determination, and on the offensive. The defensive is the death of every armed uprising; it is lost before it measures itself with its enemies. Surprise your antagonists while their forces are scattering, prepare new successes, however small, but daily; keep up the moral ascendancy which the first successful rising has given to you; rally those vacillating elements to your side which always follow the strongest impulse and which always look out for the safer side; force your enemies to a retreat before they can collect their strength against you; in the words of Danton, the greatest master of revolutionary policy yet known, *de l'audace, de l'audace, encore de l'audace!"* (*Germany: Revolution and Counterrevolution.*)

---

[1]Lenin's interpolation.—*Ed.*

We have changed all that, the "also-Marxists" of *Novaya Zhizn* might say; instead of a triple audacity we have two qualities: "Yes, sir, two—moderation and punctiliousness."

. . . .

If a revolutionary party has not a majority among the front ranks of the revolutionary classes and in the country generally, there can be no question of insurrection. Furthermore, insurrection requires: (1) that the revolution shall have assumed a national scale; (2) that the old government, for instance, the "coalition" government, shall have reached a stage of complete moral and political bankruptcy; (3) that all the intermediate elements, i.e., those who do *not* fully support the government, although they fully supported it yesterday, shall have reached an extreme state of vacillation. (*Can the Bolsheviks Retain State Power? Postscript,* October 14, 1917, *Selected Works,* VI, 291 f.)

The Central Committee recognizes that the international position of the Russian revolution (the mutiny in the German navy, which is an extreme manifestation of the growth of the world socialist revolution throughout Europe, and the threat of an imperialist peace for the purpose of strangling the revolution in Russia) and the military situation (the unquestionable decision of the Russian bourgeoisie and of Kerensky and his coadjutors to surrender Petrograd to the Germans), as well as the fact that the proletarian party has gained a majority in the Soviets—that all this, taken in conjunction with the peasant revolt and the swing of popular confidence toward our party (the elections in Moscow), and, finally, the obvious preparations being made for a second Kornilov affair (the withdrawal of troops from Petrograd, the drafting of Cossacks into Petrograd, the surrounding of Minsk by Cossacks, etc.)—that all this places armed insurrection on the order of the day.

Realizing, therefore, that armed insurrection is inevitable, and that the time for it has fully matured, the Central Committee enjoins all Party organizations to be guided accordingly, and to discuss and decide all practical questions (the Congress of Soviets of the Northern Region, the withdrawal of troops from Petrograd, the action of the people of Moscow and Minsk, etc.) from this point of view. (*Resolution Adopted by the Central Committee of the Russian Social Democratic Labor Party* (Bolsheviks), (October 23, 1917, *Selected Works*, VI, 303.)

Marxism is an extremely profound and many-sided doctrine. It is, therefore, not surprising that *scraps* of quotations from Marx—especially when the quotations are *not* to the point—can always be found among the "arguments" of those who are breaking with Marxism. A military conspiracy is Blanquism *if* it is not organized by the party of a definite class; *if* its organizers have not reckoned with the political situation in general and the international situation in particular; *if* the party in question does not enjoy the sympathy of the majority of the people, as proved by definite facts; *if* the development of events in the revolution has not led to the virtual dissipation of the illusions of compromise entertained by the petty bourgeoisie; *if* the majority of the organs of revolutionary struggle which are recognized to be "authoritative" or have otherwise established themselves, such as the Soviets, have not been won over; *if* in the army (in time of war) sentiments hostile to a government which drags out an unjust war against the will of the people have not become fully matured; *if* the slogans of the insurrection (such as "All power to the Soviets," "Land to the peasants," "Immediate proposal of a democratic peace to all the belligerent peoples, coupled with the immediate abrogation of all secret treaties and secret diplomacy," etc.) have not acquired the widest renown and popularity; *if* the advanced workers are not convinced of the desperate situation of the masses and of the support of the countryside, as demonstrated by an energetic peasant movement, or by a revolt against the landowners and against the government that defends the landowners; *if* the economic situation in the country offers any real hope of a favorable solution of the crisis by peaceful and parliamentary means. (*A Letter to the Comrades*, October 30, 1917, *Selected Works*, VI, 321 f.)

We have always said, both before the October Revolution and

during the October Revolution, that we regard ourselves, and can regard ourselves, only as one of the detachments of the world army of the proletariat, a detachment which, moreover, took up an advanced position not because of the development and training it had received, but because of the unique conditions existing in Russia; and that, therefore, the victory of the socialist revolution may be regarded as final only when the proletariat has triumphed at least in several of the advanced countries. And it is in this respect that we experienced most difficulty.

The stake, if one may so express it, we placed on the international revolution has been fully justified, if regarded generally. But from the standpoint of rate of development, the period we have passed through has been an extremely difficult one. We learned to our cost that the development of the revolution in the more advanced countries is much slower, much more difficult and much more complex. That should not astonish us, for it was naturally far easier for a country like Russia to begin the socialist revolution than it is for advanced countries. At any rate, this slower, more complex, more zigzag development of the socialist revolution in western Europe has occasioned us incredible difficulties.... Nevertheless, what more than anything else distinguishes the year under review is the fact that we gained a tremendous victory—a victory so great that one might perhaps without exaggeration say that our principal difficulties are already behind us. However great may be the dangers and difficulties that are still before us, the greatest are presumably already behind us. (*Report* ..., December 5, 1919, *Selected Works,* VIII, 51.)

During the long course of our revolutionary campaign we have seen that when our revolutionary actions were properly prepared they met with success; but when they were merely imbued with revolutionary fervor they ended in failure. (*The Cooperatives,* April 3, 1920, *Selected Works,* VIII, 226.)

IX

STRATEGY

By emphasizing the necessity, the importance and the immensity of the theoretical work Social Democrats must carry on, I do not in the least wish to suggest that this work must take precedence over *practical* work[1]; still less do I suggest that the latter be postponed until the former is finished. Only those who admire the "subjective method in sociology" and the followers of utopian socialism could arrive at such a conclusion. Of course, if the task of Socialists is presumed to be to seek "other (than the actual) paths of development" for the country, then, naturally, practical work will become possible only when some genius of a philosopher will have discovered these "other paths"; on the other hand, the discovery and indication of these paths will mark the close of theoretical work, and the work of those who are to direct the "fatherland" along the "newly discovered," "other paths" will commence. The position is altogether different when the task of the Socialists is understood to mean that they must be the

---

[1]On the contrary, the practical work of propaganda and agitation must always take precedence because: (1) theoretical work only provides the replies to the problems which practical work raises, and (2) for reasons over which they have no control, Social Democrats are too often compelled to confine themselves to theoretical work not to attach the highest value to every moment they can give to practical work whenever the opportunity for this occurs.

ideological leaders of the proletariat in its genuine struggle against real enemies, who stand on the real path of present social and economic development. In these circumstances theoretical and practical work merge into a single task, which the veteran German Social Democrat Liebknecht aptly described as: *Studieren, propagandieren, organisieren!* [To study, to propagandize, to organize]!

It is impossible to be an ideological leader without performing the above-mentioned theoretical work, just as it is impossible to be one without directing this work to meet the requirements of the cause, without propagandizing the deductions drawn from this theory among the workers and helping to organize them.

Presenting the task in this way will guard Social Democracy against the defects from which groups of Socialists frequently suffer, viz., dogmatism and sectarianism.

There can be no dogmatism where the supreme and sole criterion of a doctrine is—whether or not it corresponds to the actual process of social and economic development; there can be no sectarianism when the task undertaken is to assist to organize the proletariat, when, therefore, the role of the "intelligentsia" is reduced to the task of making special leaders from among the intellectuals unnecessary. (*What the "Friends of the People" Are*, 1894, *Selected Works*, I, 325 f.)

What do we mean when we say that the struggle of the working class is a political struggle? We mean that the workers cannot wage the struggle for their emancipation without striving to influence affairs of state, to influence the administration of the state, the passing of laws. The Russian capitalists have long understood the necessity of influencing the state, and we have shown how, in spite of all hindrances placed in their way by the police laws, they have found a thousand ways of influencing the state authorities, and how these authorities serve the interests of the capitalists. From this it logically follows that the workers cannot wage their struggle, cannot even secure a permanent improvement in their lot, unless they are able to influence the state.

We have said already that the workers' struggle against the capitalists must inevitably bring them into conflict with the government, and the government itself is doing its utmost to prove to the workers that only by fighting and by united resistance can the workers influence the state. This was most strikingly proved by the big strikes which took place in Russia in 1885–86. The government immediately set to work to examine the regulations governing workers, immediately passed new factory laws which conceded the urgent demands of the workers (for example, regulations were passed limiting the amount of fines and providing for the proper payment of wages), and similarly in the present strikes (1896), the government has taken immediate action, for it has realized that arrests and deportations are not enough, and that it is ridiculous to try to stuff the workers with stupid homilies about the generosity of the factory owners. (See circular to the factory inspectors issued by the Minister of Finance, Witte, in the spring of 1896.) The government has realized that "the united workers represent a force that has to be reckoned with," and so it has already begun to revise the factory laws and is convening a conference of chief factory inspectors in St. Petersburg to discuss the question of shortening the working day and of making other unavoidable concessions to the workers.

Thus we see that the struggle between the working class and the capitalist class must necessarily be a political struggle. Indeed, this struggle is already exercising influence upon the government and is acquiring political significance. But the more the labor movement develops, the more clearly and sharply will the workers' complete lack of political rights, to which we referred above, the complete impossibility for the workers to influence the government openly and directly, be felt. Therefore, the most urgent thing the workers must do, the first thing the working class must aim at in bringing its influence to bear upon the government is to *achieve political liberty,* i.e., the guarantee by law (constitution) that all citizens will be able directly to participate in the administration of the state; to secure for all citizens the right to assemble freely, to discuss their affairs, to influence the state affairs through the medium of associations and the press. The achievement of political liberty is becoming the *"urgent task of the workers,"* because without it the workers have not, and cannot have, any influence in the affairs of the state, and for that reason must inevitably remain a degraded and voiceless class totally without rights. And if already, when the struggle and the organization of the workers are but just beginning, the government is hastening to make concessions to the workers in order to stop further growth of the movement, there can be no doubt that when the workers rally and organize under the leadership of a single political party they will be able to compel the government to surrender, they will be able to win for themselves, and for the whole Russian people, political liberty! (*Explanation of the Program of the Social Democratic Party,* 1895–1896, *Selected Works,* I, 364 f.)

We will begin with socialist activity. One would have thought that the character of Social Democratic activity in this respect would have become quite clear since the Social Democratic League of Struggle for the Emancipation of the Working Class in St. Petersburg began its activities among the St. Petersburg workers. The socialist work of Russian Social Democrats consists of propagandizing the doctrines of scientific socialism, of spreading among the workers a proper understanding of the present social and economic system, its foundations and its development, an understanding of the various *classes* in Russian society, of the mutual relations between these classes, the struggle between them, of the role of the working class in this struggle, the attitude of this class toward the declining and developing classes, toward the past and the future of capitalism, of the historical task of international Social Democracy and of the Russian working class. Inseparably connected with propaganda is *agitation*[2] among the workers, which naturally comes to the forefront in the present

---

[2]The distinction between *propaganda* and *agitation* is as follows: *Propaganda* is the work of explaining in detail certain problems to a restricted circle; *agitation* is the work of explaining concrete issues to the masses.— *Ed*. Eng. ed.

political conditions in Russia, and with the present level of development of the masses of workers. Agitating among the workers means that the Social Democrats take part in all the spontaneous manifestations of the struggle of the working class, in all the conflicts between the workers and the capitalists over the working day, wages, conditions of labor, etc. Our task is to merge our activities with the practical everyday questions of working class life, to help the workers to understand these questions, to draw the attention of the workers to the most important abuses, to help them to formulate their demands to the employers more precisely and practically, to develop among the workers a sense of solidarity, to help them to understand the common interests and the common cause of all the Russian workers as a single class representing part of the international army of the proletariat. To organize study circles for workers, to establish proper and secret connections between these and the central group of Social Democrats, to publish and distribute literature for workers, to organize correspondence from all centers of the labor movement, to publish agitational leaflets and manifestos and to distribute them, and to train a corps of experienced agitators—such, in the main, are the manifestations of the socialist activity of Russian Social Democracy.

Our work is primarily and mainly concentrated on the urban factory workers. The Russian Social Democrats must not dissipate their forces; they must concentrate their activities among the industrial proletariat, which is most capable of absorbing Social Democratic ideas, is the most developed class intellectually and politically, and the most important from the point of view of numbers and concentration in the important political centers of the country. Hence, the creation of a durable revolutionary organization among the factory, the urban, workers is one of the first and urgent tasks that confronts the Social Democrats, and it would be very unwise indeed to allow ourselves to be diverted from this task at the present time. But, while recognizing that it is important to concentrate our forces on the factory workers and decry the dissipation of forces, we do not for a moment suggest that Russian Social Democrats should ignore other strata of the Russian proletariat and the working class. Nothing of the kind. The very conditions of life of the Russian factory workers compel them very often to come into very close contact with the *kustars,* i.e., the industrial proletariat outside of the factory, who are scattered in the towns and villages and whose conditions are infinitely worse than those of the factory workers. The Russian factory workers also come into direct contact with the rural population (very often the factory worker has his family in the country) and, consequently, cannot but come into contact with the rural proletariat, with the vast mass of professional agricultural laborers and day laborers, and also with those ruined peasants who, while clinging to their miserable plots of land, are engaged in working to pay the rent (*otrabotki*) and in casual employment, which is also wage labor. Russian Social Democrats think it inopportune to send their forces among the *kustars* and rural laborers, but they do not intend to leave them uncared for; they will try to enlighten the advanced workers on questions affecting the lives of the *kustars* and rural laborers, so that when they come into contact with the more backward strata of the proletariat they will imbue them with the ideas of the class struggle, of socialism, of the political tasks of Russian democracy in general and of the Russian proletariat in particular. It would not be practical to send agitators among the *kustars* and rural laborers when there is still so much work to be done among the urban factory workers, but in a large number of cases Socialist workers involuntarily come into contact with these rural artisans, and they must be able to take advantage of these opportunities and understand the general tasks of Social Democracy in Russia. Hence, those who accuse the Russian Social Democrats of being narrow-minded, of trying to ignore the mass of the toilers and to interest themselves entirely in the factory workers, are profoundly mistaken. On the contrary, agitation among the advanced strata of the proletariat is the surest and only way to rouse (in proportion as the movement expands) the whole of the Russian proletariat. By spreading socialism and the ideas of the class struggle among the urban workers, we shall inevitably cause these ideas to flow in the smaller and more scattered channels. To achieve this, however, it is necessary that these ideas shall become deep-rooted in better prepared soil, and that the vanguard of the Russian labor movement and of the Russian revolution shall be thoroughly imbued with them. While concentrating its forces among the factory workers, the Russian Social Democrats are prepared to support those Russian revolutionaries who, in practice, are beginning to base their socialist work on the class struggle of the proletariat; but they make no attempt to conceal the fact that practical alliances with other factions of revolutionaries cannot and must not lead to compromises or concessions on matters of theory, of the program or the flag. Convinced that the only revolutionary theory that can serve as the banner of the revolutionary movement at the present time is the theory of scientific socialism and the class struggle, the Russian Social Democrats will exert every effort to spread this theory, to guard against its false interpretation, and will combat every attempt to bind the young labor movement in Russia with less definite doctrines. Theoretical reasoning *proves* and the practical activity of the Social Democrats *shows* that all *Socialists* in Russia should become *Social Democrats*.

We will now deal with the *democratic* tasks and with the democratic work of the Social Democrats. We repeat, once again, that this work is *inseparably* connected with socialist work. In carrying on *propaganda* among the workers, the Social Democrats *cannot* ignore political questions and they would regard any attempt to ignore them or even to push them into the background as a profound mistake and a departure from the fundamental principles of international Social Democracy. Simultaneously with propaganda in favor of scientific socialism, Russian Social Democrats consider it to be their task to carry on propaganda among the masses of the workers in favor of *democratic ideas,* to spread an understanding of what absolutism means in all its manifestations, its class content, the necessity for overthrowing it, of the impossibility of waging a successful struggle for the cause of labor without achieving political liberty and the democratization of the political and social system of Russia. In carrying on *agitation* among the workers concerning their immediate *eco-*

nomic demands, the Social Democrats link this up with agitation concerning the immediate political needs, grievances and demands of the working class, agitation against the tyranny of the police, which manifests itself in every strike, in every conflict between the workers and the capitalists, agitation against the restriction of the rights of the workers as Russian citizens in general and as the most oppressed and most disfranchised class in particular, agitation against every prominent representative and flunkey of absolutism who comes into direct contact with the workers and who clearly reveals to the working class its state of political slavery. Just as there is not a question affecting the economic life of the workers that cannot be utilized for the purpose of economic agitation, so there is not a political question that cannot serve as a subject for political agitation. These two forms of agitation are inseparably bound up with each other in the activities of Social Democrats like the two sides of a medal. Both economic and political agitation are equally necessary for the development of the class consciousness of the proletariat, and economic and political agitation are equally necessary in order to guide the class struggle of the Russian workers, for every class struggle is a political struggle. Both forms of agitation, by awakening class consciousness among the workers, by organizing them and disciplining and training them for united action and for the struggle for the ideals of Social Democracy, will give the workers the opportunity to test their strength on immediate questions and immediate needs, will enable them to force their enemy to make partial concessions, to improve their economic conditions, will compel the capitalists to respect the organized might of the workers, compel the government to give the workers more right, to give heed to their demands, keep the government in constant fear of the hostile temper of the masses of the workers led by a strong Social Democratic organization.

. . . .

Support for all political opposition elements will be expressed in the propaganda of the Social Democrats by the fact that in showing that absolutism is hostile to the cause of labor, they will show that absolutism is hostile to the various other social groups;

they will show that the working class is with these groups on *this or that question, on this or that task,* etc. In their agitation this support will express itself in that the Social Democrats will take advantage of every manifestation of the police tyranny of absolutism to point out to the workers how this tyranny affects all Russian citizens *generally,* and the representatives of the particularly oppressed estates, nationalities, religions, sects, etc., in particular, and especially how that tyranny affects the *working class.* Finally, in practice, this support is expressed in that the Russian Social Democrats are prepared to enter into alliance with revolutionaries of other trends for the purpose of achieving certain partial aims, and this preparedness has been proved on more than one occasion.

While pointing out that one or another of the various opposition groups is in unison with the workers, the Social Democrats will always put the workers in a special category, they will always point out that the alliance is temporary and conditional, they will always emphasize the special class position of the proletariat which tomorrow may be the opponent of its allies of today. We may be told: This may *weaken* all the fighters of political liberty at the present time. Our reply will be: This will *strengthen* all the fighters for political liberty. Only those fighters are strong who rely on the *appreciation* of the real interests of definite *classes,* and any attempt to obscure these class interests, which already play a predominant role in modern society, will only serve to weaken the fighters. That is the first point. The second point is that in the struggle against autocracy the working class must single itself out from the rest, for it *alone* is the truly consistent and unreserved enemy of absolutism, it is *only* between the working class and absolutism that compromise is impossible, *only* in the working class has democracy a champion without reservations, who does not waver, who does not look back.

. . . .

By leading the class struggle of the proletariat, developing organization and discipline among the workers, helping them to fight for their immediate economic needs and to win position after position from capital, by politically educating the workers and systematically and unswervingly pursuing absolutism and making life a torment for every tsarist *bashibazuk* who makes the proletariat feel the heavy paw of the police government—such an organization would at one and the same time adapt itself to the conditions under which we would have to form a workers' party and be a powerful revolutionary party directed against absolutism. To discuss beforehand what methods this organization is to apply in order to strike a decisive blow at absolutism, whether, for example, it would prefer rebellion, or a mass political strike, or some other method of attack, to discuss these things beforehand and to decide this question now would be empty doctrinairism. It would be behaving like generals who called a council of war before they had recruited their army, had mobilized it and had begun the campaign against the enemy. When the army of the proletariat unswervingly, under the leadership of a strong Social Democratic organization, fights for its economic and political emancipation, that army will itself indicate to the generals the methods and means of action. Then, and then only, will it be possible to decide the question of striking a decisive blow against absolutism; for the problem depends on the state of the labor movement, on its dimensions, on the methods of struggle developed by the movement, on the character of the revolutionary organization that is leading the movement, on the attitude of other social elements toward the proletariat and toward absolutism, on the state of home and foreign politics—in short, it depends on a thousand and one things which cannot be determined and which it would be useless to determine beforehand. (*The Tasks of the Russian Social Democracy*, 1897, *Selected Works*, I, 371–375, 376 f., 384 f.)

A PROTEST BY RUSSIAN SOCIAL DEMOCRATS

AT A MEETING OF SOCIAL DEMOCRATS, SEVENTEEN IN NUMBER, HELD AT A CERTAIN PLACE (IN RUSSIA), THE FOLLOWING RESOLUTION WAS PASSED AND IT WAS RESOLVED TO PUBLISH IT AND TO SUBMIT IT TO THE COMRADES FOR THEIR CONSIDERATION.

A tendency has been observed among Russian Social Democrats recently to depart from the fundamental principles of Russian Social Democracy that were proclaimed by the founders and front-rank fighters—the members of the "Emancipation of Labor" Group—as well as in the Social Democratic publications of the Russian labor organizations of the 1890's. The *Credo* reproduced below, which is presumed to express the fundamental views of certain ("young") Russian Social Democrats represents an attempt systematically and definitely to expound "new views." The following is the *Credo.* . . .

> The handicraft and manufacture period in the West left a sharp impress on the whole of subsequent history and particularly on the history of Social Democracy. The fact that the bourgeoisie was obliged to fight for free forms, the striving for release from the guild regulations which fettered production, made the bourgeoisie a revolutionary element; everywhere in the West it began with *liberté, fraternité, egalité,* with the achievement of free political forms. By these gains, however, as Bismarck expressed it, they drew a bill on the future payable to their antipodes—the working class. Almost everywhere in the West, the working class, as a class, did not capture the democratic institutions—it used them. Against this it may be argued that the working class took part in revolutions. A reference to history will refute this opinion because, precisely in 1848, when the consolidation of constitutions took place in the West, the working class consisted of the urban artisan element, represented urban democracy: a factory proletariat hardly existed, while the proletariat employed in large-scale industry . . . represented a wild mass capable only of rioting, but not of advancing any political demands. It can be definitely stated that the constitutions of 1848 were won by the bourgeoisie and the small urban artisans. On the other hand, the working class (artisans, handicraftsmen, printers, weavers, watchmakers, etc.) since the Middle Ages have been accustomed to membership in organizations, in mutual aid societies, religious societies, etc. This spirit of organization still exists among the skilled workers in the West and sharply distinguishes them from the factory proletariat who submit to organization badly and slowly and are capable only of forming temporary and not permanent organizations with rules and regulations. These skilled handicraftsmen comprised the core of Social Democratic parties. Thus, the following picture was obtained: on the one hand, relatively easy and complete opportunity for political struggle; on the other hand, the opportunity for the systematic organization of this struggle with the aid of the workers who had

been trained in the period of manufacture. It was on this basis that theoretical and practical Marxism grew up in the West. The stimulus was given by the parliamentary political struggle with the prospect—only superficially resembling Blanquism, but of a totally different origin—with the prospect of capturing power, on the one hand, and the collapse of the socio-political system, on the other. Marxism was the theoretical expression of the prevailing practice: of the political struggle which prevailed over the economic struggle. Both in Belgium and in France, but particularly in Germany, the workers organized the political struggle with incredible ease, but organized the economic struggle with enormous difficulty and tremendous friction. Even to this day the economic organizations are extraordinarily weak and unstable (this does not apply to England) compared with the political organizations, and everywhere leave much to be desired. While the energy in the political struggle had not yet been completely exhausted, "collapse" was an essential organizational catchword destined to play an extremely important historical role. The fundamental law that can be discerned in studying the labor movement is the line of least resistance. In the West, this line was political activity, and Marxism, in the form in which it was formulated in the *Communist Manifesto,* was the best possible form the movement could assume. But when all energy had been exhausted in the political struggle, when the political movement had reached a point of intensity beyond which it was difficult and almost impossible to lead it (the slow increase in votes lately, the apathy of the public at meetings, the note of despondency expressed in literature), on the other hand, the ineffectiveness of parliamentary action and the entry into the arena of the uneducated masses of the unorganized and almost unorganizable factory proletariat gave rise in the West to what is now called Bernsteinism, the crisis of Marxism. It is difficult to imagine a more logical process of development of the labor movement from the period of the *Communist Manifesto* to the period of Bernsteinism, and a careful study of the whole of this process can determine with astronomical exactitude the outcome of this "crisis." Reference is made here, of course, not to the defeat or victory of Bernsteinism, that is of little interest, reference is made to the fundamental change in practical activity that has been gradually taking place for a long time within the parties.

This change will place not only in the direction of conducting the economic struggle with greater energy and of consolidating the economic organizations, but also, and this is the most important, in the direction of a change in the attitude of the parties towards other opposition parties. Intolerant Marxism, negative Marxism, primitive Marxism (whose conception of the class division of society is too schematic), will give way to democratic Marxism, and the social position of the parties in modern society must undergo a sharp change. The party will recognize society; its narrow corporative and, in the majority of cases, sectarian tasks will be widened to social tasks, and its striving to seize power will be transformed into a striving for change, a striving to reform present-day society in a democratic direction adapted to the present state of affairs with the object of protecting the rights (all rights) of the toiling classes in the most successful and fullest way. The concept of 'politics' will be enlarged to truly social significance, and the practical demands of the moment will acquire greater weight and will be able to count on receiving greater attention than they have been getting up to now.

From this brief description of the process of development of the labor movement in the West, it is not difficult to draw conclusions for Russia. In Russia, the line of least resistance will never tend in the direction of political activity. The incredible political oppression that prevails gives rise to much talk about it, and it is on this that attention is concentrated; but it will never result in action being taken. While, in the West, the fact that the workers were drawn into political activity served to strengthen and crystallize the weak forces of the workers, in Russia, on the contrary, these weak forces are confronted with a wall of political oppression, and not only do they lack a practical path on which to fight this oppression, and hence, a path for their development, but they are systematically strangled and cannot even give forth weak shoots. If to this we add that the working class in our country has not inherited the spirit of organization that the fighters in the West inherited, the picture will be a gloomy one that is likely to drive into despondency the most optimistic Marxist who believes that an extra factory chimney stack, by the very fact that it exists, will bring great prosperity. The economic struggle too is hard, infinitely hard, but it is possible to wage it; it is in fact being waged by the masses themselves. By learning to organize in the midst of this struggle, and coming into constant conflict with the political regime in the course of it, the Russian worker will at last create what may be called the form of the labor movement, the organization or organizations that will best conform to Russian conditions. It can now be said with certainty that the Russian labor movement is still in the amoeba state and has not yet created any form. The strike movement, which is going on with all types of organization, cannot yet be described as the crystallized form of the Russian movement, whereas the underground organizations are not worth consideration even from the mere quantitative point of view (quite apart from the question of their utility under present conditions).

That is the situation. If to this we add the famine and the ruination of the countryside, which give rise to the strike breaker, and, consequently, to even greater difficulties in the way of raising the masses of the workers to a more tolerable cultural level, then . . . well, what is the Russian Marxist to do? The talk about an independent workers' political party is nothing more nor less than the product of the attempt to transplant alien tasks and alien results to our soil. At present, the Russian Marxist presents a sad spectacle. His practical tasks at the present time are paltry, his theoretical knowledge, in so far as he utilizes it, *not as an instrument for research,* but as a scheme for activity, is worthless for the purpose of fulfilling even those paltry practical tasks. Moreover, these borrowed schemes are harmful from the practical point of view. Our Marxists forget that the working class in the West entered the field of political activity after it had already been cleared, and, consequently, are too contemptuous of the radical or liberal opposition activity of all other non-labor strata of society. The slightest attempt to concentrate attention on public manifestations of a liberal political character rouses the protests of the orthodox Marxists who forget that a number of historical conditions prevent us from being Western Marxists and compel us to be Marxists of another type, applicable to and necessary for Russian conditions. Obviously, the fact that every Russian citizen lacks political feeling and sense cannot be compensated by talk about politics or by appeals to a non-existent power. This political sense can only be acquired by training, i.e., by participating in the social life (however un-Marxian this social life may be) that is offered by Russian conditions. However opportune (temporarily) "negations" may have been in the West, they are harmful in Russia because negations coming from something that is organized and having real power is one thing, whereas negations coming from an amorphous mass of disunited individuals is another thing.

There is only one way out for the Russian Marxist: he must participate, i.e., assist in the economic struggle of the proletariat, and take part in liberal opposition activity. As a "negator," the Russian Marxist came on the scene very early, and this negation weakened that share of his energy that should be used in the direction of political radicalism. For the time being, this not terrible; but if the class scheme prevents the Russian intellectual from taking an active part in social life and removes him to too great a distance from opposition circles, it will be a serious loss to all those who are compelled to fight for constitutional forms separately from the working class, which has not yet put forward political tasks. The political innocence of the Russian Marxist intellectual which is concealed by mental exercises in political topics may land him in a mess.

We do not know whether there are many Russian Social Democrats who share these views. But there is no doubt that ideas of this kind have their adherents and that is why we feel obliged to protest categorically against such views and to warn all comrades of the danger of Russian Social Democracy being diverted from the path that it has already chosen for itself, viz., the formation of an independent political workers' party which shall be inseparable from the class struggle of the proletariat, and which shall have for its immediate aim the winning of political liberty.

The above-quoted *Credo* represents firstly, "a brief description of the process of development of the labor movement in the West," and, secondly, "conclusions to be drawn for Russia."

First of all, the conception of the history of the West European labor movement presented by the authors of the *Credo* is entirely wrong. It is not true to say that the working class in the West did not take part in the struggle for political liberty and in political revolutions. The history of the Chartist movement and the revolutions of 1848 in France, Germany and Austria prove the opposite. It is absolutely untrue to say that "Marxism was the theoretical expression of the prevailing practice: of the political struggle which prevailed over the economic struggle." On the contrary, "Marxism" appeared when non-political socialism prevailed ("Owenism," "Fourierism," "true socialism") and the *Communist Manifesto* immediately opposed non-political socialism. Even when Marxism came out fully armed with theory (*Capital*) and organized the celebrated International Workingmen's Association, the political struggle was by no means the prevailing practice (narrow trade unionism in England, anarchism and Proudhonism in the Latin countries). The great historic merit of Lassalle in Germany lay in the fact that he transformed the working class from a tail of the liberal bourgeoisie into an independent political party. Marxism linked up the economic and the political struggles of the working class into a single inseparable whole; and the efforts of the authors of the *Credo* to separate these two forms of struggle represent their most clumsy and deplorable departure from Marxism.

Furthermore, the authors of the *Credo* are utterly wrong in respect to the present state of the West European labor movement and to the theory of Marxism, under the banner of which that movement is marching. To talk about the "crisis of Marxism" is merely to repeat the nonsensical phrases of the bourgeois hacks who are doing all they can to exaggerate every disagreement among the Socialists in order to provoke a split in the socialist parties. The notorious Bernsteinism—in the sense that it is understood by the general public, and by the authors of the *Credo* in particular—is an attempt to narrow the theory of Marxism, an attempt to convert the revolutionary workers' party into a reformist party; and as was to be expected, this attempt was strongly condemned by the majority of the German Social Democrats. Opportunist trends have more than once revealed themselves in the ranks of German Social Democracy, and on every occasion they have been repudiated by the Party, which loyally guards the principles of revolutionary international Social Democracy. We are convinced that every attempt to transplant opportunist views to Russia will encounter an equally stern resistance on the part of the great majority of Russian Social Democrats.

Similarly, there can be no suggestion of a "radical change in the practical activity" of the West European workers' parties, in spite of what the authors of the *Credo* say: The tremendous importance of the economic struggle of the proletariat, and the necessity for such a struggle, was recognized by Marxism from the very outset; and even in the 1840's Marx and Engels opposed the utopian socialists who denied the importance of this struggle.

When the International Workingmen's Association was formed about twenty years later, the question of the importance of trade unions and of the economic struggle was raised at the very first Congress of the Association, at Geneva in 1866. The resolution adopted at that Congress definitely referred to the importance of the economic struggle and, on the one hand, warned the Socialists and the workers against exaggerating the importance of this struggle (which the English workers were inclined to do at that time) and against underestimating its importance (which the French and the Germans, particularly the Lassalleans, were inclined to do), on the other. The resolution recognized the trade unions to be not only a natural, but also an essential phenomenon under capitalism and regarded them as being extremely important as a means of organizing the working class for its daily struggle against capital and for the abolition of wage labor. The resolution declared that the trade unions must not devote attention exclusively to the "immediate struggle against capital," must not remain outside of the general political and social movement of the working class; they must not pursue "narrow" aims but must strive for the complete emancipation of the vast masses of the oppressed toilers. Since that time, the workers' parties in the various countries have more than once discussed the question and, of course, will discuss it again and again, as to whether to devote more or less attention at the given moment to the economic or the political struggle of the proletariat; but, in principle, the question stands today as it was presented by Marxism. The conviction that the class struggle must necessarily combine the political and the economic struggle has permeated the very flesh and blood of international Social Democracy. Moreover, the experience of history has incontrovertibly proved that the absence of liberty, or the restriction of the political rights of the proletariat, always leads to the necessity of putting the political struggle in the forefront.

Still less can there be any suggestion of any serious change in the attitude of the workers' parties toward the other opposition parties. In this respect, too, Marxism has laid down the correct position, which is equally remote from exaggerating the importance of politics, from conspiracies (Blanquism, etc.) and from decrying politics or reducing it to opportunist, reformist patching up of the social system (anarchism, utopian and petty bourgeois socialism, state socialism, professorial socialism, etc.). The proletariat must strive to form independent, political workers' parties, the main aim of which must be: the capture of political power by the proletariat for the purpose of organizing socialist society. The proletariat must not regard the other classes and parties as a "homogeneous reactionary mass": on the contrary, it must take part in the whole of political and social life, support the progressive classes and parties against the reactionary classes and parties, support every revolutionary movement against the present system, must champion the interests of every oppressed nation or race, of every persecuted religion, disfranchised sex, etc. The arguments the authors of the *Credo* advance on this subject merely reveal a desire to obscure the class character of the struggle of the proletariat, a desire to weaken this struggle by a senseless "recognition of society," to reduce revolutionary Marxism to a humdrum reformist trend. We are convinced that the overwhelming majority of Russian Social Democrats will totally reject this distortion of the fundamental principles of Social Democracy. Their incorrect premises regarding the West European labor movement led the authors of the *Credo* to draw still more erroneous "conclusions for Russia."

The assertion that the Russian working class "has not yet put forward political tasks" simply reveals ignorance of the Russian revolutionary movement. Even the North Russian Labor League formed in 1878 and the South Russian Labor League formed in 1879 put forward the demand for political liberty in their programs. After the reactionary 1880's, the working class repeatedly put forward similar demands in the 1890's. The assertion that "the talk about an independent workers' political party is nothing more nor less than the product of the attempt to transplant alien tasks and alien results to our soil" reveals a complete failure to understand the historical role of the Russian working class and the tasks of Russian Social Democracy. Apparently, the program of the authors of the *Credo* inclines to the idea that the working class, "following the line of least resistance," should confine itself to the economic struggle while the "liberal opposition elements" fight for "constitutional forms" with the "participation" of the Marxists. The carrying out of such a program would be tantamount to political suicide for Russian Social Democracy, tantamount to greatly retarding and restricting the Russian labor movement and the Russian revolutionary movement (for us the two latter terms are synonymous). The mere fact that it was possible for a program like this to appear shows how well grounded were the fears expressed by one of the front rank fighters of Russian Social Democracy. P. B. Axelrod, when, in writing on this prospect at the end of 1897, said:

> The labor movement keeps to the narrow rut of purely economic conflicts between the workers and employers, and, in itself, taken as a whole, is not of a political character, but in the struggle for political liberty the progressive strata of the proletariat follow the revolutionary circles and factions formed by the so-called intelligentsia. (Axelrod, *The Present Tasks and Tactics of the Russian Social Democrats,* Geneva, 1898, p. 19.)

Russian Social Democracy must declare determined war against the whole circle of ideas expressed in the *Credo,* for these ideas lead to this prospect becoming a fact. Russian Social Democrats must exert every effort to create another prospect, depicted by P. B. Axelrod in the following words:

> The other prospect: Social Democracy will organize the Russian proletariat in an independent political party which will fight for liberty, *partly, side by side and in alliance with* the bourgeois revolutionary factions (if such exist), and partly by recruiting directly into its ranks, or securing the following of the most democratic and revolutionary elements of the intelligentsia.

At the time P. B. Axelrod wrote the above lines, the declarations made by Social Democrats in Russia showed clearly that the overwhelming majority of them adhere to the same point of view. It is true that one paper published by the St. Petersburg workers, *Rabochaya Mysl,* seemed to incline toward the ideas of the authors of the *Credo* when, unfortunately, in a leading article on its program (in the first issue, Oct., 1897) it expressed the utterly erroneous idea, which runs counter to Social Democracy, that the "economic basis of the movement" may be "obscured by the effort constantly to keep in mind political ideals." At the same time, however, another newspaper published by St. Petersburg workers, the *St. Petersburg Rabochy Listok* (No. 2, Sept., 1897), emphatically expressed the opinion that "the overthrow of the autocracy ... can be achieved only by a well organized and numerically strong workers' party" and that "organized in a strong party" the workers will "emancipate themselves, and the whole of Russia, from all political and economic oppression." A third newspaper, the *Rabochaya Gazeta,* in its leading article in the second issue (Nov., 1897), wrote: "The fight against the autocratic government for political liberty is the immediate task of the Russian labor movement." "The Russian labor movement will increase its forces tenfold if it comes out as a single, harmonious whole, with a common name and a symmetrical organization...." "The separate workers' circles should combine into a single, common party." "The Russian workers' party will be a Social Democratic party." That the overwhelming majority of Russian Social Democrats fully share the convictions expressed by *Rabochaya Gazeta* is seen from the fact that the Congress of Russian Social Democrats which was held in the spring of 1898 formed the Russian Social Democratic Labor party, published the Manifesto of the Party and recognized the *Rabochaya Gazeta* as the official organ of the Party. Thus, the authors of the *Credo* are retreating an enormous distance from the stage of development which Russian Social Democracy has already achieved and which has been registered in the *Manifesto of the Russian Social Democratic Labor party.*

Although the desperate persecution of the Russian government has led to the temporary subsidence of the activities of the Party at the present time and to the cessation of its official organ, the task of all Social Democrats is to exert every effort finally to consolidate the Party, to draw up the Party program and to revive its official organ. In view of the wavering of opinion that is evidenced by the fact that programs like the above-examined *Credo* can appear, we think it particularly necessary to empha-size the following fundamental principles that were expounded in the Manifesto and which are of enormous importance for Russian Social Democracy.

First: Russian Social Democracy "desires to be and remain a class movement of the organized masses of workers." Hence it follows that the motto of Social Democracy must be to help the workers not only in their economic, but also in their political struggle; to carry on agitation not only in connection with immediate economic needs, but also in connection with all mani-festations of political oppression; to carry on propaganda not only in support of the ideas of scientific socialism, but also in support of the ideas of democracy. The only banner the class movement of the workers can have is the theory of revolutionary Marxism, and Russian Social Democracy must see that it is further developed and put into practice, and at the same time they must protect it against those distortions and vulgarizations to which "fashionable theories" are often subjected (and the successes which revolutionary Social Democracy in Russia has achieved have made Marxism a "fashionable" theory). While concentrating all its efforts at the present time on activity among factory workers and mine workers, Social Democrats must not forget that with the expansion of the movement they must also recruit into the ranks of the masses of the workers they organize the home workers, artisans, agricultural laborers and the millions of ruined and starving peasants.

Second: "On his strong shoulders the Russian worker must and will bear the cause of winning political liberty." Having made the overthrow of absolutism its immediate task, Social Democracy must come out as the vanguard in the fight for democracy, and this fact alone compels it to give every support to all the democratic elements of the population of Russia and to win them as allies. Only an independent workers' party can serve as a firm bulwark in the fight against the autocracy, and only in alliance with such a party, only in supporting it, can all the other fighters for political liberty display their activities.

Third and last: "As a socialist movement and trend, the Russian Social Democratic Labor party continues the cause and traditions of the whole of the preceding revolutionary movement in Russia: Setting the task of winning political liberty as the greatest of the immediate tasks of the Party as a whole, Social Democracy is marching toward the goal that was clearly indicated long ago by the glorious fighters in the old *Narodnaya Volya*." The traditions of the whole preceding revolutionary movement demand that the Social Democrats shall at the present time concentrate their efforts on the organization of the Party, on strengthening its internal discipline, and on developing the technique of secrecy. If the fighters in the old *Narodnaya Volya* managed to play an enormous role in the history of Russia in spite of the narrowness of the social strata which supported the few heroes, and in spite of the fact that that movement did not have a revolutionary theory as its banner, then Social Democracy, relying on the class struggle of the proletariat, will succeed in becoming invincible. "The Russian proletariat will throw off the yoke of autocracy in order, with still greater energy, to continue the struggle against capital and the bourgeoisie for the complete victory of socialism."

We invite all groups of Social Democrats and all workers' circles in Russia to discuss the above-quoted *Credo* and our resolution, and definitely to express their opinion on the question raised in order that all differences may be removed and in order that the work of organizing and strengthening the Russian Social Democratic Labor party may be accelerated.

Groups and circles may send their resolutions to the League of Russian Social Democrats Abroad which, on the basis of point 10 of the decision of the Congress of Russian Social Democrats held in 1898, is a part of the Russian Social Democratic Labor party and its representative abroad. (*A Protest by Russian Social Democrats*, Fall, 1899, *Selected Works*, I, 390–401.)

Rabocheye Dyelo accuses *Iskra* and *Zarya* of "setting up their program against the movement, like a spirit hovering over the formless chaos" (p. 29). But what else is the function of Social Democracy if not to be a "spirit," not only hovering over the spontaneous movement, but also *raising* the movement *to the level of "its program"*? Surely, it is not its function to drag at the *tail* of the movement: at best, this would be of no service to the movement; at the worst, it would be very, very harmful. *Rabocheye Dyelo,* however, not only follows this "tactics-process," but elevates it to a principle, so that it would be more correct to describe its tendency not as opportunism, but as *khvostism* (from the Russian word *khvost,* meaning "tail"). And it must be admitted that those who have determined always to follow behind the movement like a tail are absolutely and forever ensured against "belittling the spontaneous element of development."

.   .   .   .

He who forgets that "the Communists support every revolutionary movement," that we are obliged for that reason to expound and emphasize *general democratic tasks before the whole people,* without for a moment concealing our socialistic convictions, is not a Social Democrat. He who forgets his obligation to be *in advance of everybody* in bringing up, sharpening and solving *every* general democratic problem is not a Social Democrat.

WHAT ARE PRIMITIVE METHODS?

We shall try to answer this question by describing the activity of a typical Social Democratic circle of the period of 1894–1901. We have already referred to the manner in which the students became absorbed in Marxism at that period. Of course, these students were not only, or even not so much, absorbed in Marxism as a theory, but as an answer to the question "What is to be done?" as a call to march against the enemy. And these new warriors marched to battle with astonishingly primitive equipment and training. In a vast number of cases, they had almost no equipment and absolutely no training. They marched to war like peasants from the plough, snatching up a club. A students' circle having no contacts with the old members of the movement, no contacts with circles in other districts, or even in other parts of the same city (or with other schools), without the various sections of the revolutionary work being in any way organized, having no systematic plan of activity covering any length of time, establishes contacts with the workers and sets to work. The circle gradually expands its propaganda and agitation; by its activities it wins the sympathies of a rather large circle of workers and of a certain section of the educated classes, which provides it with money and from which the "committee" recruits new groups of young people. The charm which the committee (or the League of Struggle) exercises on the youth increases, its sphere of activity becomes wider and its activities expand quite spontaneously: the very people who a year or a few months previously had spoken at the gatherings of the students' circle and discussed the question "Whither?" who established and maintained contacts with the workers, wrote and published leaflets, now establish contacts with other groups of revolutionaries, procure literature, set to work to establish a local newspaper, begin to talk about organizing demonstrations and, finally, commence open hostilities (these open hostilities may, according to circumstances, take the form of the publication of the very first agitational leaflet, or the first newspaper, or of the organization of the first demonstration). And usually the first action ends in immediate and wholesale arrests. Immediate and wholesale, precisely because these open hostilities were not the result of a systematic and carefully thought-out and gradually prepared plan for a prolonged and stubborn struggle, but simply the result of the spontaneous growth of traditional circle work; because, naturally, the police, in almost every case, knew the principal leaders of the local movement, for they had already "recommended" themselves to the police in their schooldays, and the latter only waited for a convenient moment to make their raid. They gave the circle sufficient time to develop its work so that they might obtain a palpable *corpus delicti,* and always allowed several of the persons known to them to remain at liberty in order to act as "decoys" (which I believe, is the technical term used both by our people and by the police). One cannot help comparing this kind of warfare with that conducted by a mob of peasants armed with clubs against modern troops. One can only express astonishment at the virility displayed by the movement which expanded, grew and won victories in spite of the total lack of training among the fighters. It is true that from the historical point of view, the primitiveness of equipment was not only inevitable at first, but even *legitimate* as one of the conditions for the wide recruiting of fighters, but as soon as serious operations commenced (and they commenced in fact with the strikes in the summer of 1896), the defects in our fighting organizations made themselves felt to an increasing degree. Thrown into confusion at first and committing a number of mistakes (for example, its appeal to the public describing the misdeeds of the Socialists, or the deportation of the workers from the capital to the provincial industrial centers), the government very soon adapted itself to the new conditions of the struggle and managed to place its perfectly equipped detachments of *agents provocateurs*, spies and police in the required places. Raids became so frequent, affected such a vast number of people and cleared out the local circles so thoroughly that the masses of the workers literally lost all their leaders, the movement assumed an incredibly sporadic character, and it became utterly impossible to establish continuity and coherence in the work. The fact that the local active workers were hopelessly scattered, the casual manner in which the membership of the circles was recruited, the lack of training in and narrow outlook on theoretical, political and organizational questions were all the inevitable result of the conditions described above. Things reached such a pass that in several places the workers, because of our lack of stamina and ability to maintain secrecy, began to lose faith in the intelligentsia and to avoid them: the intellectuals, they said, are much too careless and lay themselves open to police raids!

Anyone who has the slightest knowledge of the movement

knows that these primitive methods at last began to be recognized as a disease by all thinking Social Democrats.

.   .   .   .

The revolution itself must not by any means be regarded as a single act (as Nadezhdin apparently imagines) but as a series of more or less powerful outbreaks rapidly alternating with more or less intense calm. For that reason, the principal content of the activity of our party organization, the focus of this activity should be, to carry on work that is possible and necessary in the period of the most powerful outbreaks as well as in the period of complete calm....

.   .   .   .

Picture to yourselves a popular uprising. Probably everyone will now agree that we must think of this uprising and prepare for it. But *how* to prepare for it? Surely the Central Committee cannot appoint agents to go to all the districts for the purpose of preparing for the uprising! Even if we had a central committee it could achieve nothing by making such appointments, considering the conditions prevailing in contemporary Russia. But a network of agents that would automatically be created in the course of establishing and distributing a common newspaper would not have to "sit around and wait" for the call to rebellion, but would carry on the regular work that would guarantee the highest probability of success in the event of a rebellion. Such work would strengthen our contacts with the broadest strata of the masses of the workers and with all those strata who are discontented with the autocracy, which is so important in the event of an uprising. It is precisely such work that would help to cultivate the ability properly to estimate the general political situation and, consequently, the ability to select the proper moment for the uprising. It is precisely such work that would train *all* local organizations to respond simultaneously to the same political questions, incidents and events that excite the whole of Russia, to react to these "events" in the most vigorous, uniform and expedient manner possible; for is not rebellion in essence the most vigorous, most uniform and most expedient "reaction" of the whole of the people to the conduct of the government? And finally, such work would train all revolutionary organizations all over Russia to maintain the most continuous, and at the same time the most secret, contact with each other, which would create *real* Party unity—for without such contacts it will be impossible collectively to discuss the plan of rebellion and to take the necessary preparatory measures on the eve of it, which must be kept in the strictest secrecy.

In a word, the "plan for an all-Russian political newspaper" does not represent the fruits of the work of armchair workers, infected with dogmatism and literariness (as it seemed to those who failed to study it properly), on the contrary, it is a practical plan to begin immediately to prepare on all sides for the uprising, while at the same time never for a moment forgetting the ordinary, everyday work. (*What is To Be Done? Burning Questions of Our Movement,* February, 1902, *Selected Works,* II, 73, 102, 116–118, 186–188.)

THE STAGES, TRENDS AND PROSPECTS OF THE REVOLUTION

1. The labor movement rouses the proletariat immediately under the leadership of the Russian Social Democratic Labor party and *awakens* the liberal bourgeoisie: 1895 to 1901–02.

2. The labor movement passes to open political struggle and *carries with it* the politically awakened strata of the liberal and radical bourgeoisie and petty bourgeoisie: 1901–02 to 1905.

3. The labor movement flares up into a direct *revolution,* while the liberal bourgeoisie has already united in a Constitutional Democratic party and thinks of stopping the revolution by comprising with tsarism; but the *radical* elements of the bourgeoisie and petty bourgeoisie are inclined to enter into an alliance with the proletariat for the *continuation of the revolution:* 1905 (especially the end of that year).

4. The labor movement is victorious in the *democratic* revolution, the liberals passively temporizing and the *peasants* actively assisting. To this must be added the radical republican intelligentsia and the corresponding strata of the urban petty

bourgeoisie. The uprising of the peasants is victorious, the power of the landowners is broken.

("The revolutionary-democratic dictatorship of the proletariat and the peasantry.")

5. The liberal bourgeoisie, temporizing in the third period, passive in the fourth, becomes downright counterrevolutionary, and organizes itself in order to filch from the proletariat the gains of the revolution. The whole of the well-to-do section of the peasantry and a large part of the middle peasantry also grow "wiser," quiet down and turn to the side of the counterrevolution in order to wrest power from the proletariat and the rural poor, who sympathize with the proletariat.

6. On the basis of the relations established during the fifth period, a new crisis and a new struggle blaze forth; the proletariat is now fighting to preserve its democratic gains for the sake of a socialist revolution. This struggle would be almost hopeless for the Russian proletariat alone and its defeat would be as inevitable as the defeat of the German revolutionary party in 1849–50, or as the defeat of the French proletariat in 1871, if the *European socialist proletariat* should not come to the assistance of the Russian proletariat.

Thus, at this stage, the liberal bourgeoisie and the well-to-do peasantry (and partly the middle peasantry) organize counter-revolution. The Russian proletariat *plus* the European proletariat organize revolution.

Under such conditions the Russian proletariat can win a second victory. The cause is no longer hopeless. The second victory will be the *socialist revolution in Europe.*

The European workers will show us "how to do it," and then, in conjunction with them, we shall bring about the socialist revolution. (*The Stages, Trends and Prospects of the Revolution,* 1906, *Selected Works,* III, 134 f.)

The school of civil war does not leave the people unaffected. It is a harsh school, and its complete curriculum *inevitably* includes the victories of the counterrevolution, the debaucheries of enraged reactionaries, savage punishments meted out by the old governments to the rebels, etc. But only downright pedants and mentally decrepit mummies can grieve over the fact that nations are entering this painful school; this school teaches the oppressed classes how to conduct civil war; it teaches how to bring about a victorious revolution; it concentrates in the masses of present-day slaves that hatred which is always harbored by the downtrodden, dull, ignorant slaves, and which leads those slaves who have become conscious of the shame of their slavery to the greatest historic exploits.

. . . .

The international revolutionary movement of the proletariat does not proceed and cannot proceed evenly and in the same form in different countries. The thorough and all-sided utilization of all possibilities in all spheres of activity comes only as a result of the class struggle of the workers of various countries. Every country contributes its own valuable original traits to the general stream, but in every individual country the movement suffers from some kind of one-sidedness, from some theoretical or practical shortcoming in the individual Socialist parties. (*Inflammable Material in World Politics*, August, 1908, *Selected Works*, IV, 298, 302 f.)

One of the most profound causes that periodically give rise to differences over tactics is the very growth of the labor movement itself. If this movement is not measured by the criterion of some fantastic ideal, but is regarded as the practical movement of ordinary people, it will be clear that the enlistment of larger and larger numbers of new "recruits," the enrollment of new strata of the toiling masses, must inevitably be accompanied by waverings in the sphere of theory and tactics, by repetitions of old mistakes, by temporary reversions to antiquated ideas and antiquated methods and so forth. The labor movement of every country periodically spends a varying amount of energy, attention and time on the "training" of recruits.

Furthermore, the speed of development of capitalism differs in different countries and in different spheres of national economy. Marxism is most easily, rapidly, completely and durably assimilated by the working class and its ideologists where large-scale industry is most developed. Economic relations which are backward, or which lag in their development, constantly lead to the appearance of supporters of the labor movement who master only certain aspects of Marxism, only certain parts of the new world conception, or individual slogans and demands, and are unable to make a determined break with all the traditions of the bourgeois world conception in general and the bourgeois-democratic world conception in particular.

Again, a constant source of differences is the dialectical nature of social development, which proceeds in contradictions and through contradictions. Capitalism is progressive because it destroys the old methods of production and develops productive forces; yet at the same time, at a certain stage of development, it retards the growth of productive forces. It develops, organizes and disciplines the workers—and it crushes, oppresses, leads to degeneration, poverty and so on. Capitalism creates its own gravedigger, it creates itself the elements of a new system, yet at the same time without a "leap" these individual elements change nothing in the general state of affairs and do not affect the rule of capital. Marxism, the theory of dialectical material-ism, is able to embrace these contradictions of practical life, of the practical history of capitalism and the labor movement. But needless to say, the masses learn from practical life and not from books, and therefore certain individuals or groups con-stantly exaggerate, elevate to a one-sided theory, to a one-sided system of tactics, now one and now another feature of capitalist development, now one and now another "lesson" from this development.

Bourgeois ideologists, liberals and democrats, not understand-ing Marxism, and not understanding the modern labor move-ment, are constantly leaping from one futile extreme to another. At one time they explain the whole matter by asserting that evil-minded persons are "inciting" class against class—at another they console themselves with the assertion that the workers' party is "a peaceful party of reform." Both anarcho-syndicalism and reformism—which seize upon *one* aspect of the labor movement, which elevate one-sidedness to a theory, and which declare such tendencies or features of this movement as constitute a specific peculiarity of a given period, of given conditions of working class activity, to be mutually exclusive—must be regarded as a direct product of this bourgeois world conception and its influence. But real life, real history, *includes* these different tendencies, just as life and development in nature include both slow evolution and rapid leaps, breaks in continuity.

.   .   .   .

An extremely important cause producing differences among the participants in the labor movement lies in the changes in tactics of the ruling classes in general, and of the bourgeoisie in particular. If the tactics of the bourgeoisie were always uniform, or at least homogeneous, the working class would rapidly learn to reply to them by tactics also uniform or homogeneous. But as a matter of fact, in every country the bourgeoisie inevitably works out two systems of rule, two methods of fighting for its interests and of retaining its rule, and these methods at times succeed each other and at times are interwoven with each other in various combinations. They are, firstly, the method of force, the method which rejects all concessions to the labor movement, the method of supporting all the old and obsolete institutions, the method of irreconcilably rejecting reforms. Such is the nature of the conservative policy which in western Europe is becoming less and less a policy of the agrarian classes and more and more one of the varieties of bourgeois policy in general. The second method is the method of "liberalism," which takes steps towards the development of political rights, towards reforms, concessions and so forth.

The bourgeoisie passes from one method to the other not in accordance with the malicious design of individuals, and not fortuitously, but owing to the fundamental contradictions of its own position. Normal capitalist society cannot develop successfully without a consolidated representative system and without the enjoyment of certain political rights by the population, which is bound to be distinguished by its relatively high "cultural" demands. This demand for a certain minimum of culture is created by the conditions of the capitalist mode of production itself. . . . The oscillations in the tactics of the bourgeoisie, the passage from the system of force to the system of apparent concessions, are, consequently, peculiar to the history of all European countries during the last half-century, while, at the same time, various countries chiefly develop the application of one method or the other at definite periods. For instance, England in the 1860's and 1870's was a classical country of "liberal" bourgeois policy, Germany in the 1870's and 1880's adhered to the method of force, and so on. (*Differences in the European Labor Movement,* December, 1910, *Selected Works,* XI, 738 f., 741 f.)

Let us recall the experience of 1905. Events show that the *tradition* of the revolutionary mass strike is *alive* among the workers and that the workers at once took up and revived that tradition. The strike wave of 1905, unparalleled in the world, combining both political and economic strikes, involved 810,000 strikers during the first, and 1,277,000 during the last quarter of the year. According to approximate estimates the Lena strikes involved some 300,000 workers, those of May—400,000, and strikes continue to grow in number. Every new issue of the newspapers—even of the liberal newspapers—informs us how the strike conflagration is spreading. The second quarter of 1912 is not quite over, yet even now we get definite indications of the fact that, judging by the extent of the strike movement, the beginning of the revolutionary upsurge in 1912 is *not lower but rather higher* than the corresponding upsurge beginning in 1905.

It was the Russian revolution that for the first time developed on a large scale this method of agitation, of rousing and consolidating the masses and of drawing them into the struggle. Now the proletariat is applying this method once again and with a firmer hand. No power on earth could achieve what the revolutionary vanguard of the proletariat is achieving by this method. An enormous country, with a population of 150,000,000, spread over a tremendous area, scattered, oppressed, deprived of all rights, ignorant, fenced off from "evil influences" by a swarm of authorities, police, spies—the *whole* of this country is beginning to get into a ferment. The most backward strata of the workers and peasants are coming into direct or indirect contact with the strikers. Hundreds of thousands of revolutionary agitators are suddenly appearing on the scene. Their influence is infinitely increased by the fact that they are indissolubly bound up with the lower strata, with the masses, they remain in their ranks, fight for the most urgent needs of *every* worker's family, combine with this immediate struggle for the daily economic needs a political protest and struggle against the monarchy. For counterrevolution has aroused in millions and tens of millions of people a bitter hatred for the monarchy, the rudiments of an understanding of the latter's role, and now the slogan of the advanced workers of the capitals—long live the democratic republic—is moving ever onward through thousands of channels, in the wake of every strike, into the backward strata, to the remotest places, to the "people," "into the depths of Russia"! (*The Revolutionary Revival,* June, 1912, *Selected Works,* IV, 158 f.)

The man in the street is satisfied with that undoubted, holy and *hollow* truth that it is impossible to know beforehand whether a revolution will take place or not. A Marxist is not satisfied with this; he says: Our propaganda and the propaganda of all the Social Democratic workers *is one of the factors* which will determine whether the revolution will take place or not. Hundreds of thousands of political strikers, the foremost men of various army units ask us, our party, for what they should strive, for what cause they should rebel, what they should insist upon, whether they should extend the incipient upsurge to a revolution, or whether they should direct it toward a struggle for reforms.

Revolutionary Social Democracy has given its answer to these questions; and these answers are more interesting and important than the philistine-Trotsky "nose-picking" contemplations: Will there be a revolution or not, who knows?

Our answer is—criticism of the utopia of constitutional reforms, explanation of the falsity of hopes placed in them, all possible assistance to the *revolutionary* upsurge, utilization of the election campaign *for that purpose*. Whether there will be a revolution or not *does not* depend on us *alone*. But we shall do *our* work and this work will never perish. It will sow the seeds of democracy and of proletarian independence deep among the masses, and these seeds are *bound* to shoot up either as a democratic revolution tomorrow, or as a socialist revolution the day after. (*The Platform of the Reformists* and *The Platform of the Revolutionary Social Democrats*, November, 1912, *Selected Works*, IV, 183 f.)

The supporters of reforms and improvements will always be fooled by the defenders of the old order until they realize that every old institution, however barbarous and rotten it may appear to be, is maintained by the forces of some ruling classes. And there is *only one* way of smashing the resistance of these classes, and that is to find, in the very society which surrounds us, and to enlighten and organize for the struggle, the forces which can—and, owing to their social position, *must*—constitute a power capable of sweeping away the old and creating the new. (*The Three Sources and Three Component Parts of Marxism*, March, 1913, *Selected Works*, XI, 8.)

We must *combine* the revolutionary struggle against capitalism with a revolutionary program and revolutionary tactics relative to *all* democratic demands: a republic, a militia, election of officials by the people, equal rights for women, self-determination of nations, etc. While capitalism exists, these demands can be achieved only in exceptional cases, and in an incomplete, distorted form. Basing ourselves on democracy as already achieved, exposing its incompleteness under capitalism, we demand the overthrow of capitalism, the expropriation of the bourgeoisie, as a necessary basis both for the abolition of the poverty of the masses and for the *complete* and *all-sided* achievement of *all* democratic reforms. Some of these reforms will be started before the overthrow of the bourgeoisie, others *in the process* of this overthrow, and still others after it. The social revolution is not a single battle, but represents a whole epoch of numerous battles around all the problems of economic and democratic reforms, which can be consummated only by the expropriation of the bourgeoisie. It is for the sake of this final aim that we must formulate *every one* of our democratic demands in a consistently revolutionary manner. *(The Revolutionary Proletariat and the Right of Nations to Self-Determination,* November, 1915, *Selected Works,* V, 283.)

The General Staffs in the present war assiduously strive to utilize all national and revolutionary movements in the camp of their enemy: the Germans utilize the Irish Rebellion, the French the Czech movement, etc. From their standpoint they are acting quite properly. A serious war would not be treated seriously if advantage were not taken of the slightest weakness of the enemy, if every opportunity that presented itself were not seized, the more so since it is impossible to know beforehand at what moment, where and with what force a powder magazine will "explode." We would be very poor revolutionaries if, in the great proletarian war for emancipation and socialism, we did not know how to utilize *every* popular movement against *each separate* disaster caused by imperialism in order to sharpen and extend the crisis. If, on the one hand, we were to declare and to repeat in a thousand keys that we are "opposed" to all national oppression, and, on the other hand, we were to describe the heroic revolt of the most mobile and intelligent section of certain classes in an oppressed nation against its oppressors as a "putsch," we would be sinking to the stupid level of the Kautskyists. *(Discussion on Self-Determination Summed Up,* October, 1916, *Selected Works,* V, 305.)

On a world scale, fifty years sooner or fifty years later—from the standpoint of the *world* scale—the question is a minor one. *(Imperialism and the Split in Socialism,* Fall, 1916, *Selected Works,* XI, 753.)

Who are the *allies* of the proletariat in *this* revolution?

It has *two* allies: first, the broad mass of the semiproletarian, and partly also of the small peasant population of Russia, who number scores of millions and constitute the overwhelming majority of the population. For this great mass peace, bread, freedom and land are *essential*. It is inevitable that this mass will to a certain extent be under the influence of the bourgeoisie, particularly of the petty bourgeoisie, to which it is most akin in its condition of life, vacillating between the bourgeoisie and the proletariat. . . . We must now take advantage of the freedom given by the new regime and of the existence of the Soviets of Workers' and Soldiers' Deputies to strive first of all to *enlighten and organize* this mass. Soviets of Peasants' Deputies, Soviets of Agricultural Workers—that is one of our most urgent tasks. In this connection our endeavor will be not only that the agricultural workers shall establish their own Soviets, but that the poor and propertyless peasants shall organize *separately* from the well-to-do peasants. . . . The second ally of the Russian proletariat is the proletariat of *all* the belligerent countries and of all countries in general. At present this ally is to a large degree repressed by the war; and the social chauvinists in Europe who . . . have deserted to the bourgeoisie speak all too frequently in its name. But the liberation of the proletariat from their influence has progressed with every month of the imperialist war, and it is *inevitable* that the Russian revolution will immensely accelerate this process.

With these two allies, the proletariat of Russia, *utilizing the peculiarities of the present transition moment,* can and will proceed, first, to achieve a democratic republic and the complete victory of the peasantry over the landowners, and then to *socialism,* which alone can give the war-weary peoples *peace, bread and freedom. (Letters from Afar, First Letter, The First Stage of the First Revolution,* March 20, 1917, *Selected Works,* VI, 11. f.)

Our work must be one of criticism, of *explaining* the mistakes of the petty bourgeois Socialist Revolutionary and Social Democratic parties, of preparing and welding the elements of a *class-conscious* proletarian Communist Party, and of *releasing* the proletariat from the general petty bourgeois enchantment.

This may appear to be "nothing more" than propaganda work, but in reality it is extremely practical revolutionary work; for there is no advance for a revolution that has come to a standstill, that has choked itself with phrases and that keeps marking time, *not because* of external obstacles, *not because of the violence* of the bourgeoisie (so far Guchkov only threatens to use violence against the soldiers), but because of the naive trustfulness of the masses.

Only by combating this naive trustfulness (and one can combat it only ideologically, by comradely persuasion, by pointing to the *lessons of experience*) can we escape the prevailing *orgy of revolutionary phrases* and make real progress in stimulating the class consciousness both of the proletariat and of the masses in general, as well as in stimulating their bold and determined initiative *in the localities* and the arbitrary realization, development and consolidation of liberties, democracy, and of the principle of the ownership of all the land by the people.

. . . .

The substitution of a people's militia for the police is a reform that follows from the entire course of the revolution and that is now being introduced in most localities of Russia. We must explain to the masses that in the majority of revolutions of the usual bourgeois type, this reform has never been long-lived, and that even the most democratic and republican bourgeoisie soon re-established the police of the old tsarist type, a police separated from the people, controlled by the bourgeoisie and adapted in every way to oppressing the people.

There is only one means of *preventing* the re-establishment of the police, namely, to organize a national militia and to fuse it with the army (the standing army to be replaced by the universally armed people). Service in this militia shall extend to all citizens of both sexes between the ages of fifteen and sixty-five, if these tentatively suggested age limits determine the participation of youths and old people. Capitalists must pay their workers, servants and others for the days devoted to public service in the militia. Unless women are brought to take an independent part not only in political life generally, but also in daily and universal public service, it is idle to speak even of a complete and stable democracy, let alone socialism. (*The Tasks of the Proletariat in Our Revolution*, April 23, 1917, *Selected Works*, VI, 51, 58 f.)

It is necessary:

Firstly, to carry on all propaganda and agitation from the point of view of revolution as opposed to reforms, systematically to explain this difference to the masses theoretically and practically at every step of parliamentary, trade union, co-operative, etc., work. Under no circumstances to refrain (except in special cases, as an exception) from utilizing parliamentarism and all the "liberties" of bourgeois democracy; not to reject reforms, but to regard them *only* as a *by-product* of the revolutionary class struggle of the proletariat. . . .

Secondly, legal work must be combined with *illegal* work. The Bolsheviks always taught this, and did so with particular insistence during the war of 1914–1918. The heroes of despicable opportunism ridiculed this and smugly extolled the "law," "democracy," "liberty" of the western European countries, republics, etc. Now, however, only out-and-out swindlers who deceive the workers with phrases can deny that the Bolsheviks have been proved to be right. There is not a single country in the world, even the most advanced and "freest" of the bourgeois republics, in which bourgeois terror does not reign, where freedom to carry on agitation for the socialist revolution, to carry on propaganda and organizational work precisely in this direction, are not prohibited. The party which under the rule of the bourgeoisie has not admitted this to this day and does not carry on systematic, all-sided *illegal* work in spite of the laws of the bourgeoisie and of the bourgeois parliaments is a party of traitors and scoundrels. (*The Tasks of the Third International*, July 14, 1919, *Selected Works*, X, 45 f.)

We Communists should, and will, support bourgeois liberation movements in the colonial countries only when these movements are really revolutionary, when the representatives of these move-

ments do not hinder us in training and organizing the peasants
and the broad masses of the exploited in a revolutionary spirit.

. . . .

The Communist International must lay down, and give the
theoretical grounds for, the proposition that, with the aid of the
proletariat of the most advanced countries, the backward countries may pass to the Soviet system and, after passing through a
definite stage of development, to communism, without passing
through the capitalist stage of development. (*Report* . . . , July 26,
1920, *Selected Works*, X, 241, 243.)

We must take advantage of the antagonisms and contradictions
between two capitalisms, between two systems of capitalist states,
inciting one against the other. As long as we have not conquered
the whole world, as long as, from the economic and military
standpoint, we are weaker than the capitalist world, we must
adhere to the rule that we must know how to take advantage of
the antagonisms and contradictions existing among the imperialists. Had we not adhered to this rule, every one of us would have
long ago been hanging from an aspen tree, to the satisfaction of
the capitalists.

. . . .

We took advantage of the hostility between the two imperial-
isms in such a way that in the long run both lost. Germany got
nothing from the Brest-Litovsk Peace except several million poods
of grain, but brought Bolshevik disintegration into Germany.
But we gained time, in the course of which the Red Army began
to be formed. Even the tremendous misfortunes suffered by the
Ukraine proved to be curable, although at a heavy and painful
price. That on which our antagonists counted, the rapid collapse
of the Soviet power in Russia, did not eventuate. It was just this
period, which history accorded us as a breathing space, that we
took advantage of in order so to consolidate ourselves that it
became impossible to defeat us by military force. We gained
time, we gained a little time, and only sacrificed a great deal of
space for it. At that time, I recall, people philosophized and said
that, in order to gain time, we must surrender space. It was in
accordance with the theory of time and space of the philosophers

that we acted in practice and policy: we sacrificed a great deal of space, but won time sufficient to enable us to gain strength. After this, when all the imperialists wanted to wage a big war against us, it proved impossible. They had neither the means nor the forces for a big war. At that time we did not sacrifice any fundamental interests: we sacrificed subsidiary interests and preserved the fundamental interests.

. . . .

We are at present between two foes. If we are unable to defeat them both, we must know how to dispose our forces in such a way that they fall out among themselves; because, as is always the case, when thieves fall out, honest men come into their own. But as soon as we are strong enough to defeat capitalism as a whole, we shall immediately take it by the scruff of the neck. Our strength is growing, and very rapidly.

. . . .

To support one country against another would be a crime against communism. But we Communists must use one country against another. Are we not committing a crime against communism? No, because we are doing so as a socialist state, which is carrying on communist propaganda and is obliged to take advantage of every hour granted it by circumstances in order to gain strength as rapidly as possible.

. . . .

What would have saved us still more would have been a war between the imperialist powers. If we are obliged to tolerate such scoundrels as the capitalist thieves, each of whom is preparing to plunge a knife into us, it is our direct duty to make them turn their knives against each other. When thieves fall out, honest men come into their own. (*Speech* . . . , November 26, 1920, *Selected Works,* VIII, 279 f., 281, 282, 284, 288.)

Terracini is already prepared for an attack. He says: "If the Party already has 400,000 workers, what more do we require?" Delete! He is afraid of the word "masses" and wants to expunge it. Comrade Terracini does not understand very much about the Russian revolution.

We in Russia were a small party, but, in addition to that, we had on our side the majority of the Soviets of Workers' and Peasants' Deputies all over the country. (A voice: "Quite true!") Have *you* got that? We had almost half the army, which numbered at least 10,000,000. Have you got the majority of the army? Show me the country where this is the case!

.   .   .   .

We achieved victory in Russia, and achieved it so easily, because we prepared for our revolution during the imperialist war. . . . Ten million workers and peasants were armed, and our slogan was: Immediate peace at all costs. We achieved victory because the broad masses of the peasants were in a mood of revolutionary opposition to the big landlords. In November, 1917, the Socialist Revolutionaries . . . were a big peasant party. They demanded revolutionary methods, but . . . they did not have the courage to act in a revolutionary way. In August and September, 1917, we said in effect: "Theoretically we fight against the Socialist Revolutionaries as hitherto; but practically, we are prepared to accept their theory, because we alone can carry out this program." This is what we said, and this is what we did. The peasantry, which was opposed to us in November, 1917, after our victory, and which elected a majority of Socialist Revolutionaries to the Constituent Assembly, were won over to our side, if not in a few days—as I mistakenly anticipated and foretold—at all events, in a few weeks.

.   .   .   .

We achieved victory because we adopted, not our own agrarian program, but that of the Socialist Revolutionaries, and actually put it into practice. Our victory lay in the fact that we carried out the program of the Socialist Revolutionaries; that is why it was achieved so easily. (*In Support of the Tactics of the Communist International,* July 1, 1921, *Selected Works,* X, 282, 284 f., 286.)

When we started the international revolution, we did so not because we were convinced that we could forecast its development, but because a number of circumstances compelled us to start it. . . . In actual fact . . . events did not proceed along as straight a line as we expected. (*The Tactics of the Russian Communist Party*, July 5, 1921, *Selected Works*, IX, 226 f.)

One of the biggest and most dangerous mistakes of Communists (as generally of revolutionaries who have successfully accomplished the beginning of a great revolution) is the idea that a revolution can be made by revolutionaries alone. On the contrary, to be successful every serious revolutionary work requires the understanding and translation into action of the idea that revolutionaries are capable of playing the part only of the vanguard of the truly virile and advanced class. A vanguard performs its task as vanguard only when it is able to avoid becoming divorced from the masses it leads and is able really to lead the whole mass forward. Without an alliance with non-Communists in the most varied spheres of activity there can be no question of any successful Communist constructive work. (*On the Significance of Militant Materialism*, March 12, 1922, *Selected Works*, XI, 71.)

"LEFT WING" COMMUNISM: AN INFANTILE DISORDER[3]

[February–April, 1920]
A POPULAR ESSAY IN MARXIAN STRATEGY AND TACTICS

In What Sense Can We Speak of the International Significance of the Russian Revolution?

DURING the first months after the conquest of political power by the proletariat in Russia (November 7, 1917), it might have appeared that the tremendous difference between backward Russia and the advanced countries of Western Europe would cause the proletarian revolution in these latter countries to have

---

[3]The passages from this essay, written between February and April, 1920, extend from p. 409 to p. 447 of the present selection. Only volume and page of *Selected Works* are acknowledged.

very little resemblance to ours. Now we already have very considerable international experience which very definitely shows that some of the fundamental features of our revolution have a significance which is not local, not peculiarly national, not Russian only, but international. I speak here of international significance not in the broad sense of the term: not a few, but all the fundamental and many of the secondary features of our revolution are of international significance in regard to the influence it has upon all countries. No, taking it in the narrowest sense, i.e., understanding international significance to mean the international validity or the historical inevitability of a repetition on an international scale of what has taken place here, it must be admitted that some of the fundamental features of our revolution do possess such a significance.

Of course, it would be a great mistake to exaggerate this truth and to apply it to more than a few of the fundamental features of our revolution. It would also be a mistake to lose sight of the fact that after the victory of the proletarian revolution in at least one of the advanced countries things in all probability will take a sharp turn, viz., Russia will soon after cease to be the model country and once again become a backward country (in the "Soviet" and in the Socialist sense).

But at the present moment of history the situation is precisely such that the Russian model reveals to *all* countries something, and something very essential, of their near and inevitable future. The advanced workers in every land have long understood this; most often they have not so much understood it as grasped it, sensed it, by revolutionary class instinct. Herein lies the international "significance" (in the narrow sense of the term) of the Soviet power, as well as of the fundamentals of Bolshevik theory and tactics. (*Ibid.*, 57 f.)

One of the Fundamental Conditions for the Success of the Bolsheviks

CERTAINLY nearly everyone now realizes that the Bolsheviks could not have maintained themselves in power . . . unless the strictest, truly iron discipline prevailed in our party, and unless the latter had been rendered the fullest and unreserved support of the whole mass of the working class, that is, of all its thinking, honest, self-sacrificing and influential elements who are capable of leading or of attracting the backward strata.

The dictatorship of the proletariat is a most determined and most ruthless war waged by the new class against a *more powerful* enemy, the bourgeoisie, whose resistance is increased *tenfold* by its overthrow (even if only in one country), and whose power lies not only in the strength of international capital, in the strength and durability of the international connections of the bourgeoisie, but also in the *force of habit,* in the strength of *small production.* For, unfortunately, small production is still very, very widespread in the world, and small production *engenders* capitalism and the bourgeoisie continuously, daily, hourly, spontaneously, and on a mass scale. For all these reasons the dictatorship of the proletariat is essential, and victory over the bourgeoisie is impossible without a long, stubborn and desperate war of life and death, a war demanding perseverance, discipline, firmness, indomitableness and unity of will.

I repeat, the experience of the victorious dictatorship of the proletariat in Russia has clearly shown even to those who are unable to think, or who have not had occasion to ponder over this question, that absolute centralization and the strictest discipline of the proletariat constitute one of the fundamental conditions for victory over the bourgeoisie.

This is often discussed. But far from enough thought is given to what it means, and to the conditions that make it possible.

. . . .

And first of all the question arises: How is the discipline of the revolutionary party of the proletariat maintained? How is it tested? How is it reinforced? First, by the class-consciousness of the proletarian vanguard and by its devotion to the revolution, by its perseverance, self-sacrifice and heroism. Secondly, by its ability to link itself, to keep in close touch with, and to a certain extent, if you like, to merge itself with the broadest masses of the toilers—primarily with the proletarian, *but also with the non-*

proletarian toiling masses. Thirdly, by the correctness of the political leadership exercised by this vanguard and of its political
strategy and tactics, provided that the broadest masses have been
convinced *by their own experiences* that they are correct. Without these conditions, discipline in a revolutionary party that is
really capable of being a party of the advanced class, whose mission it is to overthrow the bourgeoisie and transform the whole
of society, cannot be achieved. Without these conditions, all
attempts to establish discipline inevitably fall flat and end in
phrasemongering and grimacing. On the other hand, these conditions cannot arise all at once. They are created only by prolonged effort and hard-won experience. Their creation is facilitated by correct revolutionary theory, which, in its turn, is not a
dogma but assumes final shape only in close connection with the
practical activity of a truly mass and truly revolutionary movement. (*Ibid.*, 10, 60 f.)

*In the Struggle Against What Enemies Within the Working
Class Movement Did Bolshevism Grow, Gain Strength
and Become Steeled?*

FIRSTLY and principally, in the struggle against opportunism,
which in 1914 definitely grew into social chauvinism and definitely sided with the bourgeoisie against the proletariat. Naturally, this was the principal enemy of bolshevism in the working
class movement. This enemy remains the principal enemy on an
international scale. This enemy has claimed, and still claims,
most of the attention of the bolsheviks. This side of the activities
of the bolsheviks is now also fairly well-known abroad.

Something different, however, must be said of the other enemy
of bolshevism within the working class movement. It is not yet
sufficiently known abroad that bolshevism grew, took shape, and
became steeled in long years of struggle against *petty bourgeois
revolutionariness,* which smacks of, or borrows something from,
anarchism, and which in all essentials falls short of the conditions and requirements of a sustained proletarian class struggle.

For Marxists it is well established theoretically—and the experience of all European revolutions and revolutionary movements has fully confirmed it—that the small proprietor, the small master craftsman (a social type that is represented in many European countries on a wide, mass scale), who under capitalism suffers constant oppression and, very often, an incredibly acute and rapid deterioration in his conditions of life, ending in ruin, easily goes to revolutionary extremes, but is incapable of perseverance, organization, discipline and steadfastness. The petty bourgeois, "driven to frenzy" by the horrors of capitalism, is a social phenomenon which, like anarchism, is characteristic of all capitalist countries. The instability of such revolutionariness, its barrenness, its liability to become swiftly transformed into submission, apathy, fantasy, and even a "frenzied" infatuation with one or another bourgeois "fad"—all this is a matter of common knowledge. But a theoretical, abstract recognition of these truths does not at all free revolutionary parties from old mistakes, which always crop up at unexpected moments, in a somewhat new form, in hitherto unknown vestments or surroundings, in peculiar— more or less peculiar—circumstances. (*Ibid.,* 70 f.)

Bolshevism took over and continued the struggle against the party which more than any other expressed the tendencies of petty bourgeois revolutionariness, namely, the "Socialist Revolutionary" party, and waged this struggle on three main points. First, this party, rejecting Marxism, stubbornly refused (or, rather, was unable) to understand the need for a strictly objective estimate of the class forces and their interrelations before undertaking any political action. Secondly, this party considered itself to be particularly "revolutionary," or "Left," on account of its recognition of individual terrorism, assassination—which we Marxists emphatically rejected. Of course, we rejected individual terrorism only on the grounds of expediency. . . . Thirdly, the "Socialist-Revolutionaries" thought it very "Left" to sneer at the comparatively insignificant opportunist sins of German Social Democracy, while they themselves imitated the extreme opportunists of that party, for example, on the agrarian question, or on the question of the dictatorship of the proletariat. (*Ibid.,* 71 f.)

On two occasions the struggle that Bolshevism waged against "Left" deviations within its own party assumed particularly large proportions: in 1908, on the question of whether or not to participate in a most reactionary "parliament" and in the legal workers' societies which were restricted by most reactionary laws; and again in 1918 (the Brest-Litovsk Peace), on the question whether one or another "compromise" was admissible.

In 1908, the "Left" Bolsheviks were expelled from our party for stubbornly refusing to understand the necessity of participating in a most reactionary "parliament." The "leftists" — among whom there were many splendid revolutionaries who subsequently bore (and still bear) the title of member of the Communist party with honor—based themselves particularly on the successful experiment of the boycott in 1905. When in August, 1905, the tsar announced the convocation of an advisory "parliament," the Bolsheviks—unlike all the opposition parties and the Mensheviks—proclaimed a boycott of it, and it was actually swept away by the revolution of October, 1905. At that time the boycott proved correct, not because non-participation in reactionary parliaments is correct in general, but because we correctly estimated the objective situation that was leading to the rapid transformation of the mass strikes into a political strike, then into a revolutionary strike, and then into insurrection. Moreover, the struggle at that time centered around the question whether to leave the convocation of the first representative assembly to the tsar, or to attempt to wrest its convocation from the hands of the old government. When there was, and could be, no certainty that an analogous objective situation existed, and likewise no certainty of a similar trend and rate of development, the boycott ceased to be correct.

The Bolshevik boycott of "parliament" in 1905 enriched the revolutionary proletariat with extremely valuable political experience and showed that when combining legal and illegal, parliamentary and non-parliamentary forms of struggle, it is sometimes useful, and even essential, to be able to reject parliamentary forms. But it is a very great mistake to apply this experience blindly, imitatively and uncritically to *other* conditions and to

other circumstances. The boycott of the Duma by the Bolsheviks
in 1906 was a mistake, although small and easily remediable.[4]
The boycott of the Duma in 1907, 1908 and subsequent years was
a serious mistake and one difficult to remedy, because, on the
one hand, a very rapid rise of the revolutionary tide and its
transformation into an insurrection could not be expected, and,
on the other hand, the whole historical situation of the renovated
bourgeois monarchy called for the combining of legal and illegal
work. Now, looking back on this historical period, which is now
quite closed and the connection of which with the subsequent
periods has become fully manifest, it becomes very clear that the
Bolsheviks *could not have* preserved (let alone strengthened, developed and reinforced) the sound core of the revolutionary
party of the proletariat in 1908–14 had they not strenuously
fought for the viewpoint that it is *obligatory* to combine legal
and illegal forms of struggle, that it is *obligatory* to participate
even in the most reactionary parliament and in a number of
other institutions that were restricted by reactionary laws (benefit
societies, etc.) .

In 1918, things did not go to the lengths of a split. The "Left"
Communists at that time only formed a separate group or "faction" within our party, and that not for long. In the same year,
1918, the most prominent representatives of "Left" Communism,
for example, Comrades Radek and Bukharin, openly admitted
their mistake. It had seemed to them that the Brest-Litovsk Peace
was a compromise with the imperialists that was inadmissible on
principle and harmful to the party of the revolutionary proletariat. It really was a compromise with the imperialists, but it
was a compromise which, under the given circumstances, was
obligatory.

Today, when I hear our tactics in signing the Brest-Litovsk
Treaty assailed by the "Socialist Revolutionaries," for instance,
or when I hear the remark made by Comrade Lansbury in con-

---

[4]What applies to individuals is applicable—with necessary modifications—
to politics and to parties. It is not the man who makes no mistakes who is
wise. There are no such men, nor can there be. He is wise who makes not
very serious mistakes and who knows how to rectify them easily and quickly.

versation with me—"Our British trade union leaders say that if it was permissible for the Bolsheviks to compromise, it is permissible for them to compromise too," I usually reply by first of all giving a simple and "popular" example:

Imagine that your automobile is held up by armed bandits. You hand them over your money, passport, revolver and automobile. You are spared the pleasant company of the bandits. That is unquestionably a compromise. *"Do ut des"* ("I give" you money, firearms, automobile, "so that you give" me the opportunity to depart in peace). But it would be difficult to find a sane man who would declare such a compromise to be "inadmissible on principle," or who would proclaim the compromiser an accomplice of the bandits (even though the bandits might use the automobile and the firearms for further robberies). Our compromise with the bandits of German imperialism was a compromise of such a kind.

But when the Mensheviks and Socialist Revolutionaries in Russia, the Scheidemannites (and to a large extent the Kautskians) in Germany, Otto Bauer and Friedrich Adler (not to speak of Messrs. Renner and company) in Austria, the Renaudels and Longuet and company in France, the Fabians, the "Independents" and the "Laborites" in England, in 1914–18 and in 1918–20 entered into *compromises* with the bandits of their own, and sometimes of the "Allied," bourgeoisie *against* the revolutionary proletariat of their own country, all these gentlemen did act then as *accomplices in banditry*.

The conclusion to be drawn is clear: To reject compromises "on principle," to reject the admissibility of compromises in general, no matter of what kind, is childishness which it is difficult even to take seriously. A political leader who desires to be useful to the revolutionary proletariat must know how to single out *concrete* cases of such compromises as are inadmissible, as express opportunism and *treachery,* and direct all the force of his criticism, the edge of his merciless exposure and relentless war, against *those concrete* compromises, and not allow the highly experienced "practical" Socialists and parliamentary Jesuits to dodge and wriggle out of responsibility by resorting to arguments about "compromises in general." It is precisely in this way that Messrs. the "leaders" of the British trade unions, as well as of the Fabian Society and the "Independent" Labor party, dodge responsibility *for the treachery they have perpetrated,* for the commission of a compromise that *really* expresses the worst kind of opportunism, treachery and betrayal.

There are compromises and compromises. One must be able to analyze the situation and the concrete conditions of each compromise, or of each variety of compromise. One must learn to distinguish between a man who gave the bandits money and firearms in order to lessen the evil committed by them and to facilitate the task of getting them captured and shot, and a man who gives bandits money and firearms in order to share in the loot. In politics this is not always as easy as in this childishly simple example. But anyone who set out to invent a recipe for the workers that would provide ready-made solutions for all cases in life, or who promised that the politics of the revolutionary proletariat would never encounter difficult or intricate situations, would be simply a charlatan.

So as to leave no room for misinterpretation, I shall attempt to outline, although very briefly, a few fundamental rules for analyzing concrete compromises.

The party which concluded a compromise with the German imperialists by signing the Brest-Litovsk Treaty had been working out its internationalism in action ever since the end of 1914. It was not afraid to call for the defeat of the tsarist monarchy and to condemn "defense of the fatherland" in a war between two imperialist robbers. The parliamentary members of this party took the road of exile to Siberia rather than the road leading to ministerial portfolios in a bourgeois government. The revolution, having overthrown tsardom and established a democratic republic, put this party to a new and tremendous test; this party did not enter into any agreements with "its" imperialists, but worked for their overthrow and did overthrow them. Having taken over political power, this party did not leave a vestige either of landowner or capitalist property. Having published and repudiated the secret treaties of the imperialists, this party proposed peace to *all* nations, and yielded to the violence of the Brest-Litovsk robbers only after the Anglo-French imperialists had frustrated peace, and after the Bolsheviks had done everything humanly possible to hasten the revolution in Germany and other countries. The complete correctness of such a compromise, entered into by such a party under such circumstances, becomes every day clearer and more evident to everyone.

The Mensheviks and Socialist Revolutionaries in Russia (like the leaders of the Second International all over the world in 1914–20) began with treachery by directly or indirectly justifying the "defense of the fatherland," that is, the defense of *their own* predatory bourgeoisie. They continue their treachery by entering into a coalition with the bourgeoisie of *their own* country and fighting together with *their own* bourgeoisie against the revolutionary proletariat of their own country.... From beginning to end *their* compromise with the bandits of imperialism lay in the fact that they made themselves *accomplices* in imperialist banditry. (*Ibid.,* 73–78.)

"Left Wing" Communism in Germany:
Leaders—Party—Class—Masses

The abolition of classes not only means driving out the landowners and capitalists—that we accomplished with comparative ease—it also means *abolishing the small-commodity producers,* and they *cannot be driven out,* or crushed; we must live *in harmony* with them; they can (and must) be remoulded and re-educated only by very prolonged, slow, cautious organizational work. They encircle the proletariat on every side with a petty bourgeois atmosphere, which permeates and corrupts the proletariat and causes constant relapses among the proletariat into petty bourgeois spinelessness, disunity, individualism, and alternate moods of exaltation and dejection. The strictest centralization and discipline are required within the political party of the proletariat in order to counteract this, in order that the *organizational* role of the proletariat (and that is its *principal* role) may be exercised correctly, successfully, victoriously. The dictatorship of the proletariat is a persistent struggle—sanguinary and bloodless, violent and peaceful, military and economic, educational and administrative—against the forces and traditions of the old society. The force of habit of millions and tens of millions is a most terrible force. Without an iron party tempered in the struggle, without a party enjoying the confidence of all the honest elements in the given class, without a party capable of watching and influencing the mood of the masses, it is impossible to conduct such a struggle successfully. It is a thousand times easier to vanquish the centralized big bourgeoisie than to "vanquish" millions and millions of small proprietors, while they, by their ordinary, everyday, imperceptible, elusive, demoralizing activity achieve the *very* results which the bourgeoisie need and which *restore* the bourgeoisie. Whoever weakens ever so little the iron discipline of the party of the proletariat (especially during the time of its dictatorship) actually aids the bourgeoisie against the proletariat. (*Ibid.,* 83 f.)

. . . The rapid alternation of legal and illegal work, which made it particularly necessary to "conceal," to cloak in particular secrecy precisely the General Staff, precisely the leaders, sometimes gave rise to extremely dangerous phenomena. The worst was in 1912, when an agent-provocateur by the name of Malinovsky[5] got on to the Bolshevik Central Committee. He betrayed scores and scores of the best and most loyal comrades, caused them to be sent to penal servitude and hastened the death of many of them. He did not cause even more harm than he did just because we had established a proper combination of legal

---

[5]Malinovsky was a prisoner-of-war in Germany. When he returned to Russia under the rule of the Bolsheviks, he was instantly put on trial and shot by our workers. The Mensheviks attacked us most bitterly for our mistake in allowing an *agent-provocateur* to become a member of the Central Committee of our party. But when, under Kerensky, we demanded the arrest and trial of Rodzyanko, the speaker of the Duma, because he had known even before the war that Malinovsky was an *agent-provocateur* and *had not informed* the Trudoviks [peasant deputies] and the workers in the Duma of this fact, neither the Mensheviks nor the Socialist Revolutionaries in Kerensky's cabinet supported our demand, and Rodzyanko remained at large and went off unhindered to join Denikin.

and illegal work. As a member of the Central Committee of the Party and a deputy in the Duma, Malinovsky was forced, in order to gain our confidence, to aid us in establishing legal daily papers, which even under tsardom were able to wage a struggle against the opportunism of the Mensheviks and to preach the fundamentals of bolshevism in a suitably disguised form. While Malinovsky with one hand sent scores and scores of the best Bolsheviks to penal servitude and to death, he was obliged with the other to assist in the education of scores and score of thousands of new Bolsheviks through the medium of the legal press. It will not harm those German (as well as British, American, French and Italian) comrades who are confronted with the task of learning how to carry on revolutionary work inside the reactionary trade unions to give serious thought to this fact.

In many countries, including the most advanced, the bourgeoisie is undoubtedly now sending *agents-provocateurs* into the Communist parties, and will continue to do so. One method of combating this peril is by a skillful combination of legal and illegal work. (*Ibid.*, 85 f.)

Should Revolutionaries Work in Reactionary Trade Unions?

The German "leftists" consider that as far as they are concerned the reply to this question is an unqualified negative. In their opinion, declamations and angry ejaculations (such as uttered by K. Horner in a particularly "weighty" and particularly stupid manner) against "reactionary" and "counterrevolutionary" trade unions are sufficient "proof" that it is unnecessary and even impermissible for revolutionaries and Communists to work in yellow, social-chauvinist, compromising, counterrevolutionary trade unions of the Legien type.

But however strongly the German "leftists" may be convinced of the revolutionariness of such tactics, these tactics are in fact fundamentally wrong, and consist of nothing but empty phrasemongering.

In order to make this clear, I shall begin with our own experience—in conformity with the general plan of the present article, the object of which is to apply to Western Europe whatever is of general application, general validity and generally binding force in the history and the present tactics of bolshevism.

The correlation, leaders—party—class—masses, as well as the relation of the dictatorship of the proletariat and its party to the trade unions, now present themselves concretely in Russia in the following form: the dictatorship is exercised by the proletariat, organized in the Soviets; the proletariat is led by the Communist party (Bolsheviks), which, according to the data of the last Party Congress (April, 1920) has a membership of 611,000. The membership fluctuated considerably both before and after the October Revolution, and was formerly considerably less, even in 1918 and 1919. We are afraid of an excessive growth of the Party, as careerists and charlatans, who deserve only to be shot, inevitably strive to attach themselves to the ruling party. (*Ibid.*, 87 f.)

. . . We have a formally non-Communist, flexible, relatively wide and very powerful proletarian apparatus, by means of which the Party is closely linked up with the *class* and with the *masses,* and by means of which, under the leadership of the Party, the *dictatorship of the class* is effected. Without close contact with the trade unions, without their hearty support and self-sacrificing work, not only in economic *but also in military* affairs, it would, of course, have been impossible for us to govern the country and to maintain the dictatorship for two months, let alone two years. Of course, in practice this close contact calls for very complicated and diversified work in the form of propaganda, agitation, timely and frequent conferences. . . .

We consider that contact with the "masses" through trade unions is not enough. Our practical experience during the course of the revolution has given rise to *non-party workers' and peasants' conferences,* and we strive by every means to support, develop and extend these institutions in order to be able to watch the sentiments of the masses, to come closer to them, to respond to their requirements, to promote the best among them to state posts, etc. . . .

Then, of course, all the work of the Party is carried on through the Soviets, which embrace the toiling masses irrespective of occupation. The *uyezd* congresses of Soviets are *democratic* institutions the like of which even the best of the democratic republics of the bourgeois world has never known; and through these congresses (whose proceedings the Party endeavors to follow with the closest attention), as well as by constantly appointing class-conscious workers to all sorts of posts in the rural districts, the role of the proletariat as leader of the peasantry is exercised, the dictatorship of the urban proletariat is realized, and a systematic struggle against the rich, bourgeois, exploiting and profiteering peasantry is waged.

Such is the general mechanism of the proletarian state power viewed "from above," from the standpoint of the practical realization of the dictatorship. It is to be hoped that the reader will understand why to a Russian Bolshevik, who is acquainted with this mechanism and who for twenty-five years has watched it growing out of small, illegal, underground circles, all talk about "from above" *or* "from below," about the dictatorship of leaders *or* the dictatorship of the masses, etc., cannot but appear to be ridiculous and childish nonsense, something like discussing whether the left leg or the right arm is more useful to a man. (*Ibid.,* 88–90.)

Capitalism inevitably bequeaths to Socialism, on the one hand, old trade and craft distinctions among the workers, distinctions evolved in the course of centuries, and, on the other, trade unions which only very slowly, in the course of years and years, can and will develop into broader, industrial unions with less of the craft union about them (embracing whole industries, and not only crafts, trades and occupations), and later proceed, through these industrial unions, to the abolition of the division of labor among people, to the education, schooling and training of people with *an all-around development and an all-around* training, people *able to do everything.* Communism is marching and must march toward this goal, and *will reach it,* but only after very many years. To attempt in practice today to anticipate this future result of a fully developed, fully stabilized and formed, fully expanded and mature communism would be like trying to teach higher mathematics to a four year old child.

We can (and must) begin to build socialism not with imaginary human material, not with human material invented by us, but with the human material bequeathed to us by capitalism. That is very "difficult," it goes without saying, but no other approach to this task is serious enough to warrant discussion.

The trade unions were a tremendous progressive step for the working class at the beginning of the development of capitalism, inasmuch as they represented a transition from the disunity and helplessness of the workers to the *rudiments* of class organization. When the *highest* form of proletarian class organization began to arise, *viz.*, the *revolutionary party of the proletariat* (which will not deserve the name until it learns to bind the leaders with the class and the masses into one single indissoluble whole), the trade unions inevitably began to reveal *certain* reactionary features, a certain craft narrowness, a certain tendency to be non-political, a certain inertness, etc. But the development of the proletariat did not, and could not, proceed anywhere in the world otherwise than through the trade unions, through their interaction with the party of the working class. The conquest of political power by the proletariat is a gigantic forward step for the proletariat as a class, and the Party must more than ever, and not merely in the old way but in a new way, educate and guide the trade unions, at the same time not forgetting that they are and will long remain an indispensable "school of communism" and a preparatory school for training the proletarians to exercise their dictatorship, an indispensable organization of the workers for the gradual transfer of the management of the whole economic life of the country to the working *class* (and not to the separate trades), and later to all the toilers.

A *certain* amount of "reactionariness" in trade unions, in the sense mentioned, is *inevitable* under the dictatorship of the proletariat. He who does not understand this utterly fails to understand the fundamental conditions of the *transition* from capitalism to socialism. To fear *this* "reactionariness," try to *avoid* it, to skip it, would be the greatest folly, for it would mean fearing that function of the proletarian vanguard which consists in training, educating, enlightening and drawing into the new life the most backward strata and masses of the working class and the peasantry. On the other hand, to postpone the achievement of the dictatorship of the proletariat until a time when not a single worker with a narrow craft outlook, not a single worker with craft and craft union prejudices is left, would be a still greater mistake. The art of politics (and the Communist's correct understanding of his tasks) lies in correctly gauging the conditions and the moment when the vanguard of the proletariat can successfully seize power, when it is able, during and after the seizure of power, to obtain adequate support from adequately broad strata of the working class and of the non-proletarian toiling masses, and when it is able thereafter to maintain, consolidate and extend its rule by educating, training and attracting ever broader masses of the toilers. (*Ibid.*, 90–92.)

If you want to help "the masses" and to win the sympathy, confidence and support of "the masses," you must not fear difficulties, you must not fear the pinpricks, chicanery, insults and persecution of the "leaders" (who, being opportunists and social chauvinist, are in most cases directly or indirectly connected with the bourgeoisie and the police), but must imperatively *work wherever the masses are to be found.* You must be capable of every sacrifice, of overcoming the greatest obstacles in order to carry on agitation and propaganda systematically, perseveringly, persistently and patiently precisely in those institutions, societies and associations—even the most reactionary—in which proletarian or semiproletarian masses are to be found. And the trade unions and workers' co-operatives (the latter at least sometimes) are precisely the organizations where the masses are to be found. (*Ibid.*, 93 f.)

Should We Participate in Bourgeois Parliaments?

Parliamentarism has become "historically obsolete." That is

true as regards propaganda. But everyone knows that this is still a long way from overcoming it *practically*. Capitalism could have been declared, and quite rightly, to be "historically obsolete" many decades ago, but that does not at all remove the need for a very long and very persistent struggle *on the soil* of capitalism. Parliamentarism is "historically obsolete" from the standpoint of *world history*, that is to say, the *epoch* of bourgeois parliamentarism has come to an end and the *epoch* of the proletarian dictatorship has *begun*. That is incontestable. But when dealing with world *history*, one counts in decades. Ten or twenty years sooner or later makes no difference when measured by the scale of world history; from the standpoint of world history it is a trifle that cannot be calculated even approximately. But that is precisely why it is a howling theoretical blunder to measure questions of practical politics with the scale of world history.

Is parliamentarism "politically obsolete"? That is quite another matter. If it were true, the position of the "leftists" would be a strong one. But it has to be proved by a most searching analysis . . . that the German "leftists," as we know, considered parliamentarism to be "politically obsolete" even in January, 1919. We know that the "leftists" were mistaken. This fact alone at one stroke utterly destroys the proposition that parliamentarism is "politically obsolete." The obligation falls upon the "leftists" of proving why their error, indisputable at that time, has now ceased to be an error. They do not, and cannot, produce even the shadow of proof. The attitude a political party adopts toward its own mistakes is one of the most important and surest criteria of the seriousness of the party and of how it *in practice* fulfills its obligations toward its *class* and the toiling *masses*. Frankly admitting a mistake, disclosing the reasons for it, analyzing the conditions which led to it, and carefully discussing the means of correcting it—this is the sign of a serious party; this is the way it performs its duties, this is the way it educates and trains the *class,* and then the *masses*. By failing to fulfill this duty, by failing to give the utmost attention, care and consideration to the study of their obvious mistake, the "leftists" in Germany (and in Holland) have proved that they are not a *party of the class,* but a circle, not a *party of the masses,* but a group of intellectuals and of a few workers who imitate the worst features of intellectualism.

Secondly, . . . the Frankfurt group of "leftists" . . . [declares:]

> . . . The millions of workers who still follow the Policy of the Center [the Catholic "Center" party] are counterrevolutionary. The rural proletarians provide legions of counterrevolutionary troops.

Everything goes to show that this statement is too sweeping and exaggerated. But the basic fact set forth here is incontrovertible, and its acknowledgment by the "leftists" very clearly testifies to their mistake. How can one say that "parliamentarism is politically obsolete," when "millions" and "legions" of *proletarians* are not only still in favor of parliamentarism in general, but are downright "counterrevolutionary"!? Clearly, parliamentarism in Germany is *not yet* politically obsolete. Clearly, the "leftists" in Germany have mistaken *their desire,* their ideological-political attitude, for actual fact. That is the most dangerous mistake revolutionaries can make. In Russia—where the extremely fierce and savage yoke of tsardom for a very long time and in very varied forms produced revolutionaries of diverse shades, revolutionaries who displayed astonishing devotion, enthusiasm, heroism and strength of will—we observed this mistake of the revolutionaries very closely, we studied it very attentively and are very well acquainted with it, and we can therefore notice it very clearly in others. Parliamentarism, of course, is "politically obsolete" for the Communists in Germany; but—and that is the whole point— we must not regard what is obsolete *for us* as being obsolete *for the class,* as being obsolete *for the masses.* Here again we find that the "leftists" do not know how to reason, do not know how to conduct themselves as the party of the *class,* as the party of the *masses.* You must not sink to the level of the masses, to the level of the backward strata of the class. That is incontestable. You must tell them the bitter truth. You must call their bourgeois-democratic and parliamentary prejudices—prejudices. But at the same time you must *soberly* observe the *actual* state of class consciousness and preparedness of the whole class (not only of its

Communist vanguard), of all the toiling *masses* (not only of its advanced elements). (*Ibid.,* 97–99.)

Thirdly, the "leftist" Communists have a great deal to say in praise of us Bolsheviks. One sometimes feels like telling them to praise us less and try to understand the tactics of the Bolsheviks more; to make themselves more familiar with them! We took part in the elections to the Russian bourgeois parliament, the Constituent Assembly, in September–November, 1917. Were our tactics correct or not? If not, then it should be clearly stated and proved, for this is essential in working out correct tactics for international Communism. If they were correct, certain conclusions must be drawn. Of course, no parallel can be drawn between conditions in Russia and conditions in Western Europe. But as regards the special question of the meaning of the concept "parliamentarism has become politically obsolete," our experience must absolutely be taken into account, for unless definite experience is taken into account such concepts are very easily transformed into empty phrases. Did not we, the Russian Bolsheviks, have more right in September–November, 1917 than any western Communists to consider that parliamentarism was politically obsolete in Russia? Of course we did, for the point is not whether bourgeois parliaments have existed for a long or a short time, but to what extent the broad mass of the toilers are *prepared* (ideologically, politically and practically) to accept the Soviet system and to disperse the bourgeois-democratic parliament (or to allow it to be dispersed). That owing to a number of special conditions the urban working class and the soldiers and peasants of Russia were in September–November, 1917 exceptionally well prepared for the acceptance of the Soviet system and for the dispersal of the most democratic of bourgeois parliaments is an absolutely incontestable and fully established historical fact. Nevertheless, the Bolsheviks did *not* boycott the Constituent Assembly but took part in the elections both before and *after* the proletariat conquered political power. . . . These elections yielded exceedingly valuable (and for the proletariat, highly useful) political results. . . .

The conclusion which follows from this is absolutely incontrovertible: It has been proved that participation in a bourgeois-democratic parliament even a few weeks before the victory of a Soviet republic, and even *after* such a victory, not only does not harm the revolutionary proletariat, but actually helps it to *prove* to the backward masses why such parliaments deserve to be dispersed; it *helps* their successful dispersal, and *helps* bourgeois parliamentarism to become "politically obsolete." To refuse to take this experience into account and at the same time to claim affiliation to the Communist *International*, which must work out its tactics *internationally* (not narrow or one-sided national tactics, but international tactics), is to commit the gravest blunder and actually to retreat from real internationalism while paying lip service to it.

Now let us examine the Dutch "leftist" arguments in favor of non-participation in parliaments. The following is the text of the most important of the above-mentioned "Dutch" theses, Thesis No. 4:

> When the capitalist system of production has broken down and society is in a state of revolution, parliamentary activity gradually loses its significance compared with the action of the masses themselves. When, under these conditions, parliament becomes a center and an organ of counterrevolution, while on the other hand the working class is creating the instruments of its power in the form of Soviets, it may even become necessary to abstain from all participation in parliamentary activity.

The first sentence is obviously wrong, since the action of the masses—a big strike, for instance—is more important than parliamentary activity at *all* times, and not only during a revolution or in a revolutionary situation. This obviously untenable and historically and politically incorrect argument only very clearly shows that the authors absolutely ignore both the general European experience (the French experience before the Revolution of 1848, and 1870; the German experience of 1878 to 1890, etc.) and the Russian experience (see above) as to the importance of *combining* the legal struggle with an illegal struggle. This question is of immense importance in general, and it is of immense importance in particular because in *all* civilized and advanced countries the time is rapidly approaching when such a combination will become—and in part has already become—more and more obligatory for the party of the revolutionary proletariat owing to the fact that civil war between the proletariat and the bourgeoisie is maturing and approaching, owing to the fierce persecution of the Communists by republican governments and bourgeois governments generally, which are prepared to resort to any violation of legality. . . .

As for the second sentence, in the first place it is wrong historically. We Bolsheviks participated in the most counterrevolutionary parliaments, and experience has shown that such participation was not only useful but essential for the party of the revolutionary proletariat precisely after the first bourgeois revolution in Russia (1905), for the purpose of preparing the way for the second bourgeois revolution (February, 1917), and then for the Socialist revolution (October, 1917). In the second place, this sentence is amazingly illogical. If parliament becomes an organ and a "center" (in reality, it never has been and never can be a "center," but that by the way) of counterrevolution, while the workers are creating the instruments of their power in the form of Soviets, it logically follows that the workers must prepare—ideologically, politically and technically—for the struggle of the Soviets against parliament, for the dispersal of parliament by the Soviets. But it does not follow that this dispersal is hindered, or is not facilitated, by the presence of a Soviet opposition *within* the counterrevolutionary parliament. . . .

The authors of the theses have become utterly confused and have forgotten the experience of many, if not all, revolutions, which shows how particularly useful during a revolution is the combination of mass action outside the reactionary parliament with an opposition sympathetic to (or, better still, directly supporting) the revolution inside this parliament. (*Ibid.*, 100–103.)

. . . Without a revolutionary mood among the masses, and without conditions favoring the growth of this mood, revolutionary tactics would never be converted into action; but we in

Russia have been convinced by long, painful and bloody experience of the truth that revolutionary tactics cannot be built up on revolutionary moods alone. Tactics must be based on a sober and strictly objective estimation of *all* the class forces in a given state (and in neighboring states, and in all states the world over) as well as of the experience of revolutionary movements. Expressing one's "revolutionariness" solely by hurling abuse at parliamentary opportunism, solely by repudiating participation in parliaments, is very easy; but just because it is too easy, it is not the solution for a difficult, a very difficult, problem. It is much more difficult to create a really revolutionary parliamentary fraction in a European parliament than it was in Russia. Of course. But this is only a particular expression of the general truth that it was easy for Russia in the specific, historically very unique situation of 1917 to *start* a socialist revolution, but that it will be more difficult for Russia than for the European countries to *continue* it and consummate it. (*Ibid.*, 104 f.)

It will be more difficult to *start* a socialist revolution in western Europe than it was for us. To attempt to "circumvent" this difficulty by "skipping" the difficult job of utilizing reactionary parliaments for revolutionary purposes is absolutely childish. You want to create a new society, yet you fear the difficulties involved in forming a good parliamentary fraction, consisting of convinced, devoted, heroic Communists, in a reactionary parliament! Is that not childish? (*Ibid.*, 104.)

. . . When conditions are such that it is often necessary to hide "leaders" underground, the *development* of good, reliable, experienced and authoritative "leaders" is a very difficult task, and these difficulties *cannot* be successfully overcome without combining legal and illegal work, and *without testing the "leaders," among other ways,* in the parliamentary arena *as well.* Criticism—the keenest, most ruthless and uncompromising criticism—must be directed, not against parliamentarism or parliamentary activities, but against those leaders who are unable— and still more against those who are *unwilling*—to utilize parliamentary elections and the parliamentary tribune in a revolutionary, communist manner. Only such criticism—combined, of course, with the expulsion of worthless leaders and their replacement by capable ones—will constitute useful and fruitful revolutionary work that will simultaneously train the "leaders" to be worthy of the working class and of the toiling masses, and train the masses to be able properly to understand the political situation and the often very complicated and intricate tasks that spring from that situation. (*Ibid.*, 106 f.)

No Compromises?

Naive and utterly inexperienced people imagine that it is sufficient to admit the permissibility of compromises *in general* in order to obliterate the dividing line between opportunism, against which we wage and must wage an irreconcilable struggle, and revolutionary Marxism, or communism. But if such people do not yet know that *all* dividing lines in nature and in society are mutable and to a certain extent conventional—they cannot be assisted otherwise than by a long process of training, education, enlightenment, and by political and every-day experience. It is important to single out from the practical questions of the politics of each separate or specific historical moment those which reveal the principal type of impermissible, treacherous compromises embodying the opportunism that is fatal to the revolutionary class, and to exert all efforts to explain them and combat them. (*Ibid.*, 110 f.)

". . . To reject most emphatically all compromises with other parties . . . all policy of maneuvering and compromise," write the German "leftists" in the Frankfurt pamphlet.

It is a wonder that, holding such views, these "leftists" do not emphatically condemn bolshevism! For, the German "leftists" must know that the whole history of bolshevism, both before and after the October Revolution, is *full* of instances of maneuvering, temporizing and compromising with other parties, bourgeois parties included!

To carry on a war for the overthrow of the international bourgeoisie, a war which is a hundred times more difficult, prolonged and complicated than the most stubborn of ordinary wars between states, and to refuse beforehand to maneuver, to utilize the conflict of interests (even though temporary) among one's enemies, to refuse to temporize and compromise with possible (even though transitory, unstable, vacillating and conditional) allies—is not this ridiculous in the extreme? Is it not as though, when making a difficult ascent of an unexplored and hitherto inaccessible mountain, we were to refuse beforehand ever to move in zigzags, ever to retrace our steps, ever to abandon the course once selected to try others? (*Ibid.*, 111.)

After the first socialist revolution of the proletariat, after the overthrow of the bourgeoisie in one country, the proletariat of that country *for a long time* remains *weaker* than the bourgeoisie, simply because of the latter's extensive international connections, and also because of the spontaneous and continuous restoration and regeneration of capitalism and the bourgeoisie by the small-commodity producers of the country which has overthrown the bourgeoisie. The more powerful enemy can be conquered only by exerting the utmost effort and by *necessarily,* thoroughly, carefully, attentively and skillfully taking advantage of every, even the smallest, "rift" among the enemies, of every antagonism of interest among the bourgeoisie of the various countries and among the various groups or types of bourgeoisie within the various countries, by taking advantage of every, even the smallest, opportunity of gaining a mass ally, even though this ally be temporary, vacillating, unstable, unreliable and conditional. Those who do not understand this do not understand even a particle of Marxism, or of scientific, modern socialism *in general.* Those who have not proved by *deeds* over a fairly considerable period of time, and in fairly varied political situations, their ability to apply this truth in practice have not yet learned to assist the revolutionary class in its struggle for the emancipation of toiling humanity from the exploiters. And this applies equally to the period before and to the period after the conquest of political power by the proletariat.

Our theory is not a dogma but a *guide to action,* said Marx and Engels; and the great mistake, the great crime such "patented" Marxists as Karl Kautsky, Otto Bauer, etc., commit is that they have not understood this, have been unable to apply it at the most important moments of the proletarian revolution. "Political activity is not the pavement of the Nevsky Prospect" (the clean, broad, smooth pavement of the perfectly straight principal street of St. Petersburg) —N. G. Chernyshevsky, the great Russian Socialist of the pre-Marxian period, used to say. Since Chernyshevsky's time Russian revolutionaries have paid very dearly for ignoring or forgetting this truth. . . .

Before the downfall of tsardom the Russian revolutionary Social Democrats repeatedly utilized the services of the bourgeois liberals, that is, they concluded numerous practical compromises with them; and in 1901–02, even prior to the appearance of bolshevism, the old editorial board of *Iskra* (consisting of Plekhanov, Axelrod, Zasulich, Martov, Potresov and myself) concluded—not for long it is true—a formal political alliance with Struve, the political leader of bourgeois liberalism, while it was able at the same time to carry on incessantly a most merciless ideological and political struggle against bourgeois liberalism and against the slightest manifestation of its influence in the working class movement. The Bolsheviks have always adhered to this policy. Ever since 1905 they have systematically insisted on an alliance between the working class and the peasantry against the liberal bourgeoisie and tsardom, never, however, refusing to support the bourgeoisie against tsardom (for instance, during the second stage of elections, or during second ballots) and never ceasing their relentless ideological and political struggle against the bourgeois-revolutionary peasant party, the "Socialist Revolutionaries," exposing them as petty bourgeois democrats who falsely masqueraded as Socialists. During the Duma elections in 1907, the Bolsheviks for a brief period entered into a formal political bloc with the "Socialist Revolutionaries." Between 1903 and 1912 there were periods of several years in which we were formally united with the Mensheviks in one Social Democratic party; but we *never* ceased our ideological and political struggle against them on the grounds that they were opportunists and vehicles of bourgeois influence among the proletariat. During the war we effected certain compromises with the "Kautskians," with the leftist Mensheviks (Martov), and with a section of the "Socialist Revolutionaries" (Chernov and Natanson); we were together with them at Zimmerwald and Kienthal and issued joint manifestoes; but we never ceased and never relaxed our ideological-political struggle against the "Kautskians," Martov and Chernov (Natanson died in 1919 a "Revolutionary Communist" Narodnik who was very close to and almost in agreement with us). At the very outbreak of the October Revolution, we entered into an informal but very important (and very successful) political bloc with the petty bourgeois peasantry by adopting the *Socialist Revolutionary* agrarian program *in its entirety,* without a single alteration—that is, we effected an unquestionable compromise in order to prove to the peasants that we did not want to "steamroller" them, but to reach agreement with them. At the same time we proposed (and soon after effected) a formal political bloc, including participation in the government, with the "leftist" Socialist Revolutionaries, who dissolved this bloc after the conclusion of the Brest-Litovsk Peace and then, in July, 1918, went to the length of armed rebellion, and subsequently of armed warfare, against us. (*Ibid.,* 112–114.)

Capitalism would not be capitalism if the "pure" proletariat were not surrounded by a large number of exceedingly mixed transitional types, from the proletarian to the semiproletarian (who earns half of his livelihood by the sale of his labor power), from the semiproletarian to the small peasant (and petty artisan, handicraft worker and small proprietor in general), from the small peasant to the middle peasant, and so on, and if the proletariat itself were not divided into more or less developed strata, if it were not divided according to territorial origin, trade, sometimes according to religion, and so on. And all this makes it necessary, absolutely necessary, for the vanguard of the proletariat, its class-conscious section, the Communist party, to resort to maneuvers, arrangements and compromises with the various groups of proletarians, with the various parties of the workers and small proprietors. The whole point lies in *knowing how* to apply these tactics in such a way as to *raise,* and not lower, the *general* level of proletarian class consciousness, revolutionary spirit, and ability to fight and to conquer. Incidentally, it should be noted that the victory of the Bolsheviks over the Mensheviks demanded the application of tactics of maneuvers, arrangements and compromises not only before *but also after* the October Revolution of 1917, but such maneuvers and compromises, of course, as would facilitate, accelerate, consolidate and strengthen the Bolsheviks at the expense of the Mensheviks. The petty bourgeois democrats (including the Mensheviks) inevitably vacillate between the bourgeoisie and the proletariat, between bourgeois democracy and the Soviet system, between reformism and revolutionariness, between love for the workers and fear of the proletarian dictatorship, etc. The proper tactics for the Communists to adopt is to *utilize* these vacillations and not to ignore them; and utilizing them calls for concessions to those elements which are turning toward the proletariat, whenever and to the extent that they turn toward the proletariat, in addition to demanding a fight against those who turn toward the bourgeoisie. The result of the application of correct tactics in our country is that menshevism has disintegrated and is disintegrating more and more, that the stubbornly opportunist leaders are becoming isolated, and that the best of the workers and the best elements among the petty bourgeois democrats are being brought into our camp. This is a long process, and the hasty "decision"—"No compromise, no maneuvers!"—can only hinder the work of strengthening the influence of the revolutionary proletariat and enlarging its forces. (*Ibid.,* 115–117.)

To tie one's hand beforehand, openly to tell the enemy, who is at present better armed than we are, whether we shall fight him, and when, is stupidity and not revolutionariness. To accept battle at a time when it is obviously advantageous to the enemy and not to us is a crime; and absolutely worthless are those political leaders of the revolutionary class who are unable "to tack, maneuver and compromise" in order to avoid an obviously disadvantageous battle. (*Ibid.,* 118 f.)

Left Wing Communism in England

The fundamental law of revolution, which has been confirmed by all revolutions, and particularly by all three Russian revolutions in the twentieth century, is as follows: It is not enough for revolution that the exploited and oppressed masses should understand the impossibility of living in the old way and demand changes; what is required for revolution is that the exploiters should not be able to live and rule in the old way. Only when the *"lower classes" do not want* the old way and when the "upper classes" *cannot carry on in the old way* can revolution win. This truth may be expressed in other words: revolution is impossible without a nationwide crisis (affecting both the exploited and the exploiters). It follows that revolution requires, firstly, that a majority of the workers (or at least a majority of the class-conscious, thinking and politically active workers) should fully understand that revolution is necessary and be ready to sacrifice their lives for it; secondly, that the ruling classes should be passing through a governmental crisis which would draw even the most backward masses into politics (a symptom of every real revolution is a rapid tenfold and even hundredfold increase in the number of representatives of the toiling and oppressed masses—who have hitherto been apathetic—capable of waging the political struggle), weaken the government and make it possible for the revolutionaries to overthrow it rapidly. (*Ibid.*, 127.)

Some Conclusions

. . . The Communists of every country should quite consciously take into account both the main fundamental tasks of the struggle against opportunism and "leftist" doctrinairism and the *specific features* which this struggle assumes and inevitably must assume in each separate country in conformity with the peculiar features of its economics, politics, culture, national composition (Ireland, etc.), its colonies, religious divisions, etc. Everywhere we observe that dissatisfaction with the Second International is spreading and growing, both because of its opportunism and because of its inability, or incapacity, to create a really centralized, a really leading center that would be capable of directing the international tactics of the revolutionary proletariat in its struggle for a world Soviet republic. We must clearly realize that such a leading center cannot under any circumstances be built up on stereotyped, mechanically equalized and identical tactical rules of struggle. As long as national and state differences exist among peoples and countries—and these differences will continue to exist for a very long time even after the dictatorship of the proletariat has been established on a world scale—the unity of international tactics of the Communist working class movement of all countries demands, not the elimination of variety, not the abolition of national differences (that is a foolish dream at the present moment), but such an application of the *fundamental* principles of communism (Soviet power and the dictatorship of the proletariat) as will *correctly modify* these principles in *certain particulars,* correctly adapt and apply them to national and national-state differences. The main task of the historical period through which all the advanced countries (and not only the advanced countries) are now passing is to investigate, study, seek, divine, grasp that which is peculiarly national, specifically national in the *concrete manner* in which each country *approaches* the fulfillment of the *single* international task, the victory over opportunism and "leftist" doctrinairism within the working class movement, the overthrow of the bourgeoisie, and the establishment of a Soviet republic and a proletarian dictatorship. (*Ibid.,* 134 f.)

Victory cannot be won with the vanguard alone. To throw the vanguard alone into the decisive battle, before the whole class, before the broad masses have taken up a position either of direct support of the vanguard, or at least of benevolent neutrality toward it and one in which they cannot possibly support the enemy, would be not merely folly but a crime. And in order that actually the whole class, that actually the broad masses of toilers and those oppressed by capital may take up such a position, propaganda and agitation alone are not enough. For this the masses must have their own political experience. Such is the fundamental law of all great revolutions. . . .

The first historical task (viz., that of winning over the class-conscious vanguard of the proletariat to the side of the Soviet power and the dictatorship of the working class) could not be accomplished without a complete ideological and political victory over opportunism and social chauvinism, the second task, which now becomes the immediate task, and which consists in being able to lead *the masses* to the new position that will ensure the victory of the vanguard in the revolution, this immediate task cannot be accomplished without the liquidation of "leftist" doctrinairism, without completely overcoming and getting rid of its mistakes.

As long as the question was (and in so far as it still is) one of winning over the vanguard of the proletariat to communism, so long, and to that extent, propaganda took first place; even propaganda circles, with all the imperfections that circles suffer from, are useful under these conditions and produce fruitful results. But when it is a question of the practical activities of the masses, of the disposition, if one may so express it, of vast armies, of the alignment of *all* the class forces of the given society *for the final and decisive battle,* then propaganda habits alone, the mere repetition of the truths of "pure" communism, are of no avail. In these circumstances one must not count up to a thousand, as the propagandist who belongs to a small group that has not yet led masses really does; in these circumstances one must count in millions and tens of millions. In these circumstances we must not only ask ourselves whether we have convinced the vanguard of the revolutionary class, but also whether the historically effective forces of *all* classes—positively of all the classes of the given society without exception—are aligned in such a way that the decisive battle has fully matured; in such a way that (1) all the class forces hostile to us have become sufficiently entangled, sufficiently at loggerheads with each other, have sufficiently weakened themselves in a struggle which is beyond their strength; that (2) all the vacillating, wavering, unstable, intermediate elements—the petty bourgeoisie and the petty bourgeois democrats, as distinct from the bourgeoisie—have sufficiently exposed themselves in the eyes of the people, and

have sufficiently disgraced themselves through their practical
bankruptcy; and that (3) among the proletariat a mass sentiment
in favor of supporting the most determined, supremely bold,
revolutionary action against the bourgeoisie has arisen and begun
vigorously to grow. Then revolution is indeed ripe; then, indeed,
if we have correctly gauged all the conditions indicated, briefly
outlined above, and if we have chosen the moment rightly, our
victory is assured. (*Ibid.*, 136–138.)

The strictest loyalty to the ideas of communism must be combined with the ability to make all the necessary practical compromises, to maneuver to make agreements, zigzags, retreats and so
on, so as to accelerate the coming to power and subsequent loss
of political power of the Hendersons (the heroes of the Second
International, if we are not to mention the names of individuals;
the representatives of petty-bourgeois democracy who call themselves Socialists); to accelerate their inevitable bankruptcy in
practice, which will enlighten the masses in the spirit of our ideas,
in the direction of communism; to accelerate the inevitable friction, quarrels, conflicts and complete disintegration among the
Hendersons, the Lloyd Georges and Churchills (Mensheviks,
Socialist Revolutionaries, Constitutional Democrats, Monarchists;
Scheidemanns, the bourgeoisie, the Kappists, etc.); and to select
the proper moment when the disintegration among these "pillars
of the sacred right of private property" is at is height, in order
by a determined attack of the proletariat, to defeat them all and
capture political power.

History generally, and the history of revolutions in particular,
is always richer in content, more varied, more many-sided, more
lively and "subtle" than even the best parties and the most class-
conscious vanguards of the most advanced classes imagine. This
is understandable, because even the best vanguards express the
class consciousness, will, passion and imagination of tens of thousands, whereas the revolution is made, at the moment of its climax
and the exertion of all human capacities, by the class consciousness, will, passion and imagination of tens of millions, spurred on
by a most acute struggle of classes. From this follow two very

important practical conclusions: first, that in order to fulfil its task, the revolutionary class must be able to master *all* forms or sides of social activity without exception (completing, after the capture of political power, sometimes at great risk and very great danger, what it did not complete before the capture of power); second, that the revolutionary class must be ready to pass from one form to another in the quickest and most unexpected manner.

Everyone will agree that an army which does not train itself to wield all arms, all the means and methods of warfare that the enemy possesses, or may possess, behaves in an unwise or even in criminal manner. But this applies to politics even more than it does to war. In politics it is harder to forecast what methods of warfare will be applicable and useful to us under certain future conditions. Unless we master all means of warfare, we may suffer grave and even decisive defeat if changes in the position of the other classes that do not depend on us bring to the forefront forms of activity in which we are particularly weak. If however, we master all means of warfare, we shall certainly be victorious, because we represent the interests of the really advanced and really revolutionary class, even if circumstances do not permit us to use weapons that are most dangerous to the enemy, weapons that are most swift in dealing mortal blows. (*Ibid.*, 138 f.)

... Revolutionaries who are unable to combine illegal forms of struggle with *every* form of legal struggle are poor revolutionaries indeed. It is not difficult to be a revolutionary when the revolution has already flared up and is raging, when everybody is joining the revolution just from infatuation, because it is the fashion, and sometimes even from careerist motives. After its victory, the proletariat has to make most strenuous efforts to suffer the pains of martyrdom, one might say, to "liberate" itself from such pseudo-revolutionaries. It is far more difficult—and far more useful—to be a revolutionary when the conditions for direct, open, really mass and really revolutionary struggle *do not yet exist,* to defend the interests of the revolution (by propaganda, agitation and organization) in non-revolutionary bodies and even in downright reactionary bodies, in non-revolutionary circumstances, among the masses who are incapable of immediately appreciating the need for revolutionary methods of action. (*Ibid.*, 140.)

The Communists in western Europe and America must learn to create a new, unusual, non-opportunist, non-careerist parliamentarism; the Communist parties must issue their slogans; real proletarians, with the help of the unorganized and downtrodden poor, should scatter and distribute leaflets, canvass workers' houses and the cottages of the rural proletarians and peasants in the remote villages (fortunately there are not nearly so many remote villages in Europe as there are in Russia, and in England there are very few) ; they should go into the most common taverns, penetrate into the unions, societies and casual meetings where the common people gather, and talk to the people, not in scientific (and not in very parliamentary) language, they should not at all strive to "get seats" in parliament, but should everywhere strive to rouse the minds of the masses and to draw them into the struggle, to catch the bourgeois on their own statements, to utilize the apparatus they have set up, the elections they have appointed, the appeals to the country they have made, and to tell the people what bolshevism is in a way that has never been possible (under bourgeois rule) outside of election times (not counting, of course, times of big strikes, when, in Russia, a *similar* apparatus for widespread popular agitation worked even more intensively). It is very difficult to do this in Western Europe and America, very, very difficult; but it can and must be done, because the tasks of communism cannot be fulfilled without effort; and every effort must be made to fulfil *practical* tasks, ever more varied, ever more closely connected with all branches of social life, *winning* branch after branch and sphere after sphere *from the bourgeoisie.*

In Great Britain, too, the work of propaganda, agitation and organization among the armed forces and among the oppressed and unfranchised nationalities in "one's own" state (Ireland, the colonies) must be organized in a new way (not in a socialist, but a communist way, not in a reformist, but a revolutionary way). . . .

We do not and cannot know which spark—of the innumerable sparks that are flying around in all countries as a result of the economic and political world crisis—will kindle the conflagration, in the sense of specially rousing the masses, and we must, therefore, with the aid of our new, communist principles, set to work to "stir up" all and sundry, even the oldest, mustiest and seemingly hopeless spheres, for otherwise we shall not be able to cope with our tasks, we shall not be all-round, we shall not master all arms and we shall not be prepared either for victory over the bourgeoisie (which arranged all sides of public life—and has now disarranged them in its bourgeois way) or for the impending communist reorganization of the whole social life after the victory. (*Ibid.*, 142 f.)

The bourgeoisie practically sees only one side of bolshevism, viz., insurrection, violence, terror; it therefore strives to prepare itself for resistance and opposition particularly in *this* field. It is possible that in certain instances, in certain countries, and for more or less brief periods, it will succeed in this. We must reckon with such a possibility, and there will be absolutely nothing terrible for us if it does succeed. Communism "springs" from positively all sides of public life; its shoots are to be seen literally everywhere. The "contagion" (to use the favorite metaphor of the bourgeoisie and the bourgeois police, the one most "pleasant" to them) has very thoroughly permeated the organism and has completely impregnated it. If one of the channels is "stopped up" with special care, the "contagion" will find another, sometimes a very unexpected one. Life will assert itself. Only one thing is lacking to enable us to march forward more confidently and firmly to victory, namely, the universal and thoroughly thought-out appreciation by all Communists in all countries of the necessity of displaying the utmost *flexibility* in their tactics. Communism, which is developing magnificently in the advanced countries particularly, now lacks this appreciation and the ability to apply it in practice. (*Ibid.*, 144 f.)

We now have what from the standpoint of the development of

international communism is such a lasting, strong and powerful content of work (for the Soviet power, for the dictatorship of the proletariat) that it can *and must* manifest itself in every form, both new and old, it can and must regenerate, conquer and subjugate all forms, not only the new, but also the old—not for the purpose of reconciling itself with the old, but for the purpose of converting all and every form, new and old, into a weapon for the complete, final, decisive and irrevocable victory of communism.

The Communists must exert every effort to direct the working class movement and social development in general along the straightest and quickest path to the universal victory of the Soviet power and the dictatorship of the proletariat. That is an incontestable truth. But it is enough to take one little step further—a step that might seem to be in the same direction—and truth is transformed into error! We have only to say, as the German and British "leftist" Communists say, that we recognize only one road, only the straight road, that we do not agree with tacking, maneuvering, compromising—and it will be a mistake which may cause, and in part has already caused, and is causing, very serious harm to communism. Right doctrinairism persisted in recognizing only the old forms, and became totally bankrupt, for it did not perceive the new content. Leftist doctrinairism persists in the unconditional repudiation of certain old forms and fails to see that the new content is forcing its way through all and sundry forms, that it is our duty as Communists to master all forms, to learn how with the maximum rapidity to supplement one form with another, to substitute one for another, and to adapt our tactics to every such change not called forth by our class, or by our efforts. (*Ibid.*, 146 f.)

APPENDIX:

Incorrect Conclusions from Correct Practices

Not only in the parliamentary field, but in *all* fields of activity communism *must introduce* (and without long, persistent and stubborn effort it *will be unable* to introduce) something new in principle that will represent a radical break with the traditions of the Second International (while retaining and developing what was good in the latter).

Let us take, say, journalistic work. Newspapers, pamphlets and manifestoes perform a necessary work of propaganda, agitation and organization. Not a single mass movement can dispense with a journalistic apparatus in any at all civilized country. No outcries against "leaders," no solemn vows to preserve the purity of the masses from the influence of leaders will obviate the necessity of utilizing people who come from a bourgeois intellectual environment for this work, or will get rid of the bourgeois-democratic, "private property" atmosphere and environment in which this work is performed under capitalism. Even two and a half years after the overthrow of the bourgeoisie, after the conquest of political power by the proletariat, we still have this atmosphere around us, this mass (peasant, artisan) environment of bourgeois-democratic property relations.

Parliamentarism is one form of activity, journalism is another. The content of both can be communist, and it should be communist if those engaged in either sphere are real Communists, are real members of a proletarian mass party. Yet, in neither sphere—nor *in any other sphere of activity* under capitalism and during the period of transition from capitalism to socialism—is it possible to avoid these difficulties which the proletariat must overcome, those special problems which the proletariat must solve in order to utilize for its own purposes the services of those who have come from the ranks of the bourgeoisie, in order to gain the victory over bourgeois intellectual prejudices and influences, in order to weaken the resistance of (and, ultimately, completely to transform) the petty bourgeois environment. . . .

The childishness of those who "repudiate" participation in parliament consists precisely in the fact that they think it possible to *"solve"* the difficult problem of combating bourgeois-democratic influences *within* the working class movement by such a "simple," "easy," supposedly revolutionary method, when in reality they are only running away from their own shadow, closing their eyes to difficulties and trying to brush them aside with mere words. Shameless careerism, bourgeois utilization of parliamentary posts, glaring reformist perversion of parliamentary activity, vulgar, petty bourgeois routine are all unquestionably common and prevalent features that are engendered by capitalism everywhere, not only outside but also inside the working class movement. But this capitalism and the bourgeois environment it creates (which disappears very slowly even after the overthrow of the bourgeoisie, for the peasantry is constantly regenerating the bourgeoisie) give rise to what is also essentially bourgeois careerism, national chauvinism, petty bourgeois vulgarity, etc. — only varying insignificantly in form — in positively every sphere of activity and life.

You think, my dear boycottists and antiparliamentarians, that you are "terribly revolutionary," but in reality *you are frightened* by the comparatively small difficulties of the struggle against bourgeois influences within the working class movement, whereas your victory—i.e., the overthrow of the bourgeoisie and the conquest of political power by the proletariat—will create *these very same* difficulties on a still larger, and infinitely larger scale. Like children, you are frightened by a small difficulty which confronts you today, not understanding that tomorrow and the day after you will anyhow have to learn, and go on learning, to overcome the same difficulties, only on an immeasurably greater scale.

Under the Soviet power, your proletarian party and ours will be invaded by a still larger number of bourgeois intellectuals. They will worm their way into the Soviets, the courts, and the administration, for communism cannot be built up otherwise than with the aid of the human material created by capitalism, and the bourgeois intellectuals cannot be expelled and destroyed, but must be vanquished, remoulded, assimilated and re-educated, just as one must—in a protracted struggle waged on the basis of the dictatorship of the proletariat—re-educate the proletarians themselves, who do not abandon their petty bourgeois prejudices at one stroke, by a miracle, at the behest of the Virgin Mary, at the behest of a slogan, resolution or decree, but only in the course of a long and difficult mass struggle against mass petty bourgeois influences. Under the Soviet power these same problems, which the antiparliamentarians are now so proudly, so haughtily, so lightly and so childishly brushing aside with a wave of the hand —*these very same* problems are arising anew *within* the Soviets, within the Soviet administration, among the Soviet "attorneys" (in Russia we have abolished, and have rightly abolished, the bourgeois legal bar, but it is being revived in the guise of "Soviet" "attorneys"). Among the Soviet engineers, the Soviet school teachers and the privileged, i.e., the most highly skilled and best situated *workers* in the Soviet factories, we observe a constant revival of absolutely *all* the bad traits peculiar to bourgeois parliamentarism, and we shall gradually conquer this evil only by constant, tireless, prolonged and persistent struggle, proletarian organization and discipline.

Of course, it is very "difficult" under the rule of the bourgeoisie to overcome bourgeois habits in our own, i.e., the workers' party; it is "difficult" to expel from the party the ordinary parliamentary leaders who have been hopelessly corrupted by bourgeois prejudices; it is "difficult" to subject to proletarian discipline the absolutely essential (even if very limited) number of bourgeois intellectuals; it is "difficult" to form in a bourgeois parliament a Communist faction fully worthy of the working class; it is "difficult" to assure that the Communist parliamentarians do not play the bourgeois parliamentary game of ninepins, but concern themselves with the very urgent work of propaganda, agitation and organization of the masses. All this is "difficult," there is no doubt about it; it was difficult in Russia, and it is incomparably more difficult in western Europe and America, where the bourgeoisie is far stronger, where bourgeois-democratic traditions are stronger, and so on.

Yet all these "difficulties" are mere child's play compared with precisely *the same sort* of problems which in any event the proletariat will inevitably have to solve in order to achieve victory during the proletarian revolution, and after the seizure of power by the proletariat. Compared with *these* truly gigantic problems of re-educating, under the proletarian dictatorship, millions of peasants and small proprietors, hundreds of thousands of office employees, officials and bourgeois intellectuals, of subordinating them all to the proletarian state and to the proletarian leadership, of vanquishing their bourgeois habits and traditions—compared with these gigantic problems it is childishly easy to establish, under the rule of the bourgeoisie and in a bourgeois parliament, a really Communist faction of a real proletarian party.

If our "leftist" and antiparliamentarian comrades do not learn to overcome even such a small difficulty now, we may safely assert that either they will prove incapable of achieving the dictatorship of the proletariat, will be unable to subordinate and remould the bourgeois intellectuals and bourgeois institutions on a wide scale, or they will have to *complete their education in a hurry,* and in consequence of such haste they will do a great deal of harm to the cause of the proletariat, they will commit more errors than usual, will manifest more than the average weakness and inefficiency, and so on and so forth.

As long as the bourgeoisie has not been overthrown, and as long as small-scale economy and small-commodity production have not entirely disappeared, the bourgeois atmosphere, proprietary habits and petty bourgeois traditions will spoil proletarian work both outside and inside the working class movement, not only in one field of activity, parliamentary, but inevitably in every field of public activity, in all cultural and political spheres without exception. And the attempt to brush aside, to fence oneself off from *one* of the "unpleasant" problems or difficulties in one sphere of activity is a profound mistake, which will later most certainly have to be paid for dearly. We must study and learn how to master every sphere of work and activity without exception, to overcome all difficulties and all bourgeois habits, customs and traditions everywhere. Any other way of presenting the question is just trifling, just childishness. (*Ibid.,* 154–158.)

X

TACTICS

1. Tactics

To the followers of *Narodnaya Volya,* the term, political struggle, is synonymous with political *conspiracy!* It must be confessed that in these words P. L. Lavrov has managed to display in striking relief the fundamental difference between the tactics in political struggle adopted by the followers of *Narodnaya Volya* and those adopted by Social Democrats. The traditions of Blanquism, of conspiracies, are very strong among the followers of *Narodnaya Volya,* so much so that they cannot conceive the political struggle except in the form of political conspiracy. The Social Democrats do not hold to such a narrow point of view; they do not believe in conspiracies; they think that the period of conspiracies has long passed away, that to reduce the political struggle to a conspiracy means to restrict its scope greatly, on the one hand, and, on the other hand, it means selecting the most inefficient method of struggle. Everyone will understand that P. L. Lavrov's remark, that "the Russian Social Democrats take the activities of the West as an unfailing model," is nothing more than a debating trick, for, as a matter of fact Russian Social Democrats have never forgotten the political conditions that prevail in Russia, they have never dreamed of being able to

form an open workers' party in Russia, they never separated the
task of fighting for socialism from the task of fighting for political
liberty. But they have always thought, and continue to think,
that this fight must be waged not by conspirators, but by a revolutionary party that is based on the labor movement. They think
that the fight against absolutism must be waged not in the form
of plots, but by educating, disciplining and organizing the proletariat, by political agitation among the workers, which shall
denounce every manifestation of absolutism, which will pillory
all the knights of the police government and will compel this
government to make concessions. (*The Tasks of the Russian
Social Democrats,* 1897, *Selected Works,* I, 382 f.*)

With regard to the question of tactics, we intend to confine
ourselves here to the following: Social Democracy does not tie
its hands, it does not restrict its activities to some preconceived
plan or method of political struggle; it recognizes all methods of
struggle, as long as they correspond to the forces at the disposal
of the Party and facilitate the achievement of the greatest results
possible under the given conditions.

If we have a strongly organized party, a single strike may grow
into a political demonstration, into a political victory over the
government. If we have a strongly organized party, a rebellion
in a single locality may flare up into a victorious revolution. We
must bear in mind that the fight against the government for
certain demands, the gain of certain concessions, are merely slight
skirmishes with the enemy, slight skirmishes of outposts, but that
the decisive battle still lies ahead. (*The Urgent Task of Our
Movement,* December, 1900, *Selected Works,* II, 14.)

Tactics in carrying on agitation on some special question, or
in relation to some detail of Party organization, may be changed
within twenty-four hours; but views as to whether a militant
organization and political agitation among the masses are necessary, necessary at all times and absolutely necessary, cannot be
changed in twenty-four hours, or even in twenty-four months for
that matter—except by those who have no fixed ideas on any-

thing. It is absurd to refer to changed circumstances and changing periods. Work for the establishment of a fighting organization and for carrying on political agitation must be carried on under all circumstances, no matter how "drab and peaceful" the times may be, and no matter how low the "depression of revolutionary spirit" has sunk. More than that, it is precisely in such conditions and in such periods that this work is particularly required; for it would be too late to start building such an organization in the midst of uprisings and outbreaks. The organization must be ready to develop its activity at any moment. "Change tactics in twenty-four hours!" In order to change tactics it is necessary first of all to have tactics, and without a strong organization, tested in the political struggle carried on under all circumstances and in all periods, there can be no talk of a systematic plan of activity, enlightened by firm principles and unswervingly carried out, which alone is worthy of being called tactics. Think of it! We are now told that the "historical moment" has confronted our party with the "absolutely new" question of—terror! Yesterday the "absolutely new" question was the question of political organization and agitation; today it is the question of terror! Does it not sound strange to hear people with such short memories arguing about radical changes in tactics? (*Where To Begin?* May, 1901, *Selected Works,* II, 16 f.)

To confuse the recognition, *in principle,* of all means of struggle, of all plans and methods, as long as they are expedient —with the necessity *at a given political moment* for being guided by a strictly adhered-to plan, if we are to talk of tactics, is tantamount to confusing the recognition by medical science of all kinds of treatment of diseases with the necessity for adopting a certain definite method of treatment for a given disease. The point is, however, that *Rabocheye Dyelo,* while suffering from a disease which we have called subservience to spontaneity, refuses to recognize any "method of treatment" for *that* disease. Hence, it made the remarkable discovery that "a tactics plan contradicts the fundamental spirit of Marxism," that tactics are *"a process of growth of Party tasks, which grow with the Party."* The latter remark has every chance of becoming a celebrated maxim, a permanent monument to the tendency of *Rabocheye Dyelo*. To the question: Whither? A leading organ replies: The movement is a process of alteration in the distance between starting point and destination of the movement. This matchless example of profundity is not merely a literary curiosity (if it were, it would not be worth dealing with at length), but the *program of the whole tendency*, i.e., the program which R.M. expressed in the words: "That struggle is desirable which is possible, and the struggle which is possible is the one that is going on at the given moment." It is the tendency of unbounded opportunism, which passively adapts itself to spontaneity.

"A tactics plan contradicts the fundamental spirit of Marxism"! But this is a libel on Marxism.

.   .   .   .

As for calling the masses to action, that will come of itself immediately energetic political agitation, live and striking expo-sures are set going. To catch some criminal red-handed and immediately to brand him publicly will have far more effect than any number of "appeals"; the effect very often will be such as will make it impossible to tell exactly who it was that "ap-pealed" to the crowd, and exactly who suggested this or that plan of demonstration, etc. Calls for action, not in the general, but in the concrete sense of the term, can be made only at the place of action; only those who themselves go into action imme-diately can make appeals for action. And our business as Social Democratic publicists is to deepen, to expand and intensify political exposures and political agitation.

.   .   .   .

Here indeed is a special "struggle with the political police" required, a struggle that can never be conducted by such large masses as usually take part in strikes. Such a struggle must be organized, according to "all the rules of the art," by people who are professionally engaged in revolutionary activity. The fact that the masses are spontaneously entering the movement does not make the organization of this struggle *less necessary*. On the contrary, it makes it *more necessary;* for we Socialists would be failing in our duty to the masses if we did not prevent the police from making a secret of (and if we did not ourselves sometimes secretly prepare) every strike and every demonstration. *And we shall succeed in doing this,* precisely because the spontaneously awakening masses will *also advance from their own ranks* increasing numbers of "professional revolutionaries" (that is, if we are not so foolish as to advise the workers to keep on marking time). (*What is to be done?* February, 1902, *Selected Works,* II, 69 f., 90 f., 125 f.)

The Social Democratic party wishes to utilize the elections in order, over and over again, to *stimulate* the masses to see the need for revolution, to see precisely the revolutionary revival which has begun. (*The Platform of the Reformists and the Platform of the Revolutionary Social Democrats,* November, 1912, *Selected Works,* IV, 185.)

An episode in the Russo-Japanese War . . . will enable us to obtain a clearer picture of the relationship between the various systems and political methods in a revolution such as is taking place in our country. The episode I have in mind is the capture of Port Arthur by the Japanese General Nogi. The main thing that interests me in this episode is that the capture of Port Arthur was accomplished in two absolutely different stages. The first stage was that of furious assaults, which ended in failure and cost the celebrated Japanese commander very heavy losses. The second stage was the extremely arduous, extremely difficult and slow method of siege, according to all the rules of the art; and after a time it was precisely by this method that the problem of capturing the fortress was solved.

. . . .

If we examine the development of military operations as a whole, and the conditions in which the Japanese army operated, we shall have to come to the conclusion that the storming of Port Arthur was not only a display of great heroism on the part of the army which proved capable of suffering such great losses, but that it was the only possible tactics to adopt in the conditions then prevailing, i.e., in the beginning of operations. For that reason these tactics were necessary and useful; for without testing the strength of the fortress by the practical attempt to carry it by assault, without testing the power of resistance of the enemy, there would have been no grounds for adopting the more prolonged and arduous method of struggle, which, by the very fact that it was prolonged, harbored a number of other dangers.... What was the position of this army when the period of fighting against the enemy fortress by means of direct assault came to an end? "Thousands and thousands of men have fallen, and we shall lose more thousands, but we shall not take the fortress in this way"—such was the position when some, or the majority, began to come to the conclusion that the tactics of direct assault must be abandoned and siege tactics adopted. Since the previous tactics proved mistaken, they must be abandoned, and all that was connected with them must be regarded as a hindrance to the operations and should be dropped. Direct assaults must cease, siege tactics must be adopted, the disposition of the troops must be changed, supplies and munitions must be redistributed, and of course, certain methods and operations must be changed. What had been done before must be resolutely, precisely and clearly regarded as a mistake in order to remove all hindrances to the development of the new strategy and tactics, to the development of operations, which were now to be conducted on entirely new lines. As we know, the new tactics ended in complete victory, although it took a much longer time to achieve than was anticipated.

.   .   .   .

If an army which had become convinced that it is unable to capture a fortress by direct assault said that it refused to leave the old positions and occupy new ones, refused to adopt new methods of solving its problem, one would say about such an army that if it has learned to attack but has not learned to retreat at the dictates of certain severe conditions it will never win the war. Wars which began and ended with an uninterrupted victorious advance have never occurred in world history, or else they have been very rare exceptions. (*On the Right of Nations to Self-Determination,* October, 1921, *Selected Works,* IX, 277, 278 f., 290.)

"When living among wolves, howl like the wolves." As for exterminating all the wolves, as would be done in sensible human society, we shall act up to the wise Russian proverb: "Don't boast when going to war, boast when returning from war." (*The Importance of Gold Now and After the Complete Victory of Socialism,* November 5, 1921, *Selected Works,* IX, 300.)

2. COMPROMISES

The term compromise in politics implies the surrender of certain of one's demands, the renunciation of part of one's demands by agreement with another party.

The usual idea of the man in the street regarding the Bolsheviks, an idea fostered by the systematic calumniations of the press, is that the Bolsheviks are opposed to all compromises, no matter with whom and under what circumstances.

That idea is flattering to us as the party of the revolutionary proletariat, for it shows that even our enemies are obliged to admit our loyalty to the fundamental principles of socialism and the revolution. Nevertheless, the truth must be told: this idea does not correspond to the facts. Engels was right when, in his criticism of the manifesto of the Blanquist Communists (1873), he ridiculed their declaration, "No compromise!" That is a mere phrase, he said, for compromises are often unavoidably forced upon a fighting party by circumstances, and it is absurd once and for all to refuse "to stop at intermediate stations." The task of a truly revolutionary party is not to renounce compromises once and for all, but to be able *throughout all compromises,* when they are unavoidable, to remain true to its principles, to its class, to its revolutionary purpose, to its task of preparing the way for the revolution and of educating the masses for victory in the revolution. (*Compromises,* September 16, 1917, *Selected Works,* VI, 208.)

We must make it a rule not to make political concessions to the international bourgeoisie . . . unless we receive in return more or less equivalent concessions from the international bourgeoisie to Soviet Russia, or to the other units of the international proletariat which is fighting against capitalism. (*We Have Paid Too Much,* April 9, 1922, *Selected Works,* X, 303.)

3. INFILTRATION

Martov wrote somewhere: "You Bolsheviks hurl abuse at the Berne International but 'your' own friend Loriot is a member of it."

That is the argument of a rogue; for everybody knows that Loriot is openly, honestly and heroically fighting for the Third International. When, in 1902, Zubatov organized workers' meetings in Moscow for the purpose of fooling the workers with "police socialism," the worker, Babushkin, whom I had known since 1894, when he attended the workers' circle I conducted in St. Petersburg, who was one of the most loyal and devoted worker *Iskra*-ists, a leader of the revolutionary proletariat, and who was shot in 1906 by Rennenkampf in Siberia, *went to the Zubatov meetings* in order to fight against Zubatovism and to snatch the workers out of its clutches. Babushkin was no more a "Zubatovist" than Loriot is a "Berne-ite." (*The Task of the Third International,* July 14, 1919, *Selected Works,* X, 44.)

In all organizations without exception—unions and associations, primarily proletarian, and also organizations of the non-proletarian, toiling and exploited masses (political, industrial, military, co-operative, educational, sports, etc., etc.), groups or nuclei of Communists should be formed—mainly open groups, but also secret groups, which should be obligatory in every case when their suppression, or the arrest or deportation of their members by the bourgeoisie may be expected—and these nuclei, closely connected with each other and with the Party center, interchanging their experiences, carrying on work of agitation, propaganda and organization, adapting themselves to absolutely all spheres of public life, absolutely to all varieties and subdivisions of the toiling masses, must systematically train themselves, the Party, the class and the masses by means of this diversified work. (*Theses on the Fundamental Tasks of the Second Congress of the Communist International,* July 4, 1920, *Selected Works,* X, 169 f.)

4. MONEY

But where is the money for the newspaper to come from?

It is necessary to organize collections among the workers. These collections form a fund and show the strength of the connections of this or that group. They are an indication of the authority of the groups, the confidence placed in them by the workers, their real influence over the proletarian masses.

Such collections for a workers' newspaper were started in St. Petersburg at the beginning of 1912. Six months—from January 14 to July 13—is an adequate period. The data concerning the collections are published in all the above-named newspapers, both liquidationist and antiliquidationist.

The conclusions drawn from these data covering half a year serve as the best material—an open, complete, objective, final answer to the question of the correlation of the forces of the liquidators and of the Party in Russia. Therefore, in the appendix we have given a full translation of all the accounts of money collections for a daily workers' newspaper taken from nearly all the above-mentioned newspapers for that half year.

Here we quote only the totals.

During the half year, the antiliquidationist newspapers published accounts concerning 504 money collections among groups of workers, i.e., collections regarding which the groups of workers which made the collections are actually named. These collections were made in fifty Russian cities and factory settlements.

During the same half year—from January 14 to July 13, 1912—the liquidationist newspapers published accounts of fifteen money collections among groups of workers. These collections were made in five Russian cities.[1]

. . . .

---

[1] In spite of the gossip spread by the liquidators, it was precisely these collections, amounting to over 12,000 marks, together with the help previously rendered by the German comrades, that formed the basic fund of our Social Democratic press in Russia. The full translation, mentioned in the text, of all the accounts of money collections published by the various Social Democratic newspapers in the course of half a year was sent to the Executive Committee, the Auditing Committee and to Bebel.

No financial assistance in the world will win the sympathies of the Russian workers for the liquidators. But it goes without saying that it is possible to set up fictitious second candidatures in various places with the money supplied by the Executive Committee. In that event the responsibility for such candidatures, which will in fact be candidatures of the German Executive Committee, will rest on the Executive Committee. *The money handed out to the liquidators, who have no daily newspaper, will help them to found a competing organ. This money will be used to organize a split by those who, throughout the many years of struggle, have shown that they are nonentities; the money will be used for journeys, etc., in order to found a new party.* If the Executive Committee wants to assist the liquidators in one way or another, then, in spite of all our respect for the fraternal German Party, we shall be obliged to appeal to the International. Then we shall *prove* to the Vienna International Congress by *documents* that the Executive Committee has expressed its readiness, by means of monetary support, to help bring about a split in our party, to set up double candidatures and to galvanize that corpse—the defeated liquidators. If the German comrades want to help the Russian Social Democratic Labor party, they must transfer the money, not to those who are organizing a new party, but to the Central Committee of the old Party.

.   .   .   .

The Russian newspapers legally existing and conducted in a Marxian spirit are at the present time the most important, open organ of the masses of the Russian Social Democratic workers in connection with the agitational work of the Party.

The newspapers appearing abroad which are illegal in Russia cannot, *in essence,* claim to possess the same importance as those mentioned above, although their importance *in principle* as a means for theoretically explaining the movement is extremely great. It is well known how easily, and sometimes thoughtlessly, such newspapers are founded by small groups of Russian emigrants scattered abroad; these newspapers drag on a miserable existence amidst the same groups, and hardly ever reach the

Russian members of the Party. Therefore they cannot really be regarded as having any perceptible influence over Party life in Russia.

After half a year's struggle of the antiliquidationist newspapers (from January to June, 1912) there is now *only one* organ of the liquidators—*Nevsky Golos*. This newspaper has almost ceased to exist as a political organ. In the course of a month and a half (from June to the middle of August) only two numbers were published. It is obvious that unless a newspaper of this kind draws its vital forces from close contact with the masses of the workers, it cannot withstand the police persecution that is raging in Russia against *all* the labor and even against many quite moderate liberal newspapers.

The labor newspapers which carry great political weight and are of immediate and urgent importance are now the weekly *Nevskaya Zvezda* and the daily newspaper, *Pravda*. Both newspapers appear in St. Petersburg; our *political opponents* among the Lettish Social Democrats have contemptuously dubbed them the organs of the "Lenin group." From the objective data adduced above, which are always open for verification, it must be obvious to our German comrades that this "Lenin group" embraces, in fact, the overwhelming majority of the Russian Social Democratic workers.

Hence, it is quite understandable why all the information emanating from the liquidators, and from groups, large and small, in sympathy with them, *do not deserve the least confidence.* All the rumors spread by these small groups, together with the Jewish (Bund) and Lettish Social Democrats, who have absolutely no immediate contact with the *Russian* movement, about an alleged general conference, called or about to be called, representing all "tendencies," turn out to be pure inventions. No such conference, even if it actually took place, would play *any serious part* in the struggle of the Russian proletariat. Therefore, in essence, if we may venture to use a strong word, what we have here is a fraud. (*The Present Situation in the Russian Social Democratic Labor Party,* August, 1912, *Selected Works,* IV, 171 f., 174 f., 175 f.)

5. PROPAGANDA

A propagandist, dealing with, say, the question of unemployment, must explain the capitalistic nature of crises, the reasons why crises are inevitable in modern society, must describe how present society must inevitably become transformed into socialist society, etc. In a word, he must present "many ideas," so many indeed that they will be understood as a whole only by a (comparatively) few persons. An agitator, however, speaking on the same subject will take as an illustration a fact that is most widely known and outstanding among his audience, say, the death from starvation of the family of an unemployed worker, the growing impoverishment, etc., and utilizing this fact, which is known to everybody, will direct all his efforts to presenting a *single idea* to the "masses," i.e., the idea of the senseless contradiction between the increase of wealth and increase of poverty; he will strive to *rouse* discontent and indignation among the masses against this crying injustice, and leave a more complete explanation of this contradiction to the propagandist. Consequently, the propagandist operates chiefly by means of the *printed* word; the agitator operates with the *living* word. The qualities that are required of an agitator are not the same as the qualities that are required of a propagandist. Kautsky and Lafargue, for example, we call propagandists; Bebel and Guesde we call agitators. To single out a third sphere, or third function, of practical activity, and to include in this third function "calling the masses to certain concrete actions," is sheer nonsense, because the "call," as a single act, either naturally and inevitably supplements the theoretical tract, propagandist pamphlet and agitational speech, or represents a purely executive function. Take, for example, the struggle now being carried on by the German Social Democrats against the grain duties. The theoreticians write works of research on tariff policy and "call," say, for a fight for commercial treaties and for free trade. The propagandist does the same thing in the periodical press, and the agitator does it in public speeches. At the present time, the "concrete action" of the masses takes the form of signing petitions to the Reichstag against the raising of the grain duties. The call for this action comes directly from the theoreticians, the propagandists and the agitators, and, indirectly, from those workers who carry the petition lists to the factories and to private houses to get signatures.

.   .   .   .

It is possible to "raise the activity of the masses of the workers" *only* provided this activity *is not restricted entirely* to "political agitation on an economic basis." And one of the fundamental conditions for the necessary expansion of political agitation is the organization of *all-sided* political exposure. In *no other way* can the masses be trained in political consciousness and revolutionary activity except by means of such exposures. Hence, to conduct such activity is one of the most important functions of international Social Democracy as a whole, for even the existence of political liberty does not remove the necessity for such exposures; it merely changes the sphere against which they are directed.

.   .   .   .

In order to become a Social Democrat, a workingman must have a clear picture in his mind of the economic nature and the social and political features of the landowner, of the priest, of the high state official and of the peasant, of the student and of the tramp; he must know their strong and weak sides; he must understand all the catchwords and sophisms by which each class and each stratum camouflages its selfish strivings and its real "nature"; he must understand what interests certain institutions and certain laws reflect and how they reflect them. This "clear picture" cannot be obtained from books. It can be obtained only from living examples and from exposures, following hot after their occurrence, of what goes on around us at a given moment, of what is being discussed, in whispers perhaps, by each one in his own way, of the meaning of such and such events, of such and such statistics, of such and such court sentences, etc., etc., etc. These universal political exposures are an essential and *fundamental* condition for training the masses in revolutionary activity.

.   .   .   .

We must "go among all classes of the people" as theoreticians, as propagandists, as agitators and as organizers. No one doubts that the theoretical work of Social Democrats should be directed towards studying all the features of the social and political position of the various classes. But extremely little is done in this direction as compared with the work that is done in studying the features of factory life. In the committees and circles, you will meet men who are immersed, say, in the study of some special branch of the metal industry, but you will hardly ever find members of organizations (obliged, as often happens, for some reason or other to give up practical work) especially engaged in the collection of material concerning some pressing question of social and political life which could serve as a means for conducting Social Democratic work among other strata of the population. In speaking of the lack of training of the majority of present-day leaders of the labor movement, we cannot refrain from mentioning the point about training in this connection also, for it too is bound up with the "economic" conception of "close organic contact with the proletarian struggle." The principal thing, of course, is *propaganda and agitation* among all strata of the people.

.   .   .   .

Why is it that *not a single* political event takes place in Germany without adding to the authority and prestige of Social Democracy? Because Social Democracy is always found to be in advance of all others in its revolutionary estimation of every event and in its championship of every protest against tyranny. It does not soothe itself by arguments about the economic struggle bringing the workers up against their own lack of rights, and about concrete conditions fatalistically impelling the labor movement onto the path of revolution. It intervenes in every sphere and in every question of social and political life: in the matter of Wilhelm II's refusal to endorse a bourgeois progressive as city mayor (our economists have not yet managed to convince the Germans that this in fact is a compromise with liberalism!) ; in the question of the law against the publication of "immoral" publications and pictures; in the question of the government influencing the election of professors, etc., etc. Everywhere Social Democracy is found to be ahead of all others, rousing political discontent among all classes, rousing the sluggards, pushing on the laggards and providing a wealth of material for the development of the political consciousness and political activity of the proletariat. The result of all this is that even the avowed enemies of socialism are filled with respect for this advanced political fighter, and sometimes an important document from bourgeois and even from bureaucratic and Court circles makes its way by some miraculous means into the editorial office of *Vorwärts*. (*What Is To Be Done? Burning Questions of the Movement*, February, 1902, *Selected Works*, II, 85–87, 88, 89, 101, 114.)

For this point brings us squarely to the elucidation of the question presented by the Central Committee, namely: of permissible and impermissible statements in the press.

If the passage in the pamphlet we are examining had read: "The thirty-one were selling workers' votes to the Cadets for money"— it would have been an imputation of shameful and criminal deeds to an opponent. Anyone making such an imputation would deserve to be tried, and certainly not for "carrying confusion into the ranks of the proletariat," but for *libel*. This is perfectly clear.

On the other hand, if the passage in question had stated: "The thirty-one spoke in favor of adding workers' votes to Cadet votes on the condition that seats in the Duma were assured to the Social Democrats"— this would be an example of loyal, correct polemics, permissible to Party members.

What is the difference between *this* last quoted formulation and the one I chose? The difference is in the tone, the tone that makes the whole music. Exactly. The latter formulation is calculated to evoke in the reader hatred, aversion and contempt for people who commit such deeds. Such a formulation is calculated not to convince, but to break up the ranks of the opponent, not to correct the mistake of the opponent, but to destroy him, to wipe his organization off the face of the earth. This formulation is indeed of such a nature as to evoke the worst thoughts, the worst suspicions about the opponent and indeed, as contrasted with the formulation that convinces and corrects, it "carries confusion into the ranks of the proletariat."

I may be asked—well, do you admit that such formulations are *impermissible?* I shall answer: yes, certainly, *but only with the following little proviso:* impermissible among members of a *united party.* This proviso represents the whole crux of the question. The accusation which the Central Committee advances against me is wrong. I shall say more, it is dishonest, precisely because the Central Committee *remains silent* about the fact that at the time the pamphlet was written a united party *did not exist* in the organization from which it (not formally, but in essence) emanated, the aims of which it served. It is dishonest to advance a charge of publishing statements in the press "impermissible for a Party member" at a time when a *split* had taken place in the Party.

A split means the rupture of all organizational ties, the shifting of the struggle of ideas from the ground of influencing the organization from within to that of influencing it from without, from the ground of correcting and persuading comrades to that of destroying their organization, to the ground of inciting the masses of the workers (and the masses of the people generally) against the seceded organization.

What is impermissible among members of a united party is permissible and obligatory for the parts of a party that has been split. It is wrong to write about Party comrades in a language that systematically spreads among the working masses hatred, aversion, contempt, etc., for those who hold different opinions. But *one may and must write* in that strain about seceded organization.

Why must one? Because when a split has taken place it is one's duty to *wrest* the masses from the leadership of the seceded section. I am told: You carried confusion into the ranks of the proletariat. My answer is: I purposely and deliberately carried confusion into the ranks of the section of the St. Petersburg proletariat which followed the Mensheviks, who had seceded on the eve of the elections, and *I shall always* act in that way *whenever a split occurs.*

By my sharp offensive attacks on the Mensheviks on the eve of the elections in St. Petersburg, I actually succeeded in causing the ranks of the section of the proletariat which *trusts and follows the Mensheviks* to waver. That was my aim. That was my duty as a member of the St. Petersburg Social Democratic organization which was conducting the campaign of the Left *bloc;* because *after the split,* in order to conduct that campaign, *it was necessary* to break up the ranks of the Mensheviks who are leading the proletariat in the footsteps of the Cadets, it was necessary to carry confusion into their ranks, it was necessary to arouse among the masses hatred, aversion and contempt for these people who had ceased to be members of a united party, who had become political enemies, who were trying to put a spoke in the wheel of our Social Democratic organization in its election campaign. Against *such political* enemies I then conducted—and in the event of a repetition and development of a split *shall always conduct*—a fight of extermination.

If, after the split, which the Mensheviks engineered in St. Petersburg, we had not carried confusion into the ranks of the section of the proletariat which *followed the lead of the Mensheviks,* we would have been unable to carry on our Left *bloc* election campaign. My only regret is that, being away from St. Petersburg, I did not *sufficiently* contribute to this cause of *wresting* the masses from the influence of the seceded Mensheviks.

. . . .

They say: Fight, but not with a poisoned weapon. This is a very fine and striking expression, to be sure. But it is either a fine, empty phrase, or else it expresses in a vague and nebulous fashion the very same idea of struggle, of spreading among the masses hatred, aversion and contempt for the opponents—of a struggle that is impermissible in a united party, but inevitable and necessary when a split has occurred because of the very nature of the split, i.e., the idea which I expounded at the beginning of my speech. However much you twist this phrase, or this metaphor, you will not be able to squeeze a grain of real sense out of it except this difference between the loyal and correct method of fighting by means of argument within the organization and the method of fighting by means of a split, i.e., by destroying the enemy organization, by rousing among the masses hatred, aversion and contempt for this organization. The poisoned weapons are dishonest splits and not the war of extermination which results from a split that has already taken place.

Are there any limits to permissible struggle based on a split? There are no limits to such a struggle set by any Party standards, nor can there be such, for a split implies the cessation of the existence of the Party. The very idea that it is possible to fight against the methods of struggle that arise out of a split in the Party by Party methods, by means of Party decisions, etc., is ridiculous. The limits of the struggle based on a split are not Party limits, but general political limits, or rather general civil limits, the limits set by criminal law and nothing else.

.   .   .   .

Is it not clear that the employment of the most offensive and contemptuous mode of expression, which puts everything in the worst and not in the best light, is a method of fighting on the basis of a split, of fighting *for the extermination* of the organization which *disrupts* the political campaign of the local Social Democratic proletariat? (*Speech at the Party Trial,* February, 1907, *Selected Works,* III, 489–491, 493 f., 495.)

6. AESOPIAN LANGUAGE

When I speak of the narrow conception of Marxism, I have the Marxists themselves in mind. One cannot in this connection refrain from noting that Marxism is most atrociously narrowed and distorted by our liberals and radicals when they set about expounding it in the pages of the legal press. What sort of exposition is this! Only think how this revolutionary doctrine must be mutilated in order to fit it into the bed of Procrustes of the Russian censorship! Yet our publicists lightheartedly perform such an operation: Marxism as they expound it is reduced as it were to the doctrine of how under the capitalist system individual property, based on the labor of the owner, undergoes its dialectical development, how it becomes converted into its negation, and is then socialized. And with an air of seriousness, they assume the whole content of Marxism to lie in this "scheme," avoiding all the peculiarities of its sociological method, avoiding the doctrine of the class struggle and avoiding the direct purpose of the enquiry, namely, to expose all the forms of antagonism and exploitation in order to help the proletariat get rid of them.

It is not surprising that the result is something so pale and meager that our radicals begin to bewail the poor Russian Marxists. We should think so! Russian absolutism and Russian reaction would not be absolutism and reaction if it were possible while they exist to expound Marxism fully, exactly and completely, and to set forth all its conclusions to the full! And if our liberals and radicals knew Marxism as they should (at least, from German literature), they would have scruples to disfigure it so in the pages of the censored press. If a theory cannot be expounded—keep silent, or make the reservation that you are expounding it far from completely, that you are omitting the most essential. But when you are expounding only fragments, why cry about narrowness? (*What the "Friends of the People" Are and How They Fight the Social Democrats*, 1894, *Selected Works*, XI, 604.)

The peculiar position of Russia in regard to the point we are examining is that *the very beginning* of the spontaneous labor movement on the one hand, and the change of progressive public opinion toward Marxism on the other, was marked by the combination of obviously heterogeneous elements under a common flag for the purpose of fighting the common enemy (obsolete social and political views.) We refer to the heyday of "legal Marxism." Speaking generally, this was an extremely curious phenomenon that no one in the 1880's or the beginning of the 1890's would have believed possible. In a country ruled by an autocracy, in which the press is completely shackled, and in a period of intense political reaction in which even the tiniest outgrowth of political discontent and protest was suppressed, the theory of revolutionary Marxism suddenly forces its way into the *censored* literature, written in Aesopian[2] language, but understood by the "interested." The government had accustomed itself to regarding only the theory of (revolutionary) *Narodnaya Volya-ism* as dangerous, without observing its internal evolution, as is

---

[2] I.e., in parables, like *Aesop's Fables*.

usually the case, and rejoicing at the criticism levelled against it *no matter from what side it came.* Quite a considerable time elapsed (according to our Russian calculations) before the government realized what had happened and the unwieldy army of censors and police discovered the new enemy and flung itself upon him. Meanwhile, Marxian books were published one after another, Marxian journals and newspapers were published, nearly everyone became a Marxist, Marxism was flattered, the Marxists were courted and the book publishers rejoiced at the extraordinary, ready sale of Marxian literature. It was quite natural, therefore, that among the Marxian novices who were caught in this atmosphere, there should be more than one "author who got conceited. . . ." (*What Is To Be Done?* February, 1902, *Selected Works,* II, 39.)

The pamphlet here presented to the reader was written in Zürich in the spring of 1916. In the conditions in which I was obliged to work there I naturally suffered somewhat from a shortage of French and English literature and from a serious dearth of Russian literature. However, I made use of the principal English work, *Imperialism,* J. A. Hobson's book, with all the care that, in my opinion, that work deserves.

This pamphlet was written with an eye to the tsarist censorship. Hence, I was not only forced to confine myself strictly to an exclusively theoretical, mainly economic analysis of facts, but to formulate the few necessary observations on politics with extreme caution, by hints, in that Aesopian language—in that cursed Aesopian language—to which tsarism compelled all revolutionaries to have recourse whenever they took up their pens to write a "legal" work.[3]

It is very painful, in these days of liberty, to read these cramped passages of the pamphlet, crushed, as they seem, in an iron vise, distorted on account of the censor. Of how imperialism is the eve

---

[3]"Aesopian," after the Greek fable writer Aesop, was the term applied to the allusive and roundabout style adopted in "legal" publications by revolutionaries in order to evade the censorship.—*Ed.*

of the socialist revolution; of how social chauvinism (socialism in words, chauvinism in deeds) is the utter betrayal of socialism, complete desertion to the side of the bourgeoisie; of how the split in the labor movement is bound up with the objective conditions of imperialism, etc., I had to speak in a "slavish" tongue, and I must refer the reader who is interested in the question to the volume, which is soon to appear, in which are reproduced the articles I wrote abroad in the years 1914–17. In order to show, in a guise acceptable to the censors, how shamefully the capitalists and the social-chauvinist deserters (whom Kautsky opposes with so much inconsistency) lie on the question of annexations; in order to show with what cynicism they *screen* the annexations of *their* capitalists, I was forced to quote as an example—Japan! The careful reader will easily substitute Russia for Japan, and Finland, Poland, Courland, the Ukraine, Khiva, Bokhara, Estonia or other regions peopled by non-Great Russians, for Korea.

I trust that this pamphlet will help the reader to understand the fundamental economic question, viz., the question of the economic essence of imperialism, for unless this is studied, it will be impossible to understand and appraise modern war and modern politics. (*Imperialism, The Highest Stage of Capitalism,* Spring, 1916, *Selected Works,* V, 5 f.)

7. TERRORISM

The question of terror is certainly not a new one, and it will be sufficient briefly to recall the long-established views of Russian Social Democracy on this question to prove it.

We have never rejected terror on principle, nor can we do so. Terror is a form of military operation that may be usefully applied, or may even be essential in certain moments of the battle, under certain conditions, and when the troops are in a certain condition. The point is, however, that terror is now advocated, not as one of the operations the army in the field must carry out in close connection and in complete harmony with the whole system of fighting, but as an individual attack, completely separated from any army whatever. In view of the absence of a central revolutionary organization, terror cannot be anything but that. That is why we declare that under present circumstances such a method of fighting is inopportune and inexpedient; it will distract the most active fighters from their present tasks, which are more important from the standpoint of the interests of the whole movement, and will disrupt not the government forces, but the revolutionary forces. Recall recent events. Before our very eyes, broad masses of the urban workers and the urban "common people" rushed into battle, but the revolutionaries lacked a staff of leaders and organizers. Would not the departure of the most energetic revolutionaries to take up the work of terror under circumstances like these weaken the fighting detachments upon which alone serious hopes can be placed? Would it not threaten to break the contacts that exist between the revolutionary organizations and the disunited, discontented masses, who are expressing protest and who are ready for the fight, but who are weak simply because they are disunited? And these contacts are the only guarantee of our success. We would not for one moment assert that individual strokes of heroism are of no importance at all. But it is our duty to utter a strong warning against devoting all attention to terror, against regarding it as the principal method of struggle, as so many at the present time are inclined to do. Terror can never become the regular means of warfare; at best, it can only be of use as one of the methods of a final onslaught. (*Where To Begin,* May, 1901, *Selected Works,* II, 17 f.)

The specific arguments that *Svoboda* advanced in defense of terrorism. It "completely denies" the deterrent role of terrorism but instead stresses its "excitative significance." This is characteristic, first, as representing one of the stages of the breakup and decay of the traditional (pre-Social Democratic) cycle of ideas which insisted upon terrorism. To admit now that the government cannot be "terrified," and therefore disrupted, by terror, is tantamount to condemning terror as a system of struggle, as a sphere of activity sanctioned by the program. Secondly, it is still more characteristic as an example of the failure to understand our immediate task of "training the masses in revolutionary activity." *Svoboda* advocates terror as a means of "exciting" the labor movement, and of giving it a "strong impetus.' It is difficult to imagine an argument that disproves itself more than this one does! Are there not enough outrages committed in Russian life that a special "stimulant" has to be invented? On the other hand, is it not obvious that those who are not, and cannot be, roused to excitement even by Russian tyranny will stand by "twiddling their thumbs" even while a handful of terrorists are engaged in single combat with the government? The fact is, however, that the masses of the workers are roused to a high pitch of excitement by the outrages committed in Russian life, but we are unable to collect, if one may put it that way, and concentrate all these drops and little streams of popular excitement, which are called forth by the conditions of Russian life to a far larger extent than we imagine, but which it is precisely necessary to combine into a *single* gigantic flood. That this can be accomplished is irrefutably proved by the enormous growth of the labor movement, and the greed with which the workers devour political literature, to which we have already referred above. Calls for terror and calls to give the economic struggle itself a political character are merely two different forms of *evading* the most pressing duty that now rests upon Russian revolutionaries, namely, to organize all-sided political agitation. *Svoboda* desires to *substitute* terror for agitation, openly admitting that "as soon as intensified and strenuous agitation is commenced among the masses its excitative function will be finished." This proves precisely that both the terrorists and the Economists *underestimate* the revolutionary activity of the masses, in spite of the striking evidence of the events that took place in the spring,[4] and whereas one goes out in search of artificial "stimulants," the other talks about "concrete demands." But both, fail to devote sufficient attention to the development of *their own activity* in political agitation and organization of political exposures. And no other work can serve as a *substitute* for this work either at the present time or at any other time. (*What Is To Be Done?* February, 1902, *Selected Works,* II, 96 f.)

No verbal assurances or invocations can disprove the unques-

---

[4]This refers to the big street demonstrations which began in the spring of 1901. [Author's note to the 1908 edition.]

tionable fact that modern terrorism as it is practiced and preached by the Socialist Revolutionaries is not in any way linked with work among the masses, for the masses and together with the masses; that the organization of terroristic acts by the Party distracts the very scanty organizational forces we have from their difficult and by no means completed task of organizing a revolutionary *workers'* party; that *in practice* the terrorism of the Socialist Revolutionaries is nothing more than fighting in *single combat,* the sort of fighting that has been wholly condemned by the experience of history. Even foreign Socialists are beginning to be troubled by the noisy preaching of terrorism carried on today by our Socialist Revolutionaries. Among the masses of the Russian workers their preaching simply serves to sow harmful illusions, such as the idea that terrorism "compels people to think politically even against their will," or that it "is capable of changing the opinions of thousands of people about revolutionaries and the meaning of their activity better than months of oral propaganda," or that it is capable of "infusing new strength into those who vacillate, who have lost courage, who have been painfully struck by the sad outcome of many demonstrations," and so on. These harmful illusions can only result in early disappointment and slacken the work of preparing for the mass attack upon the autocracy. (*Why the Social Democrats Must Declare Determined and Relentless War on the Socialist Revolutionaries,* 1902, *Selected Works,* II, 196.)

If the revolution gains a decisive victory—then we shall settle accounts with tsarism in the Jacobin, or, if you like, in the plebeian way. "The terror in France," wrote Marx in 1848 in the famous *Die Neue Rheinische Zeitung,* "was nothing else than a plebeian method of settling accounts with the enemies of the bourgeoisie: with absolutism, feudalism and philistinism." Have those who, in a period of democratic revolution, try to frighten the Social Democratic workers in Russia with the bogey of "Jacobinism" ever stopped to think of the significance of these words of Marx? (*The Two Tactics of Social Democracy in the Democratic Revolution,* July, 1905, *Selected Works,* III, 84 f.)

We have always been accused of terrorism. It is a current

accusation and never leaves the pages of the press. We are accused of having established terrorism as a principle. To this we reply: "You yourselves do not believe this slander." ... We realize that the lies spread about us are beginning to lose their effect. We say that the terror was forced on us. They forget that terrorism was provoked by the attacks of the all-powerful Entente.... International imperialism has staked everything to crush the revolution; it stops at nothing and says: "One Communist for every officer, and we shall win!" And they are right. If we had tried to influence these troops, created by the international plunderers and brutalized by war, if we had tried to sway them by words and arguments, if we had tried to sway them by anything but terror, we would not have held out even for two months, we would have been fools. (*Report...*, December 5, 1919, *Selected Works*, VIII, 66.)

In connection with your report today regarding the methods of fighting saboteurs and counterrevolutionaries.

Would it not be possible to put through a decree *like the following?*

ON FIGHTING COUNTERREVOLUTIONARIES AND SABOTEURS

The bourgeoisie, the landowners and all the rich classes are making desperate efforts to undermine the revolution, the aim of which is to safeguard the interests of the workers, the toiling and exploited masses.

The bourgeoisie is prepared to commit the most heinous crimes; it is bribing the outcast and degraded elements of society and organizing them for pogroms. The supporters of the bourgeoisie, particularly among the higher employees, bank officials, and so on, are sabotaging, and are organizing strikes in order to thwart the government's measures for the realization of socialist reforms. They have even gone so far as to sabotage food distribution, thereby menacing millions of people with famine.

Special measures are necessary to fight the counterrevolutionaries and saboteurs. In virtue of this necessity, the Soviet of People's Commissars decrees:

1. Persons belonging to the wealthy classes (i.e., with incomes of 500 rubles or more per month, and owners of urban real estate, stocks and shares, or money amounting to over 1,000 rubles), and also all employees of banks, joint stock companies, state and public institutions, shall within three days present to their house committees written statements in three copies signed with their own signatures and indicating their address, income, place of employment and occupation.

2. The house committees shall countersign these statements, retain one copy and send one copy to the city administration and another to the People's Commissariat for Home Affairs (address:).

3. Persons guilty of non-observance of the present law (failing to make statements, giving false information, etc.) and members of house committees infringing the regulations governing the collection, preservation and presentation of these statements to the institutions mentioned above shall be liable to be fined a sum not exceeding 5,000 rubles for each such infringement, to imprisonment up to one year, or to be sent to the front, depending on the offense.

4. Persons sabotaging the work of, or declining to work in, banks, state and public institutions, joint stock companies, railways, etc., shall be liable to similar punishment.

5. As a first step toward universal labor service, it is decreed that the persons referred to in the first statement shall be obliged, first, constantly to carry with them a copy of the above-mentioned declaration certified by the house committees and by their chiefs or elected officials (shop committees, food committees, railway committees, employees' trade unions, etc.); the certificates must indicate what public service or work is being performed by the individual in question, or whether he is living with his family as a non-ablebodied member thereof, etc.

6. Secondly, such persons shall be obliged to acquire within one week from the issue of the present law consumers'-workers' books (specimen attached), in which shall be entered their weekly income and expenditures, and in which entries shall be made, certified by the proper committees or institutions, regarding the public duties performed by the individual in question.

7. Persons who do not come under the first statement shall present to their house committees a statement in one copy of their income and place of employment and shall carry with them another copy of this statement certified by the house committee. (*Note to F. E. Dzerzhinsky*, December 20, 1917, *Selected Works*, VI, 440 f.)

What did Crispien say about terror and violence? He said that these were two different things. Perhaps such a distinction may be drawn in textbooks on sociology, but it cannot be done in practical politics, particularly in the circumstances prevailing in Germany. Whether one likes it or not violence and terror will be employed against people who behave like the German officers who murdered Liebknecht and Rosa Luxemburg, against people who, like Stinnes and Krupp, and their like, bribe the press. It goes without saying that we need not declare beforehand that we shall resort to terror under any circumstances; but if German officers and the Kappists remain what they are now, if Krupp and Stinnes undergo no change, the employment of terror will be inevitable. (*Speech on the Condition of Affiliation to the Communist International*, July 30, 1920, *Selected Works*, X, 210.)

The deviation to the bad side is shown by the abuses committed by former government officials, landowners, bourgeois and other scum who have attached themselves to the Communists and whose conduct toward the peasantry is sometimes disgraceful and outrageous. Here there must be a terroristic purging; summary trial and death by shooting. Let the Martovs, the Chernovs, and the non-Party philistines like them, beat their breasts and exclaim: "I thank Thee, Lord, that I am not as one of 'these'; that I have never recognized, nor do I recognize, terror." These fools "do not recognize terror" because they chose for themselves the role of servile accomplices of the White Guards in fooling the workers and peasants. The Socialist Revolutionaries and Mensheviks "do not recognize terror" because under the flag of "socialism" they are fulfilling their function of *leading the masses into the reign of White Guard terror*. This was proved by the Kerensky and Kornilov regime in Russia, by the

Kolchak regime in Siberia, by menshevism in Georgia; it was proved by the heroes of the Second International and of the "Two-and-a-Half" International in Finland, Hungary, Austria, Germany, Italy, England, etc. Let the flunkey accomplices of White Guard terror praise themselves for repudiating all terror. We shall speak the bitter and undoubted truth; in countries that are experiencing an unprecedented crisis, the collapse of old ties, and the intensification of the class struggle after the imperialist war of 1914–18—and such are all the countries of the world— terror cannot be dispensed with notwithstanding the hypocrites and phrase-mongers. Either the White Guard, bourgeois terror of the American, British (Ireland), Italian (the fascists), German, Hungarian and other types, or Red proletarian terror. There is no middle course, no "third" course, nor can there be. (*The Food Tax. The Significance of the New Policy and Its Conditions*, April 21, 1921, *Selected Works*, IX, 192.)

8. PARTISAN WARFARE

The question of partisan actions has aroused great interest within the party and among the workers. . . . What are the basic questions every Marxist must ask when he analyzes the problem of the types of struggle? First of all, unlike primitive forms of socialism, Marxism does not tie the movement to any particular combat method. It recognizes the possibility that struggle may assume the most variegated forms. For that matter, Marxism does not "invent" those forms of struggle. It merely organizes the tactics of strife and renders them suitable for general use. It also renders the revolutionary classes conscious of the forms of the clashes which emerge spontaneously from the activities of the movement. Marxism rejects all abstract thinking and doctrinaire prescriptions about types of struggle. It calls for a careful study of the *mass struggle* which actually is taking place. As the movement develops, as the consciousness of the masses grows, and as the economic and political crises are becoming more intense, ever new and different methods of defense and attack will be used in the conflict. Hence, Marxism never will reject any particular combat method, let alone reject it forever. Marxism does not limit itself to those types of struggle which, at a given moment, are both practical and traditional. It holds that, due to changes in social conditions, new forms of battle will arise *inevitably,* although no one can foresee what the character of these future encounters will be. In this field, if we may say so, Marxism is *learning* from the practice of the masses. It is far from claiming that it should *teach* the masses tactics elaborated in the abstract by strategists of the pen. We know . . . that the coming crisis will present us with new and unpredictable forms of action.

Second, Marxism asks that the various types of struggle be analyzed within their *historical* framework. To discuss conflict outside of its historical and concrete setting is to misunderstand elementary dialectic materialism. At various junctures of the economic evolution, and depending upon changing political, national, cultural, social and other conditions, differing types of struggle may become important and even predominant. As a result of those [sociological] transformations, secondary and sub-ordinate forms of action may change their significance. To try and answer positively or negatively the question of whether a certain tactic is usable, without at the same time studying the concrete conditions confronting a given movement at a precise point of its development, would mean a complete negation of Marxism.

Those are the two basic concepts which must serve as our guide. The soundness of this approach has been confirmed by numerous examples from the history of western European Marxism. At present, European Socialists regard parliamentarism and trade unionism as their main method of struggle. Previously, they favored the armed uprising. . . . The European Socialists are perfectly willing to favor the uprising again should the situation change in the future.

During the 1870's, Social Democrats rejected the idea that the general strike could be used as a panacea tactic and as a non-political method suitable for the immediate overthrow of the bourgeoisie. But after the experience of 1905, the Social Democrats fully recognized the political mass strike as *a* means which, under *certain* conditions, could become necessary. Similarly, during the 1840's the Social Democrats recognized the utility of barricades. By the end of the nineteenth century, conditions had changed and the Socialists rejected the barricades as unsuitable. However, after the experience of the Moscow rising . . . they were willing to revise their position and again acknowledged the usefulness of barricades.

.   .   .   .

What is armed struggle? What are its forms and its causes? When did it originate? What has been the frequency of its occurrence? What is its significance for the general course of the revolution? What is its connection with the proletarian class struggle organized and waged by social democracy? After having described the general background of the problem, we shall now address ourselves to these questions.

Armed struggle is waged by small groups and individuals, some of whom are members of revolutionary parties. In certain regions of Russia, however, the *majority* [of the partisans] are not affiliated with any revolutionary organization. Armed struggle aims at two *different* objectives which must be distinguished *sharply* from one another. The first objective is to kill individuals such as high officials and lower-ranking members of the police and army. The second objective is to confiscate money from the government as well as from private persons. Portions of the captured money are used for party purposes, other portions for arms and the preparation of the rising, and the rest for the sustenance of persons engaging in the struggle. . . .

.   .   .   .

The aggravation of the political crisis to the point of armed insurrection, and especially the ever growing pauperization, famine and unemployment in villages and cities, were among the most potent causes leading to the emergence of armed combat. The *declassé* elements of the population, the *Lumpenproletariat* and anarchist groups, chose this struggle as the main and even *only* form of the social war. Autocracy answered with the tactics of martial law, conscription of younger military classes, Black Hundreds pogroms (Siedliec) and court martials.

Armed struggle often is considered to be anarchism, Blanquism, old-style terrorism and, at any rate, an activity perpetrated by isolated individuals out of touch with the masses.

. . . .

Those actions are related not only to the economic crisis but also to the political crisis. Traditional Russian terrorism was the work of plotting intellectuals. Now, workers or unemployed persons who are members of combat groups usually are leading this struggle. People who like to generalize according to abstract patterns easily may think of anarchism or Blanquism. In the face of an insurrectionist situation . . . such phrases learned by rote obviously are meaningless.

. . . .

The movement has not been disorganized by partisan struggles but by the weakness of the party, which does not know how to *take those actions into its own hands.* Consequently, the indictments against partisan warfare, so customary among us Russians, go together with secret, accidental and unorganized partisan actions which, indeed, do disorganize the party. If we do not understand the historical conditions of partisan warfare, then we shall be unable to eliminate its darker sides. In spite of everything, partisan operations occur [because they] are created by powerful economic and political causes. Since we are unable to get rid of those causes, we are unable to prevent this type of struggle. Our complaints about partisan warfare are nothing but complaints about the weakness of our party [which is incapable of] organizing the uprising.

What we said about disorganization also applies to demoralization. Partisan struggle as such does not produce demoralization, which results rather from *disorganization,* undisciplined armed actions and from lack of party leadership. Demoralization, which *unquestionably* has set in, cannot be overcome by disapproving and rejecting the [concept of] partisan struggle.

. . . .

In periods of grave economic and political crisis, the class struggle develops into civil war—that is, into an armed struggle between two parts of the people. In such periods, every Marxist is *obliged* to endorse the cause of civil war. From the Marxist point of view, moral condemnations of civil war are entirely unacceptable.

In situations of civil war, a *combat party* is the ideal type of a proletarian party.

.   .   .   .

One must accept assertions that partisan warfare disorganizes the [socialist] movement with skepticism. *Every* new form of struggle which involves new dangers and new sacrifices inevitably will "disorganize" organizations unprepared for the new tactics. Our old study groups became disorganized when agitational methods were adopted. Later on, our party committees were disorganized when the party took to demonstrations. In every war, new tactics carry a degree of disorganization into the battle ranks. Yet this is no argument against fighting a war. It merely follows that one must *learn* how to wage war. That is all there is to it.

.   .   .   .

. . . If a social democratic theoretician or writer fails to be saddened by . . . lack of preparedness and, on the contrary, displays proud self-satisfaction, and conceitedly and enthusiastically repeats slogans on anarchism, Blanquism and terrorism which he memorized in his early youth, then I consider this to be a degradation of the world's most revolutionary doctrine.

It is asserted that partisan actions lower the class-conscious proletariat to the level of drunkards and bums. This is correct. But from this follows only that the party of the proletariat never should consider partisan warfare to be its only or even its chief means of struggle. This particular technique must be integrated with other tactics and be in harmony with the most important methods of combat. Partisan warfare should be ennobled by the enlightening and organizing influence of socialism. (*The Guerilla Warfare*, September, 1906. Compare with *Collected Works*, 4th ed., II, 213–222.)

9. ANTIMILITARISM

No Social Democrat at all familiar with history, who has studied Engels, the great expert on this matter, ever doubted the tremendous importance of military knowledge, the tremendous importance of military technique and military organization as an instrument in the hands of the masses of the people and classes of the people for deciding the issue of great historical conflicts. Social Democracy never stooped to the game of military conspiracies, it never advanced military questions to the forefront until the conditions of incipient civil war had arisen. *But now all* Social Democrats have advanced military questions, if not to the very first, at least to one of the first places, and are now making it their business to study these questions and to popularize them among the masses of the people. The revolutionary army must employ military knowledge and military weapons in deciding the fate of the Russian people and in deciding the first and most urgent question of all, the question of liberty. (*The Revolutionary Army and the Revolutionary Government,* July, 1905, *Selected Works,* III, 315.)

The connection between the principles of militarism and of capitalism has been firmly established among Socialists, and there are no differences of opinion on that point. However, the recognition of this connection does not concretely define the antimilitarist *tactics* of the Socialists and does not solve the practical problem of how the struggle against the burden of militarism is to be carried on and how wars are to be prevented. And it is precisely in the answers to this question that one notes considerable divergence in the views of the Socialists. At the Stuttgart Congress these differences could be observed in a particularly palpable manner.

At one extreme we find German Social Democrats of the Vollmar type. They argue that since militarism is the child of capitalism, since wars are a necessary concomitant of capitalist development, there is no need for any special antimilitarist activity. That is exactly what Vollmar declared at the Essen *Parteitag.* On the question of what the Social Democrats are to do in the event of a declaration of war, the majority of the German Social Democrats—with Bebel and Vollmar at their head —persistently maintain that Social Democrats must defend their fatherland from attacks, that they are in duty bound to take part in a "defensive" war. This postulate led Vollmar to declare in Stuttgart that "all our love for humanity cannot prevent us from being good Germans," and led the Social Democratic deputy, Noske, to proclaim in the Reichstag that in the event of a war against Germany "the Social Democrats will not lag behind the bourgeois parties and will shoulder the rifle." From this position Noske had to take only one step more to declare: "We want Germany to be as well armed as possible."

The other extreme is represented by the small group of followers of Hervé. The Hervéists argue that the proletariat has no fatherland. Hence, all wars are waged in the interests of the capitalists; hence, the proletariat must fight against every kind of war. The proletariat must reply to every declaration of war by declaring a military strike and insurrection. This is what the antimilitarist propaganda must amount to in the main. Hence, in Stuttgart, Hervé proposed the following draft resolution:

> The congress demands that *every declaration of war, from whatever quarter it may emanate,* be answered *by a military strike and insurrection.*

Such are the two "extreme" positions on this question held among the western Socialists. The two diseases, which still cripple the activity of the socialist proletariat in the West, are reflected in them "like the sun in a drop of water": opportunist tendencies on one side, anarchist phrase-mongering on the other.

First of all, a few remarks about patriotism. That the "proletarians have no fatherland" is actually stated in the *Communist Manifesto*; that the position of Vollmar, Noske and Company is a "flagrant violation" of this fundamental proposition of *international* socialism is equally true. But it does not follow from this that Hervé and the Hervéists are right when they assert that it is immaterial to the proletariat in which fatherland it lives: whether it lives in monarchist Germany, republican France or despotic Turkey. The fatherland, i.e., the given political, cultural and social environment, is the most powerful factor in the class struggle of the proletariat, and if Vollmar is wrong in establishing a kind of "truly German" attitude of the proletariat towards the "fatherland," Hervé is not less wrong in treating such an important factor of the proletarian struggle for emancipation in an unpardonably uncritical fashion. The proletariat cannot treat the political, social and cultural conditions of its struggle with indifference or equanimity, consequently, it cannot remain indifferent to the destiny of its country. But it is interested in the destiny of its country only *insofar as* it affects its class struggle, and not by virtue of some bourgeois "patriotism," which sounds altogether indecent on the lips of a Social Democrat.

The other question is more complicated—the attitude toward militarism and war. It is obvious at the very first glance that Hervé confuses these two questions unpardonably and forgets the cause and effect as between capitalism and war; if the proletariat had adopted Hervé's tactics, it would have condemned itself to futile work: it would have used all its fighting preparedness (he talks of insurrection, does he not?) to fight the consequences (war), while allowing the cause (capitalism) to continue.

The anarchist method of reasoning is revealed here in full measure. The blind faith in the miraculous power of every *"action directe,"* the abstraction of this "direct action" from the general social and political situation without analyzing it in the least—in a word, "the arbitrary mechanical conception of social phenomena" (according to K. Liebknecht's expression) is obvious.

Hervé's plan is "very simple": On the day of the declaration of war the Socialist soldiers desert, and the reservists declare a strike and stay at home.

> [But] a reservists' strike is not passive resistance: the working class would soon pass on to open resistance, to insurrection, and this latter would have more chances of success, because the active army would be on the frontier of the country. (G. Hervé, *Leur Patrie.*)

Such is this "effective, direct and practical plan," and, certain of its success, Hervé proposes to reply to every declaration of war by a military strike and insurrection.

As is clearly seen from the above, the question here is not whether the proletariat should, when it deems it expedient, reply to a declaration of war by a strike and insurrection. The controversy centers around the question as to whether the proletariat should be bound by an obligation to reply to *every* war by insurrection. To adopt the latter policy means depriving the proletariat of the choice of the moment for the decisive battle and leaving that choice to its enemies. It is not the proletariat that is to choose the moment of struggle in accordance with its own interests, when its general socialist class-consciousness is at its height, when it is well organized, when the ground is favorable, etc., etc.; no, the bourgeois governments could provoke it to an uprising even when the conditions were unfavorable for it....

The proletariat may reply to the declaration of war by a military strike if it finds it expedient and appropriate; it may, among other methods of achieving the social revolution, resort also to a military strike; but it is not in the interests of the proletariat to bind itself down to this "tactical recipe."

.   .   .   .

While the views of the Hervéists are "heroic folly," the position of Vollmar, Noske and their adherents of the "right wing" is, on the other hand, opportunist cowardice. Since militarism is the offspring of capital and will fall with it—they argued in Stuttgart, and especially in Essen—there is no need for special antimilitarist agitation: no such agitation should be carried on. But—was the rejoinder made to them in Stuttgart—the radical solution of the labor and women's problems, for instance, is also impossible so long as the capitalist system prevails; nevertheless, we are fighting for labor legislation, for the extension of civil rights to women, etc. Special antimilitarist propaganda must be conducted all the more energetically because cases of the intervention of military forces in the struggle between labor and capital become increasingly frequent, and the importance of militarism not only during the present struggle of the proletariat, but also in the future, at the moment of the social revolution, becomes increasingly obvious.

The need for special antimilitarist propaganda is supported not only by proof based on principles but also by important historical experience....

Simultaneously with agitation in the press, intense oral agitation is carried on. . . . Antimilitarist propaganda does not stop at the doorstep of the barracks; the Socialist soldiers form groups for the purpose of carrying on propaganda in the army. . . .

Special antimilitarist activity is not only particularly necessary, but practically expedient and useful. Therefore, inasmuch as Vollmar opposed it, pointing to the impossible police conditions in Germany and to the danger of the Party organizations being smashed on this account, the question was reduced to a concrete analysis of the conditions in the given country, to a question of fact and not to a question of principle. (*Militant Militarism and the Antimilitarist Tactics of Social Democracy*, August, 1908, *Selected Works*, IV, 326–331.)

It must be the task of the Social Democrats in every country, first of all, to fight against the chauvinism of their own country. In Russia this chauvinism has wholly affected bourgeois liberalism (the "Cadets") and partly the Narodniki, right down to the Socialist Revolutionaries and the "Right" Social Democrats. In particular, it is necessary to brand the chauvinist declarations of such men as E. Smirnov, P. Maslov and G. Plekhanov, for example, which have been taken up and widely utilized by the bourgeois "patriotic" press.

Under present conditions, it is impossible to determine, from the standpoint of the international proletariat, whether the defeat of one or the other group of belligerent nations is the lesser evil for socialism. For us Russian Social Democrats, however, there cannot be the slightest doubt that, from the standpoint of the working class and of the toiling masses of all nations of Russia, the lesser evil would be the defeat of the tsarist monarchy, of the most reactionary and barbarous government that is oppressing the greatest number of nations and the largest mass of the population of Europe and Asia. (*The War and Russian Social Democracy*, October, 1914, *Selected Works*, V, 128 f.)

A revolutionary class in a reactionary war cannot but desire the defeat of its government.

This is an axiom. It is disputed only by the conscious partisans or the helpless satellites of the social-chauvinists. . . . To desire Russia's defeat, Trotsky says, is "an uncalled-for and unjustifiable concession to the political methodology of social patriotism which substitutes for the revolutionary struggle against the war and the conditions that cause it, what, under present conditions, is an extremely arbitrary orientation toward the lesser evil."

This is an example of the high-flown phraseology. . . . A "revolutionary struggle against the war" is an empty and meaningless exclamation, . . . *unless* it means revolutionary action against *one's own government* even in time of war. One has only to think a little in order to understand this. And revolutionary action in wartime against one's own government undoubtedly and incontrovertibly means not only desiring its defeat, but really facilitating such defeat. . . .

Revolution in wartime is civil war; and the *transformation* of war between governments into civil war is, on the one hand, facilitated by military reverses ("defeats") of governments; on the other hand, it is *impossible* really to strive for such a transformation without thereby facilitating defeat. (*Defeat of One's Own Government in the Imperialist War*, August, 1915, *Selected Works*, V, 142 f.)

Not a single great revolution has ever refrained from "disorganizing" the army and cannot now refrain from doing so; because the army is the most rigid instrument for supporting the old regime, the most hardened bulwark of bourgeois discipline, of the rule of capital, of preserving among the toiling masses and imbuing them with the servile spirit of submission and subjection to capital. Counterrevolution has never tolerated, and never could tolerate, the armed workers side by side with the army. Engels wrote that in France, after each revolution, the workers were armed: "Therefore the disarming of the workers was the first commandment for whatever bourgeois group was at the helm of the state."

The armed workers were the embryo of a *new* army, the nucleus of the organization of a *new* social order. The first commandment of the bourgeoisie was: Crush this nucleus, prevent it from growing. The first commandment of every victorious revolution, as Marx and Engels repeatedly emphasized, was: Smash the old army, dissolve it and replace it by a new one. In rising to power the new social class never could, and cannot now, attain power or consolidate it except by absolutely disintegrating the old army ("disorganization!" the reactionary or cowardly philistines will howl), except by passing through a most difficult and painful period without any army (as was the case also during the French Revolution) and by gradually building up in the midst of the civil war a new army, a new discipline, a new military organization of the new class. (*The Proletarian Revolution and the Renegade Kautsky*, 1918, *Selected Works*, VII, 174.)

The recognition of internationalism in words, and substituting for it in deeds, in all propaganda, agitation and practical work, petty bourgeois nationalism and pacifism, is a common occurrence, not only among the parties affiliated to the Second International, but also among those which have withdrawn from that International, and not infrequently, even among those which now call themselves Communist parties. The struggle against this evil, against these most deep-rooted petty bourgeois national prejudices, comes more and more to the forefront in proportion as the task of transforming the dictatorship of the proletariat from a national one (i.e., existing in one country and incapable of determining world politics) into an international one (i.e., the dictatorship of the proletariat covering at least several advanced countries and capable of exercising decisive influence upon the whole of world politics) becomes the question of the day. Petty bourgeois nationalism declares the recognition of the equality of nations, and nothing else, to be internationalism, while preserving intact national egoism (quite apart from the purely verbal character of this recognition), whereas proletarian internationalism demands, firstly, the subordination of the interests of the proletarian struggle in one country to the interests of the struggle on a world scale; and secondly, it calls for the ability and readiness on the part of the nations which are achieving victory over the bourgeoisie to make the greatest national sacrifices for the sake of overthrowing international capital. (*Preliminary Draft of Theses on the National and Colonial Question,* June, 1920, *Selected Works,* X, 235 f.)

Only a revolutionary party which has been built up beforehand is well tried and has a good illegal apparatus can successfully wage a struggle against war, . . . the means of combating war are not a strike against war, but the formation of revolutionary nuclei in the combatant armies, their training for the purpose of bringing about revolution. (*The Question of Combating War,* February 4, 1922, *Selected Works,* X, 315.)

10. War

In this question (as also in views on "patriotism") it is not the offensive or defensive character of the war, but the interests of the class struggle of the proletariat, or rather, the interests of the international movement of the proletariat that represent the only possible point of view from which the question of the attitude of Social Democracy toward a given phenomenon in international relations can be considered and solved. (*Militant Militarism and the Antimilitarist Tactics of Social Democracy,* August, 1908, *Selected Works,* IV, 332.)

One of the forms of deception of the working class is pacifism and the abstract preaching of peace. Under capitalism, particularly in its imperialist stage, wars are inevitable. On the other hand, Social Democrats cannot deny the positive significance of revolutionary wars, i.e., not imperialist wars, but such as were conducted, for instance, between 1789 and 1871, for the purpose of abolishing national oppression and creating national capitalist states out of the separate feudal states, or of possible wars for the defense of the gains of the victorious proletariat in the struggle against the bourgeoisie.

Propaganda of peace at the present time, if not accompanied by a call for revolutionary mass action, is only capable of spreading illusions, of demoralizing the proletariat by imbuing it with belief in the humanitarianism of the bourgeoisie, and of making it a plaything in the hands of the secret diplomacy of the belligerent countries. In particular, the idea that a so-called democratic peace is possible without a series of revolutions is profoundly mistaken. (*Conference of the Sections of the Russian Social Democratic Labor Party Abroad,* March, 1915, *Selected Works,* V, 135.)

Applied to wars, the main thesis of dialectics . . . is that *"war is simply the continuation of politics by other* (i.e., violent) *means."* This formula belongs to Clausewitz, one of the greatest writers on the history of war, whose ideas were fertilized by Hegel. And this was always the standpoint of Marx and Engels, who regarded *every* war as the *continuation* of the politics of the given interested powers—and the *various classes* within these countries—at a given time. (*The Collapse of the Second International,* June, 1915, *Selected Works,* V, 179 f.)

Just as all war is but the continuation by violent means of the politics which the belligerent states and the classes that rule in them have been conducting for many years, sometimes for decades before the outbreak of war, so the peace that succeeds every war can be nothing else than a summing up and registration of the changes in the relation of forces brought about in the course of, and in consequence of, the given war. (*Proposals . . . ,* April, 1916, *Selected Works,* V, 232.)

. . . Socialists, without ceasing to be Socialists, cannot oppose any kind of war. In the first place, Socialists never have and never could oppose revolutionary wars. . . . In the second place civil wars are also wars. He who accepts the class struggle cannot fail to recognize civil wars which under any class society represent the natural, and under certain conditions, inevitable continuation of the development and aggravation of class struggle. . . . In the third place, socialism, victorious in one country does not exclude forthwith all wars in general. On the contrary, it presupposes them. The development of capitalism proceeds highly unevenly in various countries. This cannot be otherwise under the conditions of commodity production. From this follows the unavoidable conclusion: Socialism cannot win simultaneously *in all* countries. It will win initially in one or several countries, while the remainder will remain for some time, either bourgeois or pre-bourgeois. This should result not only in frictions, but also in the direct striving of the bourgeoisie of other countries to smash the victorious proletariat of the socialist state. In such cases, a war on our part would be lawful and just. This would be a war for socialism, for the liberation of other peoples from the bourgeoisie. Engels was completely right when in his letter to Kautsky of September 12, 1882, he directly recognized the possibility of "defensive wars" by *already victorious* socialism. He had in mind exactly the defense of the victorious proletariat against the bourgeoisie of other countries.

Only after we overthrow, completely defeat and expropriate the bourgeoisie in the entire world, and not only in one country, will wars become impossible. And from the scientific point of view, it would be completely incorrect and completely unrevolutionary to by-pass or tone down the most important, the suppression of the resistance of the bourgeoisie—which is the most difficult, the most struggle-requiring (aspect) of transition to socialism. "Social" priests and opportunists are always ready to dream of future peaceful socialism, but this is precisely the way they differ from revolutionary Social Democrats, because they do not wish to think and ponder the embittered class struggle and class wars which are required in order to bring about this wonderful future.

Theoretically, it would be absolutely mistaken to forget that every war is merely a continuation of politics by other means; that the present imperialistic war is a continuation of imperialistic policies of two groups of great powers, and this policy has been engendered and is fed by the totality of relations of the imperialistic epoch. But the same epoch must necessarily also engender and feed the policy of struggle against national oppression and of the struggle of the proletariat against the bourgeoisie, and consequently the possibility and inevitability, in the first place, of revolutionary national uprisings and wars; in the second place, of wars and uprisings of the proletariat against the bourgeoisie; in the third place, of unification of both types of revolutionary wars, etc. . . . (*Military Program of Proletarian Revolution*, 1916 (pub. 1917), *Collected Works* (New York: International Publishers, 1942), XIX, 362–366.)

The war is not a product of the evil will of rapacious capitalists, although it is undoubtedly being fought *solely* in their interests and they alone are enriched by it. The war is a product of half a century of development of world capitalism and of its million threads and connections. One *cannot* escape from the imperialist war, one *cannot* achieve a democratic, non-oppressive peace without first overthrowing the power of capital and without the transfer of the power of state to another class, the proletariat.

The Russian revolution of February–March, 1917, was the beginning of the transformation of the imperialist war into a civil war. The revolution took the *first* step toward ending the war; but it requires a *second* step, namely, the transfer of the power of state to the proletariat, to make the end of the war a certainty. This will be the beginning of a "breach in the front" on a worldwide scale, a breach in the front of the interests of capital; and only after having broken *this* front *can* the proletariat save mankind from the horrors of war and endow it with the blessings of a durable peace. (*How Can the War Be Ended?* April 23, 1917, *Selected Works,* VI, 55.)

We are not pacifists and cannot renounce revolutionary war. Wherein does a revolutionary war differ from a capitalist war? Chiefly by the class that has an interest in the war and by the policy that the interested class pursues in the war. . . . When we address the masses, we must give them concrete answers. How can one distinguish a revolutionary war from a capitalist war? The rank-and-file masses do not grasp the distinction, do not realize that the distinction is one of classes. We must not confine ourselves to theory, but must demonstrate in practice that we can wage a truly revolutionary war only when the proletariat is in power. It seems to me that by putting the matter thus we give a clearer answer to the question of what the nature of the war is and who is waging it. (*Report* . . . , May, 1917, *Selected Works*, VI, 96.)

History suggests that peace is a respite for another war, war is a method of obtaining a somewhat better or somewhat worse peace. (*War and Peace*, March 7, 1918, *Selected Works*, VII, 302.)

Marxists have never forgotten that violence will be an inevitable accompaniment of the collapse of capitalism on its full scale and of the birth of a socialist society. And this violence will cover a historical period, a whole era of wars of the most varied kinds—imperialist wars, civil wars within the country, the interweaving of the former with the latter, national wars, the emancipation of the nationalities crushed by the imperialists and by various combinations of imperialist powers which will inevitably form various alliances with each other in the era of vast state-capitalist and military trusts and syndicates. This is an era of tremendous collapses, of wholesale military decisions of a violent nature, of crises. It has already begun, we see it clearly—it is only the beginning. (*Report* . . . , March 8, 1918, *Selected Works*, VIII, 315 f.)

Socialism is opposed to violence against nations. That is indisputable. But socialism is opposed to violence against men in general. Apart from Christian Anarchists and Tolstoyans, however, no one has yet drawn the conclusion from this that socialism is opposed to *revolutionary* violence. Hence, to talk about "violence" in general, without examining the conditions which distinguish reactionary from revolutionary violence, means being a petty bourgeois who renounces revolution, or else it means simply deceiving oneself and others by sophistry.

The same holds good about violence against nations. Every war is the exercise of violence against nations, but that does not prevent socialists from being in *favor* of a revolutionary war. The class character of the war—that is the fundamental question which confronts a Socialist.

.   .   .   .

All philistines, and all stupid and ignorant yokels argue: . . . "The enemy has invaded my country; I do not care about anything else."[5]

The Socialist, the revolutionary proletarian, the internationalist, argues differently. He says: "The character of the war (whether reactionary or revolutionary) is not determined by who the aggressor was, or whose territory the 'enemy' has occupied; it is *determined by the class* that is waging the war, and the politics of which this war is a continuation." If the war is a reactionary, imperialist war, that is, if it is being waged by two world coalitions of the imperialist, violent, predatory reactionary bourgeoisie, then every bourgeoisie (even of the smallest country) becomes a participant in the plunder, and my duty as a representative of the revolutionary proletariat is to prepare for the *world proletarian revolution* as the *only* escape from the horrors of a world war. I must argue, not from the point of view of "my" country (for this is the argument of a poor, stupid, nationalist philistine who does not realize that he is only a plaything in the hands of the imperialist bourgeoisie), but from the point of view of *my share* in the preparation, in the propaganda and in the accelerations of the world proletarian revolution.

This is what internationalism is, and this is the duty of the internationalist, of the revolutionary worker, of the genuine

---

[5]The social-chauvinists (the Scheidemanns, Renaudels, Hendersons, Gompers and company) absolutely refuse to talk about the "International" during the war. They regard the enemies of their respective bourgeoisies as "traitors" to socialism. They *support* the policy of conquest of their respective bourgeoisies. The social pacifists (*i.e.*, the socialists in words and petty bourgeois pacifists in practice) express all sorts of "internationalist" sentiments, protest against annexations, etc., but in practice, they continue to support their respective imperialist bourgeoisies. The difference between the two types is slight. It is like the difference between two capitalists—one with rude, and the other with sweet words on his lips.

Socialist. (*The Proletarian Revolution and the Renegade Kautsky*, 1918, *Selected Works*, VII, 175, 177.)

The building up of a Red Army was an entirely new question, one which had never been treated even theoretically. . . . We have undertaken a task which nobody in the world has ever attempted on so large a scale.

That is also true of the Red Army. When, upon the conclusion of the war, the army began to disintegrate, many people thought that this was a purely Russian phenomenon. But we see that the Russian revolution was in fact the dress rehearsal, or one of the rehearsals, for the world proletarian revolution. . . .

We proceeded from experiment to experiment; we endeavored to create a volunteer army, feeling our way, testing the ground and experimenting how the problem could be solved in the given situation. And the nature of the problem was clear. Unless we defended the socialist republic by force of arms, we could not exist. A ruling class will never surrender its power to an oppressed class. And the latter must prove in practice that it is capable not only of overthrowing the exploiters, but also of organizing its self-defense and of staking everything for that purpose. We have always said that there are wars and wars. We condemned the imperialist war, but we did not reject *war in general*. Those who attempted to accuse us of militarism got themselves hopelessly muddled. And when I had occasion to read the report on the Berne Conference of the yellow Socialists, where Kautsky declared that what the Bolsheviks had was militarism and not socialism, I smiled and shrugged my shoulders. As though history has ever known a big revolution that was not involved in war! Of course not. We are living not merely in a state, but in *a system of states,* and the existence of the Soviet Republic side by side with imperialist states for a long time is unthinkable. One or the other must triumph in the end. And before that end supervenes, a series of frightful collisions between the Soviet Republic and the bourgeois states will be inevitable. That means that if the ruling class, the proletariat, wants to hold sway, it must prove its capacity to do so by its military organization also. . . . How was a class which had hitherto served as cannon fodder for the military commanders of the dominant imperialist class to create its own commanders? How was it to solve the problem of combining the enthusiasm and the new revolutionary creative spirit with the employment of the stock of bourgeois science and military technique in its worst form, without which it is incapable of mastering the modern technique and the modern methods of conducting war? . . . I do not recall that the old teachers of socialism, who foresaw a great deal of what would take place in the future socialist revolution and discerned many of its features, ever expressed themselves on this question. It did not exist for them, for it arose only when we proceeded to create a Red Army. That meant creating out of an oppressed class, which had been turned into cannon fodder, an army inspired by enthusiasm and compelling that army to make use of all that was most coercive and abhorrent in what we had inherited from capitalism. (*Report* . . . , March 18, 1919, *Selected Works*, VIII, 32–34.)

We must declare to the other nations that we are out-and-out internationalists and are striving for a voluntary union of the workers and peasants of all nations. This in no way precludes wars. . . . We have never said that a socialist republic can exist without military force. War may be a necessity under certain conditions. (*Reply* . . . , May 19, 1919, *Selected Works*, VIII, 366.)

The imperialist war was a continuation of the imperialist policy and therefore led to revolution. During the imperialist war everybody felt that it was being waged by the bourgeoisie on behalf of its own rapacious interests, that while the people were perishing in the war the bourgeoisie was piling up wealth. That is its fundamental motive, the motive that inspires its policy in every country, and that is what is ruining it and will ruin it completely. But our war is a continuation of the policy of the revolution, and every worker and peasant knows—and if he does not know it he instinctively feels and sees it—that this war is being waged as a defense against the exploiters, that it is a war which is imposing burdens most of all on the workers and peasants, but which will stop at nothing to transfer those burdens to other classes. We know that it is much more difficult for them than for the workers and peasants because they belonged to a privileged class. But we assert that when it is a matter of liberating millions of toilers from exploitation, a government which would hesitate to lay the burden of sacrifice on other classes would be not a socialist government, but a government of traitors. We are laying the burden on the middle classes because the governments of the Entente have placed us in an incredibly difficult situation. And—as we see from the experience of our revolution, although I cannot dwell on it now—every stage in our victory is accompanied by the fact that, in spite of all their waverings and innumerable attempts to turn back, larger and larger numbers of representatives of the vacillating elements are becoming convinced that there is indeed no choice except between a dictatorship of the toilers and the power of the exploiters. If times have been difficult for these elements, it is not the Bolshevik government that is to blame, but the White Guards and the Entente. And a victory over them will be a real and durable condition for the improvement of the position of these classes. . . . Our war is a continuation of the policy of the revolution, of the policy of overthrowing the exploiters, the capitalists and the landowners. That is why our war, unutterably difficult though it may be, is earning us the sympathies of the workers and peasants. War is not only a continuation of politics but also a summation of politics; it is an education in politics. (*Report . . .*, December 5, 1919, *Selected Works,* VIII, 67 f.)

We have waged the war for peace with extreme vigor. This war is producing excellent results. We have made a very good showing in this sphere of the struggle, at any rate not worse than in the sphere of the operations of the Red Army, on the bloody front. . . . But the measures we take for peace must be accompanied by an intensification of our military preparedness, and in no case must our army be disarmed. Our army offers a real guarantee that not the slightest attempt will be made on us by the imperialist powers; for although they may count on certain ephemeral successes at first, not one of them will escape defeat at the hands of Soviet Russia. That we must realize, that must be made the basis of our agitation and propaganda, that is what we must prepare for. And we must solve the problem which ... compels us to combine the one with the other. (*Report* ..., March 29, 1920, *Selected Works,* VIII, 86 f.)

That war is brewing, that war is inevitable, is beyond doubt. The pacifists are trying to evade this question, to obscure it by general phrases; but anybody who studies the history of economic relations and diplomacy cannot entertain the slightest doubt that an economic war is ripe and is being prepared politically. One cannot take up a single book devoted to this question without seeing that war is ripening. (*Speech* ..., November 26, 1920, *Selected Works,* VIII, 283.)

Hitherto, the fate of all revolutions, of all great revolutions, has been decided by long series of wars. Our revolution is one of these great revolutions. We have passed through one period of war and we must prepare for a second. But we do not know when it will come, and we must see to it that when it does come we shall be prepared for all eventualities. It is for this reason that we must not refuse to resort to measures of compulsion. (*Report* ..., December 22, 1920, *Selected Works,* VIII, 261.)

Can we save ourselves from a future conflict with these imperialist states? Do we have any hope that internal contradictions and conflicts among the prosperous imperialist states of the West and the prosperous imperialist states of the East will give us another time period as they gave us once before when the campaign of western European counterrevolution directed toward supporting the Russian counterrevolution miscarried due to the contradictions in the Western and Eastern counterrevolutionary camp, in the camp of Eastern exploiters and Western exploiters, in the camp of Japan and America?

One should reply to this question, it seems to me, by saying that the solution depends in this instance on too many circumstances, and the outcome of the struggle, in its entirety and generally speaking, may be foreseen only on the grounds that the gigantic majority of the population of the earth finally becomes educated and trained for struggle by capitalism itself.

The outcome of the struggle depends, in its final account, on the fact that Russia, India, China, etc., compose the gigantic majority of the population. And it is precisely this majority of the population which is being drawn with uncommon speed during the last few years into struggle for its liberation, so that in this respect there can be not a shadow of doubt as to the final conclusion of the world struggle. In this respect, the final victory of socialism is fully and unconditionally guaranteed. (*Better Less, But Better,* March, 1923. Compare with *Collected Works,* 4th ed., XXXIII, 458.)

Were an army, which is convinced that it is incapable of taking a fort by storm, to declare that it refuses to abandon former positions, will not occupy new ones, and will not shift to other methods of solving a problem—one would say about such an army that anyone who has learnt to advance and has not learnt to retreat under certain difficult conditions adapting oneself thereto, will fail to end the war victoriously. There were never in world history wars which started and ended in a completely victorious offensive, or if such wars occurred they were exceptions. And this refers only to ordinary wars. As to a war where the fate of a whole class is at stake, where the question of whether it is to be socialism or capitalism is being decided—are there any reasonable foundations to suppose that a people resolving this problem for the first time can immediately find the only correct unerring method? What basis is there for such suppositions? None! Experience says the contrary. There was not a single task of those we solved which failed to demand of us repeated decision to tackle it. The way we worked, the way one should continue to work is, after experiencing defeat, to tackle the problem a second time, to redo everything, and to find a way of approaching the solution of the problem, not the final correct solution, but a solution which would at least be satisfactory.... (*Report* ..., October 29, 1921. Compare with *Collected Works,* 4th ed., XXXIII, 74.)

XI

CULTURE

Popularization . . . is very different from vulgarization, from currying general favor. The popular writer leads his reader toward profound thoughts, toward profound study, proceeding from simple and generally known facts; with the aid of simple arguments or striking examples he demonstrates how the main conclusions are to be drawn from those facts and always generates in the mind of the thinking reader new questions. The popular writer does not presuppose a reader who does not think, who cannot or does not wish to think; on the contrary, he assumes in the undeveloped reader a serious intention to use his head and aids him in his serious and difficult work, leads him, helps him take his first steps and teaches him how to proceed independently. The vulgar writer assumes that his reader does not think and is incapable of thinking; he does not help him take his first steps toward serious knowledge, but in a distorted and simplified form, interlarded with jokes and facetiousness, hands out "ready-made" *all* the conclusions of a given theory, so that the reader does not even have to chew but merely to swallow. (Autumn, 1901, *Collected Works* (1961), V, 311–312.)

What is this principle of party literature? It is not simply that, for the socialist proletariat, literature cannot be a means of enriching individuals or groups: it cannot, in fact, be an individual undertaking, independent of the common cause of the proletariat. Down with non-partisan writers! Down with literary supermen! Literature must become part of the common cause of the proletariat, "a cog and a screw" of one single great Social Democratic mechanism set in motion by the entire politically conscious vanguard of the entire working class. Literature must become a component of organized, planned and integrated Social Democratic party work.

"All comparisons are lame," says a German proverb. So is my comparison of literature with a cog, of a living movement with a mechanism. And I daresay there will ever be hysterical intellectuals to raise a howl about such a comparison, which degrades, deadens, "bureaucratizes" the free battle of ideas, freedom of criticism, freedom of literary creation, etc., etc. Such outcries, in point of fact, would be nothing more than an expression of bourgeois-intellectual individualism. There is no question that literature is least of all subject to mechanical adjustment of leveling, to the rule of the majority over the minority. There is no question, either, that in this field greater scope must undoubtedly be allowed for personal initiative, individual inclination, thought and fantasy, form and content. All this is undeniable; but all this simply shows that the literary side of the proletarian party cause cannot be mechanically identified with its other sides. This, however, does not in the least refute the proposition, alien and strange to the bourgeoisie and bourgeois democracy, that literature must by all means and necessarily become an element of Social Democratic party work, inseparably bound up with the other elements. Newspapers must become the organs of the various party organizations, and their writers must by all means become members of these organizations. Publishing and distributing centers, bookshops and reading rooms, libraries and similar establishments—must all be under Party control. The organized socialist proletariat must keep an eye on all this work, supervise it in its entirety, and, from beginning to end, without any exception, infuse into it the life-stream of the living proletarian cause, thereby cutting the ground from under the old, semi-Oblomov, semi-shopkeeper Russian principle: the writer does the writing, the reader does the reading. . . .

What! some intellectual, an ardent champion of liberty, may shout. What, you want to impose collective control on such a delicate, individual matter as literary work! You want workmen to decide questions of science, philosophy or aesthetics by a majority of votes! You deny the absolute freedom of absolutely individual ideological work!

Calm yourselves, gentlemen! First of all, we are discussing Party literature and its subordination to Party control. Everyone is free to write and say whatever he likes, without any restrictions. But every voluntary association (including a pary) is also free to expel members who use the name of the party to advocate anti-Party views. Freedom of speech and the press must be complete. But then freedom of association must be complete too. I am bound to accord you, in the name of free speech, the full right to shout, lie and write to your heart's content. But you are bound to grant me, in the name of freedom of association, the right to enter into, or withdraw from, association with people advocating this or that view. The Party is a voluntary association, which would inevitably break up, first ideologically and then physically, if it did not cleanse itself of people advocating anti-Party views. And to define the border line between Party and anti-Party there is the Party program, the Party's resolutions on tactics and its rules and lastly, the entire experience of international Social Democracy, the voluntary international association of the proletariat, which has constantly brought into its parties individual elements and trends not fully consistent, not completely Marxist and not altogether correct and which, on the other hand, has constantly conducted periodical "cleansings" of its ranks. So it will be with us too, supporters of bourgeois "freedom of criticism," within the Party. We are now becoming a mass party all at once, changing abruptly to an open organization, and it is inevitable that we shall be joined by many who are inconsistent (from the Marxist standpoint), perhaps we shall be joined even by some Christian elements, and even by some mystics. We have sound stomachs and we are rock-like Marxists. We shall digest those inconsistent elements. Freedom of thought and freedom of criticism within the Party will never make us forget about the freedom of organizing people into those voluntary associations known as parties.

Secondly, we must say to you bourgeois individualists that your talk about absolute freedom is sheer hypocrisy. There can be no real and effective "freedom" in a society based on the power of money, in a society in which the masses of working people live in poverty and the handful of rich live like parasites. Are you free in relation to your bourgeois publisher, Mr. Writer, in relation to your bourgeois public, which demands that you provide it with pornography in frames and paintings, and prostitution as a "supplement" to "sacred" scenic art? This absolute freedom is a bourgeois or an anarchist phrase (since, as a world outlook, anarchism is bourgeois philosophy turned inside out). One cannot live in society and be free from society. The freedom of the bourgeois writer, artist or actress is simply masked (or hypocritically masked) dependence on the money-bag, on corruption, on prostitution.

And we Socialists expose this hypocrisy and rip off the false labels, not in order to arrive at a non-class literature and art (that will be possible only in a socialist extra-class society), but to contrast this hypocritically free literature, which is in reality linked to the bourgeosie, with a really free one that will be openly linked to the proletariat.

It will be a free literature, because the idea of socialism and sympathy with the working people, and not greed or careerism, will bring ever new forces to its ranks. It will be a free literature, because it will serve, not some satiated heroine, not the bored "upper ten thousand" suffering from fatty degeneration, but the millions and tens of millions of working people—the flower òf the country, its strength and its future. It will be a free literature, enriching the last word in the revolutionary thought of mankind with the experience and living work of the socialist proletariat, bringing about permanent interaction between the experience of the past (scientific socialism, the completion of the development of socialism from its primitive, utopian forms) and the experience of the present (the present struggle of the worker comrades). (November 13, 1905, *Collected Works*, (1962), X, 45-49.)

Tolstoy's indictment of the ruling classes was made with tremendous power and sincerity; with absolute clearness he laid bare the inner falsity of all those institutions by which modern society is maintained: the church, the law courts, militarism, "lawful" wedlock, bourgeois science. But his doctrine proved to be in complete contradiction to the life, work and struggle of the gravedigger of the modern social system, the proletariat. Whose then was the point of view reflected in the teachings of Leo Tolstoy? Through his lips there spoke that multitudinous mass of the Russian people who already detest the masters of modern life but have not yet advanced to the point of intelligent, consistent, thoroughgoing, implacable struggle against them.

The history and the outcome of the great Russian revolution have shown that such precisely was the mass that found itself between the class-conscious socialist proletariat and the out-and-out defenders of the old regime. This mass, consisting mainly of the peasantry, showed in the revolution how great was its hatred of the old, how keenly it felt all the inflictions of the modern regime, how great within it was the spontaneous yearning to be rid of them and to find a better life.

At the same time, however, this mass showed in the revolution that it was not politically conscious enough in its hatred, that it was not consistent in its struggle and that its quest for a better life was confined within narrow bounds.

This great human ocean, agitated to its very depths, with all its weaknesses and all its strong features found its reflection in the doctrine of Tolstoy.

By studying the literary works of Leo Tolstoy the Russian working class will learn to know its enemies better, but in examining the doctrine of Tolstoy, the whole Russian people will have to understand where their own weakness lies, the weakness which did not allow them to carry the cause of their emancipation to its conclusion. This must be understood in order to go forward.

This advance is impeded by all those who declare Tolstoy a "universal conscience," a "teacher of life." This is a lie that the liberals are deliberately spreading in their desire to utilize the anti-revolutionary aspect of Tolstoy's doctrine. This lie about

Tolstoy as a "teacher of life" is being repeated after the liberals by some former Social Democrats.

The Russian people will secure their emancipation only when they realize that it is not from Tolstoy they must learn to win a better life but from the class, the significance of which Tolstoy did not understand, and which alone is capable of destroying the old world which Tolstoy hated. That class is the proletariat. (December 18, 1910, *Collected Works* (1963), XVI, 353–354.)

Precisely, in its true historical meaning, Tolstoyism is the ideology of the Oriental system, of the Asiatic system. Hence—asceticism, non-resistance to evil, the profound notes of pessimism, the conviction that "all is nothing, everything material is nothing" ("The Meaning of Life"), faith in the "Spirit," "the principle underlying everything," in relation to which principle man is only "a laborer . . . who has been set the task of saving his soul," and so forth. Tolstoy remains true to this philosophy in *The Kreuzer Sonata* when he says that "woman's emancipation lies not in study courses and not in having a profession, but in the bedroom," and in an article written in 1862 in which it is stated that the universities train only "irritable and sickly liberals," who are "entirely useless to the people," are "aimlessly torn from their former environment," "cannot find a place for themselves in life," etc.

Pessimism, non-resistance, appeals to the "Spirit" constitute an ideology which inevitably appears in an era when the old order has been entirely "overturned," and when the masses who were educated under this old order and who imbibed with their mother's milk the principles, customs, traditions and beliefs of the old order, do not and cannot discern what the new order that is "taking shape" is, what social forces are "shaping" it and how exactly, and what social forces are capable of bringing salvation from the innumerable and very acute misfortunes that are peculiar to times of "break-up." (January 22, 1911, *Selected Works*, XI, 688–689.)

The Social Democrats demand the promulgation of a law,

operative throughout the state, protecting the rights of every national minority in no matter what part of the state. This law must declare inoperative any measure by means of which the national majority might attempt to establish privileges for itself or restrict the rights of a national minority (in the sphere of education, in the use of a specific language, in matters of budget, etc.), and forbid the implementation of any such measure by making it a punishable offence. . . .

It is impermissible, from the standpoint of social democracy, to issue the slogan of national culture either directly or indirectly. The slogan is incorrect because, already under capitalism, all economic, political, and intellectual life is becoming more and more international. Socialism will make it completely international. International culture, which is already being systematically created by the proletariat of all countries, does not absorb "national culture" (no matter of what national group) as a whole, but accepts from *each* national culture *exclusively* those of its elements that are consistently democratic and socialist. (June 1913, *Collected Works* (1963), XIX, 246–247.)

Politically conscious workers have understood that the slogan "national culture" is clerical or bourgeois deception—no matter whether it concerns Great-Russian, Ukrainian, Jewish, Polish, Georgian or any other culture. A hundred and twenty-five years ago, when the nation had not been split into bourgeoisie and proletariat, the slogan "national culture" could have been a clear and uniting call to struggle against feudalism and clericalism. Since that time, however, the class struggle between the bourgeoisie and the proletariat has gained momentum everywhere. The division of the "single" nation into the exploiters and exploited has become an accomplished fact.

Only the clerical partisans and the bourgeoisie can speak of national culture in general. The working people can speak only of the international culture of the world working-class movement. This is the only culture that means full, real, sincere equality of nations, the absence of national oppression and the realization of democracy. Only the unity and solidarity of workers of all nations in all working-class organizations in the struggle against capital will lead to "the solution of the national problem." (September 13, 1913, *Collected Works* (1963), XIX, 380–381.)

If a Ukrainian Marxist allows himself to be swayed by his quite legitimate and natural hatred of the Great Russian oppressors to such a degree that he transfers even a particle of this hatred, even if it be only estrangement, to the proletarian culture and proletarian cause of the Great Russian workers, then such a Marxist will get bogged down in bourgeois nationalism. Similarly, the Great-Russian Marxists will be bogged down, not only in bourgeois, but also in Black-Hundred nationalism, if he loses sight, even for a moment, of the demand for complete equality for the Ukrainians or of their right to form an independent state. (October-December 1913, *Collected Works* (1964), XX, 33.)

One feels embittered on reading this letter which is permeated with ordinary philistine prejudices. On many occasions, the present writer, in meeting with Gorky on the Island of Capri, warned him against and reproached him for his political errors. Gorky parried these reproaches with his inimitably sweet smile and the candid admission: "I know that I am a bad Marxist. Moreover, all of us artists are a bit irresponsible." It is not easy to argue against this. Gorky has, no doubt, great artistic talent that has been and will be of great use to the proletarian movement of the world. But why should Gorky dabble in politics? (March 12, 1917, *Collected Works* (1929), XX, i, 56–57.)

Much too much space is devoted to political agitation on old themes—political fireworks. Too little space is devoted to the building of a new life, to facts and facts about this. . . .

Less politics. Politics have been fully "cleared up" and have been reduced to the struggle between two camps: the camp of the proletariat in rebellion and that of a handful of capitalist slave-owners (with their pack of hounds, including the Mensheviks and others). I repeat, these politics can and should be dealt with very briefly.

More economics. But not economics in the sense of "general" arguments, scientific reviews, plans drawn up by intellectuals, and other twaddle of that sort, which, unfortunately, is too often just twaddle. No, we want economics in the sense of collecting, carefully testing and studying the facts of the actual building up of the new life. . . .

It is the same with the war. Do we denounce cowardly officers and men? Have we disgraced the inefficient regiments in the eyes of Russia? Have we "caught" a sufficient number of the worst examples which should, with the greatest possible publicity, be expelled from the army, as being useless, negligent, unpunctual, etc.? We are not waging a practical, ruthless and truly revolutionary war against the concrete carriers of evil. . . .

Less political fireworks. Less intellectual arguments. Get closer to life. More attention to the way the masses of the workers and peasants are actually building something new in their everyday work. More testing to ascertain to what extent this something new is Communistic. (September 20, 1918, *Collected Works* (1959), XXVIII, 86–88.)

One of these bourgeois hypocrisies is the belief that the school can stand aloof from politics. You know how false this belief is. The bourgeoisie itself, which advocated this principle, made its own bourgeois politics the cornerstone of the school system, and tried to reduce education to the drilling of docile and efficient servants of the bourgeoisie, to reduce even universal education from top to bottom to the drilling of docile and efficient servants for the bourgeoisie, of slaves and tools of capital, and never gave a thought to making the school an instrument of human personality, irrespective of class. And now it is clear to all that this can be done only by a Socialist school having inseparable bonds with all the toiling and exploited and wholeheartedly supporting the Soviet platform. (January 18, 1919, *Collected Works* (1945), XXIII, 498–499.)

We are fully aware of the effects of Russia's lack of cultural development, what it is doing to Soviet government—which in principle has provided an immeasurably higher proletarian democracy, which serves as a model of such democracy for the whole world—how this lack of culture is depreciating Soviet government and reviving bureaucracy. The Soviet apparatus is accessible to all the toilers in word, but in fact it is far from accessible to all of them, as we all know. And not because the laws prevent it from being so, as was the case under the bourgeoisie; on the contrary, the laws assist in this respect. But here laws alone are not enough. A vast amount of educational, organizational and cultural work is required, which cannot be done rapidly by legislation and which demands a vast amount of prolonged work. (*Selected Works,* VIII, 349.)

In the period of the dictatorship of the proletariat, that is, in the period when the conditions for the complete implementation of communism are being created, the school should teach not only the general principles of communism, but must impart the ideological, organizational and educational influence of the proletariat on the semi-proletarian and non-proletarian strata of the toiling masses, in order to raise a generation able to accomplish the final realization of communism.

The next tasks on this road are:

1. For all children of both sexes till the age of 16 (and to provide knowledge of the theoretical and practical foundations of all main branches of production), free and compulsory general and polytechnical education.

2. Establishment of close contacts between instruction and socially productive labor.

3. Supplying by the state of all students with food, clothing and teaching materials.

4. Stepped-up agitation and propaganda among the teachers.

5. Training of cadres of new teachers who are imbued with the ideas of communism.

6. Ever more active participation of the toiling population in

educational programs (development of educational soviets, mobilization of literate people, etc.).

7. Full support by the Soviet government to workers and toiling peasants engaged in self-study and self-development (establishment of libraries, schools and universities for adult education, lecture courses, movies, workshops, etc.).

8. Widest propaganda of communist ideas. . . . (February-March, 1919, *O Literaturye i Iskustvye* (1957), p. 347 f.)

Soviet apparatus—this term means that the toiling masses are united in such a manner that capitalism will be smashed through the might and weight of their union. And they did smash it. But crushed capitalism cannot feed us. We must take possession of the culture left to us by capitalism, and out of it we must create socialism. We must take over, in their entirety, science and technology, knowledge and art. Otherwise we will not be able to construct the communist society. But science, technology and art are held in the hands and heads of the experts. . . .

The utilization of the whole apparatus of bourgeois capitalist society requires more than effective coercion. It also requires organization, discipline, loyal discipline of the masses and the organized influence of the proletariat on the rest of the population; as well as the creation of new social conditions to persuade the bourgeois specialist that there is no choice, and no retreat to the old social order, and that he will be able to perform only if he sides with the Communists who are directing the masses, who are enjoying their absolute confidence and who are working toward the objective of making accessible the fruits of bourgeois science and technology, the fruits of thousands of years of progress of civilization not only to a handful of people who are abusing those benefits for their own glory and enrichment, but to the whole of the working population. (April 17, 1919, *O Literaturye i Iskustvye* (1957), pp. 351–352.)

We must take up the simple and urgent task of mobilizing all those who are able to read and write for the struggle against illiteracy. We must use those books which we do possess and set out to establish an organized network of libraries which should help the people to read every one of the existing books. . . . The basic task of our revolution is reflected in this little matter. (May 6, 1919, *O Literaturye i Iskustvye* (1957), p. 357.)

We are spoiling the Russian language. We are using foreign words without necessity and we are using them incorrectly. . . . Naturally, if a person only very recently learned how to read, in particular to read newspapers, and if he reads them avidly, he cannot help but adopt newspaper style and phraseology. But, precisely, newspaper language is beginning to deteriorate with us, too. A person who just learned to read may be forgiven for his use of foreign words. He is undergoing a new experience. But publicists cannot be excused. . . . Has the time not come to wage war on the corruption of the Russian language? (1919 or 1920, *O Literaturye i Iskustvye* (1957), p. 374.)

There was a time when representatives of the medical profession were suspicious of the working class and were dreaming about the restitution of the bourgeois order. Now they have become convinced that Russia can be led toward cultural flowering only by working together with the proletariat. Cooperation between science and labor, and only such cooperation, can eliminate the burden of misery, disease and filth. And this will happen. None of the dark forces will be able to resist the alliance of the representatives of science, of the proletariat, and of technology. (March 1, 1920, *Über Kultur und Kunst* (Berlin: Dietz, 1960), p. 348 f.)

It is said that the cultural standard is measured best by the legal status of women. There is profound truth in this assertion. By this criterion, only the dictatorship of the proletariat, only the socialist state, had the capability to achieve, and did indeed achieve, a higher cultural standard. (March 4, 1920, *Über Kultur und Kunst,* (Berlin: Dietz, 1960), p. 350.)

In the Soviet workers' and peasants' republic, the whole system of education, in the political-educational sphere in general as well as in the special sphere of art, must be imbued with the spirit of the class struggle of the proletariat for the successful achievement of the aims of its dictatorship—the overthrow of the bourgeoisie, the abolition of classes and the abolition of all exploitation of man by man.

Therefore the proletariat, personified by its vanguard, the Communist party, as well as by all the various kinds of proletarian organizations in general, must take a most active and leading part in the whole work of popular education.

The whole experience of modern history, and particularly the more than half a century of revolutionary struggle of the proletariat in all countries in the world since the appearance of *The Communist Manifesto,* has indisputably proved that the Marxian world outlook is the only correct expression of the interests, the point of view and culture of the revolutionary proletariat.

Marxism won for itself its world-historical significance as the ideology of the revolutionary proletariat by the fact that it did not cast aside the valuable gains of the bourgeois epoch, but on the contrary assimilated and re-worked all that was valuable in the more than two thousand years of development of human thought and culture. Further work on this basis and in this direction, inspired (practically) by the experience of the dictatorship of the proletariat as its last struggle against all exploitation, can alone be regarded as the development of really proletarian culture.

Adhering unswervingly to the point of view of these principles, the All-Russian Congress of Proletarian Culture most emphatically rejects as theoretically wrong and practically harmful all attempts to invent a special culture, all attempts to isolate itself in an exclusive organization, to restrict the work of the People's Commissariat for Education and the Proletcult to separate sphere, etc., or to establish the Proletcult as an "autonomous" organization within the People's Commissariat for Education, etc. On the contrary, the Congress imposes upon all organizations of the Proletcult the absolute duty of regarding themselves as being entirely auxiliary organs in the system of institutions of the People's Commissariat for Education, and performing their duties under the general guidance of the Soviet government (in particular, the People's Commissariat for Education) and of the Russian Communist party, as part of the duties of the proletarian dictatorship. (October 8, 1920, *Selected Works,* IX, 484–485.)

We must put hundreds of thousands of useful people to work in the service of communist education. This is what has been done at the front, in our Red Army, in which tens of thousands of the old army were enrolled. In the course of a long process, a process of re-education, they became welded into the Red Army, as they proved in the long run by their victories. And we must follow this example in our cultural and educational work. True, this work is not so spectacular, but it is even more important. We need every agitator and propagandist; he will be fulfilling his function if he works in a strict Party spirit, but does not at the same time confine himself to the Party only and remembers that it is his duty to direct hundreds of thousands of teachers, to arouse their interests, to overcome their old bourgeois prejudices, to enlist them in the work we are doing, to fire them with the knowledge of the immensity of our task. It is only by proceeding to do this that we can lead these masses, whom capitalism crushed and drew away from us, on to the right path. (November 3, 1920, *Selected Works in Three Volumes* (Moscow: 1961), III, 526.)

Unreservedly adhering to the position defined by the program of the Russian Communist party in regard to polytechnical education . . . the Party must regard the reduction of the age for general and polytechnical education from seventeen to fifteen exclusively as a temporary measure of practical necessity called forth by the poverty and ruin of the country caused by the war imposed upon us by the Entente.

The introduction of vocational education for persons of 15

years of age and upward "in conjunction" with "general poly-technical education" . . . is absolutely obligatory everywhere, as soon as the slightest opportunity for it occurs.

The principal defect of the People's Commissariat for Education is its lack of practical efficiency, inadequate accounting and verification of practical experience, the absence of system in applying the lessons of this experience and the predominance of general arguments and abstract slogans. The attention of the People's Commissar and of the collegium should be directed mainly toward combating these defects.

The enlistment of specialists, i.e., of pedagogues having theoretical and long practical training, and of persons having such training in the sphere of vocational-technical (including agronomic) education at the center, is improperly organized in the People's Commissariat for Education in general, and in the Chief Vocational Educational Board in particular.

The registration of such workers, the study of their experience, the verification of the results of their work and their systematic enlistment for responsible posts in local and, particularly, in central work must be organized immediately. Not a single serious measure should be carried out without the opinion of these specialists being first obtained and without their constant co-operation.

It goes without saying that the enlistment of specialists must be carried out under two unfailing conditions: first, specialists who are not Communists must work under the control of Communists; secondly, the content of the tuition, insofar as this concerns general educational subjects, and particularly philosophy, the social sciences and Communist training, must be determined exclusively by Communists. . . .

Very unsatisfactory also is the organization of the distribution of newspapers, pamphlets, magazines and books in school and other libraries and reading rooms. The result is that only a thin stratum of Soviet employees are able to obtain newspapers and books, while workers and peasants obtain extremely few. This business must be fundamentally reorganized. (February, 1921, *Selected Works,* IX, 491–492.)

It is not sufficient to liquidate illiteracy; it is necessary to build up Soviet economy, and in this literacy alone will not carry you very far. We must raise culture to a very much higher level. A man must make use of his ability to read and write, he must have something to read, newspapers and propaganda pamphlets, which should be properly distributed and should reach the people and not get lost in transit, as they do now, so that not more than half of them are read and the rest are used in offices for some purpose or other; perhaps not more than one-fourth reach the people. We must learn to make full use of the scanty resources that we do possess.

That is why, in connection with the New Economic Policy, we must ceaselessly propagate the idea that political education calls for the raising of the level of culture at all costs. We must try to make the ability to read and write serve the purpose of raising the level of culture, try to make the peasant learn to read and write for the purpose of improving his farm and his state. (October 17, 1921, *Selected Works,* IX, 270–271.)

Yesterday I casually read in *Izvestiya* a political poem by Mayakovsky. I am not an admirer of his poetical talent, although I fully admit that I am not a competent judge in this field. But it is a long time since I experienced such pleasure from the point of view of politics and administration. In his poem Mayakovsky pours scorn on meetings and taunts the Communists with continually sitting at meetings. I am not sure about the poetry; but as for the politics, I vouch for its absolute correctness. We are indeed in the position (and it must be said that it is a very absurd position) of those who are continually meeting, setting up commissions, drawing up plans without end. There was a character in Russian life—Oblomov. He was always lolling on his bed and mentally drawing up plans. That was a long time ago. Since then Russia has passed through three revolutions; but the Oblomovs have remained, for there were Oblomovs not only among the landlords but also among the peasants, and not only among the peasants but among the intellectuals, and not only among the intellectuals, but also among the workers and

Communists. It is sufficient to watch us at our meetings, at our work on commissions, to be able to say that the old Oblomov has remained, and it will be necessary to give him a good washing and cleaning, a good rubbing and drubbing to make a man of him. In this respect we must look upon our position without any illusions. We have not copied any one of those who write the word "revolution" with a capital R, as the Socialist Revolutionaries do. We could quote the words of Marx to the effect that many foolish things are done during a revolution, more perhaps than at any other time. We revolutionaries must learn to regard these foolish acts soberly and fearlessly. (March 6, 1922, *Selected Works*, IX, 316–317.)

It will be seen from what has been said that a magazine that sets out to be an organ of militant materialism must be a fighting organ in the first place, in the sense of unflinchingly exposing and indicting all modern "graduated flunkeys of clericalism," irrespective of whether they appear as the representatives of official science or as free-lances calling themselves "democratic Left or ideologically Socialist" publicists.

In the second place, such a magazine must be an organ of militant atheism. We have departments, or at least state institutions, which are in charge of this work. But this work is being carried on extremely apathetically and extremely unsatisfactorily, and is apparently suffering from the general conditions of our truly Russian (even though Soviet) bureaucracy. It is therefore highly essential that in addition to the work of these state institutions, and in order to improve and infuse life into this work, a magazine which sets out to be an organ of militant materialism should carry on untiring atheist propaganda and an untiring atheist fight. . . .

It would be the biggest and most grievous mistake a Marxist could make to think that the millions (especially the peasants and artisans), who have been condemned by all modern society to darkness, ignorance and prejudice, can emancipate themselves from this darkness only along the straight line of a purely Marxist education. These millions should be supplied with the most varied atheist propaganda material, they should be made acquainted with facts from the most varied spheres of life, they should be approached in this way and in that way so as to interest them, rouse them from their religious torpor, stir them from the most varied angles and by the most varied methods and so forth.

The keen, vivacious and talented writings of the old atheists of the eighteenth century, which wittily and openly attacked the prevailing clericalism, will very often prove to be a thousand times more suitable for arousing people from their religious torpor than the dull and dry paraphrases of Marxism, almost completely unillustrated by skillfully selected facts, which predominate in our literature and which (it is no use hiding the fact) frequently distort Marxism. We have translations of all the bigger works of Marx and Engels. . . .

Extremely important is all material relating to the United States of America, where the official, state connection between religion and capital is less manifest. But, on the other hand, it makes it clearer to us that so-called modern democracy (which the Mensheviks, the Socialist Revolutionaries, partly also the anarchists, etc., so unreasonably worship) is nothing but the freedom to preach what it is to the advantage of the bourgeoisie to preach, namely, the most reactionary ideas, religion, obscurantism, defense of the exploiters, etc. (March 12, 1922, *Selected Works*, XI, 72–76.)

What then is lacking? That is clear; what is lacking is culture among that stratum of the Communists who perform the work of administration. But if we take Moscow, with its 4,700 responsible Communists, and if we take that huge bureaucratic machine, that huge pile, we must ask: Who is leading whom? I doubt very much whether it could be said that the Communists were guiding this pile. To tell the truth, it is not they who are leading, they are being led. (March 27, 1922, *Selected Works*, IX, 348.)

[Marx] critically studied all that had been created by human society and did not ignore a single point of it. He studied all that had been created by the human mind, subjected it to criticism, tested it on the working class movement and arrived at conclusions at which those who were restricted within bourgeois limits, or bound by bourgeois prejudices, could not arrive.

This is what we must bear in mind when we talk about proletarian culture, for example. Unless we clearly understand that only by an exact knowledge of the culture created by the whole development of mankind, that only by re-working this culture, is it possible to build proletarian culture, unless this is understood, we shall not be able to solve our problem. Proletarian culture is not something that has sprung from nowhere, it is not an invention of those who call themselves experts in proletarian culture. That is all nonsense. Proletarian culture must be the result of the natural development of the stores of knowledge which mankind has accumulated under the yoke of capitalist society, landlord society and bureaucratic society. All these roads and paths have led, are leading and continue to lead, to proletarian culture in the same way as the political economy re-worked by Marx showed us what human society must arrive at, showed us the transition to the class struggle, to the beginning of the proletarian revolution.

When we sometimes hear representatives of the youth and certain advocates of a new system of education attacking the old school and saying that it taught by rote, we say to them that we must take what was good in the old school. We must not take from the old school the system whereby the young man's mind was crammed with knowledge nine-tenths of which was useless and one-tenth of which was distorted. But this does not mean that we must confine ourselves to Communist conclusions and learn only Communist slogans. We shall not create communism by this means. One can become a Communist only when one enriches one's mind with the knowledge of all the wealth created by mankind. (October 2, 1922, *Selected Works*, IX, 470–471.)

While we are chattering about proletarian culture and its relation to bourgeois culture, facts present us with figures which show that things are bad with us even in regard to bourgeois culture. It turns out, as was to be expected, that we are still very backward in regard to general literacy and that even our progress compared with tsarist times (1897) has been too slow. This serves as a severe warning and reproach to those who are soaring in the empiric heights of "proletarian culture." It shows what imperative spadework still confronts us in order to reach the level of an ordinary West European civilized state. It also shows what an enormous amount of work confronts us today in order to achieve anything like a real cultural level on the basis of our proletarian gains. . . .

Our village school teachers should be placed on a level that has never been achieved, and can never be achieved, in bourgeois society. This is a truism that requires no proof. We must strive toward this by means of systematic, steady and persistent work in raising the spiritual level of the teachers, of training them thoroughly for their really high calling, and, principally, principally, principally, by raising their material level.

We must systematically increase our work of organizing the village school teachers in order to transform them from the bulwark of the bourgeois system that they still are in all capitalist countries without exception into the bulwark of the Soviet system, in order, through their agency, to win the peasantry away from their alliance with the bourgoisie and to bring them into alliance with the proletariat. (January 2, 1923, *Selected Works*, IX, 486, 488.)

Our opponents have told us more than once that we are undertaking the senseless task of implanting socialism in an insufficiently cultured country. But they were misled by the fact that we did not go about it in a way that was demanded by theory (the theory of all sorts of pedants), and that in our country the political and social revolution preceded the cultural revolution, the cultural revolution which now confronts us.

This cultural revolution would be sufficient to transform us into a completely socialist country; but this cultural revolution confronts us with immense difficulties of a purely educational (for we are illiterate) and material character (for in order to be cultured we must have reached a certain level of development of the material means of production, we must have a certain material base). (January 4-6, 1923, *Selected Works*, IX, 408–409.)

What if the complete hopelessness of the situation, by intensifying tenfold the energies of the workers and peasants, offered us the possibility of proceeding to create the fundamental requisites of civilization in a way different from that of West European countries? Has that changed the general line of development of world history? Has that changed the fundamental relations between the basic classes of every state that is being drawn, or has been drawn, into the general course of world history?

If a definite level of culture is required for the creation of socialism (although nobody can tell what that definite level of culture is), why cannot we begin by achieving the prerequisites for that definite level of culture in a revolutionary way, and then, with the help of a workers' and peasants' government and a Soviet system, proceed to overtake the other nations? (January 16–17, 1923, *Selected Works*, VI, 511.)

The first five years have fairly crammed our heads with disbelief and scepticism. Involuntarily, we are inclined to display these latter qualities toward those who talk very fine and large about "proletarian" culture, for example. For a start we would be satisfied with real bourgeois culture, for a start we would be satisfied to be able to dispense with the particularly crude types of pre-bourgeois culture, i.e., bureaucratic or serf culture, etc. In matters of culture haste and bustle are the worst possible things. Many of our young writers and Communists should get this well into their heads. (March 2, 1923, *Selected Works*, IX, 387.)

INDEX